Photograph courtesy of Colorsport

Published by Queen Anne Press
Macdonald and Jane's Publishing Group Limited
Paulton House
8 Shepherdess Walk
London N1 7LW

ISBN 0 354 09084 4

Typeset in Monotype Times, printed and bound in England
by C. Nicholls & Company Ltd
The Philips Park Press, Manchester

PLAYFAIR
FOOTBALL ANNUAL

1979-80

Compiled by Peter Dunk and Lionel Francis

BIRTH OF THE ALLIANCE

The birth of the Alliance Premier League marks a great step forward for all those ambitious clubs who for years have dreamed of being elected to the Football League. This new League will not fulfil all the dreams of all the aspiring clubs, but it does mean considerable progress has been made.

Since the early 1920s, after the enlargement of the Third Division into the North and South Sections, non-League clubs have been striving, largely unsuccessfully, to get elected to the Football League.

At first each and every club was concerned only for its own advancement, and so they proved by default one of life's truisms, that in seeking the good of others, we can best look after ourselves. After the Second World War we saw, year after year, several clubs from the same League each striving for election, and year after year we watched them fail, sometimes getting a derisory two, one, or even no votes. From time to time some clubs, particularly those in the Southern League, realised that the way into the Football League was to allow only one club from their League to apply for election each year. Motions to this effect were put forward at more than one of their Annual General Meetings, but always pride and personal ambition prevailed, and so the system continued.

In 1968/69 a new League was formed, the Northern Premier League, and after two seasons, Gordon Graham was appointed as Secretary. This was to herald the start of a new era. It was not long before he had a clear view of what he wanted to see created, and it was not long before other people knew about it. For the next few years he worked unceasingly towards a new structure which would enable the senior non-League clubs to win promotion to the Football League. Against all the odds, all the doubts, and all the disappointments, he never wavered. He was certain in his own quiet and determined way. Never did he doubt, for one minute, the sense and the practicability of his vision.

4

Eventually, as the Football League started to elect non-League clubs into the Fourth Division with some regularity, these non-League clubs began to sense that after all these years of frustration the dream was at least within reach. It needed only a little more effort and faith on their part to bring it to reality. Many people had worked towards the same goal, but to us there is no doubt who was the driving force.

The Alliance Premier League will consist of 20 clubs, with 13 places reserved for the Southern League and seven for the Northern Premier. There were 16 applications from the Northern Premier League, and 31 from the Southern League. The Football League had previously decided on their own scheme of putting clubs into grades, A, B, or C. It was the intention of the Football League to inspect each club, but this was not possible due to the very bad winter of 1978/79. Clubs have therefore been graded on the results of a very detailed questionnaire which they completed. All 20 clubs are considered to be at least Grade B, and some Grade A. The clubs elected to the Alliance were chosen on the basis of their grading, plus their performance over the last two years.

At the end of the 1979/80 season the winner of the Alliance will be eligible, provided it obtains a Grade A marking from the Football League Management Committee, to seek election to the League, together with the four clubs seeking re-election. If the Alliance Champions do not get a Grade A, then the highest-placed club that does will be eligible. However, a club going forward to the Football League AGM without having won the Alliance will probably not stand a very high chance of being elected. It is hoped that in the very near future, promotion and relegation between the Football League and the Alliance Premier League will be automatic.

From the start, the bottom three clubs in the Alliance Premier will be relegated, one to the Northern Premier League and the other two to the two divisions of the Southern League (which will henceforth consist of Midland Premier and Southern Premier Divisions). The top clubs of these three divisions will, of course be promoted to the Alliance Premier.

The Alliance Premier League will need a lot of support, especially financial. We hope it receives it.

In February 1905 a young man called Alf Common was transferred from Sunderland to Middlesbrough for £1,000. At the time this was a transfer record – the first time that the magic four-figure barrier had been reached. Of course, inflation has taken its toll since then, and we have just broken through the seven-figure barrier. The alarming fact is that this increase is not altogether taken care of by inflation.

It is surprisingly difficult to estimate the exact rate of inflation over the past 74 years, but the average, according to official figures, shows an increase to the factor of 18. The most startling increase (apart from footballers) has been in the cost of houses, which have gone up by a factor of 90 since about 1940. Where did the rest of Trevor Francis' million come from?

Pressure from wealthy overseas clubs, notably in the USA, has, of course, had its effect. Once Real Madrid had put in their offer of about £900,000 for Laurie Cunningham, it was pointless any other British club coming in with a bid below that. Real Madrid are a wealthy and successful club, and their supporters (average home gate 90,000) pay more per head than we do in this country. Unfortunately, this situation has led to panic, which at the time of writing has been most notably displayed by Manchester City. This ambitious club, a long-serving member of our First Division, has lived in the shadow of Old Trafford for many years, and after a relatively poor season in 1978/79 they did two significant things; they 'promoted' Tony Book and brought in Malcolm Allison as Team Manager, and they paid a staggering £756,000 for Mick Robinson, whose *total League career to date* consists of only 36 games and 13 goals as a central striker for Preston North End in the Second Division.

We deplore these desperate tactics and, in particular, that the value of footballers has escalated so disproportionately. The outside factors mentioned above have played a significant part, of course, but we in this country simply cannot afford to keep pace with the sort of transfer fees bandied about on the continent (example: Paulo Rossi, the young player who came to prominence with Italy in the 1978 World Cup, recently sold for £3,500,000). The next couple of seasons will be very interesting.

6

FINAL HONOURS 1978-79

BRITISH CHAMPIONSHIP
Winners: England

EUROPEAN CUP
Winners: Nottingham F.; Runners-up: Malmoe

EUROPEAN CUP-WINNERS' CUP
Winners: Barcelona; Runners-up: Fortuna Dusseldorf

UEFA CUP
Winners: Borussia Mœnchengladbach; Runners-up: Red Star Belgrade

FOOTBALL LEAGUE
Division I: Champions: Liverpool; Runners-up: Nottingham F.
Relegated: Q.P.R., Birmingham, Chelsea

Division II: Champions: Crystal Palace; Also promoted: Brighton & H. A., Stoke C.
Relegated: Sheffield U., Millwall, Blackburn R.

Division III: Champions: Shrewsbury; Also promoted: Watford, Swansea
Relegated: Peterborough U., Walsall, Tranmere R., Lincoln C.

Division IV: Champions: Reading; Also promoted: Grimsby T., Wimbledon, Barnsley
Re-elected: Darlington; Doncaster, Halifax, Crewe Alex.

SCOTTISH LEAGUE
Premier Division: Champions: Celtic; Runners-up: Rangers
Relegated: Hearts, Motherwell.

Division I: Champions: Dundee; Also promoted: Kilmarnock
Relegated: Montrose, Queen of the South

Division II: Champions: Berwick Rangers; Also promoted: Dunfermline Ath.

FA CUP
Winners: Arsenal; Runners-up: Manchester U.

LEAGUE CUP
Winners: Nottingham F.; Runners-up: Southampton

FA CHARITY SHIELD
Winners: Nottingham F.; Runners-up: Ipswich T.

ANGLO-SCOTTISH CUP
Winners: Burnley; Runners-up: Oldham Ath.

FA CHALLENGE VASE
Winners: Billericay T.; Runners-up: Almondsbury Greenway

FA CHALLENGE TROPHY
Winners: Stafford Rangers; Runners-up: Kettering T.

SCOTTISH CUP
Winners: Rangers; Runners-up: Hibernian

SCOTTISH LEAGUE CUP
    Winners: Rangers; Runners-up: Aberdeen

WELSH FA CUP
    Winners: Shrewsbury T.; Runners-up: Wrexham

SOUTHERN LEAGUE
    Premier Division Champions: Worcester C.; Runners-up: Kettering T.
    Division I (N) Champions: Grantham; Runners-up: Merthyr T.
    Division I (S) Champions: Dover; Runners-up: Folkestone & Shepway

NORTHERN PREMIER LEAGUE
    Champions: Mossley; Runners-up: Altrincham

IRISH CUP
    Winners: Portadown; Runners-up: Cliftonville.

FA YOUTH CUP
    Winners: Millwall; Runners-up: Manchester C.

FA SUNDAY CUP
    Winners: Lobster; Runners-up: Carlton U.

IRISH LEAGUE
    Champions: Linfield; Runners-up: Glenavon.

FOOTBALL LEAGUE CLUBS AND THEIR PLAYERS

ALDERSHOT   DIV. 4

BAMBRIDGE, Stephen M.
BRODIE, Murray
CROSBY, Malcolm
DIXON, William
DODDS, Kenneth
DUNGWORTH, John H.
DWARDS, Nigel S.

GREEN, Adrian
HOWITT, David J.
JOHNSON, Glenn W.
JOPLING, Joseph
LONGHORN, Dennis
LUCAS, Brian A.
McGREGOR, Alexander G. P.

NEEDHAM, Andrew
SCOTT, Peter W.
SHANAHAN, Terence C.
TOMLIN, David
WOOLER, Alan T.
YOULDEN, Thomas F.

LEAGUE APPEARANCES: Brodie, M. 38; Crosby, M. 30(4); Dixon, W. 36(5); Dungworth, J. H. 46; Earls, M. M. 3; Edwards, N. S. 31; Green, A. –(2); Hooper, W. 3(3); Howitt, D. J. 28(2); Johnson, G. W. 46; Jopling J, 39; Longhorn, D. 30(5); McGregor, A. G. P. 41; Needham, A. 29; Scott, P. W. 9; Shanahan, T. C. 14; Tomlin, D. 9(3); Wooler, A. T. 31(1); Youlden, T. F. 43.

GOALS—League (63): Dungworth 26 (5 pens.), Needham 9, Brodie 6, Shanahan 4, Dixon 3, Edwards 2, Longhorn 2, McGregor 2, Tomlin 2, Wooler 2, Crosby 1, Howitt 1, Jopling 1, Own goals 2.
F.A. Cup (11): Dungworth 8 (1 pen.), Shanahan 2, Crosby.
League Cup: Nil.

Ground: Recreation Ground, Aldershot GU11 1TW. (Aldershot 20211).
Nearest station: Aldershot.
Team Manager: Tom McAnearney   Secretary/Commercial Manager: M. A. Cosway.
Colours: Red shirts with blue and white trim; white shorts with blue and red trim
Record home gate: 19,138 v. Carlisle, January, 1970 (F.A. Cup).
Honours—Champions: Nil.
          F.A. Cup Winners: Nil.

ARSENAL   DIV. 1

BARRON, Paul G.
BRADY, William L.
BRIGNALL, Stephen J. C.
CANT, Clifford W. H.
DEVINE, John A.
DRUMMY, Dermott
FLIGHT, Keith A.
GATTING, Stephen P.
HARVEY, James

HEELEY, Mark D.
JENNINGS, Patrick A.
McDERMOTT, Brian J.
MACDONALD, Malcolm I.
NELSON, Samuel
O'LEARY, David A.
POWLING, Richard
PRICE, David J.
RICE, Patrick J.

RIX, Graham
STAPLETON, Francis A.
STEAD, Kevin
SULLIVAN, Nicholas
SUNDERLAND, Alan
TALBOT, Brian
WALFORD, Stephen J.
YOUNG, William D.

9

LEAGUE APPEARANCES: Barron, P. 3; Brady, W. 37; Brignall, S. J. C. –(1); Devine, J. A. 7; Gatting, S. P. 19(2); Harvey, J. 1(1); Heeley, M. D. 6(4); Jennings, P. A. 39; Kosmina, A. J. –(1); McDermott, B. J. –(2); MacDonald, M. I. 4; Nelson, S. 33; O'Leary, D. A. 37; Price, D. J. 39; Rice, P. J. 39; Rix, G. 39; Stapleton, F. A. 41; Stead, K. 1(1); Sunderland, A. 37; Talbot, B. 20; Vaessen, P. L. 1; Walford, S. J. 26(7); Young, W. D. 33.

GOALS—League (61): Stapleton 17, Brady 13 (4 pens.), Sunderland 9, Price 8, Rix 3, Macdonald 2, Nelson 2, O'Leary 2, Walford 2, Gatting 1, Heeley 1, Rice 1.

F.A. Cup (20): Stapleton 6, Sunderland 6, Brady 2, Talbot 2, Young 2, Gatting, Price.

League Cup (1): Stapleton.

Ground: Arsenal Stadium, Avenell Road, N5 1BU. (01-226 0304).
Nearest stations: Arsenal (Piccadilly Line), Drayton Park (Northern Line) or Finsbury Park (B.R., Piccadilly Line or Victoria Line).
Manager: Terry Neill. Secretary: Ken Friar.
Colours: Red shirts, white sleeves; white shorts.
Record home gate: 73,295 v. Sunderland, March, 1935 (League).
Honours—Champions: Div. 1: 1930–31, 1932–33, 1933–34, 1934–35, 1937–38, 1947–48, 1952–53, 1970–71.
F.A. Cup Winners: 1929–30, 1935–36, 1949–50, 1970–71, 1978–79.
Fairs Cup Winners: 1969–70.

ASTON VILLA   DIV. 1

CARRODUS, Frank
COWANS, Gordon S.
CRAIG, Thomas B.
CROPLEY, Alexander J.
CUNNINGHAM, David
DEACY, Eamonn
DEEHAN, John M.
EVANS, Allan
EVANS, David G.
GIBSON, Colin
GIDMAN, John
GRAY, Andrew M.
GREGORY, John C.
JENKINS, Lee
LINTON, Ivor
LITTLE, Brian
McNAUGHT, Kenneth
MORTIMER, Dennis G.
O'DOWD, Adrian G.
ORMSBY, Brendan T. C.
READY, Kevin P.
RIMMER, John J.
SHAW, Gary R.
SHELTON, Gary
SPINK, Nigel P.
STIRLAND, Gary
SWAIN, Kenneth
WARD, Joseph
WILLIAMS, Gary
YOUNG, William J.

LEAGUE APPEARANCES: Carrodus, F. 6; Cowans, G. S. 34; Craig, T. B. 23; Cropley, A. J. 15(2); Deehan, J. M. 25(1); Evans, A. 36(1); Evans, D. G. 2; Gibson, C. 11(1); Gidman, J. 36; Gray, A. M. 15; Gregory, J. C. 38(1); Jenkins, L. –(2); Linton, I. 4(4); Little, B. 24; McNaught, K. 32; Mortimer, D. G. 38; Ormsby, B. T. C. 2; Phillips, L. 3(2); Rimmer, J. J. 42; Shaw, G. R. 2(1); Shelton, G. 19; Smith, G. M. 6(1); Swain, K. 24; Ward, J. 1; Williams, G. 21(2); Young, W. J. 3.

GOALS—League (59): Deehan 10, Gregory 7, Shelton 7 (1 pen.), Evans (A) 6, Gray 6 (1 pen.), Cowans 4, Gidman 3 (3pens.), Mortimer 3, Craig 2 (1 pen.), Cropley 2, Swain 2, Little 1, McNaught 1, Own goals 5.

F.A. Cup: Nil.

League Cup (5): Gray 2, Shelton, Little, Gregory.

10

Ground: Villa Park, Trinity Road, Birmingham B6 6HE. (021-327 6604).
Nearest station: Birmingham, New Street.
Manager: Ron Saunders. Secretary: Steven Stride.
Colours: Claret shirts with light blue sleeves; white shorts.
Record home gate: 76,588 v. Derby, March, 1946 (F.A. Cup).
Honours—Champions: Div. 1: 1893–94, 1895–96, 1896–97, 1898–99,
    1899–1900, 1909–10. Div. 2: 1937–38, 1959–60. Div. 3: 1971–72.
    F.A. Cup Winners: 1886–87, 1894–95, 1896–97, 1904–05, 1912–13,
    1919–20, 1956–57. (Seven wins stands as the record).
    League Cup Winners: 1960–61, 1974–75, 1976–77.

BARNSLEY   DIV. 3

BANKS, Ian F.
BELL, Derek M.
CLARKE, Allan J.
COLLINS, John L.
GRAHAM, Thomas
LITTLE, Alan

McCARTHY,
  Michael
MARTIN-
  CHAMBERS,
  Philip
MILLAR, Alistair

PUGH, John G.
RILEY, Glyn
SPEEDIE, David R.
SPRINGETT,
  Peter J.

LEAGUE APPEARANCES: Banks, I. F. –(2); Bell, D. M. 32; Clarke,
A. J. 34; Collins, J. L. 46; Copley, G. 1; Graham, T. 27; Joicey, B. 6(5);
Little, A. 40; McCarthy, M. 46; Mallender, G. –(1) Martin-Chambers, P.
45; Millar, A. 43; Peachey, J. M. 12(1); Prendergast, M. J. 1(8); Pugh, J. G.
42; Reed, G. 1; Riley, G. 34(7); Saunders, J. G. 46; Speedie, D. R. 5(5);
Springett, P. J. 45.
GOALS—League: (73): Bell, 18 (3 pens.), Clarke 12 (1 pen.), Graham 12,
  Little 7, Millar 4, Pugh 4, Joicey 3, Riley 3, McCarthy 2,
  Peachey 2, Saunders 2, Chambers 1, Collins 1, Own goals 2.
  F.A. Cup (7): Clarke 2, Reed 2, Bell, Riley, Own goal 1.
  League Cup (1): Little.
Ground: Oakwell, Grove Street, Barnsley S71 1ET. (Barnsley 84113).
Nearest station: Barnsley.
Player/manager: Allan Clarke. Secretary/General Manager: J. Steele.
Colours: Red shirts; white shorts.
Record home gate: 40,255 v. Stoke, 1936 (F.A. Cup).
Honours—Champions: Div. 3 North: 1933–34, 1938–39, 1954–55.
    F.A. Cup Winners: 1911–12.

BIRMINGHAM CITY   DIV. 2

AINSCOW, Alan
BARROWCLOUGH,
  Stewart J.
BERTSCHIN,
  Keith E.
BRADY, Paul J.
BROADHURST,
  Kevan
BUCKLEY, Alan P.

CALDERWOOD,
  James
COTON, Anthony P.
DARK, Trevor C.
DENNIS, Mark E.
DILLON, Kevin P.
FREEMAN, Neil
GALLAGHER,
  Joseph A.

GIVENS, Daniel J.
IVEY, Paul H. W.
PAGE, Malcolm E.
PENDREY,
  Garry J. S.
TOWERS, Mark A.
VAN DEN HAUWE,
  Patrick W. R.

LEAGUE APPEARANCES: Ainscow, A. 27(4); Barrowclough, S. J. 26(3);
Bertschin, K. E. 9; Briggs, M. D. –(1); Broadhurst, K. 13(3); Buckley,
A. P. 24(4); Calderwood, J. 24(1); Dark, T. C. 2(3); Dennis, M. E. 31;
Dillon, K. P. 35(1); Emmanuel, J. G. 12(1); Fox, S. D. 13(1); Francis, T. J.
8(1); Freeman, N. 29; Gallagher, J. A. 41; Givens, D. J. 38(1); Howard, P.
5; Ivey, P. H. W. 3(2); Lynex, S. C. 2; Montgomery, J. 13; Page, M. E. 32;
Pendrey, G. J. S. 9(1); Rathbone, M. J. 2; Rioch, B. D. 3; Tarantini, A. C.
23; Towers, M. A. 31(1); Van Den Hauwe, P. W. R. 7(1).
GOALS—League (37): Buckley 8, Givens 7, Francis 3 (1 pen.), Gallagher
3, Ainscow 2, Barrowclough 2 (1 pen.), Bertschin 2, Dillon 2,
Towers 2 (1 pen.), Broadhurst 1, Calderwood, 1, Darke 1,
Lynex 1, Tarantini 1, Own goal 1.
F.A. Cup: Nil.
League Cup (2): Gallagher, Francis.
Ground: St. Andrews, Birmingham B9 4NH. (021-772 0101 and 2689).
Nearest station: Birmingham New Street.
Manager: Jim Smith. Secretary: A. G. Instone.
Colours: Royal blue shirts with 3 white vertical stripes on sleeves; white
shorts with blue trim.
Record home gate: 66,844 v. Everton, February, 1939 (F.A. Cup).
Honours—Champions: Div. 2: 1892–93, 1920–21, 1947–48, 1954–55.
League South: 1945–46.
F.A. Cup Winners: Nil.
League Cup Winners: 1962–63.

BLACKBURN ROVERS   DIV. 3

ASTON, John	FOWLER, Martin	PARKES, Tony
BAILEY, John A.	GARNER, Simon	PARKIN, Timothy J.
BROTHERSTON,	KEELEY, Glenn M.	RATHBONE,
Noel	McKENZIE, Duncan	Michael J.
BUTCHER, John M.	METCALFE,	ROUND, Paul G.
COUGHLIN,	Stuart M.	WADDINGTON,
Russell J.	MORAN,	John
CRAIG, Joseph	Bernard F.	WAGSTAFFE,
FAZACKERLEY,	MORLEY, Brian J.	David
Derek W.	MORRIS, Peter A.	

LEAGUE APPEARANCES: Aston, J. 10(3); Bailey, J. A. 39; Birchenhall,
A. J. 17(1); Brotherston, N. 34(1); Butcher, J. M. 32; Coughlin, R. J. 11;
Craig, J. 28(2); Curtis, J. 2; Fazackerley, D. W. 37; Fowler, M. 32(2);
Garner, S. 20(5); Gregory, D. H. 5; Hird, K. 22; Keeley, G. M. 26;
McKenzie, D. 13; Metcalfe, S. M. 24(1); Morley, B. J. 3; Morris, P. A.
2(2); Parkes, T. 12; Parkin, T. J. 12; Radford, J. 23; Ramsbottom, N. 10;
Rathbone, M. J. 15; Round, P. G. 17(2); Taylor, R. 3; Waddington, J.
11(2); Wagstaffe, D. 2.
GOALS—League (41): Garner 8, Hird 6 (2 pens.), Radford 6, Craig 5,
Fazackerley 3 (3 pens), Gregory 3, Aston 2, Brotherston 2,
McKenzie 2, Metcalfe 1, Round 1, Taylor 1, Waddington 1.
F.A. Cup (2): Brotherston, Radford.
League Cup (1): Gregory.

Ground: Ewood Park, Blackburn BB2 4JF. (Blackburn 55432/3).
Nearest station: Blackburn.
Manager: Howard Kendall. Secretary: John W. Howarth.
Colours: Blue and white halved shirts; white shorts.
Record home gate: 61,783 v. Bolton Wanderers, March, 1929 (F.A. Cup).
Honours—Champions: Div. 1: 1911–12, 1913–14. Div. 2: 1938–39. Div. 3: 1974–75.

    F.A. Cup Winners: 1883–84, 1884–85, 1885–86, 1889–90, 1890–91, 1927–28.

BLACKPOOL   DIV. 3

BOWEY, Keith A.
CHANDLER, Jeffrey G.
COYLE, Patrick J.
FLEMING, Robert L. P.
GARDNER, Paul A.
HALL, James
HESFORD, Iain
HOCKADAY, David
HOWARTH, Carl
JACKSON, Brian
JONES, Garry E.
KELLOW, Tony
KERR, Robert
McEWAN, Stanley
MALONE, Richard P.
MAY, Jonathan
PASHLEY, Terence
RONSON, William
ROWLAND, Shaun B.
SERMANNI, Thomas D.
SPENCE, Derek W.
SUDDABY, Peter
THOMPSON, Maxwell
TYNAN, Robert A.
WESTON, James J.
WILSON, Brian

LEAGUE APPEARANCES: Bissell, S. J. 1; Bowey, K. A. 1; Chandler, J. G. 18(6); Davidson, V. 23(2); Gardner, P. A. 22(1); Hall, J. 1; Hesford, I. 33; Hockaday, D. 13(5); Holden, M. G. 2(1); Jones, G. E. 11(8); Kellow, T. 25; Kerr, R. 7; McEwan, S. 46; Malone, R. P. 29; May, J. 4; Milligan, L. C. 2; Pashley, T. 35; Ronson, W. 32; Sermanni, T. D. 6(4); Spence, D. W. 42; Suddaby, P. 42; Thompson, M. 38(1); Tong, D. J. 2; Wagstaffe, D. 17(2); Waldron, A. 5; Ward, R. A. 13; Weston, J. J. 29(2); Wilson, B, 7(3).

GOALS—League (61): Spence 16, Kellow 11, Chandler 5, McEwan 5 (2 pens.), Hockaday 4, Weston 4, Davidson 3, Jones 3, Ronson 3, Suddaby 2, Malone 1, Thompson 1, Wagstaffe 1, Wilson 1, Own goal 1.

    F.A. Cup (3): Chandler, Kellow, McEwan (pen.).

    League Cup (7): Davidson 3, McEwan 2 (2 pens.), Spence, Own goal 1.

Ground: Bloomfield Road, Blackpool FY1 6JJ. (Blackpool 46118).
Nearest station: Blackpool North.
Manager: Bob Stokoe. Secretary: W. Smith.
Colours: Tangerine shirts with white stripe on sleeves, white collar and cuffs; white shorts.
Record home gate: 39,118 v. Manchester U., April, 1952 (League).
Honours—Champions: Div. 2: 1929–30.

    F.A. Cup Winners: 1952–53.

    Anglo-Italian Cup Winners: 1971.

13

BOLTON WANDERERS   DIV. 1

ALLARDYCE, Samuel
BURKE, David I.
CARTER, Michael
FELGATE, David W.
GOWLING, Alan E.
GRAHAM, Michael A.
GREAVES, Roy
HEANEY, Roy

JONES, Paul B.
KEIGHLEY, John P.
McDONAGH, James
McNAB, Neil
MOORES, James C.
MORGAN, William
NICHOLSON, Peter
NOWAK, Tadeusz
POOLE, Terence
REID, Peter

SMITH, Brian
THOMPSON, Christopher D.
WALSH, Michael T.
WHATMORE, Neil
WILSON, Philip
WORTHINGTON, Frank S.

LEAGUE APPEARANCES: Allardyce, S. 18(2); Burke, D. I. 19(1); Dunne, A. P. 24(2); Gowling, A. E. 36; Graham, M. A. 9; Greaves, R. 41; Jones, G. E. –(1); Jones, P. B. 31(1); McDonagh, J. 42; McNab, N. 22(1); Morgan, W. 41; Nicholson, P. 34; Nowak, T. 1(1); Reid, P. 14; Smith, B. 18(2); Train, R. 5; Walsh, M. T. 42; Whatmore, N. 23(6); Worthington, F. S. 42.

GOALS—League (54): Worthington 24 (5 pens.), Gowling 15, McNab 3, Whatmore 3, Morgan 2, Allardyce 1, Burke 1, Greaves 1, Jones (P.) 1, Smith 1, Walsh 1, Own goal 1.
    F.A. Cup (1): Smith.
    League Cup (3): Worthington 2 (1 pen.), Gowling.
Ground: Burnden Park, Bolton BL3 2QR. (Bolton (0204) 389200).
Nearest station: Bolton.
Team Manager: Ian Greaves. **Secretary:** Des McBain.
Colours: White shirts; navy blue shorts.
Record home gate: 69,912 v. Manchester City, February, 1933 (F.A. Cup).
Honours—Champions: Div. 2: 1908–09, 1977–78. Div. 3: 1972–73.
    F.A. Cup Winners: 1922–23, 1925–26, 1928–29, 1957–58.

AFC BOURNEMOUTH   DIV. 4

ALLEN, Kenneth
BENJAFIELD, Brian J.
BORTHWICK, Gary M.
BROWN, Kenneth G.

BROWN, Roger W.
BUTLER, Michael A.
FERNS, Philip D.
HOLDER, Philip
IMPEY, John E.

MacDOUGALL, Edward J.
MASSEY, Stephen
MILLER, Keith R.
SCOTT, Joseph

LEAGUE APPEARANCES: Allen, K. 46; Barton, F. 22; Benjafield, B. J. 2; Benson, J. H. 1(1); Borthwick, G. M. 42; Brown, K. G. 28(2); Brown, R. W. 45; Butler, G. 6; Butler, M. A. 28; Cunningham, I. 39; Ferns, P. D. 14(1); Finnigan, T. T. 3(2); Holder, P. 15; Impey, J. E. 38; Johnson, P. J. 20(8); Lennard, D. 18(3); MacDougall, E. J. 29; Massey, S. 29(7); Miller, K. R. 46; Scott, J. 18(3); Showers, D. 14(2); Weeks, G. J. 3.

GOALS—League (47): Butler (M.) 8, MacDougall 8, Massey 6 (1 pen.), Brown (K.) 4, Scott 4, Brown (R.) 3, Johnson 3, Barton 2, Lennard 2, Showers 2, Borthwick 1, Finnigan 1, Impey 1, Own goals 2.
    F.A. Cup (4): MacDougall 2, Butler (M.), Massey (pen.).
    League Cup (1): Brown.

14

Ground: Dean Court, Bournemouth, Hants, BH7 7AF. (Bournemouth (0202) 35381).
Nearest station: Bournemouth.
Manager: Alec Stock. Secretary: G. H. MacKrell.
Colours: Red shirts with white trim; black shorts.
Record home gate: 28,799 v. Man. United, March, 1957 (F.A. Cup).
Honours—Champions: Nil.
  F.A. Cup Winners: Nil.

BRADFORD CITY   DIV. 4

BAINES, Stephen J.   HUTCHINS, Donald   ROBERTSON,
BATES, Michael J.   JACKSON, Peter A.   Archibold L.
DOLAN, Terence P.   McNIVEN, David S.   SMITH, Stephen J.
DOWNSBOROUGH,   MARTINEZ, Eugene   WATSON, Garry
  Peter   PODD, Cyril M.   WOOD, Michael J.
GALLAGHER,   REANEY, Paul
  Barry P.

LEAGUE APPEARANCES: Baines, S. J. 43; Bates, M. J. 30; Cook, J. W. 8; Cooke, J. 16; Dolan, T. P. 40; Downsborough, P. 25; Gilliver, A. H. 1 (1); Hutchins, D. 37; Jackson, D. 9(3); Jackson, P. A. 8(1); Johnson, R. 24(2); McNiven, D. S. 42(1); Martinez, E. 15(7); Middleton, J. 23(1); Podd, C. M. 39; Reaney, P. 33; Robertson, A. L. 14; Smith, S. J. 21; Szabo, T. 8(5); Watson, G. 28(1); Wood, M. J. 42.
GOALS—League (62): McNiven 15, Baines 10, Dolan 9 (2 pens.), Cooke 8, Hutchins 6, Jackson (P.) 4, Robertson 3, Wood 3, Martinez 2, Johnson 1, Szabo 1.
  F.A. Cup (3): Dolan 2 (1 pen.), Cooke.
  League Cup (6): Cooke 2, Baines, Dolan(pen.), Hutchins, Johnson,

Ground: Valley Parade, Bradford BD8 7DY. (Bradford (0274) 26565).
Nearest station: Bradford Exchange.
Team Manager: George Mulhall. Secretary: T. F. Newman.
Colours: White shirts amber/maroon trim; white shorts.
Record home gate: 39,146 v. Burnley, March, 1911 (F.A. Cup).
Honours—Champions: Div. 2: 1907–08, Div. 3 North: 1928–29.
  F.A. Cup Winners: 1910–11. (First holders of present trophy).

BRENTFORD   DIV. 3

ALLDER, Douglas S.   KRUSE, Patrick K.   SALMAN,
BOND, Leonard A.   McCULLOCH,   Danis M. M.
BOOKER, Robert   Andrew   SHRUBB, Paul J.
CARLTON, David G.   McNICHOL,   SMITH, Dean
FRASER, John   James A.   TUCKER,
GLOVER, Allan R.   PHILLIPS,   William B.
GRAHAM, Jack J.   Stephen E.   WALKER, Paul J.
GRAHAM,   PORTER, Trevor J.
  William V.

LEAGUE APPEARANCES: Allder, D. S. 18(12); Allen, M. 5(2); Bond, L. A. 35; Booker, R. 2(1); Carlton, D. G. 36(1); Eames, W. A. 2; Fraser, J. 21(2); Frost, L. A. 5(1); Glover, A. R. 18(1); Graham, J.J. 35; Graham,

15

W. V. 8(3); Kruse, P. K. 44; McCulloch, A. 39; McNichol, J. 32; Phillips, S. E. 46; Porter, T. J. 11; Rolph, G. L. 1; Salman, D. M. M. 39(1); Shrubb, P. J. 39; Silman, D. A. 1; Smith, D. 22(3); Smith, N. P. 2(1); Tucker, W. B. 43; Walker, P. J. 2(5).

GOALS—League (53): Phillips, 14 (1 pen.), McCulloch 13, Smith 9, Kruse 4, McNichol 4, Carlton 2, Glover 2, Shrubb 2, Eames 1, Graham (J.) 1, Salman 1.

    F.A. Cup: Nil.

    League Cup (1): Rolph.

Ground: Griffin Park, Braemar Road, Brentford TW8 0NT. (01-560 2021).

Nearest stations: Brentford (B.R.) or South Ealing (Piccadilly Line).

Team Manager: William Dodgin. **Chief Administrator/Secretary:** D. R. Piggott.

Colours: Red and white striped shirts; black shorts.

Record home gate: 39,626 v. Preston North End, March, 1938 (F.A. Cup).

Honours—Champions: Div. 2: 1934–35. Div. 3 South: 1932–33. Div. 4: 1962–63.

    F.A. Cup Winners: Nil.

BRIGHTON & HOVE ALBION   DIV. 1

CATTLIN, Christopher J.	MAYBANK, Edward G.	SAYER, Peter A.
CHIVERS, Martin H.	MOSELEY, Graham	STEELE, Eric G.
CLARK, Paul P.	O'SULLIVAN, Peter A.	TILER, Kenneth D.
GEARD, Glen J. H.		WARD, Peter D.
HORTON, Brian	POSKETT, Malcolm	WILLIAMS, Peter G.
KERSLAKE, Michael L.	ROLLINGS, Andrew N.	WINSTANLEY, Graham
LAWRENSON, Mark T.	RING, Michael P.	
	RYAN, Gerard J.	

LEAGUE APPEARANCES: Cattlin, C. J. 27; Chivers, M. H. 3; Clark, P. P. 28(5); Horton, B. 39(1); Lawrenson, M. T. 39; Maybank, E. G. 35(2); Moseley, G. 17; O'Sullivan, P. A. 37; Poskett, M. 21(8); Rollings, A. N. 37; Ryan, G. 34(1); Sayer, P. A. 26(6); Steele, E. G. 25; Tiler, K. D. 17; Towner, A. J. 4(2); Ward, P. D. 27(5); Williams, P. G. 42; Winstanley, G. 4.

GOALS—League (72): Horton 11 (5 pens.), Maybank 10, Ward 10, Poskett 9, Ryan 9, Sayer 5, Clark 4, Rollings 3, Lawrenson 2, Williams 2, Chivers 1, O'Sullivan 1, Own goals 5.

    F.A. Cup (2): Lawrenson, Ryan.

    League Cup (6): Ward 3, Lawrenson, Maybank, O'Sullivan.

Ground: Goldstone Road, Old Shoreham Road, Hove, Sussex BN3 7DE. (0273-739 535).

Nearest station: Hove.

Team Manager: Alan Mullery, M.B.E. **Secretary:** Kenneth J. Calver.

Colours: Blue and white striped shirts, white sleeves; blue shorts.

Record home gate: 36,747 v. Fulham, December, 1958 (League).

Honours—Champions: Div. 3 South: 1957–58. Div. 3: 1971–72. Div. 4: 1964–65.

    F.A. Cup Winners: Nil.

16

BRISTOL CITY

CASHLEY, Alec R.
CHANDLER, Ricky D.
COLLIER, Gary B.
COOPER, Terence
CORMACK, Peter B.
DOYLE, Ian P.
GARLAND, Christopher S.
GILLIES, Donald G.
GOW, Gerard

HAY, Alan B.
HUNTER, Norman
JANTUNEN, Pertti K.
MABBUTT, Kevin R.
MANN, James A.
MEIJER, Geert
MERRICK, Geoffrey
MOGG, David J.
PENNY, Shaun
PRITCHARD, Howard K.

RITCHIE, Thomas G.
RODGERS, David M.
ROYLE, Joseph
SHAW, John
STEVENS, Paul D.
SWEENEY, Gerald
TAINTON, Trevor K.
WHITEHEAD, Clive R.

LEAGUE APPEARANCES: Bain, J. 3(1); Cashley, A. R. 2; Collier, G. B. 9; Cooper, T. 11; Cormack, P. B. 14(3); Garland, C. S. 4(1); Gillies, D. G. 27; Gow, G. 38; Hunter, N. 39; Jantunen, P. K. –(1); Mabbutt, K. R. 26(1); Mann, J. A. 23(5); Meijer, G. 9; Pritchard, H. K. 1; Ritchie, T. G. 39(1); Rodgers, D. M. 36; Royle, J. 40; Shaw, J. 40; Sweeney, G. 42; Tainton, T. K. 37; Whitehead, C. R. 22(8).

GOALS—League (47): Mabbitt 9, Ritchie 9 (2 pens.), Royle 7, Gow 5, Rodgers 5, Cormack 3 (2 pens.), Meijer 2, Whitehead 2, Garland 1, Gillies 1, Hunter 1, Mann 1, Tainton 1.
    F.A. Cup (3): Gow, Ritchie, Rodgers.
    League Cup (1): Ritchie.

Ground: Ashton Gate, Bristol BS3 2EJ. (Bristol 632812).
Nearest station: Bristol Temple Mead or Parson Street.
Manager: Alan Dicks. **Secretary:** A. E. Rance.
Colours: Red shirts; white shorts.
Record home gate: 43,335 v. Preston, February, 1935 (F.A. Cup).
Honours—Champions: Div. 2: 1905–06. Div. 3 South: 1922–23, 1926–27, 1954–55.
    F.A. Cup Winners: Nil.

BRISTOL ROVERS

AITKEN, Peter G.
BATER, Philip T.
BROWN, Keith T.
CLARKE, Gary
DENNEHY, Jeremiah
EMMANUEL, John G.
ENGLAND, Michael

GRIFFITHS, Ashley R.
HARDING, Stephen J.
HENDRIE, Paul
JONES, Glyn A.
JONES, Vaughan
MABBUTT, Gary V.
PALMER, David J.
PRINCE, Francis A.

PULIS, Anthony R.
SHAW, Martin J.
STANIFORTH, David A.
TAYLOR, Stuart
THOMAS, Martin R.
WHITE, Stephen J.
WILLIAMS, David M.

LEAGUE APPEARANCES: Aitken, P. G. 31(1); Barry, M. J. 12; Bater,
P. T. 36; Brown, K. T. 1(2); Clarke, G. 2(4); Day, G. G. 24; Dennehy, J.
29(3); Emmanuel, J. G. 21; England, M. 1; Gould, R. A. 3(1); Harding,
S. J. 10; Hendrie, P. 13(5); Jones, V. 21(1); Lythgoe, P. 6; Mabbutt, G. V.
8(3); Palmer, D. J. 1; Petts, P. A. 9(1); Prince, F. A. 26; Pulis, A. R. 7;
Randall, P. 21; Shaw, M. J. 1(1); Staniforth, D. A. 31(2); Taylor, S. 41;
Thomas, M. R. 42; White, S. J. 23(4); Williams, D. M. 42.
GOALS—League (48): Randall 13, White 10, Williams 10, Staniforth 6,
Gould 2, Prince 2, Aitken 1, Barry 1, Hendrie 1, Jones 1 (pen.),
Own goal 1.
F.A. Cup (3): White 3.
League Cup (2): Aitken, Staniforth.
Ground: Eastville Stadium, Bristol BS5 6NN. (Bristol 558620).
Nearest stations: Bristol Temple Mead or Stapleton Road.
Team Manager: Bobby Campbell. **Secretary:** E. Peter Terry.
Colours: Blue and white quartered shirts; white shorts.
Record home gate: 38,472 v. Preston, January, 1960 (F.A. Cup).
Honours—Champions: Div. 3 South: 1952–53.
F. A. Cup Winners: Nil.

BURNLEY   DIV. 2

ARINS, Anthony F.
BRENNAN, Ian
BURKE, Marshall
DIXON, Paul K.
FLETCHER, Paul J.
GARDINER,
  James D.
HALL, Brian W.
HIGGINS, Robert J.
INGHAM,
  William C.
JAKUB, Yanek
JAMES, Leighton

KINDON,
  Stephen M.
McADAM, Steven
McGREGOR, Neil
MORLEY,
  Anthony W.
NOBLE, Peter
NORMAN,
  Anthony J.
O'ROURKE,
  William J.
OVERSON,
  Richard J.

PICKERILL, Stuart
ROBERTSON,
  Stuart
ROBINSON, Peter
RODAWAY,
  William V.
SCOTT, Derek E.
SMITH, Malcolm
STEVENSON, Alan
TAIT, David J.
TATE, Jeffrey
THOMSON, James S.

LEAGUE APPEARANCES: Arins, A. F. 7; Brennan, I. 38; Cochrane,
G. 6; Fletcher, P. J. 34(1); Hall, B. W. 25(3); Ingham, W. C. 37; Jakub, Y.
13; James, L. 37; Kindon, S. M. 37(1); Morley, W. A. 12(7); Noble, P. 41;
Robertson, S. –(1); Robinson, P. 8(5); Rodaway, W. V. 39; Scott, D. E.
35; Smith, M. 9; Stevenson, A. 42; Thomson, J. S. 41; Young, K. 1.
GOALS—League (51): Noble 14 (7 pens.), Fletcher 9, Ingham 9, Brennan
4, James 3, Kindon 3, Hall 2, Morley 2, Cochrane 1, Robinson
1, Scott 1, Smith 1, Thomson 1.
F.A. Cup (6): Fletcher, Ingham, James, Kindon, Morley, Thomson.
League Cup (5): Cochrane 2, Brennan, Ingham, Noble.
Ground: Turf Moor, Burnley BB10 4BX. (0282 27777 and 38021).
Nearest station: Burnley Central.
Manager: Harry Potts. **Secretary.** A. Maddox.
Colours: Claret shirts with sky blue V, white shorts.
Record home gate: 54,775 v. Huddersfield, February, 1924 (F.A. Cup).
Honours—Champions: Div. 1: 1920–21, 1959–60. Div. 2: 1897–98, 1972–73.
F.A. Cup Winners: 1913–14.

18

BURY   DIV. 3

BAILEY, Anthony D.
BEAMISH,
  Kenneth G.
CONSTANTINE,
  David
EVANS, Ronald
FORREST, John A.
GREGORY, David
HILTON, Paul

JOHNSON,
  Stephen A.
KENNEDY,
  Keith V.
LATCHFORD,
  David
LUGG, Raymond
MADDEN, Craig

MULLEN,
  Stephen A.
RITSON, John
STANTON, Brian
TAYLOR, Gordon
TUCKER, William
WHITEHEAD, Alan
WILSON, Daniel

LEAGUE APPEARANCES: Bailey, A. D. 16; Beamish, K. G. 35;
Constantine, D. 16; Farrell, P. 8(3); Forrest, J. A. 44; Gregory, D. 36;
Hamstead, G. W. 10; Hatton, D. H. 12(1); Hilton, P. 6(3); Johnson, S. A.
3(5); Keenan, G. P. 5; Kennedy, K. V. 33; Latchford, D. 2; Lugg, R. 45;
Madden, C. 4(9); Mullen, S. A. 2(1); Ritson, J. 31; Robins, I. 4; Rowland,
A. A. 7; Stanton, B. 36(3); Taylor, G. 45; Tucker, W. 36; Whitehead, A.
24; Wilson, D. 46; Woolfall, A. F. –(1).
GOALS—League (59): Beamish 16 (3 pens.), Gregory 10, Wilson 7,
  Stanton 4, Whitehead 3, Lugg 2, Ritson 2, Taylor 2, Tucker 2,
  Constantine 1, Farrell 1, Hatton 1, Hilton 1, Johnson 1,
  Keenan 1, Kennedy 1, Madden 1, Robins 1, Rowland 1, Own
  goal 1.
    F.A. Cup (11): Gregory 6, Beamish Kennedy, Lugg, Wilson (pen),
    Own goal 1.
    League Cup (1): Rowland.
Ground: Gigg Lane, Bury BL9 9HR. (061-764 4881/2).
Nearest station: Bury.
Player/manager: Dave Hatton. **Secretary:** John Heap.
Colours: White shirts; royal blue shorts.
Record home gate: 35,000 v. Bolton, January, 1960 (F.A. Cup).
Honours—Champions: Div. 2: 1894–95. Div. 3: 1960–61.
    F.A. Cup Winners: 1899–1900, 1902–03.

CAMBRIDGE UNITED   DIV. 2

AVERY, Roger J.
BILEY, Alan P.
BUCKLEY, Ian
CHRISTIE,
  Derrick H. M.
COZENS, John W.
FALLON, Stephen P.
FINNEY, Tom
GARNER,
  William D.

GRAHAM, Peter
HOWARD,
  Trevor E.
KEY, Richard M.
LEACH,
  Michael J. C.
MURRAY,
  James G.
O'NEIL, Thomas
SMITH, Lindsay J.

SMITH, Nigel P.
SPRIGGS, Stephen
STREETE, Floyd A.
STRINGER,
  David R.
SWEETZER,
  Gordon E. P.
WEBSTER,
  Malcolm W.

LEAGUE APPEARANCES: Adams, S. T. –(1); Biley, A. P. 41; Buckley,
I. 22(3); Christie, D. H. M. 20(1); Corbin, K. D. 3; Cozens, J. W. 23(4);
Fallon, S. P. 42; Finney, T. 42; Garner, W. D. 17(5); Graham, P. 28(2);
Howard, T. E. 15; Key, R. M. 1; Leach, M. J. C. 18(1); Murray, J. G. 23(3);

19

O'Neil, T. 1(1); Smith, L. J. 40; Smith, N. P. –(1); Spriggs, S. 40; Streete,
F. A. 9(4); Stringer, D. R. 36; Watson, G. S. –(1); Webster, M. W. 41.
GOALS—League (44): Biley 20 (4 pens.), Finney 8, Christie 3, Garner 3,
     Spriggs 2, Buckley 1, Cozens 1, Leach 1, Murray 1, Streete 1,
     Own goals 3.
    F.A. Cup (1): Biley.
    League Cup (3): Biley (pen.), Finney, Morgan.
Ground: Abbey Stadium, Newmarket Road, Cambridge CB5 8LL.
   (Teversham (02205) 2170).
Nearest station: Cambridge.
Manager: John Docherty. Secretary: L. S. Holloway.
Colours: Black and amber vertical striped shirts; black shorts.
Record home gate: 14,000 v. Chelsea (friendly), May, 1970.
Honours—Champions: Div. 4: 1976–77.
    F.A. Cup Winners: Nil.

CARDIFF CITY   DIV. 2

BISHOP, Raymond J.	JOSEPH, Antone D.	PONTIN, Keith
BUCHANAN, John	LARMOUR,	ROBERTS, David F.
CAMPBELL, Alan J.	Albert A. J.	SHERMAN,
DAVIES, John G.	LEACH, Phillip D.	Robert G.
DAVIES, Paul A.	LEWIS, John	STEVENS, Gary M.
DWYER, Philip J.	MICALEFF,	SULLIVAN, Colin J
EVANS, Anthony	Constantinous	THOMAS,
FRIDAY, Robin	MILLER, Paul E.	Roderick J.
GRAPES, Stephen P.	MOORE, Ronald D.	WILLIAMS,
HARRIS, Gary W.	PARSONS,	Christopher
HEALEY, Ronald	Anthony M.	
JONES, Linden	PIPER, Dean W.	

LEAGUE APPEARANCES: Attley, B. R. 8(2); Barber, K. 2; Bishop, R.
J. 26(5); Buchanan, J. 36; Burns, M. E. 6; Byrne, G. 2; Campbell, A. J.
40; Davies, J. G. 4; Dwyer, P. J. 39; Evans, A. 30(1); Giles, D. C. 4;
Grapes, S. P. 22(2); Harris, G. W. 1; Healey, R. 32; Jones, L. 14; Larmour,
A. A. J. 15; Lewis, J. 13(3); Micalleff, C. 1(1); Moore, R. D. 18; Pethard,
F. J. 14(5); Platt, J. A. 4; Pontin, K. 27; Roberts, D. F. 28; Stevens, G. M.
32(2); Sullivan, C. J. 19; Thomas, R. J. 22(1); Went, P. F. 3.
GOALS—League (56): Buchanan 16 (5 pens.), Stevens 13, Evans 7 (2 pens.),
    Bishop 6, Dwyer 4, Moore 3, Roberts 2, Grapes 1, Sullivan 1,
    Went 1, Own goals 2.
    F.A. Cup: Nil.
    League Cup (2): Bishop, Buchanan.
Ground: Ninian Park, Cardiff CF1 8SX. (Cardiff 28501, 33230 and
   397997).
Nearest station: Cardiff Central.
Team Manager: Richie Morgan. Secretary: L. G. Hayward.
Colours: Blue shirts with a single yellow and white stripe; blue shorts
  with yellow and white trim.
Record home gate: 61,566 Wales v. England, October 1961. (Club record)
  57,800 v. Arsenal, Div. 1 April 22, 1953.
Honours—Champions: Div. 3 South: 1946–47.
    F.A. Cup Winners: 1926–27.

CARLISLE UNITED   DIV. 3

BANNON, Paul A.
BONNYMAN,
  Philip
COLLINS,
  Andrew B.
FELL, Geoffrey M.
HAMILTON, James
HARRISON,
  Anthony L.

HOOLICKIN,
  Stephen
KEMP, David M.
LUDLAM, Steven J.
LUMBY, James A.
McCARTNEY,
  Michael
MACDONALD,
  Ian C. A.

McLEAN, David J.
McVITIE, George J.
PARKER, Robert
SAWYERS, Keith W.
SWINBURNE,
  Trevor
TAIT, Michael P.

LEAGUE APPEARANCES: Bannon, P. A. 2; Bonnyman, P. 45; Clarke, D. –(1); Collins, A. B. 3; Hamilton, J. 31(1); Hoolickin, S. 46; Kemp, D. M. 45; Ludlam, S. J. 38(1); Lumby, J. A. 22(3); McCartney, M. 44; McLean, D. J. 6(3); McVitie, G. J. 46; MacDonald, I. C. A. 41; Parker, R. 46; Ross, J. A. 1; Sawyers, K. W. –(1); Swinburne, T. 45; Tait, M. P. 45(1).

GOALS—League (53): Kemp 18, Bonnyman 7 (1 pen.), Tait 7, Lumby 6, McCartney 5 (5 pens.), Ludlam 3, McVitie 2, Hamilton 1, McDonald 1, Parker 1, Own goals 2.
  F.A. Cup (6): Kemp 2, Lumby 2, McCartney (pen.), Tait.
  League Cup (3): Bonnyman, Kemp, Lumby.
Ground: Brunton Park, Carlisle CA1 1LL. (Carlisle 26237).
Nearest station: Carlisle.
Manager: Bobby Moncur. Secretary: J. D. Dent.
Colours: Blue shirts with broad white vertical stripe and red trim; white shorts.
Record home gate: 27,500 v. Birmingham, January, 1957 (F.A. Cup), and v. Middlesbrough, February, 1970 (F.A. Cup).
Honours—Champions: Div. 3: 1964–65.
  F.A. Cup Winners: Nil.

CHARLTON ATHLETIC   DIV. 2

ABRAHAMS,
  Lawrence A. M.
BERRY, Leslie D.
BOOTH, Anthony J.
BRISLEY,
  Terence W.
CAMPBELL,
  David A.

CHURCHOUSE,
  Gary
DUGDALE, Alan
FLANAGAN,
  Michael A.
GRITT, Stephen J.
HALES, Derek D.
MADDEN,
  Lawrence D.

NEWSON, Mark J.
ROBINSON,
  Martin J.
SHAW, Peter K.
SHIPPERLEY,
  David J.
TYDEMAN, Richard
WARMAN, Philip R.
WOOD, Jeffrey R.

LEAGUE APPEARANCES: Berry, L. D. 36(2); Booth, A. J. –(2); Brisley, T. W. 29(3); Campbell, D. A. 39; Churchouse, G. 9; Dugdale, A. 4; Flanagan, M. A. 25; Gritt, S. J. 38(1); Hales, D. D. 20; Johns, N. 10; Madden, L. D. 37(1); Peacock, K. 25(5); Penfold, M. 4(2); Powell, C. D. 21(7); Robinson, M. J. 35; Shaw, P. K. 33(1); Shipperley, D. J. 33; Tydeman, R. 21; Warman, P. R. 11; Wood, J. R. 32.

21

GOALS—League (60): Robinson 15, Flanaghan 13 (1 pen.), Hales 8 (2
pens.), Brisley 3, Gritt 3, Madden 3, Shipperley 3, Campbell 2,
Peacock 2 (1 pen.), Tydeman 2, Warman 2, Berry 1, Powell 1,
Shaw 1, Own goal 1.
F.A. Cup (3): Campbell, Flanagan, Robinson.
League Cup (12): Peacock 3, Robinson 3, Flanagan 2, Shipperley 2,
Brisley, Hales.
Ground: The Valley, Floyd Road, Charlton, SE7 8AW. (01-858 3711/2).
Nearest station: Charlton (S.R.).
Team Manager: Andy Nelson. General Manager/Secretary: Benny R. V.
Fenton.
Colours: Red shirts; white shorts.
Record home gate: 75,031 v. Aston Villa, February, 1938 (F.A. Cup).
Honours—Champions: Div. 3 South: 1928–29, 1934–35.
F.A. Cup Winners: 1946–47.

CHELSEA   DIV. 2

AYLOTT,   FROST, Lee A.   PHILLIPS,
 Trevor K. C.   HALES, Kevin P.   Thomas J. S.
BANNON,   HARRIS, Ronald E.   SITTON, John E.
 Eamonn J. P.   HAY, David   SPARROW, John P.
BONETTI, Peter P.   ILES, Robert J.   STANLEY, Garry E.
BOROTA, Petar   JENKINS, Ioreth C.   STRIDE, David R.
BRITTON, Ian   JOHNSON, Gary J.   SULLEY,
BUMSTEAD, John   LANGLEY,   Christopher S. L.
CHIVERS, Gary   Thomas W.   WALKER, Clive
CLARE, James E.   LOCKE, Gary R.   WILKINS,
DOCHERTY, James   NUTTON,   Graham G.
DROY, Michael R.   Michael W.   WILKINS,
FILLERY,   OSGOOD, Peter L.   Raymond C.
 Michael C.   PENNY, Clive A.   WILSON, Richard.

LEAGUE APPEARANCES: Aylott, T. K. C. 13(2); Bannon, E. J. P. 19;
Bonetti, P. P. 16; Borota, P. 12; Britton, I. 9(4); Bumstead, J. 6(2);
Chivers, G. 5; Docherty, J. 2(1); Droy, M. R. 14; Fillery, M. C. 6(1);
Frost, L. A. 2(1); Garner, W. D. 1; Harris, R. E. 38(2); Hay, D. 8; Iles,
R. J. 7; Johnson, G. J. 1; Langley, T. W. 40(1); Lewington, R. K. 10;
Locke, G. R. 8; McKenzie, D. 15; Nutton, M. W. 15; Osgood, P. L. 9;
Phillips, T. J. S. 7; Sitton, J. E. 11(1); Stanley, G. E. 32(4); Stride, D. R.
32; Swain, K. 15; Walker, C. 23(7); Wicks, S. J. 23; Wilkins, G. 28;
Wilkins, R. C. 35.
GOALS—League (44): Langley 15 (1 pen.), Stanley 5 (1 pen.), McKenzie
4, Swain 4, Walker 4, Wilkins (R.) 3, Osgood 2, Bannon 1.
Bumstead 1, Johnson 1, Wicks 1, Wilkins (G.) 1, Own goals 2.
F.A. Cup: Nil.
League Cup (1): Langley.
Ground: Stamford Bridge, Fulham Road, London SW6 1HS (01-385
5545/6), also information service 381-0111.
Nearest station: Fulham Broadway (District Line).
Manager: Danny Blanchflower. General Manager: Ron Suart. Secretary:
Christine Mathews.

Colours: Blue shirts; blue shorts with white stripe.
Record home gate: 82,905 v. Arsenal, October, 1935 (League).
Honours—Champions: Div. 1: 1954–55.
F.A. Cup Winners: 1969–70.
League Cup Winners: 1964–65.
European Cup Winners Cup: 1970–71.

CHESTER   DIV. 3

BURNS, David
EDWARDS, Robert I.
GENDALL, Richard M.
HENDERSON, Peter
HOWAT, Ian S.
JEFFRIES, Derek
JONES, Brynley
LEWIS, Paul
LIVERMORE, Douglas E.
LLOYD, Brian W.
MELLOR, Ian
MILLINGTON, Grenville R.
NICKEAS, Mark
OAKES, Alan A.
PHILLIPS, Ronald D.
PRESTIDGE, Ronald D.
RAYNOR, Paul E.
STORTON, Trevor G.
SUTCLIFFE, Peter D.
WALKER, James M.

LEAGUE APPEARANCES: Burns, D. 7(2); Delgado, R. A. 15; Edwards, R. I. 39; Felix, G. M. 8; Henderson, P. 25; Howat, I. S. 5; Jeffries, D. 40; Jones, B. 26(3); Livermore, D. E. 39; Lloyd, B. W. 41; Mellor, I. 21(2); Millington, G. R. 5; Nickeas, M. 33(1); Oakes, A. A. 37; Phillips, R. D. 40; Raynor, P. E. 36(1); Rush, I. J. 1; Storton, T. G. 46; Sutcliffe, P. D. 11(3); Walker, J. M. 31(1).
GOALS—League (57): Edwards 20, Phillips 10 (1 pen.), Henderson 7, Mellor 6, (2 pens.), Oakes 4, Raynor 4 (3 pens.), Jones 2, Delgado 1, Jeffries 1, Livermore 1, Walker 1.
F.A. Cup (7): Mellor 3, Phillips 2, Howatt, Jones.
League Cup (6): Edwards 3, Livermore, Mellor, Phillips.
Ground: The Stadium, Sealand Road, Chester CH1 4LW. (Chester (0244) 371376).
Nearest station: Chester.
Manager: Alan Oakes. Secretary: S. Gandy.
Colours: Royal blue shirts with white stripes; royal blue shorts with red and white trim.
Record home gate: 20,500 v. Chelsea, January, 1952 (F.A. Cup).
Honours—Champions: Nil.
F.A. Cup Winners: Nil.

CHESTERFIELD   DIV. 3

BURTON, Kenneth O.
CAMMACK, Stephen R.
CHAMBERLAIN, Glyn
COTTAM, John
DEARDEN, William
FERN, Rodney
FLAVELL, Robert W.
HEPPOLETTE, Richard A. W.
HIGGINS, Andrew M.
HUNTER, Leslie
KOWALSKI, Andrew M.
LETHEREN, Glan
MOSS, Ernest
O'NEILL, James J.
POLLARD, Gary
PROPHETT, Colin G.
SALMONS, Geoffrey
SIMPSON, Gary
TARTT, Colin
TINGAY, Philip
WALKER, Phillip A.

LEAGUE APPEARANCES: Burton, K. O. 40(2); Cammack, S. R. 13(9); Chamberlain, G. 1; Cottam, J. 36; Dearden, W. 1(4); Fern, R. 39(1); Flavell, R. W. 27(2); Heppolette, R. A. W. 13(1); Higgins, A. M. 1; Hunter, L. 40; Kowalski, A. M. 42(2); Letheren, G. 34; Moss, E. 22(1); O'Neill, J. J. 23(1); Pollard, G. 1; Prophett, C. G. 35; Salmons, G. 37; Simpson, G. 10(5); Tartt, C. 42; Tingay, P. 12; Walker, P. A. 37(3).

GOALS—League (51): Fern 11 (3 pens.), Walker 9, Kowalski 5, Moss 5, Salmons 5, Cammack 4, Simpson 3 (1 pen.), Cottam 2, Flavell 2, Burton 1, Prophett 1, Tartt 1, Own goals 2.

F.A. Cup (1): Flavell.

League Cup (8): Fern 2, Tartt 2, Cammack, Cottam, Flavell, Walker.

Ground: Recreation Ground, Saltergate, Chesterfield S40 4SX. (Chesterfield 32318).

Nearest station: Chesterfield.

Team Manager: Arthur Cox. **General Manager-Secretary:** A. G. Sutherland.

Colours: Royal blue shirts; white shorts.

Record home gate: 30,968 v. Newcastle U., April, 1939 (League).

Honours—Champions: Div. 3 North: 1930–31, 1935–36. Div. 4: 1969–70.

F.A. Cup Winners: Nil.

COLCHESTER UNITED   DIV. 3

ALLINSON, Ian J. R.
BUNKELL, Raymond K.
COOK, Michael
COTTON, Russell A.
DOWMAN, Stephen J.
DYER, Paul D.

EVANS, Anthony W.
FOLEY, Stephen P.
GOUGH, Robert G.
HAMILTON, Robert H. M.
HODGE, Robert W.
LEE, Trevor C.

LESLIE, Steven R. W.
PACKER, Michael D.
ROWLES, Edward A. J.
WALKER, Michael S. G.
WIGNALL, Steve L.
WRIGHT, Stephen P.

LEAGUE APPEARANCES: Allinson, I. J. R. 45(1); Bunkell, R. K. 10(2); Cook, M. 46; Cotton, R. A. 1; Dowman, S. J. 37(1); Dyer, P. D. 37(3); Evans, A. W. 8(1); Foley, S. P. 34; Gough, R. G. 42; Hodge, R. W. 31; Lee, T. C. 27; Leslie, S. R. W. 3; Packer, M. D. 40(2); Rowles, E. A. J. 19(2); Sharkey, P. G. 5(1); Walker, M. S. G. 46; Wignall, S. L. 42; Wright, S. P. 33(2).

GOALS—League (60): Gough 16, Lee 11, Foley 6, Allinson 5 (1 pen.), Rowles 4, Wignall 4, Hodge 3 (1 pen.), Dowman 2, Dyer 2, Evans 2, Bunkell 1 Cook 1, Packer 1, Wright 1, Own goal 1.

F.A. Cup (11): Gough 6, Dowman 2, Foley, Hodge, Lee.

League Cup (2): Dowman, Rowles.

Ground: Layer Road, Colchester CO2 7JJ. (Colchester (0206) 74042).

Nearest station: Colchester.

Manager: Bobby Roberts. **Secretary:** Mrs. E. Scott.

Colours: Blue and white vertical striped shirts; blue shorts.

Record home gate: 19,072 v. Reading, November, 1948 (F.A. Cup).

Honours—Champions: Nil.

F.A. Cup Winners: Nil.

COVENTRY CITY   DIV. 1

BANNISTER, Gary
BLAIR, Andrew
BLYTH, James A.
COOP, Michael A.
COOPER, Kevin J.
DYSON, Paul I.
FERGUSON,
  Michael J.
GILLESPIE, Gary T.
GOODING,
  Raymond
HAGAN, James
HATELEY, Mark W.

HAYWOOD, Clive
HOLTON, James A.
HUNT, Stephen K.
HUTCHISON,
  Thomas
JACOBS, Steven D.
McDONALD,
  Robert W.
MURCOTT, Stephen
NARDIELLO,
  Donato
OAKEY, Graham
OSGOOD, Keith

PHILLIPS, Nicholas
POWELL, Barry I.
ROBERTS,
  Brian L. F.
SEALEY, Leslie J.
THOMAS, Daniel J.
THOMPSON,
  Garry L.
WALLACE, Ian A.
WHITTON,
  Stephen P.
YORATH,
  Terence C.

LEAGUE APPEARANCES: Bannister, G. 3(1); Beck, J. A. 5(1); Blair,
A. 25(1); Blyth, J. A. 6; Coop, M. A. 36; Dyson, P. I. 2; Ferguson, M. J.
16(2); Gillespie, G. T. 14(1); Gooding, R. 2(2); Green, A. P. 6(5); Hagan,
J. 12(1); Hateley, M. W. 1; Holton, J. A. 34; Hunt, S. K. 20(4); Hutchison,
T. 42; McDonald, R. W. 42; Nardiello, D. 16; Osgood, K. 11; Powell,
B. I. 38; Roberts, B. L. F. 17; Sealey, L. J. 36; Thompson, G. L. 19(1);
Wallace, I. A. 38; Yorath, T. C. 21.
GOALS—League (58): Wallace 15, Powell 9 (3 pens.), Thompson 8,
  Ferguson 6, Hutchison 6, Hunt 5, McDonald 4, Bannister 1,
  Beck 1, Blair 1, Green 1, Own goal 1.
  F.A. Cup (2): Blair, Green.
  League Cup (1): Thompson.
Ground: Highfield Road, Coventry CV2 4GU. (Coventry 57171).
Nearest station: Coventry.
Team Manager: Gordon Milne. **Secretary:** J. D. Dent.
Colours: Sky blue shirts and shorts, with navy blue and white trim.
Record home gate: 51,457 v. Wolverhampton, April, 1967 (League).
Honours—Champions: Div. 2: 1966–67. Div. 3: 1963–64. Div. 3 South:
  1935–36.
  F.A. Cup Winners: Nil.

CREWE ALEXANDRA   DIV. 4

BEVAN, Paul
BOWLES,
  Paul M. A.
CHEETHAM,
  Hugh D.

COYNE, Peter D.
DAVIES, David L.
DULSON, Garry
MAYMAN, Paul
NELSON, Dennis N.

PURDIE, Bernard
RAFFERTY,
  Kevin B.
WARNOCK, Neil
WILKINSON, Neil

LEAGUE APPEARANCES: Bevan, P. 44; Bowles, P. M. A. 45; Brand,
A. 1; Caswell, P. D. 22; Cheetham, H. D. 22; Coyne, P. D. 32(4); Davies,
D. L. 38; Dulson, G. 28(1); Hughes, R. D. 12(1); Nelson, D. N. 31(4);
Nicholls, P. R. 10(3); Purdie, B. C. 39; Rafferty, K. B. 20; Rimmer, W.
20(3); Roberts, I. 34(3); Robertson, J. G. 32(1); Rogan, M. 3; Spence, C.
1; Tully, K. F. 6; Warnock, N. 20(1); White, E. A. 1; Wilkinson, N. 25(1);
Wilshaw, S. E. 20(2).

GOALS—League (43): Coyne 16, Bowles 8 (2 pens.), Davies 8, Nelson 5 (1 pen.), Purdie 2, Bevan 1, Warnock 1, Wilshaw 1, Own goal 1, F.A. Cup (2): Bowles, Coyne.
League Cup (8): Nelson 3, Bowles 2 (1 pen.), Coyne, Davies. Wilshaw.
Ground: Gresty Road, Crewe CW2 6EB. (Crewe 3014).
Nearest station: Crewe.
Manager: Tony Waddington. **Secretary:** Ken Dove.
Colours: Red shirts; white shorts.
Record home gate: 20,000 v. Tottenham, January, 1960 (F.A. Cup).
Honours—Champions: Nil.
F.A. Cup Winners: Nil.

CRYSTAL PALACE   DIV. 1

BOYLE,
  Terence D. J.
BURRIDGE, John
CANNON, James A.
CARTER, Leslie A.
DARE, Kevin J.
ELWISS, Michael
EVANS, Ian P.
FENWICK,
  Terence W.
FRY, David P.
GILBERT,
  William A.

GRAHAM, George
HAZELL,
  Anthony P.
HILAIRE,
  Vincent M.
HINSHELWOOD
  Paul A.
HORN, Robert I.
KEMBER,
  Stephen D.
LEAHY, Stephen D.
LOVELL, Stephen J.
LOWE, Gary W.

MURPHY,
  Jeremiah M.
NICHOLAS, Peter
PAUL, Anthony G.
SANSOM,
  Kenneth G.
SEALY, Anthony J.
SMILLIE, Neil
SPARKS,
  Christopher J.
SWINDLEHURST,
  David
WALSH, Ian P.

LEAGUE APPEARANCES: Burridge, J. 42; Cannon, J. A. 41; Chatterton, N. J. 13; Elwiss, M. 19(1); Fenwick, T. W. 20(4); Gilbert, W. A. 41; Hazell, A. P. 5; Hilaire, V. M. 25(6); Hinshelwood, P. A. 31; Kember, S. D. 29; Murphy, J. M. 40(1); Nicholas, P. 37; Sansom, K. G. 42; Sealy, A. J. 4(1); Silkman, B. –(1); Smillie, N. 3(5); Swindlehurst, D. 40; Walsh, I. P. 30(3).

GOALS—League (51): Swindlehurst 14 (1 pen.), Walsh 8, Elwiss 7, Hilaire 6, Murphy 5, Chatterton 3 (2 pens.), Nicholas 3, Cannon 2, Gilbert 1, Hinshelwood 1, Smillie 1.
F.A. Cup (5): Fenwick, Kember Nicholas, Sansom, Walsh.
League Cup (3): Chatterton (pen.), Murphy, Swindlehurst.
Ground: Selhurst Park, SE25 6PU. (01-653 2223/4).
Nearest stations: Selhurst, Norwood Junct. or Thornton Heath.
Team Manager: Terry Venables. **Secretary:** Alan J. Leather.
Colours: Shirts, white with 4 inch diagonal band red over blue from left shoulder, white shorts.
Record home gate: 49,498 v. Chelsea, December, 1969 (League).
Honours—Champions: Div. 2: 1978–79. Div. 3 South: 1920–21.
F.A. Cup Winners: Nil.

DARLINGTON   DIV. 4

BURLEIGH, Martin S.
COCHRANE, James K.
CROSSON, David
CRAIG, Derek M.
FERGUSON, Ronald C.
HAGUE, Neil
LYONS, Barry
MAITLAND, Lloyd C.
NATTRESS, Clive
OWERS, Philip
PATERSON, Thomas
PEACHEY, John M.
PROBERT, Eric W.
SEAL, James
STONE, John G.
TAYLOR, Philip A.
WALSH, Alan
WANN, John D.

LEAGUE APPEARANCES: Burleigh, M. S. 42; Cochrane, J. K. 39; Craig, D. M. 44; Crosson, D. 14(7); Ferguson, R. C. 31(3); Hague, N. 34; Hedley, G. 14; Lyons, B. 26; Maitland, L. C. 19(6); Nattress, C. 45; Owers, P. 4; Paterson, T. 6(1); Peachey, J. M. 13(1); Probert, E. W. 19(1); Seal, J. 35(5); Stone, J. G. 41; Taylor, P. A. 2(3); Walsh, A. 32(1); Wann, J. D. 46.

GOALS—League (49): Stone 9, Walsh 9, Seal 8, Ferguson 6, Peachey 6, Lyons 2, Paterson 2, Wann 2, Cochrane 1, Hague 1, Hedley 1 Maitland 1, Nattress 1.
    F.A. Cup (4): Ferguson 3, Craig.
    League Cup (6): Craig 2, Lyons 2 (1 pen.), Stone, Wann.
Ground: Feethams, Darlington DL1 5JB (Darlington (0325) 65097 and 67712).
Nearest station: Darlington.
Manager: Billy Elliott. **Secretary:** Andrew W. Rowell.
Colours: White shirts with red trim; black shorts.
Record home gate: 21,023 v. Bolton, November, 1960 (League Cup).
Honours—Champions: Div. 3, North: 1924–25.
    F.A. Cup Winners: Nil.

DERBY COUNTY   DIV. 1

BARTLETT, Paul J.
BLADES, Stephen M.
BOWERS, Robert
BUCKLEY, Steven
CARTER, Stephen C.
CASKEY, William
CHERRY, Steven R.
CHESTERS, Colin W.
CLARK, Jonathan
CLAYTON, John
CRAWFORD, Andrew
DALY, Gerard A.
DUNCAN, John P.
EMSON, Paul
FALCONER, Keith
GREENWOOD, Roy T.
HILL, Gordon A.
LANGAN, David
McCAFFERY, Aidan
McFARLAND, Roy L.
McKELLAR, David
MIDDLETON, John
MORELAND, Victor
MURRAY, Kevin
POWELL, Stephen
RIOCH, Bruce D.
SHERIDAN, Frank M.
SPOONER, Stephen A.
WEBB, David J.
WICKS, Stephen J.

LEAGUE APPEARANCES: Bartlett, P. J. 3; Buckley, S. 42; Carter, S. C. 29; Caskey, W. 22(2); Chesters, C. W. –(1); Clayton, J. 1; Clark, J. 17; Crawford, A. 12(1); Daly, G. A. 37; Daniel, P. A. 6(1); Duncan, J. P. 16(1); Emson, P. 6; George, C. F. 8; Greenwood, R. T. 19(1); Hill, G. A.

12(2); Langan, D. 40; McCaffrey, A. 6; McFarland, R. L. 24; McKellar, D. 16; Middleton, J. 26; Moreland, V. 27(4); Nish, D. J. 6(4); Powell, S. 41; Rioch, B. D. 7(1); Ryan, G. 6; Spooner, S. A. 1; Todd, C. 4; Webb, D. J. 9(1); Wicks, S. J. 19.

GOALS—League (44): Daly 13 (4 pens.), Duncan 5, Buckley 4, Caskey 3, Crawford 3, McFarland 3, Powell 3, George 2, Daniel 1, Greenwood 1, Hill 1, Nish 1, Webb 1, Own goals 3.

    F.A. Cup: Nil.

    League Cup (1): Hill.

Ground: The Baseball Ground, Derby DE3 8NB. (Derby 40105).

Nearest station: Derby.

Manager: To be announced.   General Secretary: To be announced.

Colours: White shirts; blue shorts.

Record home gate: 41,826 v. Tottenham, September 1969 (League).

Honours—Champions: Div. 1: 1971–72, 1974–75; Div. 2: 1911–12, 1914–15; 1968–69; Div. 3 North: 1956–57.

    F.A. Cup Winners: 1945–46.

DONCASTER ROVERS   DIV. 4

BENTLEY, David A.
BRADLEY, David
CORK, David
FLANAGAN, Shaun
FRENCH, Michael J.

LAIDLAW, Joseph D.
LALLY, Patrick A. M.
LEWIS, Frederick J.

MEAGAN, Thomas P.
PACKER, Leslie J.
PEACOCK, Dennis
PUGH, Daral J.
SNODIN, Glynn

LEAGUE APPEARANCES: Austin, R. L. 3; Bentley, D. A. 32(1); Bowden, P. W. 5(1); Bradley, D. 42; Cannell, S. 11(1); Cork, D. 7; Cox, M. L. 10(5); Flanagan, S. 14; French, M. J. 36; Gilligan, A. A. 1; Habbin, R. L. 16(3); Hemsley, E. J. O. 9; Jones, C. M. N. 4; Lally, P. A. M. 33; Laidlaw, J. D. 38; Lewis, F. J. 24(8); Lister, S. H. 9; Meagan, T. P. 27(4); Olney, K. J. 32; Owen, R. 29(2); Packer, L. J. 4(1); Peacock, D. 46; Pugh, D. J. 16(5); Read, S. E. 11; Robinson, F. J. 6; Snodin, G. 28(6); Taylor, B. 13.

GOALS—League (50): Owen 10, Laidlaw 7, French 5 (1 pen.), Lewis 5, Bradley 3, Cox 3, Snodin 3, Bentley 2, Habbin 2, Jones 2, Packer 2, Cork 1, Olney 1, Pugh 1, Reed 1, Taylor 1, Own goal 1.

    F.A. Cup (2): Laidlaw, Lewis.

    League Cup (1): French.

Ground: Belle Vue Ground, Doncaster DN4 5HT. (Doncaster 55281).

Nearest station: Doncaster.

Manager: Billy Bremner. General Manager-Secretary: J. E. Bennison.

Colours: Red shirts with white trim; white shorts.

Record home gate: 37,149 v. Hull City, October, 1948 (League).

Honours—Champions: Div. 3 North: 1934–35, 1946–47, 1949–50. Div. 4: 1965–66, 1968–69.

    F.A. Cup Winners: Nil.

EVERTON   DIV. 1

ANDERSON, John
BARTON, John S.
BRAND, Andrew S.
DEAKIN,
  Raymond J.
DOBSON, John M.
EASTOE, Peter R.
HEARD, Timothy P.
HIGGINS, Mark N.
JACK, James R.
JONES, David R.

KIDD, Brian
KING, Andrew E.
LATCHFORD,
  Robert D.
LODGE, Paul
LYONS, Michael
McBRIDE, Joseph
MURRAY,
  Martin P.
NULTY,
  Geoffrey O.

PEJIC, Michael
RATCLIFFE, Kevin
ROBINSON, Neil
ROSS, Trevor W.
TELFER, George A.
THOMAS, David
THOMAS, John W.
TODD, Colin
VARADI, Imre
WOOD, George
WRIGHT, William

LEAGUE APPEARANCES: Barton, J. S. 9(1); Darracott, T. M. 7; Dobson, J. M. 40; Eastoe, P. R. 7(1); Heard, T. P. 9(1); Higgins, M. N. 20(1); Jack, J. R. 1; Jones, D. R. 11; Kenyon, R. N. 3; Kidd, B. 9; King, A. E. 40; Latchford, R. D. 36; Lyons, M. 37; Nulty, G. O. 13(5); Pejic, M. 19; Robinson ,N. 4(3); Ross, T. W. 26(1); Telfer, G. A. 10(2); Thomas, D. 33; Todd, C. 29; Walsh, M. A. 18(2); Wood, G. 42; Wright, W. 39.
GOALS—League (52): King 12 (1 pen.), Latchford 11, Lyons 6, Ross 6 (2 pens.), Dobson 4, Kidd 2, Telfer 2, Thomas 2, Wright 2, Higgins 1, Jack 1, Nulty, 1, Todd 1, Walsh 1.
  F.A. Cup (1): Dobson.
  League Cup (11): Latchford 6 (1 pen.), Dobson 4, Own goal 1.
Ground: Goodison Park, Liverpool L4 4EL. (051-521 2020).
Nearest station: Liverpool Lime Street.
Manager: Gordon Lee. **Secretary:** Jim Greenwood.
Colours: Royal blue shirts with white trim; white shorts with blue trim.
Record home gate: 78,299 v. Liverpool, September, 1948 (League).
Honours—Champions: Div. 1: 1890–91, 1914–15. 1927–28, 1931–32, 1938–39, 1962–63, 1969–70; Div. 2: 1930–31.
  F.A. Cup Winners: 1905–06, 1932–33, 1965–66.

EXETER CITY   DIV. 3

BAUGH, John R.
BOWKER, Keith
DELVE, John F.
GILES, James A.
HATCH, Peter D.
HORE, Kenneth J.

IRELAND, Roy P.
NEVILLE, Steven F.
O'KEEFE, James V.
PEARSON, Ian T.
RANDELL, Colin
ROBERTS, Lee J.

ROGERS, Peter P.
SIMS, John
TEMPLEMAN,
  John H.

LEAGUE APPEARANCES: Bowker, K. 26(3); Delve, J. F. 42; Forbes, R. J. 7(1); Giles, J. A. 43; Hatch, P. D. 45; Hodge, R. W. 4; Holman, H. W. 4(4); Hore, K. J. 44; Ingham, F. R. –(2); Ireland, R. P. –(1); Kellow, T. 17; Main, I. 13; Mitchell, A. J. 10; O'Keefe, J. V. 33; Neville, S. F. 36; Pearson, I. T. 18; Randell, C. 38; Roberts, L. J. 41; Roberts, P. S. 2; Rogers, P. P. 11(1); Sims, J. 25; Templeman, J. H. 45; Williams, O. J. 2(1).
GOALS—League (61): Bowker 11, Sims 9, Neville 9 (4 pens.), Kellow 7, Delve 6, Pearson 3, Randell 3, Roberts 3, Rogers 3, Hatch 2, Giles 1, Holman 1, Templeman 1.

F.A. Cup (1): Forbes.
League Cup (6): Delve 3, Kellow 2, Bowker.
Ground: St. James Park, Exeter, Devon EX4 6PX. (Exeter 54073).
Nearest station: Exeter Central or St. David's.
Manager: Brian Godfrey. **Secretary:** P. R. Wakeham.
Colours: White shirts with 3 red stripes on sleeve; white shorts.
Record home gate: 20,984 v. Sunderland, March, 1931 (F.A. Cup).
Honours—Champions: Nil.
F.A. Cup Winners: Nil.

FULHAM   DIV. 2

BANTON, Geoffrey
BECK, John
BEST, George
BOYD, Gordon
BULLIVANT,
    Terence P.
CORNER, Brian
DAVIES, Gordon J.
DAY, Clive A.
DIGWEED, Perry M.
EVANS, Raymond L.
EVANSON, John M.
GALE, Anthony P.

GIBSON, Brian G.
GREENAWAY,
    Brian J.
GUMMER, John M.
GUTHRIE,
    Christopher W.
HATTER, Steven
KITCHEN,
    Michael P.
LOCK, Kevin J.
LOVELL, Mark A.
MAHONEY,
    Anthony J.

MARGERRISON,
    John W.
MARINELLO, Peter
MASON,
    Thomas R. J.
MONEY, Richard
O'DOHERTY,
    Peter D.
PEYTON, Gerald J.
RICHARDSON,
    James F.
SCRIVENS, Steven J.
STRONG, Leslie

LEAGUE APPEARANCES: Banton, G. 7; Beck, J. 32; Boyd, G. 1(2); Bullivant, T. P. 28; Davies, G. J. 32; Digweed, P. M. 2; Evans, R. L. 35; Evanson, J. M. 16(7); Gale, A. P. 36; Greenaway, B. J. 14(2); Guthrie, C. W. 34; Hatter, S. 5; Kitchen, M. P. 17; Lock, K. J. 39; Lovell, M. A. 2; Mahoney, A. J. 7; Margerrison, J. W. 20(6); Marinello, P. 8(1); Mason, T. J. R. 4; Money, R. 42; Peyton, G. J. 40; Strong, L. 41.
GOALS—League (50): Guthrie 13, Davies 9, Margerrison 6 (2 pens.), Kitchen 5, Greenaway 3, Lock 3 (2 pens.), Evans 2, Gale 2, Beck 1, Evanson 1, Mahoney 1, Money 1, Strong 1, Own goals 2.
F.A. Cup (3): Margerrison 2, Davies.
League Cup (2): Davies, Mahoney.
Ground: Craven Cottage, Fulham SW6 6HH. (01-736 6561).
Nearest station: Putney Bridge (District) or Hammersmith (Met., District and Piccadilly).
Manager: Robert Campbell. **Secretary:** George Noyce.
Colours: White shirts with black collars and 3 black stripes on shoulders; black shorts with three white stripes down seam.
Record home gate: 49,335 v. Millwall, October 1938 (League).
Honours—Champions: Div. 2: 1948–49. Div. 3, South: 1931–32.
F.A. Cup Winners: Nil.

GILLINGHAM DIV. 3

ARMSTRONG, Gary S.
BARKER, Allan M.
BRUCE, Stephen R.
CRABBE, Stephen A.
FORD, Colin
FUNNELL, Anthony
HILLYARD, Ronald W.
HOBDAY, Peter B. E.
HUGHES, Stephen J.
JOLLEY, Terence A.
KNIGHT, Graham J.
NICHOLL, Terence
OVERTON, John
PRICE, Kenneth G.
RICHARDSON, Damien J.
SHARPE, John W. H.
WALKER, Patrick J.
WEATHERLY, Colin M.
WESTWOOD, Daniel R.
WHEATLEY, Stephen J.
WHITE, Dean
YOUNG, Charles F.

LEAGUE APPEARANCES: Armstrong, G. S. 24(2); Barker, A. M. 22; Buttress, M. D. –(1); Crabbe, S. A. J. 34; Funnell, A. 12; Hillyard, R. W. 46; Hughes, S. J. 38(2); Jolley, T. A. 9(4); Knight, G. J. 3; Nicholl, T. 43; Overton, J. 43; Price, K. G. 41(1); Richardson, D. J. 28; Sharpe, J. W. H. 37; Walker, P. J. 4(6); Weatherley, C. M. 46; Westwood, D. R. 43(2); White, D. 26(1); Williams, N. J. 1; Young, C. F. 6.
GOALS—League (65): Westwood 18 (2 pens.), Price 14, Funnell 7, Jolley 5, Nicholl 4, Richardson 4, White 3 (2 pens.), Crabbe 2 (2 pens.), Hughes 2, Overton 2, Weatherley 2, Armstrong 1, Barker 1.
        F.A. Cup (1): Westwood.
        League Cup (2): Price, Young.
Ground: Priestfield Stadium, Gillingham, Kent ME7 4DD. (Medway (0634) 51854).
Nearest station: Gillingham.
Manager: Gerry Summers. **Secretary:** R. J. Dennison.
Colours: Blue shirts; white shorts.
Record home gate: 23,002 v. Q.P.R., January, 1948 (F.A. Cup).
Honours—Champions: Div. 4; 1963–64.
        F.A. Cup Winners: Nil.

GRIMSBY TOWN DIV. 3

BATCH, Nigel A.
BROLLY, Michael J.
CROMBIE, Dean M.
CUMMING, Robert
DONOVAN, Terence C.
DRINKELL, Kevin S.
FORD, Tony
LESTER, Michael J. A.
LIDDELL, Gary
MAWER, Shaun K.
MITCHELL, Robert
MOORE, David
MOORE, Kevin T.
WAINMAN, William H.
WAINWRIGHT, Peter L.
WATERS, Joseph L. W.
WIGGINTON, Clive A.
YOUNG, Martin

LEAGUE APPEARANCES: Barker, G. A. 28; Batch, N. A. 46; Brolly, M. J. 44; Crombie, D. M. 46; Cumming, R. 31(3); Donovan, T. C. 4(1); Drinkell, K. S. 20(8); Ford, T. 43(2); Lester, M. J. A. 30; Liddell, G. 21(5); Mawer, S. K. 15; Mitchell, R. 24; Moore, D. 30; Moore, K. T. 46; Partridge, M. 7(1); Waters, J. J. W. 46; Wigginton, C. A. 18; Young, M. 7(2).

31

GOALS—League (82): Ford 15, Waters 10 (2 pens.), Brolly 9, Cumming 9 (1 pen.), Drinkell 7, Lester 7, Liddell 6, Moore (K.) 6, Donovan 3, Mitchell 2, Barker 1, Crombie 1, Mawer 1, Young 1, Own goals 4.
    F.A. Cup: Nil.
    League Cup (5): Cumming, Donovan, Lester, Mitchell, Waters (pen.).

Ground: Blundell Park, Cleethorpes, Lincs. DN35 7PY. (Cleethorpes (0472) 61420 and 61803).
Nearest stations: Cleethorpes or Grimsby Town.
Manager: John H. E. Newman. **Secretary:** D. J. Dowse.
Colours: Black and white striped shirts; black shorts.
Record home gate: 31,657 v. Wolves, February, 1937 (F.A. Cup).
Honours—Champions: Div. 2: 1900–01, 1933–34, Div. 3, North: 1925–26, 1955–56. Div. 4: 1971–72.
    F.A. Cup Winners: Nil.

HALIFAX TOWN   DIV. 4

BULLOCK, Michael E.
BURKE, Peter
CAMPBELL, Robert M.
DUNLEAVY, Christopher
FIRTH, Francis M.
HUTT, Geoffrey
JOHNSON, Kevin P.
KENNEDY, Michael F.
LEONARD, Michael C.
MOUNTFORD, Robert W.
SIDEBOTTOM, Arnold
SMITH, Stephen
STAFFORD, Andrew

LEAGUE APPEARANCES: Bell, D. M. 11; Bradley, L. H. 19(1); Bullock, M. E. 10(1); Burke, P. 31; Campbell, R. M. 19(3); Carroll, J. 9(3); Dunleavy, C. 46; Firth, F. M. 33(2); Hutt, G. 31(1); Johnson, K. P. 37(2); Johnston, J. 5(2); Kennedy, M. F. 28(2); Kilner, J. I. 21; Lawson, J. J. 12; Leonard, M. C. 25; Loska, A. S. 34(1); Mountford, R. W. 23(3); Nixon, J. C. 12(7); Prendergast, M. J. 4; Sidebottom, A. 21; Smith, S. 38(2); Stafford, A. G. 7(1); Trainer, J. 30.

GOALS—League (39): Johnson 7 (2 pens.), Mountford 4, Bell 3, Bradley 3, Campbell 3, Bullock 2, Burke 2, Dunleavy 2, Firth 2, Sidebottom 2, Trainer 2, Carroll 1, Lawson 1, Nixon 1, Prendergast 1, Own goals 3.
    F.A. Cup: Nil.
    League Cup (1): Bullock.

Ground: The Shay, Halifax HX1 2YS. (Halifax 53423).
Nearest station: Halifax.
Manager: George Kirby. **Secretary:** D. Holland.
Colours: Royal blue shirts with white trim; white shorts with blue trim.
Record home gate: 36,885 v. Tottenham, February, 1953 (F.A. Cup).
Honours—Champions: Nil.
    F.A. Cup Winners: Nil.

HARTLEPOOL UNITED DIV. 4

AYRE, William
BROOKES, Stephen M.
BROWN, Phillip
CRUMPLIN, Ian
EVANS, David T.
GOLDTHORPE, Wayne
GORRY, Martin C.
HARDING, Alan
HEWITT, Samuel
HOGAN, Roy D.
HOUCHEN, Keith
LARKIN, Gordon T.
LAWRENCE, Mark
LINACRE, John
LOADWICK, Derek
LOWE, Kenneth
NEWTON, Robert
NORMANTON, Graham S.
NORTON, David J.
RICHARDSON, Graham C.
SMITH, George
SPELMAN, Michael T.
WATSON, John

LEAGUE APPEARANCES: Ayre, W. 42; Brookes, S. M. 34; Crumplin, I. 25(4); Edgar, E. 3; Evans, D. T. 1(2); Goldthorpe, W. 37(4); Gorry, M. C. 41; Guy, K. 7(3); Harding, A. 15; Hogan, R. D. 20(3); Houchen, K. 38(1); Larkin, G. T. 1(2); Lawrence, M. 34(4); Linacre, J. 45; Loadwick, D. 28(1); Malone, R. P. 3; Newton, R. 23; Norton, D. 8(3); Platt, J. A. 13; Richardson, G. C. 18; Smith, G. 43; Smith, T. M. 15(2); Watson, J. 12.
GOALS—League (57): Houchen 12, Lawrence 9, Newton 8 (4 pens.), Goldthorpe 6 (1 pen.), Ayre 5, Crumplin 5, Linacre 5, Brooks 1, Harding 1, Morgan 1, Norton 1, Smith (T.) 1, Own goals 2.
    F.A. Cup (4): Newton 2 (2 pens.), Crumplin, Goldthorpe.
    League Cup (1): Newton.
Ground: Victoria Ground, Clarence Road, Hartlepool (Hartlepool 72584).
Office: 5 Scarborough Street, Hartlepool TS24 7DA. (3492).
Nearest station: Hartlepool.
Manager: Billy Horner. **Secretary:** W. P. Hillan.
Colours: Blue shirts; white shorts.
Record home gate: 17,426 v. Manchester United, January, 1957 (F.A. Cup).
Honours—Champions: Nil.
    F.A. Cup Winners: Nil.

HEREFORD UNITED DIV. 4

BAILEY, Michael A.
BOUSTON, Bryan J.
BURROWS, Philip A.
CORNES, James S.
CROMPTON, Stephen W.
DIXON, David R.
EMERY, Stephen R.
GOULD, Robert A.
HENDRY, Ian
HOLMES, Kyle J.
HOLMES, William G.
HUGHES, Thomas A.
HUNT, Paul L.
JONES, David J.
KNIGHT, Lyndon A.
LAYTON, John H.
McGRELLIS, Francis
MARSHALL, Julian P.
POWELL, Wayne
PRICE, Christopher J.
SPIRING, Peter J.
STEPHENS, Kenneth J.
THOMAS, Valmore N.
WHITE, Eric W.

LEAGUE APPEARANCES: Bailey, M. A. 13(3); Barton, F. 4; Burrows, P. A. 34; Cornes, J. S. 23; Crompton, S. W. 6(2); Emery, S. R. 43(1); Feeley, A. J. 25(1); Gould, R. A. 39(1); Hendry, I. 15; Hill, H. –(1); Holmes, K. J. 19(2); Holmes, W. G. 12(4); Hughes, T. A. 44; Hunt, P. L.

33

9; Jones, D. J. 25(1); Knight, L. A. 2; Layton, J. H. 38; McGrellis, F. 11;
Marshall, J. P. 14; O'Brien, C. 1(1); O'Hara, G. 1; Phillips, S. G. 5(3);
Powell, W. 6; Price, C. J. 29; Roberts, P. S. 3; Spiring, K. M. 24(1);
Stephens, K. J. 25(3); Strong, S. 10; Thomas, V. N. 11(1); White, E. W. 15.
GOALS—League (53): Gould 13, Jones 8, Emery 5 (4 pens.), Spiring 5,
  Holmes (K.) 3, Holmes (W.) 3, McGrellis 3, White 3, Powell 2,
  Bailey 1, Barton 1 (pen.), Burrows 1, Crompton 1, Layton 1,
  Stephens 1, Thomas 1, Own goal 1.
  F.A. Cup: Nil.
  League Cup (5): Barton, Emery, Holmes (W.), Jones, Layton.
Ground: Edgar Street, Hereford HR4 9JU. (0423 4037).
Nearest station: Hereford.
Player/Manager: Mike Bailey. Secretary: Bill Stevens.
Colours: White shirts with red and black trim; black shorts.
Record home gate: 18,114 v. Sheffield Wednesday, 1958 (F.A. Cup).
Honours—Champions: Div. 3: 1975–76.
  F.A. Cup Winners: Nil.

HUDDERSFIELD TOWN   DIV. 4

ARMSTRONG,
  Terry
BEILBY, Paul A.
BRANAGHAN,
  James P. S.
BROOK, Daryl
BROWN, Malcolm
COWLING,
  David R.
FLETCHER, Peter

GARTLAND,
  Paul E.
GIBSON, Paul
GRAY, Terence I.
HANVEY, Keith
HART, Peter O.
HOLMES, Ian M.
LILLIS, Mark A.
MELLOR, Robert B.
ROBINS, Ian

SANDERCOCK,
  Philip J.
SMITH, Thomas E.
STARLING, Alan
SUTTON, David
TAYLOR,
  Richard H.
TOPPING,
  Christopher

LEAGUE APPEARANCES: Armstrong, T. 15(2); Bielby, P. A. 29(2);
Branagan, J. P. S. 13(1); Brook, D. 1; Brown, M. 42; Campbell, R. M. 7;
Cowling, D. R. 25(1); Fletcher, P. 31(4); Gartland, P. E. 4; Gray, T. I. 22
(4); Hanvey, K. 32; Hart, P. O. 46; Holmes, I. M. 31(3); Howey, P. 10;
Lillis, M. A. 11(1); McGrellis, F. 4(1); Ripley, K. A. 2(3); Robins, I. 37(1);
Sandercock, P. J. 36; Smith, T. E. –(1); Starling, A. 45; Sutton, D. 39;
Taylor, R. H. 1; Topping, C. 23.
GOALS—League (57): Robins 16, Fletcher 12, Holmes 11, Bielby 5
  (3 pens.), Campbell 3, Hanvey 2, Armstrong 1, Cowling 1,
  Gray 1, Hart 1, Howey 1, Sutton 1, Topping 1, Own goal 1.
  F.A. Cup (1): Fletcher.
  League Cup (2): Holmes (pen.), Ripley.
Ground: Leeds Road, Huddersfield HD1 6PE. (Huddersfield 20335/6).
Nearest station: Huddersfield.
Team Manager: Mick Buxton. Secretary: G. S. Binns.
Colours: Shirts; Blue/white striped; white shorts.
Record home gate: 67,037 v. Arsenal, February, 1932 (F.A. Cup).
Honours—Champions: Div. 1: 1923–24, 1924–25, 1925–26. Div. 2: 1969–
  70.
  F.A. Cup Winners: 1921–22.

HULL CITY   DIV 3.

BANNISTER, Bruce I.
BLACKBURN, Edwin H.
BOYD, William
CROFT, Stuart D.
DE VRIES, Roger S.
DOBSON, Ian
EDWARDS, Keith
FARLEY, John D.
HAIGH, Paul
HAWKER, David
HOOD, Derek
HORSWILL, Michael F.
LEADBEATER, David R.
LORD, Malcolm
McCLAREN, Stephen
McDONALD Robert R.
MARWOOD, Brian
NISBET, Gordon J. M.
NORRIE, Craig T.
ROBERTS, Garreth W.
SKIPPER, Peter D.
WARBOYS, Alan
WEALANDS, Jeffrey A.

LEAGUE APPEARANCES: Bannister, B.I. 43(3); Blackburn, E. H. 18; Croft, S. D. 24; De Vries, R. S. 29; Dobson, I. 22(2); Edwards, K. 46; Farley, J. D. 32; Galvin, C. 15(4); Haigh, P. 45; Hawker, D. 22; Hood, D. 14(3); Horswill, M. F. 40; Lord, M. 23(1); McDonald, R. R. 8(2); Nisbet, G. J. M. 46; Norrie, C. T. –(1); Roberts, G. W. 18(1); Skipper, P. D. 17; Stewart, D. C. 2(3); Warboys, A. 14(4); Wealands, J. A. 28.

GOALS—League (66): Edwards 24, Bannister 15 (2 pens.), Horswill 6, Galvin 4, Lord 3, Roberts 3, McDonald 2, Skipper 2, Warboys 2, Farley 1, Haigh 1, Hawker 1, Nisbet 1, Stewart 1.
  F.A. Cup (2): Edwards 1, own goal 1.
  League Cup (2): Bannister, Haigh.

Ground: Boothferry Park Hull, HU4 6EU. (0482 52195/7).
Nearest stations: Hull or Boothferry Park Halt.
Manager: Ken Houghton. **General Manager/Secretary:** M. T. Stone.
Colours: Shirts: black and amber stripes; white shorts.
Record home gate: 55,019 v. Manchester United, February, 1949 (F.A. Cup).
Honours—Champions: Div. 3 North: 1932–33, 1948–49. Div. 3: 1965–66.
  F.A. Cup Winners: Nil.

IPSWICH TOWN   DIV. 1

BAKER, Kieron R.
BEATTIE, Thomas K.
BRAZIL, Alan B.
BURLEY, George E.
BUTCHER, Terry I.
COOPER, Paul D.
CROUCH, Nigel J.
ENDERSBY, Scott A. G.
GATES, Eric L.
GEDDIS, David
HUBBICK, David
HUNTER, Allan
KLUG, Bryan P.
LAMBERT, Michael A.
McCALL, Stephen H.
MARINER, Paul
MILLS, Michael D.
MUHREN, Arnoldous J. H.
OSBORNE, Roger C.
OSMAN, Russell C.
PARKIN, Thomas A.
PARKINSON, Noel D.
ROBERTS, James D.
SHIELDS, Peter
SIVELL, Laurence
SOUTER, Don D.
STEGGLES, Kevin P.
THIJSSEN, Fransiscus J.
TURNER, Robin D.
WARK, John
WHARTON, Anthony D.
WOODS, Clive R.

35

LEAGUE APPEARANCES: Beattie, T. K. 19(1): Brazil, A. B. 14(5);
Burley, G. E. 38; Butcher, T. I. 21; Cooper, P. D. 41; Gates, E. L. 20(2);
Geddis, D. 6(9); Hunter, A. 4; Lambert, M. A. 1(3); Mariner, P. 33;
Mills, M. D. 42; Muhren, A. J. H. 41; Osman, R. C. 39; Parkin, T. A.
3(1); Sivell, L. 1; Talbot, B. E. 21; Thijssen, F. J. 16; Tibbott, L. 11; Wark,
J. 42; Whymark, T. J. 8(5); Woods, C. R. 41.
GOALS—League (63): Mariner 13, Brazil 9, Muhren 8, Gates 7, Wark 6
(2 pens.), Woods 5, Talbot 3, Butcher 2, Mills 2, Osman 2,
Beattie 1, Burley 1, Geddis 1, Thijssen 1, Whymark 1, Own
goals 1.
      F.A. Cup (11): Mariner 3, Brazil 2, Muhren 2, Beattie, Geddis,
Mills, Wark.
      League Cup: Nil.
Ground: Portman Road, Ipswich IP1 2DA. (Ipswich 51306 and 57107).
Nearest station: Ipswich.
Manager: Bobby Robson. **Secretary:** D. C. Rose.
Colours: Blue shirts with three white stripes down each arm; white shorts
with three blue stripes.
Record home gate: 38,010 v. Leeds Utd., March, 1975 (F.A. Cup).
Honours—Champions: Div. 1: 1961–62. Div. 2: 1960–61, 1967–68. Div. 3.
South: 1953–54, 1956–57.
      F.A. Cup Winners: 1977–78.

LEEDS UNITED   DIV. 1

BENNETT, David
CHERRY, Trevor J.
CLARKE, Alan
CURRIE,
   Anthony W.
DALY, Peter
FIRM, Neil J.
FLYNN, Brian
GRAHAM, Arthur
GRAY, Edwin
GRAY, Francis T.
HAMPTON, Peter J.
HANKIN, Raymond

HARRIS, Carl S.
HART, Paul A.
HARVEY, David
HAWLEY, John E.
HIRD, Kevin
LUKIC, Jovan
McGHIE,
   William L.
MADELEY, Paul E.
PARKER, Neil
PARKINSON,
   Keith J.

PORTHOUSE,
   Philip E.
REID, David
REYNARD,
   Duncan E.
SAVILL, Peter
SMITH, Henry G.
STEVENSON,
   William B.
THOMAS, David G.
TYREMAN, Barry
WHYTE, David

LEAGUE APPEARANCES: Cherry, T. J. 38; Currie, A. W. 32; Flynn,
B. 41; Graham, A. 39; Gray, E. 25(3); Gray, F. T. 41; Hampton, P. J. 4;
Hankin, R. 29(1); Harris, C. S. 29(2); Hart, P. A. 40; Harvey, D. 39;
Hawley, J. E. 29(3); Hird, K. 13(1); Lorimer, P. P. 3; Madeley, P. E.
39; Parkinson, K. J. 3(2); Stevenson, W. B. 14(1); Stewart, D. S. 3;
Thomas, D. G. 1(1).

GOALS—League (70): Hawley 16, Hankin 9, Graham 8, Currie 7,
Cherry 6, Gray (F.) 6 (5 pens.), Hart 5, Gray (E.) 4, Flynn
3, Harris 3, Madeley 1, Stevenson 1, Own goal 1.
      F.A. Cup (9): Graham 2, Gray E. 2, Gray F. 2 (1 pen.), Harris 2,
Hart.
      League Cup (13): Currie 3, Gray E. 3, Gray F. 2 (1 pen.), Hankin 2,
Cherry, Hart, Hawley.

Ground: Elland Road, Leeds LS11 0ES. (Leeds 716037/9).
Nearest station: Leeds.
Manager: Jimmy Adamson. General Manager/Secretary: K. Archer.
Colours: White shirts, blue and yellow trim; white shorts with blue and yellow trim.
Record home gate: 57,892 v. Sunderland, March, 1967 (F.A. Cup).
Honours—Champions: Div. 1: 1968–69, 1973–74. Div. 2: 1923–24, 1963–64.
  F.A. Cup Winners: 1971–72.
  League Cup Winners: 1967–68.
  European Fairs Cup Winners: 1967–68, 1970–71.

LEICESTER CITY   DIV. 2

ALLEN, John
BROTHERTON, Alan R.
CARR, Everton D.
CHRISTIE, Trevor
COLE, Francis P.
CONVEY, Stephen C.
DUFFY, Michael K.
EDMUNDS, Paul
FARMER, Kevin J.
GEDDES, Paul
GOODWIN, Mark A.
HAMILTON, Stephen T.

HENDERSON, William M. M.
HUGHES, William
HUMPHRIES, Stephen R.
KELLY, Edward P.
KIRK, David
LEE, Alan R.
LINEKER, Gary W.
McGOWAN, Gerald K.
McSHANE, Patrick
MAY, Lawrence C.
MUNRO, Malcolm G.

O'NEILL, John P.
PEAKE, Andrew M.
RAFTER, Sean
RATCLIFFE, Mark T.
RIDLEY, John
ROFE, Dennis
SMITH, Robert
WALLINGTON, Francis M.
WELSH, Peter M.
WILLIAMS, Thomas E.
WILSON, Ian W.

LEAGUE APPEARANCES: Armstrong, G. 3; Buchanan, D. 17(2); Carr, E. D. 2(1); Christie, T. 23(3); Davies, R. 8; Duffy, M. K. 7(4); Goodwin, M. A. 23(5); Grewcock, N. 1; Henderson, W. M. M. 31(2); Hughes, W. 18(1); Kelly, E. P. 27; Kember, S. D. 8(1); Lee, A. R. 3; Lineker, G. W. 7; May, L. C. 36; O'Neill, J. P. 23; Peake, A. M. 17(1); Reed, K. D. –(1); Ridley, J. 17(7); Rofe, D. 39; Sims, S. F. 8; Smith, R. 17; Wallington, F. M. 42; Webb, D. J. 3; Weller, K. 16; Welsh, P. M. 4(2); White, W. E. 1(1); Whitworth, S. 29; Williams, T. E. 32(3).
GOALS—League (43): Christie 8, Smith 6 (1 pen.), Buchanan 5, Henderson 4, May 4, Hughes 3 (2 pens.), Weller 3, Davies 2, Peake 2, Williams 2, Duffy 1, Goodwin 1, Grewcock 1, Lineker 1.
  F.A. Cup (4): Henderson 2, May, Weller.
  League Cup: Nil.
Ground: City Stadium, Filbert Street, Leicester LE2 7FL. (Leicester 57111/2; match information 539199).
Nearest station: Leicester.
Manager: Jock Wallace. Secretary: J. R. Smith.
Colours: Blue shirts with white collar and cuffs; white shorts.
Record home gate: 47,298 v. Tottenham, February, 1928 (F.A. Cup).
Honours—Champions: Div. 2: 1924–25, 1936–37, 1953–54, 1956–57, 1970–71.
  F.A. Cup Winners: Nil.
  League Cup Winners: 1963–64.

LINCOLN CITY   DIV. 4

BURROWS,   HARFORD,   SMITH, Michael
   David W.   Michael G.   SUNLEY, David
COCKERILL, Glenn   HOBSON, Gordon   WARD, John P.
COOPER, Terence   HUGHES, David T.   WATSON,
EDEN, Alan   LAYBOURNE,   Graham S.
FLEMING, John J.   Keith E.   WRIGHT, William S.
FOX, Kevin   LOXLEY,
GROTIER, Peter D.   Anthony D.
GUEST, Brendan J.   NEALE, Phillip A.

LEAGUE APPEARANCES: Burrows, D. W. 1; Cockerill, G. 34(1);
Cooper, T. 35; Creane, G. M. 2(1); Cross, G. F. 19; Eden, A. 1; Fleming,
J. J. 28(3); Grotier, P. D. 32; Guest, B, J. 39(2); Harding, A. 17; Harford,
M. G. 28(3); Hobson, G. 27(6); Hubbard, P. J. 21(1); Hughes, D. T. 13;
Jones, A. 1(2); Laybourne, K. E. 17; Leigh, D. 29; Loxley, A. D. 1;
McCalliog, J. 9; Neale, P. A. 10(1); Sivell, L. 2; Smith, M. 17(3); Sunley,
D. 27(2); Turner, I. 7; Turner, C. R. 5; Tynan, T. E. 9; Ward, J. P. 32(1);
Watson, G. S. 21; Wigginton, C. A. 19; Wright, W. S. 3.
GOALS—League (41): Cockerill 6, Fleming 6 (4 pens.), Harford 6,
     Hobson 6, Sunley 4, Ward 3, Watson 2, Wigginton 2 (1 pen.).
     Cooper 1, Harding 1, Laybourne 1, Leigh 1, Neale 1, Tynan 1
   F.A. Cup (1): Ward.
   League Cup (1): Hughes.
Ground: Sincil Bank, Lincoln LN5 8LD. (Lincoln 22224).
Nearest station: Lincoln Central and St. Mark's.
Team Manager: Colin Murphy. Secretary: J. H. Sorby.
Colours: Red and white striped shirts; black shorts.
Record home gate: 23,196 v. Derby, November, 1967 (League Cup).
Honours—Champions: Div. 3 North: 1931–32, 1947–48, 1951–52. Div. 4:
     1975–76.
   F.A. Cup Winners: Nil.

LIVERPOOL   DIV. 1

AINSWORTH,   GAYLE, Howard   McCARTNEY, Gary
   Jeffrey T.   HANSEN, Alan D.   McDERMOTT,
BRADDISH,   HARPER, Alan   Terence
   Synan F. J.   HEIGHWAY,   McGARVEY,
BROWN, John O.   Stephen D.   Francis P.
CARROLL,   HUGHES,   NEAL, Philip G.
   Derek F. D.   Emlyn W.   OGRIZOVIC,
CASE, James R.   IRWIN, Colin T.   Steven
CLEMENCE,   JOHNSON,   RUSSELL, Colin
   Raymond N.   David E.   SAVAGE, Robert J.
CRIBLEY,   KENNEDY, Alan P.   SHEEDY, Kevin M.
   Alexander   KENNEDY,   SOUNESS,
DALGLISH,   Raymond   Graeme J.
   Kenneth M.   KETTLE, Brian   THOMPSON,
DUFF, Brian F.   LE CORNU,   Philip B.
FAIRCLOUGH,   Craig D.   WILLIAMS, James T.
   David   LEE, Samuel

LEAGUE APPEARANCES: Case, J. R. 37; Clemence, R. N. 42; Dalglish, K. M. 42; Fairclough, D. 3(1); Hansen, A. D. 34; Heighway, S. D. 26(2); Hughes, E. W. 16; Johnson, D. E. 26(4); Kennedy, A. P. 37; Kennedy, R. 42; Lee, S. 1(1); McDermott, T. 34(3); Neal, P. G. 42; Souness, G. J. 41; Thompson, P. B. 39.

GOALS—League (85): Dalglish 21, Johnson 16, Kennedy (R.) 10, McDermott 8 (2 pens.), Souness 8, Case 7, Neal 5 (2 pens.), Heighway 4, Kennedy (A.) 3, Fairclough 2, Hansen 1.

F.A. Cup (10): Dalglish 4, Johnson 2, Case, R. Kennedy, Souness, Hansen 1.

League Cup: Nil.

Ground: Anfield Road, Liverpool L4 0TH (051-263 2361/2).

Nearest stations: All stations, Liverpool.

Manager: Bob Paisley. **Secretary:** P. Robinson.

Colours: Red shirts with white trim; red shorts.

Record home gate: 61,905 v. Wolves, February, 1952 (F.A. Cup).

Honours—Champions: Div. 1: 1900–01, 1905–06, 1921–22, 1922–23, 1946–47, 1963–64, 1965–66, 1972–73, 1975–76, 1976–77, 1978–79. Div. 2: 1893–94, 1895–96, 1904–05, 1961–62.

F.A. Cup Winners: 1964–65, 1973–74.

European Champions Cup: 1976–77, 1977–78.

U.E.F.A. Cup Winners: 1972–73, 1975–76.

LUTON TOWN DIV. 2

AIZLEWOOD, Mark
BIRCHENALL, Alan J.
CARR, David
DONAGHY, Malachy
FINDLAY, John W.
FUCCILLO, Pasquale
GOODYEAR, Clive

HARRIOTT, Leslie A.
HATTON, Robert J.
HEALE, Gary J.
HEATH, Seamus J. M. P.
HILL, Ricky A.
INGRAM, Godfrey P. A.
JONES, Graham
JUDGE, Alan G.

MOSS, David J.
PEARSON, Andrew J.
PRICE, Paul T.
SISMAN, Gary
STEIN, Brian
STEPHENS, Kirk W.
TAYLOR, Steven J.
TURNER, Wayne L.
WEST, Alan

LEAGUE APPEARANCES: Aizlewood, M. 39; Aleksic, M. A. 14; Birchenall, A. J. 8; Boersma, P. 1; Carr, D. 13(2); Donaghy, M. 40; Findlay, J. W. 23; Fuccillo, P. 16(2); Hatton, R. J. 41; Hill, R. A. 38; Ingram, G. P. A. 2(1); Jones, G. 6(4); Lawson, D. 5; McNichol, J. A.—(1); Moss, D. J. 29(1); Philipson-Masters, F. E. 10; Price, P. T. 34; Sherlock, S. E. 2; Silkman, B. 3; Stein, B. 31(3); Stephens, K. W. 24(1); Taylor, S. J. 15(5); Turner, C. J. 30; Turner, W. L. 1; West, A. 37(3).

GOALS—League (60): Moss 13 (1 pen.), Hatton 11, Stein 10, Fuccillo 7, (4 pens.), Turner 5, Hill 3, West 3, Price 2, Taylor 1, Own goals 5.

F.A. Cup: Nil.

League Cup (7): Stein 4, Hatton 2, Hill.

Ground: 70–72 Kenilworth Road, Luton LU1 1DH. (0582 411622).

Nearest station: Luton.

Manager: David Pleat. **Secretary:** John Wilkinson.

Colours: Orange shirts with one navy and one white stripe down left hand
  side; navy blue shorts.
Record home gate: 30,069 v. Blackpool, March, 1959 (F.A. Cup).
Honours—Champions: Div. 3 South: 1936–37. Div. 4: 1967–68.
  F.A. Cup Winners: Nil.

MANCHESTER CITY   DIV. 1

BARNES, Peter S.
BELL, Colin
BENNETT, David
BOOTH, Thomas A.
BRADLEY, Noel B.
BUCKLEY, Gary
CHANNON,
  Michael R.
CLEMENTS,
  Kenneth H.

CORRIGAN,
  Joseph T.
DEYNA,
  Kazimierz
DONACHIE,
  William
FUTCHER, Paul
HARTFORD,
  Richard A.
HENRY, Anthony

MACRAE, Keith A.
OWEN, Gary A.
PALMER, Roger N.
POWER, Paul C.
RANSON, Raymond
REID, Nicholas
SILKMAN, Barry
VILJOEN, Colin
WATSON, David V.

LEAGUE APPEARANCES: Barnes, P. S. 29; Bell, C. 10; Bennett, D.
–(1); Booth, T. A. 20; Channon, M. R. 36; Clements, K. H. 15; Corrigan,
J. T. 42; Deyna, K. 11(2); Donachie, W. 38; Futcher, P. 24; Futcher, R.
10(7); Hartford, R. A. 39; Henry, A. 13(2); Keegan, G. A. 4; Kidd, B.
19(1); Owen, G. A. 34(1); Palmer, R. N. 10(4); Power, P. C. 32; Ranson,
R. 8; Reid, N. S. 7(1); Silkman, B. 12; Viljoen, C. 16; Watson, D. V. 33.

GOALS—League (58): Channon 11, Owen 11 (6 pens.), Futcher (R.) 7,
  Kidd 7 (1 pen.), Denya 6, Palmer 4, Hartford 3, Power 3,
  Silkman 3, Barnes 1, Watson 1, Own goal 1.
  F.A. Cup (4): Kidd 2, Barnes, Owen.
  League Cup (10): Channon 3, Owen 2 (1 pen.), Barnes, Booth,
  Palmer, Own goals 2.
Ground: Maine Road, Moss Side, Manchester M14 7WN. (061-226
  1191/2).
Nearest station: Manchester Piccadilly.
Team Manager: Tony Book. Secretary: J. B. Halford.
Colours: Sky blue shirts with white trim white strip down sleeve; sky blue
  shorts with white trim.
Record home gate: 84,569 v. Stoke City, March, 1934 (F.A. Cup).
Honours—Champions: Div. 1: 1936–37, 1967–68. Div. 2: 1898–99, 1902–
  03, 1909–10, 1927–28, 1946–47, 1965–66.
  F.A. Cup Winners: 1903–04, 1933–34, 1955–56, 1968–69.
  League Cup Winners: 1969–70, 1975–76.
  European Cup Winners' Cup: 1969–70.

MANCHESTER UNITED DIV. 1

ALBISTON, Arthur R.
BAILEY, Gary R.
BUCHAN, Martin M.
CONNELL, Thomas E.
COPPELL, Stephen J.
DAVIES, Alan
DUXBURY, Michael
GREENHOFF, Brian
GREENHOFF, James
GRIMES, Ashley A.
HAGGETT, David L.

HOUSTON, Stewart M.
JORDAN, Joseph
KEEN, Nigel J.
KNOX, Barry W.
LYNAM, Christopher A.
McCREERY, David
McGRATH, Roland C.
McILROY, Samuel B.
McQUEEN, Gordon
MACARI, Luigi
MICKLEWHITE, Gary
MORAN, Kevin B.

NICHOLL, James M.
PATERSON, Steven W.
PEARS, Stephen
PEARSON, Stuart J.
RITCHIE, Andrew T.
ROBERTS, Christopher O.
ROCHE, Patrick J.
ROGERS, Martyn
SLOAN, Thomas
THOMAS, Michael R.
WORRALL, Garry G.
WRAY, Andrew P.

LEAGUE APPEARANCES: Albiston, A. R. 32(1); Bailey, G. R. 28; Buchan, M. M. 37; Connell, T. E. 2; Coppell, S. J. 42; Greenhoff, B. 32(1); Greenhoff, J. 33; Grimes, A. A. 5(11); Houston, S. M. 21(1); Jordan, J. 30; McCreery, D. 14(1); McGrath, R. C. –(2); McIlroy, S. B. 40; McQueen, G. 36; Macari, L. 31(1); Moran, K. B. 1; Nicholl, J. M. 19(2); Paterson, S. W. 1(2); Ritchie, A. T. 16(1); Roche, P. J. 14; Sloan, T. 3(1); Thomas, M. R. 25.

GOALS—League (60): Coppell 11, Greenhoff (J.) 11, (1 pen.), Ritchie 10, Jordan 6, McQueen 6, Macari 6, McIlroy 5, Buchan 2, Greenhoff (B.) 2, Thomas 1.

F.A. Cup (14): J. Greenhoff 5, McIlroy 2, Jordan 2, Coppell, Grimes, Thomas, McQueen, B. Greenhoff.

League Cup (4): Jordan 2, McIlroy, J. Greenhoff (pen.).

Ground: Old Trafford, Manchester M16 0RA. (061-872 1661/2).

Nearest stations: All stations Manchester.

Team Manager: David Sexton. **Secretary:** R. L. Olive.

Colours: Red shirts with red and white trim; white shorts.

Record home gate: 76,962 F.A. Cup semi-final (Wolves v. Grimsby) March, 1939.

Honours—Champions: Div. 1: 1907–08, 1910–11, 1951–52, 1955–56, 1956–57, 1964–65, 1966–67. Div. 2: 1935–36, 1974–75.

F.A. Cup Winners: 1908–09, 1947–48, 1962–63, 1976–77.

European Champions Cup: 1967–68.

MANSFIELD TOWN DIV. 3

ALLEN, Russell P.
ARNOLD, Roderick J.
AUSTIN, Terence W.
BIRD, Kevin
CURTIS, Robert D.
DAWKINS, Derek A.

FOSTER, Barry
FOSTER, Colin
GOODWIN, David
HAMILTON, Neville R.
McCLELLAND, John

MILLER, John T.
MORRIS, Peter J.
NEW, Martin P.
SAXBY, Gary P.
SAXBY, Michael W.
WOOD, Ian N.

LEAGUE APPEARANCES: Allen, R. P. 26(10); Arnold, R. J. 28;
Austin, T. W. 16; Bird, K. 44; Carter, M. 18; Coffey, M. J. J. 2(1); Curtis,
R. D. 33(1); Dawkins, D. A. 26; Foster, B. 39; Foster, C. 9(4); Goodwin,
D. 26(2); Grattan, J. 1; Hamilton, N. R. 16(2); Hodgson, G. H. 6;
McClelland, J. 33(3); Martin, D. W. 33; Miller, J. T. 28(3); Moss, E. 12(1);
New, M. P. 18; Phillips, I. A. 3(2); Saxby, G. P. 14(2); Saxby, M. W. 46;
Syrett, D. K. 23; Wood, I. N. 6(11).
GOALS—League (51): Curtis 6 (5 pens.), Allen 5, Austin 5, Bird 4,
    Carter 4, Goodwin 4, Miller 4, Saxby (M.) 4, Syrett 4, Martin 3,
    Moss 2, Hamilton 1, McClelland 1, Saxby (G.) 1, Own goals 3.
    F.A. Cup: Nil.
    League Cup (2): Miller, Bird.
Ground: Field Mill, Quarry Lane, Mansfield. (Mansfield 23567).
Nearest station: Alfreton and Mansfield Parkway.
Manager: Billy Bingham. **Secretary:** J. D. Eaton.
Colours: Amber shirts; blue shorts.
Record home gate: 24,467 v. Nottingham Forest, January 1953 (F.A. Cup).
Honours—Champions: Div. 3: 1976–77. Div. 4: 1974–75.
    F.A. Cup Winners: Nil.

MIDDLESBROUGH   DIV. 1

ANGUS, Michael A.
ARMSTRONG,
  David
ASHCROFT, William
ASKEW, William
BAILEY, Ian C.
BELL, Anthony J.
BELL, Ian C.
BOAM, Stuart W.
BROWN, David J.
BURNS, Michael E.

COCHRANE,
  George T.
CRAGGS, John E.
CUMMINS, Stanley
HEDLEY, Graeme
HODGSON,
  David J.
JANKOVIC, Bozo
JOHNSON, Peter E.
JOHNSTON,
  Craig P.

McANDREW,
  Anthony
MAHONEY, John F.
PETERS, Jeffrey
PLATT, James A.
PROCTOR, Mark G
RAMAGE, Alan
SHEARER, David J
STEWART, James
STOKOE, Ian D.
WOOF, William

LEAGUE APPEARANCES: Armstrong, D. 42; Ashcroft, W. 33(4);
Bailey, I. C. 18(1); Bell, I. C. 1; Boam, S. W. 40; Burns, M. E. 31; Cochrane, G. T. 18(1); Craggs, J. E. 41; Cummins, S. 11(1); Hedley, G. –(1);
Hodgson, D. J. 13(6); Jankovic, B. 4(4); Johnson, P. E. 21; Johnston, C. P.
1(1); McAndrew, A. 38; Mahoney, J. F. 40; Mills, D. J. 17; Platt, J. A.
15; Proctor, M. G. 31(2); Ramage, A. 14; Shearer, D. J. 2(3); Stewart, J.
27; Woof, W, 4(1).
GOALS—League (57): Burns 14, Armstrong 11 (1 pen.), Proctor 9,
Ashcroft 6, Mills 6, Cochrane 3, Boam 1, Cummins 1, Hodgson 1, Janko-
vic 1, McAndrew 1, Shearer 1, Woof 1, Own goal 1.
    F.A. Cup (1): Ashcroft.
    League Cup: Nil.
Ground: Ayresome Park, Middlesbrough TS1 4PB. (Middlesbrough 89659
  and 85996).
Nearest station: Middlesbrough.
Manager: John Neal. **Secretary:** T. H. C. Green.
Colours: Red shirts with three narrow stripes down sleeve in white; red
  shorts with same markings.
Record home gate: 53,596 v. Newcastle U., December, 1949 (League).
Honours—Champions: Div. 2: 1926–27, 1928–29, 1973–74.
    F.A. Cup Winners: Nil.

MILLWALL   DIV. 3

ALLEN, Peter C.
BLYTH, Melvyn B.
CHAMBERS,
  Brian M.
CHATTERTON,
  Nicholas J.
COLEMAN, Philip
CUFF, Patrick J.
DIBBLE,
  Christopher
DONALDSON,
  David J.

GALE, Ian J.
GLEASURE, Peter
GREGORY,
  David P.
HORRIX, Dean V.
KINSELLA,
  Anthony S.
KITCHENER,
  Barry R.
McKENNA, Alan M.
MASSEY, Andrew
MEHMET, David

MITCHELL, John
O'CALLAGHAN,
  Kevin
ROBERTS, Paul A.
SEASMAN, John
TAGG, Anthony P.
TOWNER,
  Anthony J.
WALKER, Philip

LEAGUE APPEARANCES: Allen, P. C. 4(1); Blyth, M. B. 13; Chambers,
  B. M. 26(2); Chatterton, N. J. 27; Coleman, P. 2; Cross, R. G. 1(1);
  Cuff, P. J. 42; Dibble, C. 5(2); Donaldson, D. J. 41; Gale, I. J. 4(1);
  Gregory, D. P. 23; Hamilton, B. 12(1); Hamilton, J. T. 1(1); Hazell, A. P.
  7; Kinsella, A. S. –(1); Kitchener, B. R. 40; Lee, T. C. 4(1); McKenna,
  A. M.–(1); Mehmet, D. 20(13); Mitchell, J. 32; Moore, J. 11; O'Callaghan,
  K. 7(3); Pearson, I. T. 8(1); Roberts, P. A. 1(1); Seasman, J. 35; Sparrow,
  J. P. 7; Tagg, A. P. 26(2); Towner, A. J. 25; Walker, P. 38.
GOALS—League (42): Seasman 10, Mitchell 5, Walker 5, Chambers 4
  (2 pens.), Chatterton 4 (2 pens.), Mehmet 4, Hamilton, B. 2,
  Kitchener 2, Lee 1, Tagg 1, Towner 1, Own goals 3.
    F.A. Cup (1): Walker.
    League Cup (2): Mitchell, Seasman (pen.).
Ground: The Den, Cold Blow Lane, London SE14 5RH. (01-639 3143/4).
Nearest stations: New Cross or New Cross Gate (S.R. and Metropolitan
  Line).
Manager: George Petchey. Secretary:
Colours: Blue shirts with white trim; white shorts.
Record home gate: 48,672 v. Derby, February, 1937 (F.A. Cup).
Honours—Champions: Div. 3 South: 1927–28, 1937–38. Div. 4: 1961–62.
  F.A. Cup Winners: Nil.

NEWCASTLE UNITED   DIV. 2

ARMSTRONG,
  Robin J.
BALDWIN, Kevin P.
BARTON, David
BIRD, John C.
BROWNLIE, John
CARR, Kevin
CASSIDY, Thomas
CONNOLLY, John
FAIRLESS, Stephen
FERGUSON, Brian
HALLIDAY, Bruce
HARDWICK, Steven

HIBBIT, Terence A.
KELLY, Peter A.
LATTY, Brian
MacFARLANE,
  Craig J.
MANNERS, Peter J.
MARTIN,
  Michael P.
MITCHELL,
  Kenneth
MULGROVE,
  Keith A.
NATTRASS, Irving

NICHOLSON,
  Gary A.
PEARSON, James F.
PUGH, Kevin J.
ROBINSON,
  Stuart A.
SCOTT, James A.
SHOULDER, Alan
SUGGETT, Colin
WALKER, Nigel S.
WHARTON,
  Kenneth
WITHE, Peter

LEAGUE APPEARANCES: Barker, A. M. 5(1); Barton, D. 21(1); Bird, J. C. 27; Blackley, J. H. 28; Brownlie, J. 34; Carr, K. 8; Cassidy, T. 19; Connolly, J. 34; Guy, A. –(1); Hardwick, S. 31; Hibbitt, T. A. 40; Kelly, P. A. 15; McGhee, M. 4(6); Mahoney, M. J. 3; Manners, P. J. 2; Martin, M. P. 23; Mitchell, K. 26(5); Mulgrove, K. A. –(1); Nattrass, I. 21; Nicholson, G. A. 5(3); Parkinson, A. J. –(1); Pearson, J. F. 9; Robinson, S. A. 4; Scott, J. A. 2; Shoulder, A. 24; Suggett, C. 20(3); Walker, N. S. 18(2); Wharton, K. –(2); Withe, P. 39.

GOALS—League (51): Withe 14, Shoulder 11 (2 pens.), Connolly 8, Bird 3, Pearson 3, Barton 2, McGhee 2, Nattrass 2, Walker 2, Cassidy 1, Martin 1, Mitchell 1, Robinson 1.

    F.A. Cup (4): Withe 2, Nattrass (pen.), Robinson.

    League Cup (1): Pearson.

Ground: St. James' Park, Newcastle-upon-Tyne NE1 4ST. (0632 28361/2 answer service 611571).

Nearest station: Newcastle.

Manager: Bill McGarry. **Secretary:** R. Cushing.

Colours: Black and white vertical striped shirts; black shorts.

Record home gate: 68,386 v. Chelsea, September, 1930 (League).

Honours—Champions: Div. 1: 1904–05, 1906–07, 1908–09, 1926–27, Div. 2: 1964–65.

    F.A. Cup Winners: 1909–10, 1923–24, 1931–32, 1950–51, 1951–52, 1954–55.

    European Fairs' Cup Winners: 1968–69.

    Anglo-Italian Cup Winners: 1973.

NEWPORT COUNTY   DIV. 4

ALDRIDGE, John W.
BAILEY, Neil
BRUTON, David E.
DAVIES, Grant
DOWLER, Michael J.
GODDARD, Howard
LOWNDES, Stephen R.
MOORE, Kevin J.
PLUMLEY, Gary E.
OAKES, Keith B.
RELISH, John D.
THOMPSON, John T.
TYNAN, Thomas E.
VAUGHAN, Nigel M.
WALDEN, Richard
WARRINER, Stephen

LEAGUE APPEARANCES: Armstrong, K. T. 3(1); Bailey, N. 20(1); Brown, J. 2(1); Bruton, D. E. 34; Byrne, A. B. 26; Clark, B. D. 1(3); Cosslett, M. 1; Davies, G. 38; Elliott, D. –(2); Goddard, H. 46; Jones, R. 2; Lee, T. W. G. 1; Lowndes, S. R. 43; McGeady, J. 2; Moore, K. J. 21; Oakes, K. B. 34; Plumley, G. E. 45; Relish, J. D. 20(7); Sinclair, C. M. 14(1); Thompson, J. T. 26(2); Tynan, T. E. 20; Vaughan, N. M. 23(4); Walden, R. 40; Walker, R. L. 6; Warriner, S. 16(4); Williams, M. 3(1); Woods, E. 19.

GOALS—League (66): Goddard 19 (6 pens.), Lowndes 8, Tynan 7, Bruton 5, Oakes 5, Sinclair 4, Vaughan 4, Moore 3, Woods 2, Bailey 1, Clark 1, Davies 1, Thompson 1, Walden 1, Warriner 1, Williams 1, Own goals 2.

    F.A. Cup (5): Goddard 3 (1 pen.), Woods, Own goal 1.

    League Cup (2): Williams, Woods.

Ground: Somerton Park, Newport NPT 0HZ. (Newport 71543 and 71271).

Nearest station: Newport.

Manager: Len Ashurst. Secretary: K. L. Saunders.
Colours: Amber shirts; black shorts.
Record home gate: 24,268 v. Cardiff, October, 1937 (League).
Honours—Champions: Div. 3 South: 1938–39.
    F.A. Cup Winners: Nil.

NORTHAMPTON TOWN   DIV. 4

ASHENDEN,   JAYES, Carl G.   SAUNDERS, Paul B.
    Russell H.   McCAFFREY, James   WALKER,
FARRINGTON,   McNICOL, James   Richard P.
    John R.   PERKINS, Glen S.   WILLIAMS, Keith
FROGGATT,   POOLE, Andrew J.   WOOLLETT, Alan
    John L.   REILLY, George G.

LEAGUE APPEARANCES: Ashenden, R. H. 4(9); Bowen, K. 2(3);
Bryant, S. P. 28; Christie, D. H. M. 15; Cordice, N. A. 4(4); Farrington,
J. R. 46; Froggatt, J. L. 42; Geidmintis, A. 45; Jayes, C. G. 29; Liddle, D.
3(1); McCaffry, J. 25; Matthews, P. W. 13; Mead, P. S. 38(1); Perkins,
G. S.–(1); Poole, A. J. 17; Reilly, G. G. 43; Robertson, S. J. 38; Saunders,
P. B. 24(4); Waldock, D. H. 3; Walker, R. P. 10(3); Wassell, K. 10(3);
Williams, K. 44; Woollett, A. 23.
GOALS—League (64): Reilly 19, Froggatt 13, Farrington 8, Robertson 5,
    McCaffrey 4, Bryant 3, Christie 3, Mead 3, Williams 2,
    Cordice 1, Geidmintis 1 (pen.), Liddle 1, Own goal 1.
    F.A. Cup: Nil.
    League Cup (6): Reilly 4, Christie, Farrington.
Ground: County Ground, Abington Avenue, Northampton NN1 4PS.
    (Northampton 31553).
Nearest station: Northampton.
Manager: Clive Walker. Secretary/General Manager: Dave Bowen.
Colours: White shirts with claret trim; white shorts.
Record home gate: 24,523 v. Fulham, April 1966 (League).
Honours—Champions: Div. 3: 1962–63.
    F.A. Cup Winners: Nil.

NORWICH CITY   DIV. 1

BAKER, Clive E.   HALSEY, Mark A.   NIGHTINGALE,
BENNETT, David P.   HANSBURY, Roger   Mark B. D.
BIRD, Kevan J.   HOADLEY,   PADDON,
BOND, Kevin J.   Philip F. W.   Graham C.
CARTER, Robert M.   JONES, David E.   PETERS, Martin S.
CORDICE, Alan R.   LYTHGOE, Philip   POWELL, Anthony
DAVIES, Ian C.   McGUIRE, Michael   REEVES, Kevin P,
DOWNS, Gregory   MENDHAM,   ROBSON, Keith
EVANS, David D.   Peter S.   SHEPHERD,
FASHANU,   MOUNTFORD,   Jamie G.
    Justinus S.   Peter   STEELE,
FORBES, Duncan S.   NEIGHBOUR,   William M.
GOBLE, Stephen R.   James E.   SYMONDS, Richard

LEAGUE APPEARANCES: Baker, C. E. 2; Bennett, D. P.–(1); Bond, K. J. 42; Chivers, M. H. 11; Davies, I. C. 26(1); Downs, G. 1(2); Evans, D. D. 4; Fashanu, J. S. 13(3); Forbes, D. S. 3(1); Hansbury, R. 18; Hoadley, P. F. W. 39; Keelan, K. D. 22; Lythgoe, P. 3; McGuire. M. 22(2); Mendham, P. S. 7(1); Neighbour, J. E. 33(1); Paddon, G.C. 16(1); Peters, M. S. 38(1); Powell, A. 42; Reeves, K. P. 38; Robb, D.T. 4(1); Robson, K. 26(3); Ryan, J. G. 25; Sullivan, C. J. 10; Symonds, M. 17(2).
GOALS—League (51): Peters 10, Reeves 9, Ryan 9 (4 pens.), Fashanu 5, Chivers 4, Robson 4, Bond 2, Davies 2, Neighbour 2, Evans 1, Paddon 1, Powell 1, Robb 1.
    F.A. Cup: Nil.
    League Cup (6): Peters 2, Ryan 2, Reeves, Own goal 1.
Ground: Carrow Road Stadium, Norwich NOR 22T (Norwich 612131).
Nearest station: Norwich.
Manager: John Bond. **Secretary:** A. E. Westwood.
Colours: Yellow shirts, green collar and cuffs; green shorts with yellow trim.
Record home gate: 43,984 v. Leicester, March, 1963 (F.A. Cup).
Honours—Champions: Div. 2: 1971–72. Div. 3 South: 1933–34.
    F.A. Cup Winners: Nil.
    League Cup Winners: 1961–62.

NOTTINGHAM FOREST   DIV. 1

ANDERSON,
  Vivian A.
BARRETT, Colin
BIRTLES, Garry
BOWYER, Ian
BURKE, Steven J.
BURNS, Kenneth
CLARK, Frank A.
FRANCIS,
  Trevor J.

GEMMILL,
  Archibald
GUNN, Brynley C.
LLOYD,
  Lawrence V.
McGOVERN,
  John P.
MILLS, Gary R.
NEEDHAM, David
O'HARE, John

O'NEILL,
  Martin H. M.
ROBERTSON,
  John N.
SHILTON, Peter L.
WOODCOCK,
  Anthony S.
WOODS,
  Christopher C. E.

LEAGUE APPEARANCES: Anderson, V. A. 40; Barrett, C. 11; Birtles, G. 35; Bowyer, I. 26(3); Burns, K. 25; Clarke, F. A. 20; Elliott, S. B. 4; Francis, T. J. 19(1); Gemmill, A. 24; Gunn, B. C. 1; Lloyd, L. V. 36; McGovern, J. P. 36; Mills, G. R. 4; Needham, D. 23(3); O'Hare, J. 9(3); O'Neill, M. H. M. 28; Robertson, J. N. 42; Shilton, P. L. 42; Withe, P. 1; Woodcock, A. S. 36.
GOALS—League (61): Birtles 14, O'Neill 10, Woodcock 10, Robertson 9 (3 pens.), Francis 6, Bowyer 4, Needham 2, Anderson 1, Barrett 1, Gemmill 1, Mills 1, Own goals 2.
    F.A. Cup (5): Lloyd, McGovern, Needham, O'Neill, Own goal 1.
    League Cup (21): Birtles 6, Robertson 4 (1 pen.), Woodcock 3, Anderson 2, McGovern 2, Burns, Lloyd, Needham, O'Neill.
Ground: City Ground, Nottingham NG2 5FJ. (Nottingham (0602) 868236/8; Information Desk 860232).
Nearest station: Nottingham.
Manager: Brian Clough. **Secretary:** K. Smales.
Colours: Red shirts, white shorts.
Record home gate: 49,945 v. Manchester Utd., October, 1967 (League).

Honours—Champions: Div. 1: 1977–78; Div. 2: 1906–07, 1921–22. Div. 3
South: 1950–51.
F.A. Cup Winners: 1897–98, 1958–59.
League Cup Winners: 1977–78, 1978–79.
European Champions Cup: 1978–79.

NOTTS COUNTY   DIV. 2

BENJAMIN, Tristam   McMANUS,   RICHARDS,
BLOCKLEY,   Charles E.   Lloyd G.
  Jeffrey P.   McVAY, David R.   RICHARDS, Peter
GREEN, Richard   MAIR, Gordon   SMITH, David F.
HOOKS, Paul   MANN, Arthur F.   STUBBS, Brian H.
HUNT, David   MASSON, Donald S.   VINTER, Michael
KING, Colin   O'BRIEN, Raymond   WOOD, Gary T.
McCULLOCH, John

LEAGUE APPEARANCES: Benjamin, T. 24(3); Blockley, J. P. 27(2);
Carter, S. C. 2; Green, R. 6(3); Hooks, P. 36(2); Hunt, D. 36(1); Mc-
Culloch, J. 42; McManus, C. E. 42; McVay, D. R. 3(8); Mair, G. 4;
Mann, A. F. 37(3); Masson, D. S. 37; O'Brien, R. 41; Richards, P. 40;
Stubbs, B. H. 42; Vinter, M. 41; Wood, G. T. 2.
GOALS—League (48): Vinter 12, Hooks 10, McCulloch 8, O'Brien 6
(4 pens.), Blockley 3, Mann 3, Masson 3, Hunt 2, Mair 1.
    F.A. Cup (4): Hooks, Mann, Mason, Vinter.
    League Cup (4): Carter 2, Hooks 2.
Ground: Meadow Lane, Nottingham NG2 3HJ. (Nottingham 864152).
Nearest station: Nottingham.
Manager: Jimmy Sirrel. Secretary: Dennis Marshall.
Colours: Black and white striped shirts; black shorts.
Record home gate: 47,310 v. York, March, 1955 (F.A. Cup).
Honours—Champions: Div. 2: 1896–97, 1913–14, 1922–23. Div. 3 South:
1930–31, 1949–50. Div. 4: 1970–71.
    F.A. Cup Winners: 1893–94.

OLDHAM ATHLETIC   DIV. 2

BLAIR, Ronald V.   HOOLIKIN, Garry J.   SINCLAIR,
EDWARDS,   HURST, John   Nicholas J. T.
  Stephen G.   JORDAN,   STAINROD,
GARDNER,   Timothy E.   Simon A.
  Stephen D.   KEEGAN,   STEEL,
HALOM, Victor L.   Gerard A.   William J.
HEATON, Paul J.   McDONNELL,   WOOD, Ian T.
HICKS, Keith   Peter A.   YOUNG,
HILTON, Mark G. J.   PLATT, John R.   Alexander F.
HOLT, David

LEAGUE APPEARANCES: Bell, G. T. 22(1); Bernard, M. P. 2; Blair,
R. V. 35; Chapman, L. 42; Edwards, S. G. 21; Gardner, S. D. 20(4);
Halom, V. L. 28(2); Heaton, P. J. 20(3); Hicks, K. 34; Hilton, M. G. J.
10(1); Holt, D. 5; Hoolickin, G. J. 1; Hurst, J. 41; Jordan, T. E. 2(2):
Keegan, G. A. 19(1); McDonnell, P. A. 42; Sinclair, N. J. T. 1; Stainrod,

47

S. A. 14; Steel, W. J. 6(1); Taylor, S. J. 13(2); Valentine, C. H. 11; Wood,
I. T. 36; Young, A. F. 37.
GOALS—League (52): Young 10 (1 pen.), Halom 5, Heaton 5, Stainrod 5,
       Taylor 5, Hicks 4, Steel 4, Chapman 3 (1 pen.), Bell 2, Hilton 2,
       Wood 2, Gardner 1, Hoolickin 1, Hurst 1, Valentine 1, Own
       goal 1.
    F.A. Cup (4): Young 3, Wood.
    League Cup (2): Halom, Young.
Ground: Boundary Park, Oldham OL1 2PA. (061-624 4972).
Nearest station: Oldham, Werneth.
Manager: Jimmy Frizzel. Gen. Manager/Secretary: W. Griffiths.
Colours: Blue shirts; white shorts.
Record home gate: 47,671 v. Sheffield Wednesday, January, 1930 (F.A.
    Cup).
Honours—Champions: Div. 3 North: 1952–53. Div. 3: 1973–74.
    F.A. Cup Winners: Nil.

ORIENT   DIV. 2

BANJO, Tunji B.	GRAY, Mark S.	HURLEY,
BENNETT, Peter L.	GRAY, Nigel R.	William H.
BLACKHALL,	GREALISH,	JACKSON, John K.
Mark C.	Anthony P.	KANE, John P.
BRIGHT, Michael I.	HAMBERGER,	MAYO, Joseph
CHIEDOZIE,	Stephen M.	MOORES, Ian R.
John O.	HENNEY,	ROFFEY, William R.
COATES, Ralph	Christopher	WENT, Paul F.
FISHER, Robert P.	HUGHTON,	WHITTLE, Alan
GODFREY, Kevin	Henry T.	

LEAGUE APPEARANCES: Banjo, T. B. 13(4); Bennett, P. L. 6; Chiedo-
zie, J. O. 33(3); Clarke, D. 4(2); Coates, R. 30; Fisher, R. P. 37; Godfrey,
K. 3(3); Gray, M. S. 1(1); Gray, N. R. 42; Grealish, A. P. 39; Hughton,
H. T. 33; Jackson, J. K. 42; Kane, J. P. –(1); Kitchen, M. P. 22(1); Mayo,
J. 40; Moores, I. R. 30; Roffey, W. R. 39; Smith, M. S. 1; Went, P. F. 37;
Whittle, A. 10.
GOALS—League (51): Moores 13 (1 pen.), Mayo 11, Kitchen 7 (2 pens.),
       Chiedozie 6, Grealish 5, Coates 3, Hughton 2, Went 2 (1 pen.),
       Banjo 1,Whittle 1.
    F.A. Cup (3): Kitchen 2, Chiedozie.
    League Cup (1): Fisher.
Ground: Leyton Stadium, Brisbane Road, Leyton, E10 5NE. (01-539
    2223/4).
Nearest station: Leyton (Central Line).
Manager: Jimmy Bloomfield. Secretary: Peter Barnes.
Colours: White shirts with a red vertical stripe on each side of chest; white
    shorts.
Record home gate: 34,345 v. West Ham, January, 1964 (F.A. Cup).
Honours—Champions: Div. 3: 1969–70. Div. 3 South: 1955–56.
    F.A. Cup Winners: Nil.

OXFORD UNITED   DIV. 3

BERRY, Paul A.
BODEL, Andrew C.
BRIGGS, Gary
BURTON, Royston
DOYLE, John J.
DUNCAN, Colin J.
EMSDEN, Philip J.
FOGG, David
FOLEY, Peter J.
FOYSTER,
   Stephen R.

GRAYDON,
   Raymond J.
HODGSON,
   Gordon H.
JEFFREY,
   William G.
KINGSTON,
   Andrew K.
McGROGAN, Hugh
McINTOSH,
   Malcolm P.

MERRY, Nicholas
MILKINS, Albert J.
SEACOLE, Jason P.
SWEETZER,
   James E.
TAYLOR, Leslie
WATSON, Gary
WHITE, Archibald

LEAGUE APPEARANCES: Berry, P. A. 16(3); Bodel, A. C. 40; Briggs,
G. 39; Burton, R. 39; Curran, H. P. 1(1); Doyle, J. J. 5; Duncan, C. J. 43;
Fogg, D. 44; Foley, P. J. 31(1); Graydon, R. J. 18; Hodgson, G. H. 31;
Jeffrey, W. G. 40(2); Kingston, A. K. 3; McGrogan, H. 21(3); McIntosh,
M. P. 23; Milkins, A. J. 7; Seacole, J. P. 45(1); Stott, I. 2; Sweetzer, J. E.
–(8); Taylor, L. 46; Watson, G. 9; White, A. 3(5).
GOALS—League (44): Foley 8, Seacole 8, Graydon 5 (1 pen.), Berry 4,
   McGrogan 4, Duncan 3, Bodel 2, Fogg 2 (1 pen.), Hodgson 1,
   Jeffrey 1, Sweetzer 1, Taylor 1, White 1, Own goals 3.
   F.A. Cup (2): Foley, Seacole.
   League Cup (7): Seacole 2, Duncan, Fogg (pen.), Foley, Sweetzer,
   Taylor.
Ground: Manor Ground, Beech Road, Headington, Oxford OX3 7RS.
  (0865 61503).
Nearest station: Oxford.
Team Manager: Mike Brown. Secretary: Jim A. Hunt.
Colours: Yellow shirts with blue trim; blue shorts.
Record home gate: 22,730 v. Preston, February, 1964 (F.A. Cup).
Honours—Champions: Div. 3: 1967–68.
   F.A. Cup Winners: Nil.

PETERBOROUGH UNITED   DIV. 4

ANDERSON, Trevor
BUTLIN, Barry D.
BYATT, Dennis J.
CARMICHAEL, Jack
CHARD, Phillip
CLISS, Tony
COOKE, Joseph
DOYLE, Robert
GREEN, William

GUY, Alan
GYNN, Michael
HOLMAN, Harry W.
McEWAN,
   William J.
QUOW, Trevor
ROBSON,
   Thomas H.
SARGENT, Gary S.

SHARKEY,
   Patrick G.
SLOUGH, Alan P.
SMITH, Anthony
STYLES, Arthur
WAUGH, Keith
WINTERS, John M.

LEAGUE APPEARANCES: Anderson, T. 23; Butlin, B. D. 30; Byatt,
D. J. 2(1); Carmichael, J. 25(2); Chard, P. 5(1); Cliss, T. 15(4); Collins
S. M. 5; Cooke, J. 18; Cunningham, D. 4; Doyle, R. 41; Green, W. 30;
Guy, A. 13(2); Gynn, M. 9(2); Hindley, P. 30; Holman, H. W. 9; McEwan,

W. J. 33(1); Quow, T. 5(3); Robertson, A. L. 12(3); Robson, T. H. 29(7); Ross, I. 45; Sargent, G. S. 9(2); Sharkey, P. 11; Slough, A. P. 10(1); Smith, A. 15; Styles, A. 32; Waugh, K. 46.

GOALS—League (44): Butlin 5, Cooke 5, Guy 4, Robson 4, Slough 4 (1 pen.), Doyle 3, Cliss 2, Gynn 2, McEwan 2, Sargent 2, Smith 2, Anderson 1, Chard 1, Cunningham 1, Holman 1, Robertson (1 pen.), Ross 1 (pen.), Styles 1, Own goals 2.

F.A. Cup (2): Anderson, Butlin.

League Cup (7): Slough 2 (1 pen.), Styles 2, Butlin, Doyle, Robson.

Ground: London Road Ground, Peterborough PE2 8AL. (0733 63947).

Nearest station: Peterborough.

Manager: Peter Morris. **Secretary:** A. V. Blades.

Colours: Shirts: blue and white stripes; shorts: blue.

Record home gate: 30,096 v. Swansea, February, 1965 (F.A. Cup).

Honours—Champions: Div. 4: 1960–61, 1973–74.

F.A. Cup Winners: Nil.

PLYMOUTH ARGYLE   DIV. 3

BALL, Stephen G.
BASON, Brian
BINNEY, Frederick E.
BRENNAN, Stephen A.
CLARKE, Colin
ELLIOTT, William
FEAR, Keith W.
FORDE, Clevere

FOSTER, George W.
GRAVES, Mark T.
HARRISON, Christopher C.
HODGE, Martin J.
HODGES, Kevin
JAMES, Tyrone S.
JOHNSON, Brian F.
LEVY, Anthony S.

McCORMICK, Steven
McNEILL, Brian
MEGSON, Gary J.
PERRIN, Steven C.
ROGERS, Alan J.
TRUSSON, Michael S.
UPTON, Colin C.
UZZELL, John E.

LEAGUE APPEARANCES: Bason, B. 36; Binney, F. E. 42(1); Brennan, S. A. 6; Burns, A. J. 8; Clarke, C. 35; Chapman, L. R. 3(1); Fear, K. W. 22(5); Forde, C. 4(1); Foster, G. W. 28; Graves, M. T. 5(5); Harrison, C. C. 22(2); Hodge, M. J. 38; Hodges, K. 11(1); James, T. S. 15; Johnson, B. F. 33; Levy, A. S. –(1); McNeill, B. 27; Megson, G. J. 42; Perrin, S. C. 23; Rogers, A. J. 38; Silkman, B. 14; Taylor, B. J. 8; Trusson, M. S. 24(3); Upton, C. C. 2(1); Uzzell, J. E. 20(1).

GOALS—League (67): Binney 26 (5 pens.), Johnson, 9 Megson 8, Trusson 5, Bason 4, Clarke 3, Fear 3, Perrin 3, Silkman 2, Harrison 1, Rogers 1, Own goals 2.

F.A. Cup: Nil.

League Cup (5): Binney 2, Fear 2 (1 pen.), own goal 1.

Ground: Home Park, Plymouth, Devon PL2 1BQ. (0752 52561/3).

Nearest station: Plymouth.

Team Manager: Bobby Saxton. **Secretary:** Graham Little.

Colours: Green shirts; white shorts.

Record home gate: 43,596 v. Aston Villa, October, 1936 (League).

Honours—Champions: Div. 3 South: 1929–30, 1951–52. Div. 3: 1958–59.

F.A. Cup Winners: Nil.

50

PORTSMOUTH DIV. 4

BARNARD, Leigh K.
BRYANT, Steven P.
DAVEY, Stehhen R.
DENYER, Peter R.
ELLIS, Peter J.
FOSTER, Stephen B.
GARWOOD, Colin A.
HEMMERMAN, Jeffrey L.
KNIGHT, Alan E.
LATHAN, John G.
McILWRAITH, James M.
MELLOR, Peter J.
PIPER, Stephen P.
PULLAR, David H.
ROBERTS, Trevor L.
SHOWERS, Derek
VINEY, Keith B.

LEAGUE APPEARANCES: Barnard, L. K. 28; Bryant, S. P. 15; Davey, S. R. 42(4); Denyer, P. R. 39(3); Ellis, P. J. 44; Foster, S. B. 35 (1); Garwood, C. A. 27(8); Hand, E. K. 3(2); Hemmerman, J. L. 37; James, K. A. 3(1); Lathan, J. G. 43(2); McCaffery, J. –(1); McIlwraith, J. 16(3); Mellor, P. J. 46; Milligan, L. C. 7; Piper, S. P. 14; Pullar, D. H. 35(3); Roberts, T. L. –(1); Showers, D. 19(1); Viney, K. B. 38(1); Wilson, W. 15(3).

GOALS—League (62): Garwood 15 (3 pens.), Hemmerman 14, Barnard 7, Davey 7, Denyer 6, Lathan 4, Foster 2, Showers 2, Viney 2 (1 pen.), Hand 1, Pullar 1, Wilson 1.

    F.A. Cup (2): Hemmerman 2.

    League Cup (2): Gilchrist, Pullar.

Ground: Fratton Park, Frogmore Road, Portsmouth, PO4 8RA. (Portsmouth 31204/5).

Nearest stations: Fratton or Portsmouth and Southsea.

Manager: Frank Burrows. **Secretary:** Mr. W. J. B. Davis.

Colours: Blue shirts with white trim; white shorts.

Record home gate: 51,385 v. Derby, February, 1949 (F.A. Cup).

Honours—Champions: Div. 1: 1948–49, 1949–50. Div. 3 South: 1923–24. Div. 3: 1961–62.

    F.A. Cup Winners: 1938–39.

PORT VALE DIV. 4

BEECH, Kenneth
BENNETT, Paul
BENTLEY, William J.
BLOOR, Alan
BROMAGE, Russel
CHAMBERLAIN, Mark
CHAMBERLAIN, Neville P.
CONNAUGHTON, Patrick J.
DANCE, Trevor
DELGADO, Robert A.
ELSBY, Ian C.
FARRELL, Peter
GRIFFITHS, Neil
HAWKINS, Graham N.
HEALY, Patrick J.
KEENAN, Gerrard
SINCLAIR, Brian W.
SPROSON, Philip J.
STENSON, Gerard P.
TODD, Kenneth
TULLY, Kevin F.
WRIGHT, Bernard P.

LEAGUE APPEARANCES: Beamish, K. G. 6; Beech, K. 20(3); Bentley, W. J. 30(1); Bloor, A. 5(1); Bromage, R. 19(1); Chamberlain, M. 6(2); Chamberlain, N. P. 22(4); Connaughton, P. J. 19; Dance, T. 27; Delgado, R. A. 24; Elsby, I. C. 3(2); Farrell, P. 28; Froggatt, J. L. 1(1); Griffiths, N. 26; Harris, D. 10(1); Hawkins, G. N. 43; Healy, P. J. 23; Keenan, G. 32;

51

Proudlove, G. 5; Ridley, J. 6(1); Sinclair, B. W. 14(4); Sproson, P. 22(1); Stenson, G. P. 10(1); Sutcliffe, P. D. 7(1); Todd, K. 40(1); Tully, K. F. 5(3); Wilkinson, N. 7; Wright, B. P. 46.

GOALS—League (57): Wright 14, Todd 8, Chamberlain (N.) 7, Beamish 4, Beach 4, Farrell 4 (2 pens.), Bromage 2, Hawkins 2, Healy 2, Keenan 2, Sinclair 2, Bloor 1, Griffiths (1 pen.), Sutcliffe 1, Tully 1, Own goals 2.
    F.A. Cup: Nil.
    League Cup (1): Wright.
Ground: Vale Park, Burslem, Stoke-on-Trent ST6 1AW. (Stoke (0782) 814134).
Nearest station: Stoke-on-Trent.
Manager: Dennis Butler. Secretary: Andrew Waterhouse.
Colours: White shirts with black trim; black shorts.
Record home gate: 50,000 v. Aston Villa, February, 1960 (F.A. Cup).
Honours—Champions: Div. 3 North: 1929–30, 1953–54. Div. 4: 1958–59.
    F.A. Cup Winners: Nil.

PRESTON NORTH END   DIV. 2

BAXTER, Michael J.
BELL, Graham T. A.
BRUCE, Alexander R.
BURNS, Francis
CAMERON, Daniel
COCHRANE, John
COLEMAN,
  Gordon M.
DOYLE, Stephen C.
ELLIOTT,
  Stephen B.

HASLEGRAVE,
  Sean M.
HOUSTON,
  Graham R.
KILNER, John I.
LITCHFIELD, Peter
McATEER,
  Andrew W.
McMAHON, John J.
O'RIORDAN,
  Donald J.

POTTS, Eric T.
ROBINSON,
  Michael J.
SPAVIN, Alan
TAYLOR, Brian J.
THOMSON,
  Richard B.
TUNKS, Roy W.
UZELAC, Steven
WILSON, Harry

LEAGUE APPEARANCES: Baxter, M. J. 37; Bell, G. T. A. 10; Bruce, A. R. 40; Burns, F. 21; Cameron, D. 36; Cochrane, J. 2(2); Coleman, G. M. 37; Cross, G. F. 5; Doyle, S. C. 25(4); Elliott, S. B. 5(2); Haslegrave, S. M. 41; McMahon, J. 8; O'Riordan, D. J. 32; Potts, E. T. 25(4); Robinson, M. J. 36; Smith, J. 1(3); Spavin, A. 2; Taylor, B. J. 29(1); Thomson, R. B. 13(4); Tunks, R. W. 42; Uzelac, S. 7; Wilson, H. 8(4).
GOALS—League (59): Bruce 21, Robinson 13 (1 pen.), Coleman 7, Baxter 4, Potts 4, Thomson 4, Doyle 2, Bell 1, Cochrane 1, Haslegrave 1, Own goal 1.
    F.A. Cup (3): Bruce 2, Burns.
    League Cup (6): Bruce 3, Baxter, Fisher, Thomson.
Ground: Deepdale, Preston PR1 6RU. (Preston (0772) 795919).
Nearest station: Preston.
Manager: Nobby Stiles. Secretary: Ron Severs.
Colours: White shirts with blue collars and cuffs; white shorts with blue stripes.
Record home gate: 42,684 v. Arsenal, April, 1938 (League).
Honours—Champions: Div. 1: 1888–89, 1889–90. Div. 2: 1903–04, 1912–13, 1950–51. Div. 3: 1970–71.
    F.A. Cup Winners: 1888–89, 1937–38.

QUEEN'S PARK RANGERS   DIV. 2

ABBOTT, Ronald F.
ALLEN, Clive D.
BOWLES, Stanley
BUSBY, Martyn G.
CLEMENT, David T.
ELSEY, Karl W.
FRANCIS,
  Gerald C. J.
GILLARD, Ian T.

GODDARD, Paul
HAMILTON,
  William R.
HARKOUK,
  Rachid P.
HOLLINS, John W.
HOWE, Ernest J.
HUCKER, Peter I.
McGEE, Paul

NUTT, Philip J.
RICHARDSON,
  Derek
ROEDER, Glenn V.
SHANKS, Donald
WALLACE, Barry D.
WALSH, Michael A.

LEAGUE APPEARANCES: Abbott, R. F. –(2); Allen, C. D. 4(6);
Bowles, S. 30; Busby, M. G. 29(6); Clement, D. T. 29; Cunningham, T. E.
9; Eastoe, P. R. 26; Elsey, K. W. 2(1); Francis, G. C. J. 31; Gillard, I. T.
38; Goddard, P. 20(3); Hamilton, W. R. 8(3); Harkouk, R. P. 14(1);
Hollins, J. W. 41; Howe, E. J. 38; James, L. 1; McGee, P. 18(4); Parkes,
P. B. 24; Richardson, D. 18; Roeder, G. V. 27; Shanks, D. 41; Wallace,
B. D. 4(1); Walsh, M. A. 10.
GOALS—League (45): Busby 6, Goddard 6, Allen 4, Roeder 4, Eastoe 3,
    Gillard 3, Harkouk 3, McGee 3, Shanks 3, Walsh 3 (1 pen.),
    Francis 2, Hamilton 2, Bowles (1 pen.), Clement 1, Howe 1.
  F.A. Cup: Nil.
  League Cup (5): Eastoe 3, McGee, Own goal 1.
Ground: Rangers Stadium, South Africa Road, Shepherds Bush, W12
7PA. (01-743 2618 and 2670).
Nearest stations: Shepherds Bush (Metropolitan and Central Lines); White
City (Central Line).
Manager: Tommy Docherty. **Secretary:** R. J. Phillips.
Colours: Blue and white hooped shirts; white shorts.
Record home gate: 35,353 v. Leeds U., April, 1974 (League).
Honours—Champions: Div. 3: 1966–67. Div. 3 South: 1947–48.
  F.A. Cup Winners: Nil.
  League Cup Winners: 1966–67.

READING   DIV. 3

ALEXANDER,
  John E.
BENNETT, Paul R.
BOWMAN,
  Richard D.
DEATH,
  Stephen V.
EARLES, Patrick J.

HENDERSON,
  James S.
HETZKE,
  Stephen E. R.
HICKS, Martin
KEARNEY,
  Michael J.
KEARNS, Oliver A.
LEWIS, Alan T.

MORELINE, David
PETERS, Gary D.
SANCHEZ,
  Lawrence P.
WANKLYN,
  Edward W.
WHITE, Mark I.
WILLIAMS,
  Jeremy S.

LEAGUE APPEARANCES: Alexander, J. E. 15(1); Bennett, P. R. 45;
Bowman, R. D. 34; Britten, M. E. W. –(1); Death, S. V. 46; Earles, P. J.
37(2); Hetzke, S. E. R. 42; Hicks, M. 46; Kearney, M. J. 31(2); Kearns,
O. A. 20(7); Lewis, A. T. 40; Peters, G. D. 45; Sanchez, L. 34(5); Shipley,
G. 11(1); Wanklyn, E. W. 13; White, M. I. 46; Williams, J. S. 1.

GOALS—League (76): Earles 15, Kearns 11 (3 pens.), Bowman 10 (5 pens.), Kearney 10, Hetzke 9, Alexander 8, Lewis 4, Sanchez 4, Bennett 1, Hicks 1, Peters 1, Shipley 1, Own goal 1.

F.A. Cup (5): Kearney 3, Alexander, Lewis.

League Cup (9): Earles 4, Hetzke 2, Kearns, Lewis, Own goal 1.

Ground: Elm Park, Norfolk Road, Reading RG3 2EF. (Reading 57878/80).

Nearest station: Reading.

Team Manager: Morris Evans. **Secretary-Manager:** R. Bentley.

Colours: Blue and white hooped shirts; white shorts.

Record home gate: 33,042 v. Brentford, February, 1927 (F.A. Cup).

Honours—Champions: Div. 3 South: 1925–26. Div. 4: 1978–79.

F.A. Cup Winners: Nil.

ROCHDALE   DIV. 4

ASHWORTH, Philip A.	HART, Brian P.	SCAIFE, Robert H.
BANNON, Ian	HILDITCH, Mark	SLACK, Andrew
COLLINS, John D.	HOY, Robert	SNOOKES, Eric
ESSER, Edward D.	JONES, Christopher M. N.	TAYLOR, Brian
HALLOWS, Paul C. R.	OLIVER, Edmund A.	WRIGHT, Graham
	O'LOUGHLIN, Nigel	

LEAGUE APPEARANCES: Ashworth, P. A. 9(2); Bannon, I. 15(5); Collins, J. D. 6(2); Creamer, P. 18(2); Esser, E. D. 37(3); Felgate, D. W. 35; Forster, G. P. –(1); Hallows, P. C. R. 18; Hart, B. P. 39; Hilditch, M. 19(8); Hoy, R. 39(2); Jones, C. M. N. 21; Milne, M. 1(1); Morrin, A. J. 1; Mullington, P. T. 8(1); Oliver, E. A. 8; O'Loughlin, N. 45; Owen, L. T. 41; Price, J. 9(1); Scaife, R. H. 34; Scott, R. W. 31; Shyne, C. 10; Slack, A. 1; Snookes, E. 35; Taylor, B. 26.

GOALS—League (47): Owen 11, Hoy 10 (2 pens.), Jones 10, Esser 5, Hilditch 3, Scaife 2, Scott 2, Oliver 1, O'Loughlin 1, Snookes 1, Taylor 1.

F.A. Cup: Nil.

League Cup (2): Ashworth, O'Loughlin.

Ground: Spotland, Willbutts Lane, Rochdale OL11 5DS. (Rochdale 44648/9).

Nearest station: Rochdale.

Player-Manager: Doug Collins. **Secretary:** T. Nichol.

Colours: Royal blue shirts with white trim; white shorts with blue trim.

Record home gate: 24,231 v. Notts County, December, 1949 (F.A. Cup).

Honours—Champions: Nil.

F.A. Cup Winners: Nil.

ROTHERHAM UNITED   DIV. 3

BRECKIN, John	GALLOWAY, Steven	NIX, Peter
CARR, Peter	GREEN, John R.	PHILLIPS, Trevor
CRAWFORD, Alan P.	GWYTHER, David G. A.	RHODES, Mark N.
DAWSON, Richard	McALISTER, Thomas G.	SMITH, David
EVANS, Stewart J.	MOON, Richard A.	STANCLIFFE, Paul I.
FINNEY, John R.	MOUNTFORD, Raymond	TAYLOR, Ashley
FLYNN, John E.		WINN, Stephen
FORREST, Gerald		YOUNG, Thomas M.

LEAGUE APPEARANCES: Breckin, J. 45; Carr, P. 18; Crawford, A. P. 39; Dawson, R. 7(3); Finney, J. R. 41; Flynn, J. E. 29(1); Forrest, G. 46; Green, J. R. 46; Gwyther, D. G. A. 41; McAllister, T. G. 45; Mountford, R. 1; Phillips, T. 46; Pugh, D. 3; Rhodes, M. N. 20; Smith, D. 31(1); Stancliffe, P. I. 33; Vaughan, I. 1; Winn, S. 6(2); Young, T. 8.

GOALS—League (49): Phillips 14, Gwyther 13, Finney 9 (2 pens.), Smith 3 (2 pens.), Crawford 2, Breckin 1, Carr 1, Dawson 1, Flynn 1, Green 1, Rhodes 1, Young 1, Own goal 1.

F.A. Cup (8): Gwyther 3, Breckin 2, Crawford, Green, Phillips.

League Cup (11): Finney 5 (1 pen.), Crawford 2, Gwyther 2, Green Phillips.

Ground: Millmoor, Rotherham S60 1HR. (Rotherham 2434).

Nearest station: Rotherham.

Manager: Jimmy McGuigan. **Secretary:** G. A. Somerton.

Colours: Red shirts with white trim; white shorts.

Record home gate: 25,000 v. Sheffield United, December, 1952 and Sheffield Wednesday, January, 1952 (League).

Honours—Champions: Div. 3: North: 1950–51.

F.A. Cup Winners: Nil.

SCUNTHORPE UNITED   DIV. 4

COUCH, Geoffrey R.	EARL, Steven	KEELEY, Nolan B.
CRAWFORD, Peter G.	GIBSON, David	KILMORE, Kevin
CZUCZMAN, Michael	GORDON, James S.	OATES, Robert A.
DAVY, Stephen	GRIMES, Vincent	O'DONNELL, Jonathan D.
DEERE, Stephen H.	HALL, David A.	PEACOCK, John C.
	KAVANAGH, Eamon A.	PILLING, Anthony S.

LEAGUE APPEARANCES: Armstrong, K. T. –(1); Bloomer, B. M. 3(4); Couch, G. R. 14(4); Crawford, P. G. 46; Czuczman, M. 39; Davy, S. 12 (2); Deere, S. H. 45; Earl, S. 23; Gibson, D. 14(4); Grimes, V. 45; Hall, D. A. 10(1); Kavanagh, E. A. 37(2); Keeley, N. B. 25; Kilmore, K. 44(2); Oates, R. A. 45; O'Donnell, J. D. 32; Peacock, J. C. 26(2); Pilling, A. S. 29(1); Wigg, R. G. 17(1).

GOALS—League (54): Kilmore 17 (8 pens.), Earl 8, Couch 5, Grimes 5, Pilling 5, Oates 3, Wigg 3, Kavanagh 2, Keeley 2, Bloomer 1, Deere 1, Gibson 1, Own goal 1.

F.A. Cup (1): Pilling.

League Cup: Nil.

Ground: Old Show Ground, Scunthorpe DN15 7RH. (Scunthorpe 2954).

Nearest station: Scunthorpe.

Manager: Ron Ashman. **Secretary:** Mrs. S. Louth.

Colours: Red shirts with white trim, red shorts.

Record home gate: 23,935 v. Portsmouth, January, 1954 (F.A. Cup).

Honours—Champions: Div. 3 North: 1957–58.

F.A. Cup Winners: Nil.

SHEFFIELD UNITED DIV. 3

BROWN, Douglas A.
CLARK, Graham J.
CONROY, Stephen H.
CUTBUSH, William J.
FINNIESTON, Stephen J.
FLOOD, John G.
GARNER, Paul
GUY, Michael
HAMSON, Gary
HARWOOD, Richard
KEELEY, Andrew J.
KENWORTHY, Anthony D.
LARNER, Keith D.
McGARRY, Brian J.
McPHAIL, John
MATTHEWS, John
RENWICK, Craig
SABELLA, Alexandro
SPEIGHT, Michael
TIBBOTT, Leslie
WINDRIDGE, David H.

LEAGUE APPEARANCES: Anderson, P. 28(2); Benjamin, I. T. 1(1); Brown, D. A. 7(2); Calvert, C. A. 21; Conroy, S. H. 41; Cutbush, W. J. 26; Finnieston, S. J. 23; Flood, J. G. 5(2); Franks, C. J. 15(2); Garner, P. 19; Guy, M. 12(3); Hamson, G. 41; Harwood, R. A. 2(1); Johns, N. 1; Jones, P. H. 1; Keeley, A. J. 10; Kenworthy, A. D. 37; McPhail, J. 15; Matthews, J. 31(1); Renwick, C. 6(1); Rioch, B. D. 8; Sabella, A. 39; Smith, T. E. 2(1); Speight, M. 39; Stainrod, S. A. 9(5); Tibbott, L. 12; Varadi, I. 6(4); Woodward, A. 5.
GOALS—League (52): Anderson 12, Matthews 5, Finnieston 4, Hamson 4 (2 pens.), Varadi 4, Kenworthy 3, Sabella 3, Stainrod 3, Benjamin 2, (2 pens.), Guy 2, Speight 2, Brown 1, Calvert 1, Franks 1, Garner 1, McPhail 1, Rioch 1, Smith 1, Own goal 1.
    F.A. Cup: Nil.
    League Cup (2): Calvert, Hamson.
Ground: Bramhall Lane, Sheffield S2 4SU. (0742 738955).
Nearest station: Sheffield.
Manager: Harry Haslam. Secretary:
Colours: Red and white striped shirts with thin black stripes; black shorts.
Record home gate: 68,287 v. Leeds, February, 1936 (F.A. Cup).
Honours—Champions: Div. 1: 1897–98. Div. 2: 1952–53. Div. 3 North: 1945–46.
    F.A. Cup Winners: 1898–99, 1901–02, 1914–15, 1924–25.

SHEFFIELD WEDNESDAY DIV. 3

BLACKHALL, Raymond
BOLDER, Robert J.
COX, Brian R.
CURRAN, Edward
DOWD, Hugh O.
FLEMING, John H.
GRANT, David
HORNSBY, Brian G.
JOHNSON, Jeffrey D.
LEMAN, Denis
LOWEY, John A.
MULLEN, James
NIMMO, Ian W.
OWEN, Gordon
PICKERING, Michael J.
PORTERFIELD, John
RUSHBURY, David G.
SHIRTLIFF, Peter A.
SMITH, Mark C.
STRUTT, Brian
TAYLOR, Kevin
TURNER, Christopher R.
WYLDE, Rodger J.

LEAGUE APPEARANCES: Blackhall, R. 21; Bolder, R. J. 19; Cox, B. 4; Curran, E. 11(1); Dowd, H. O. 7; Fleming, J. H. 6; Grant, D. 26(1); Hornsby, B. G. 44(1); Johnson, J. D. 37(1); Leman, D. 16(1); Lowey, J. A.

24(5); Mullen, J. 35; Nimmo, I. W. 8(7); Owen, G. 14(8); Pickering, M. J. 35; Porterfield, J. 45(1); Rushbury, D. G. 36(1); Shirtliff, P. A. 26; Smith, M. C. 20(1); Sterland, M. 1(1); Taylor, K 4(1); Turner, C. R. 23; Tynan, T. E. 8; Wylde, R. J. 36(2)

GOALS—League (53): Hornsby 16 (6 pens.), Wylde 14, Nimmo 4, Johnson 3, Lowey 3, Owen 3, Porterfield 2, Curran 1, Fleming 1, Grant 1, Mullen 1, Rushbury 1, Shirtliff 1, Sterland 1, Tynan 1.

    F.A. Cup (14): Hornsby 4 (3 pens.), Wylde 3, Lowey 2, Nimmo 2, Johnson, Leman, Rushbury.

    League Cup (2): Hornsby, Own goal 1.

Ground: Hillsborough, Sheffield S6 1SW. (0742 343123, Box office 343122).

Nearest station: Sheffield.

Team Manager: Jack Charlton, O.B.E. Secretary: Eric England.

Colours: Royal blue and white striped shirts; royal blue shorts.

Record home gate: 72,841 v. Manchester City, February, 1934 (F.A. Cup).

Honours—Champions: Div. 1: 1902–03, 1903–04, 1928–29, 1929–30.
    Div. 2: 1899–1900, 1925–26, 1951–52, 1955–56, 1958–59.
    F.A. Cup Winners: 1895–96, 1906–07, 1934–35.

SHREWSBURY TOWN   DIV. 2

ATKINS, Ian L.
BIGGINS, Stephen J.
BIRCH, Trevor N.
CROFT, Brian G.
CROSS, Stephen C.
GRIFFIN, Colin R.
HAYES, Stephen C.
KEAY, John P.
KING, John
LARKIN, Anthony G.
LEONARD, Carleton C.
LINDSAY, James Y.
MAGUIRE, Paul B.
MULHEARN, Kenneth J.
NEIL, Michael
ROBERTS, Michael J.
TONG, David J.
TURNER, Graham J.
WARDLE, Robert I.

LEAGUE APPEARANCES: Atkins, I. L. 44; Biggins, S. J. 44(1); Birch, T. N. 13(1); Chapman, R. D. 24(1); Cross, S. C. 14(5); Griffin, C. R. 46; Hayes, S. C. 21; Keay, J. P. 27(1); King, J. 39; Larkin, A. G. 25; Leonard, C. C. 26; Lindsay, J. Y. 27(3); Loughnane, P. B. 3; Maguire, P. B. 40; Mulhearn, K. J. 26; Roberts, M. J. –(1); Tong, D. J. 35(2); Turner, G. J. 32; Wardle, R. I. 20.

GOALS—League (61): Maguire 13, Atkins 11 (5 pens), Biggins 9, King 6, Tong 5, Turner 5, Chapman 4, Birch 2, Cross 2 (1 pen.), Griffin 2, Keay 2.

    F.A. Cup (17): Maguire 5, Biggins 3, Chapman 3, Atkins 2 (1 pen.), Keay, Leonard, Tong, Turner.

    League cup: (2), Cross 1, Own goal 1.

Ground: Gay Meadow, Shrewsbury SY2 6AB. (0743 56068).

Nearest station: Shrewsbury.

Player-Manager: Graham Turner. Secretary: M. J. Starkey.

Colours: Shirts: blue with amber trim. Shorts: blue with amber trim.

Record home gate: 18,917 v. Walsall, April, 1961 (League).

Honours—Champions: Div. 3: 1978–79.

    F.A. Cup Winners: Nil.

SOUTHAMPTON   DIV. 1

ANDRUSZEWSKI,
  Emanuel F.
BAKER, Graham E.
BALL, Álan J.
BOYER, Phillip J.
DAWTRY, Kevin A.
GENNOE,
  Terence W.
GEORGE, Charles F.
GOLAC, Ivan
HARRISON,
  Mark S.
HAYES,
  Austin W. P.

HEBBERD,
  Trevor N.
HOLMES,
  Nicholas C.
McGRATH,
  Martin L.
NICHOLL,
  Christopher J.
O'DONOGHUE,
  Michael G.
PEACH, David S.
PHILLIPSON-
  MASTERS,
  Forbes E.

PRATT, Wayne
PUCKETT, David C.
SHIPLEY,
  George M.
WALDRON,
  Malcolm R.
WELLS, Peter A.
WHITLOCK, Mark
WILLIAMS,
  Oshor J.
WILLIAMS,
  Steven C.

LEAGUE APPEARANCES: Andruszewski, E. F. 10; Baker, G. E. 20(2); Ball, A. J. 42; Boyer, P. J. 42; Curran, E. 25(1); Dawtry, K. A. –(1); Funnell, A. 2; Gennoe, T. W. 23; George, C. F. 2; Golac, I. 36; Hayes, A. W. P. 13(2); Hebberd, T. N. 16(6); Holmes, N. C. 38; MacDougall, E. J. 10; Nicholl, C. J. 38; Peach, D. S. 38; Pickering, M. J. 3; Sealey, A. J. –(5); Shipley, G. M. –(1); Waldron, M. R. 42; Wells, P. A. 19; Williams, O. J. 4(1); Williams, S. C. 39.
GOALS—League (47): Holmes 8, Boyer 7, Waldron 6, Baker 5, MacDougall 5, Peach 5 (5 pens), Hayes 3, Nicholl 3, Ball 2 (1 pen.), Hebbard 2, Own goals 1.
    F.A. Cup (7): Boyer 4, Ball, Hayes, Peach (pen.).
    League Cup (15): Boyer 4, Hebberd 2, Holmes 2, MacDougall 2, Peach 2, Curran, Nicholl, Williams.
Ground: The Dell, Milton Road, Southampton SO9 4XX. (0703 23408).
Nearest station: Southampton.
Team Manager: Lawrie McMenemy. Secretary: B. Truscott.
Colours: Red and white vertical striped shirts; black shorts.
Record home gate: 31,044 v. Manchester Utd., October, 1969 (League).
Honours—Champions: Div. 3 South: 1921–22. Div. 3: 1959–60.
    F.A. Cup Winners: 1975–76.

SOUTHEND UNITED   DIV. 3

ABBOTT, Peter A.
CAWSTON,
  Mervyn, W.
CUSACK, David S.
DUDLEY, Philip W.
FELL, Gerald C.
FRANKLIN,
  Graham N.
GOODWIN,
  Stephen A.

HADLEY,
  Antony P. F.
HORN, Graham R.
HULL, Jeff
LAVERICK,
  Michael G.
MOODY, Alan
MORRIS, Colin
OTULAKOWSKI
  Anton

PARKER, Derrick
POLYCARPOU,
  Andrew
POUNTNEY,
  Ronald A.
STEAD, Michael J.
WALKER, John
YATES, Stephen

LEAGUE APPEARANCES: Abbott, P. A. 7(1); Cawston, M. W. 39; Cusack, D. S. 37; Dudley, P. W. 46: Fell, G. C. 22(1); Franklin, G. N. –(1); Goodwin, S. A. 2; Hadley, A. P. F. 33(3); Horn, G. R. 7; Hull, J. 1; Laverick, M. G. 29(2); Moody, A. 34; Morris, C. 44; Otulakowski, A. 9; Parker, D. 43; Polycarpou, A. 21(5); Pountney, R. A. 40(2); Stead, M. J. 38; Townsend, N. R. 1; Walker, J. 11(8); Yates, S. 42.

GOALS—League (51): Parker 10, Fell 7, Morris 7 (3 pens.), Laverick 6, Polycarpou 5, Pountney 5, Dudley 3, Moody 3 (3 pens.), Stead 2, Abbott 1, Cusack 1, Yates 1.

> **F.A. Cup (5):** Parker 2, Polycarpou, Pountney, Own goal 1.
> **League Cup (2):** Own goals 2.

Ground: Roots Hall Ground, Victoria Avenue, Southend SS2 6NQ. (Southend 40707).

Nearest station: Prittlewell or Southend Central.

Manager: Davis Smith. **Secretary:** K. Holmes.

Colours: Shirts: royal blue with red and white trim. Shorts: white with blue and red trim.

Record home gate: 28,059 v. Birmingham, January, 1957 (F.A. Cup).

Honours—Champions: Nil.

> **F.A. Cup Winners:** Nil.

STOCKPORT COUNTY   DIV. 4

ARMSTRONG, George	GALVIN, Christopher	ROGAN, Leslie M.
BRADD, Leslie J.	HENSON, Philip M.	RUTTER, John T.
CONNOR, James T.	LAWSON, David	SUMMERBEE, Michael G.
EDWARDS, Paul F.	LEE, Frederick S.	THORPE, Andrew
	PRUDHAM, Edward	

LEAGUE APPEARANCES: Armstrong, G. 34; Bradd, L. J. 45; Cahill, P. G. 3; Cassidy, A. D. 4; Connor, J. T. 1(1); Edwards, P. F. 40; Fogarty, K. A. 20(1); Galvin, C. 1; Goodfellow, J. 2(1); Halford, C. 21(9); Henson, P. M. 34(2); Lawson, D. 18; Lee, F. S. 45; Loadwick, D. 11; Park, T. 29(2); Prudham, E. 19(5); Rogan, L. M. 24; Rutter, J. T. 45; Seddon, A. J. 1(3); Smith, G. L. 19; Summerbee, M. G. 33; Sumner, A. 3(2); Thompson, W. A. 16(1); Thorpe, A. 38.

GOALS—League (58): Lee 20 (1 pen.), Bradd 18, Henson 5, Park 4, Thompson 4, Edwards 2, Halford 2, Prudham 1, Summerbee 1, Own goal 1.

> **F.A. Cup (11):** Park 5, Bradd 2, Lee 2, Fogarty, Prudham.
> **League Cup (5):** Lee 2, Bradd, Park, Thompson (pen.).

Ground: Edgeley Park, Stockport SK3 9DD. (061-480 8888/9).

Nearest station: Stockport.

Player-Manager: Mike Summerbee. **Secretary:** T. R. McCreery.

Colours: White shirts with royal blue trim; royal blue shorts.

Record home gate: 27,833 v. Liverpool, February, 1950 (F.A. Cup).

Honours—Champions: Div. 3 North: 1921–22, 1936–37. Div. 4: 1966–67.

> **F.A. Cup Winners:** Nil.

STOKE CITY DIV. 1

BOWERS, Ian
BRISSETT, Trevor A.
BUSBY, Vivian D.
CHAPMAN, Lee R.
COOK, Jeffrey
CROOKS, Garth A.
DODD, Alan
DOYLE, Michael
FOX, Peter D.

HEATH, Adrian P.
IRVINE, Samuel
JOHNSON, Paul
JOHNSON, Paul A.
JONES, Roger
KENDALL, Howard
McGROARTY, James M.
MORGAN, Andrew J.

O'CALLAGHAN, Brendan R.
PEJIC, Melvyn
RANDALL, Paul
RICHARDSON, Paul
SCOTT, Geoffrey
SIMPSON, Gary J.
SMITH, Denis
THORLEY, Dennis

LEAGUE APPEARANCES: Busby, V. D. 8(10); Conroy, G. A. 3(4); Cook, J. 1(2); Crooks, G. A. 38(2); Dodd, A. 34(4); Doyle, M. 41; Fox, P. D. 1; Heath, A. P. 1(1); Irvine, S. 41; Johnson, P. 7(1); Johnson, P. A. 2; Jones, R. 41; Kendall, H. 40; McGroarty, J. M. 3(1); Marsh, J. H. 24; O'Callaghan, B. R. 40(1); Randall, P. 20; Richardson, P. 40; Scott, G. 37(1); Sheldon, K. J. –(1); Smith, D. 38; Waddington, S. 2.

GOALS—League (58): O'Callaghan 16, Crooks 12 (3 pens.), Irvine 8, Richardson 6, Busby 5, Randall 5, Kendall 2, Smith 2, Doyle 1, McGroarty 1.

    F.A. Cup: Nil.

    League Cup (9): Irvine 2, Busby, Crooks (pen.), Dodd, Doyle, Kendall, O'Callaghan, Richardson.

Ground: Victoria Ground, Stoke-on-Trent ST4 4EG. (Stoke 44660).
Nearest station: Stoke-on-Trent.
Manager: Alan Durban. Secretary: M. J. Potts.
Colours: Red and white striped shirts; white shorts.
Record home gate: 51,380 v. Arsenal, March, 1937 (League).
Honours—Champions: Div. 2: 1932–33, 1962–63. Div. 3 North: 1926–27.
    F.A. Cup Winners: Nil.
    League Cup Winners: 1971–72.

SUNDERLAND DIV. 2

ARNOTT, Kevin W.
ASHURST, Jack
BOLTON, Joseph
BROWN, Alan
BUCKLEY, Michael J.
CHISHOLM, Gordon W.
CLARKE, Jeffrey D.
COADY, Michael L.
CRAWFORD, Colin

DOCHERTY, Michael
DUNCAN, John A.
ELLIOTT, Shaun
ENTWISTLE, Wayne P.
GILBERT, Timothy H.
GREGOIRE, Roland B.
HAMILTON, David
HENDERSON, Michael R.

HINDMARCH, Robert
HUTTON, Vincent
LEE, Robert G.
MAIN, John C.
RODDY, Joseph P.
ROSTRON, John W.
ROWELL, Gary
SIDDALL, Barry
WATSON, Ian
WEIR, Alan
WHITWORTH, Stephen

LEAGUE APPEARANCES: Arnott, K. W. 15; Ashurst, J. 10(1); Bolton, J. 32; Brown, A. 14(8); Buckley, M. J. 30; Chisholm, G. W. 27; Clarke,

J. D. 33(1); Coady, M. L. 3; Docherty, M. 26(1); Elliott, S. 41; Entwistle, W. P. 34(2); Gilbert, T. H. 12; Greenwood, R. T. 3(5); Gregoire, R. B. 1(1); Henderson, M. R. 30; Kerr, R. 3; Lee, R. G. 30(3); Rostron, J. W. 34; Rowell, G. 32; Siddall, B. 41; Watson, I. 1; Whitworth, S. 10.
GOALS—League (70): Rowell 21 (6 pens.), Entwistle 11, Rostron 11 (2 pens.), Brown 6, Lee 6, Docherty 4, Bolton 3, Clarke 2, Greenwood 2, Ashurst 1, Chisholm 1, Elliott 1, Gilbert 1.
    F.A. Cup (3): Entwistle, Lee, Rowell (pen.).
    League Cup: Nil.
Ground: Roker Park, Sunderland SR6 9SW. (Sunderland 72077 58638).
Nearest station: Sunderland or Seaburn.
Manager: Ken Knighton. **Secretary:** R. M. Linney.
Colours: Red and white striped shirts; black shorts.
Record home gate: 75,118 v. Derby, March, 1933 (F.A. Cup).
Honours—Champions: Div. 1: 1891–92, 1892–93, 1894–95, 1901–02, 1912–13, 1935–36.
    F.A. Cup Winners: 1936–37, 1972–73.

SWANSEA CITY DIV. 2

ATTLEY, Brian R.	CRUDGINGTON,	MORRIS, Steven G.
BAKER, Mark	Geoffrey	PHILLIPS, Leighton
BARTLEY, Daniel R.	CURTIS, Alan T.	REEVES, Peter P.
BOERSMA, Philip	EVANS,	SMITH, Thomas
CALLAGHAN,	Wyndham E.	STEVENSON,
Ian R.	JAMES,	Nigel C.
CHAPPELL,	Anthony R.	TOSHACK, John B.
Leslie A.	JAMES, Robert M.	WADDLE, Alan R.
CHARLES,	MARUSTIK,	
Jeremy M.	Christopher	

LEAGUE APPEARANCES: Attley, B. R. 19(1); Baker, M. 2(3); Bartley, D. R. 40(2); Boersma, P. 15(3); Bruton, D. E. 7(1); Callaghan, I. R. 40; Charles, J. M. 36(4); Crudgington, G. 46; Curtis, A. T. 34; Evans, W. E. 35; James, A. R. 1(1); James, R. M. 43; Lally, P. A. M. 1; Marustik, C. 2(2); Moore, K. J. 14(1); Morris, S. G. 7(2); Phillips, L. 28; Reeves, P. P. 2(2); Smith, T. 34(2); Stevenson, N. C. 36(3); Toshack, J. B. 24(4); Waddle, A. R. 40(2).
GOALS—League (83): Waddle 19, James (R.) 14 (1 pen.), Curtis 13, Toshack 13, Charles 12, Baker 2, Bartley 2, Smith 2, Stevenson 2, Attley 1, Boersma 1, Moore 1, Own goal 1.
    F.A. Cup (11): Curtis 5, Charles 2, James 2, Toshack, Waddle.
    League Cup (11): James (R.) 4 (1 pen.), Curtis 3, Charles 2, Toshack, Waddle.
Ground: Vetch Field, Swansea SA1 3SU. (Swansea 42855).
Nearest station: Swansea.
Team Manager: John Toshack. **Secretary:** G. J. Daniels.
Colours: White shirts with black trim; white shorts with black trim.
Record home gate: 32,796 v. Arsenal, February, 1968 (F.A. Cup).
Honours—Champions: Div. 3 South: 1924–25, 1948–49.
    F.A. Cup Winners: Nil.

SWINDON TOWN   DIV. 3

AIZLEWOOD,   KAMARA,   OGDEN,
  Steven   Christopher   Christopher J.
ALLAN, James   LEWIS, Russell   ROBERTS, Kevin J.
BATES, Philip D.   McHALE, Raymond   ROWLAND,
CARTER, Roy W.   McLAUGHLIN,   Andrew A.
DORNAN, Peter   John   STROUD,
FORD, Andrew C.   MAYES, Alan K.   Kenneth A.
GILCHRIST,   MILLER, Ian   TROLLOPE,
  Paul A.   NORMAN,   Norman J.
HAMILTON, Bryan   Kenneth A.   WILLIAMS, Brian

LEAGUE APPEARANCES: Aizlewood, S. 39(1); Allan, J. 24; Bates, P.
D. 34(8); Carter, R. W. 46; Cunningham, D. 1(1); Dornan, P. –(1);
Ford, A. C. 46; Gilchrist, P. A. 10(6); Guthrie, C. W. 6; Hamilton, B. 18
(3); Kamara, C. 22(6); Lewis, R. 5(4); McHale, R. 46; McLaughlin, J.
18; Mayes, A. K. 21; Miller, I. 44; Ogden, C. J. 22; Rowland, A. A. 28;
Stroud, K. A. 44; Trollope, N. J. 16(2); Williams, B. 16(9).
GOALS—League (74): Bates 14, Rowland 13, Mayes 11, Carter 10, (1 pen.)
      Gilchrist 6, McHale 5, Miller 3, Aizlewood 2, Kamara 2,
      Williams 2, Hamilton 1, McLaughlin 1, Own goals 4.
    F.A. Cup (9): Bates 2, Gilchrist 2, Kamara 2, Carter, McHale,
    Rowland.
    League Cup (7): Aizlewood 2, Guthrie 2, Miller 2, Williams.
Ground: County Ground, Swindon SN1 1AA. (Swindon 22118).
Nearest station: Swindon.
Team Manager: Bob Smith. **Secretary:** R. Jefferies.
Colours: Red shirts; white shorts.
Record home gate: 32,000 v. Arsenal, January, 1972 (F.A. Cup).
Honours—Champions: Nil.
    F.A. Cup Winners: Nil.
    League Cup Winners: 1968–69.
    Anglo-Italian Cup Winners: 1970.

TORQUAY UNITED   DIV. 4

BOULTON,   DUNNE, James C.   PAYNE, Jeremy
  Clinton W.   GREEN,   RITCHIE,
CLARKE, Stuart A.   Michael C.   Stephen K.
COFFILL, Peter T.   LAWRENCE,   TURNER, John
COOPER, Steven M.   Leslie O.   TWITCHIN, Ian R.
DAVIES, Roy   MURPHY, Donal P.

LEAGUE APPEARANCES: Bicknell, S. J. –(3); Boulton, C. W. 11;
Clarke, S. A. 4(1); Coffill, P. T. 27(8); Cooper, S. M. 28(5); Cox, N. 2;
Darke, P. G. 33; Davies, R. 39(2); Dunne, J. C. 43; Green M. C. 33; John-
son B. F. 5; Lawrence L. O. 42(3); Murphy, D. P. 37(4); Parsons, L. W. 13;
Payne, J. 21; Raper, K. 21; Ritchie, S. K. 17; Turner, J. 46; Twitchin, I. R.
45; Vassallo, B. E. 1(1); Wilson, A. 38(4).

GOALS—League (58): Lawrence 17, Cooper 14, Murphy 10 (1 pen.), Coffill 3, Davies 3, Green 3, Cox 2, Johnson 2, Wilson 2, Payne 1, Raper 1.

F.A. Cup (4): Cooper, Lawrence, Twitchin, Wilson.

League Cup (2): Lawrence, Murphy.

Ground: Plainmoor, Torquay, Devon TQ1 3PS. (0803 38666/7).

Nearest stations: Torquay or Torre.

Player-Manager: Mike C. Green. **Secretary**: D. J. Easton.

Colours: White shirts with blue and yellow vertical stripes on sleeve; blue shorts with yellow and white stripes on side.

Record home gate: 21,908 v. Huddersfield, January, 1955 (F.A. Cup).

Honours—Champions: Nil.

F.A. Cup Winners: Nil.

TOTTENHAM HOTSPUR   DIV. 1

ALEKSIC, Milija A.	HODDLE, Glenn	MAZZON, Georgio
ARDILES,	HOLMES, James A.	MILLER, Paul R.
Osvaldo C.	HUGHTON,	NAYLOR,
ARMSTRONG,	Christopher W. G.	Terence M. P.
Gerard J.	JONES,	PERRYMAN,
BEAVON, Stuart M.	Christopher H.	Stephen J.
BROOKE, Garry J.	KENDALL, Mark	PRATT, John A.
DAINES, Barry R.	LACY, John	SMITH, Gordon M.
FALCO, Mark P.	LEE, Colin	TAYLOR, Peter J.
GALVIN, Anthony	McALLISTER,	VILLA, Julio R.
HAZARD, Michael	Donald	

LEAGUE APPEARANCES: Aleksic, M. A. 5; Ardiles, O. C. 38; Armstrong, G. J. 7(3); Beavon, S. M. 1; Daines, B. R. 14; Duncan, J. P. 2; Falco, M. P. 1; Galvin, A. 1; Gorman, J. 15; Hoddle, G. 34(1);Holmes, J. A. 33; Jones, C. H. 18(1); Kendall, M. 23; Lacy, J. 35; Lee, C. 26(1); McAllister, D. 38; McNab, N. 2; Miller, P. R. 7; Moores, I. R. 2; Naylor, T. M. P. 22; Perryman, S. J. 42; Pratt, J. A. 37(1); Smith, G. M. 1(1); Taylor, P. J. 32(1); Villa, J. R. 26(6).

GOALS—League (48): Taylor 10 (2 pens.), Lee 8, Hoddle 7 (2 pens.), Jones 5, Pratt 4, Ardiles 3, Villa 2, Armstrong 1, Duncan 1, Falco 1, Holmes 1, McAllister 1, Perryman 1, Own goals 3.

F.A. Cup (12): Jones 4, Lee 3, Ardiles, Hoddle, Perryman, Taylor (pen.), Own goal 1.

League Cup (3): Armstrong, Hoddle, Villa.

Ground: White Hart Lane, 748 High Road, Tottenham, N17 0AP. (01-088 2046).

Nearest stations: White Hart Lane (E.R.), Northumberland Park (E.R.) or Seven Sisters (Victoria Line) thence by bus.

Manager: Keith Burkinshaw. **Secretary**: G. W. Jones.

Colours: White shirts; navy blue shorts.

Record home gate: 75,038 v. Sunderland, March, 1938 (F.A. Cup).

Honours—Champions: Div. 1: 1950–51, 1960–61. Div. 2: 1919–20, 1949–50.

F.A. Cup Winners: 1900–01, 1920–21, 1960–61, 1961–62, 1966–67.

League Cup Winners: 1970–71, 1972–73.

European Cup Winners' Cup: 1962–63.

U.E.F.A. Cup Winners: 1971–72.

TRANMERE ROVERS DIV. 4

BRAMHALL, John
CLIFF, Edward
CRAVEN, Stephen
EATON, Stephen P.
EVANS, Andrew C.
FLOOD, Edward D.
GRIFFITHS, Ian J.

JOHNSON,
  Richard R.
KERR, John
McAULEY, Hugh A.
MATHIAS,
  Raymond
O'NEIL, Thomas P.

PALIOS, Mark
PARRY, Leslie I.
PEPLOW,
  Stephen T.
POSTLEWHITE,
  Dennis J.
WEST, Gordon

LEAGUE APPEARANCES: Bramhall, J. 35; Cahill, P. G. 5; Cliff, E. 6(1); Craven, S. 26(4); Eaton, S. P. 1; Evans, A. C. 46; Flood, E. D. 40; Griffiths, I. J. 3; Johnson, R. R. 41; Kerr, J. 22(3); McAuley, H. A. 41(2); Mathias, R. 45; Moore, R. D. 26; O'Neil, T. P. 32; Palios, M. 21(3); Parry, L. I. 46; Peplow, S. T. 23(5); Postlewhite, D. J. 31(1); Thomas, J. W. 10(1); West, G. 5; Whittingham, S. P. –(1); Williams, W. J. 1.

GOALS—League (45): Evans 11, Moore 8 (1 pen.), Peplow 8, Kerr 6, Bramhall 2, Craven 2, O'Neil 2 (1 pen.), Thomas 2, Cliff 1, Palios 1, Parry 1, Postlewaite 1.

    F.A. Cup (3): Moore 2, McAuley.

    League Cup (2): McAuley, O'Neil.

Ground: Prenton Park, 14 Prenton Road West, Birkenhead, Wirral, L42 8NR. (051-608 3677/4194).

Nearest station: Birkenhead, Hamilton Square.

Manager: John King. **Secretary:** D. Johnson.

Colours: White shirts with blue edgings; royal blue shorts.

Record home gate: 24,424 v. Stoke, February, 1972 (F.A. Cup).

Honours—Champions: Div. 3 North: 1937–38.

    F.A. Cup Winners: Nil.

WALSALL DIV. 4

BIRCH, Alan
CASWELL, Brian L.
GREEN, Ronald R.
HARRISON,
  Colin G.
JONES, Stephen R.
KEARNS, Michael
KELLY, James
KING, Jeffrey

McDONOUGH, Roy
MACKEN, Anthony
MOWER,
  Kenneth M.
PAUL, Ian K.
PENN, Donald
SBRAGIA, Richard
SERELLA, David E.
SYRETT, David K.

TURNER, Ian
WADDINGTON,
  David P.
WADDINGTON,
  Steven F.
WILLIAMS,
  James L.

LEAGUE APPEARANCES: Austin, T. W. 33; Birch, A. 45; Buckley, A. P. 13; Caswell, B. L. 41(1); Clarke, K. L. 1(1); Green, R. R. 1; Harrison, C. G. 30; Jones, S. R. 15; Kearns, M. 24; Kelly, J. 18(7); King, J. 34(1); McDonough, R. 31(3); Macken, A. 42; Mower, K. M. 1; Paul, I. K. 13(1); Penn, D. 10(3); Rees, M. 7(3); Sbragia, R. 32; Serella, D. E. 43; Syrett, D. K. 11; Turner, I. 21; Waddington, D. P. –(2); Waddington, S. F. 33; Williams, J. L. 7(2).

GOALS—League (56): Austin 13, Birch 9 (4 pens.), McDonough 7, Buckley 5 (1 penl), King 3, Penn 3, Sbragia 3, /Syrett 3, Kelly 2, Serella 2, Waddington (S.) 2, Caswell 1, Williams 1, Own goals 2.

64

F.A. Cup: Nil.
    League Cup (5): Buckley 3 (1 pen.), Birch, Paul.
Ground: Fellows Park, Walsall WS2 9DB (0922-22791).
Nearest station: Walsall or Bescot (15 mins. walk. No public transport).
Player/manager: Alan Buckley. Secretary: H. J. Westmancoat.
Colours: Red shirts, white shorts.
Record home gate: 25,453 v. Newcastle, August, 1961 (League).
Honours—Champions: Div. 4: 1959–60.
    F.A. Cup Winners: Nil.

WATFORD   DIV. 2

BLISSETT, Luther L.   HOW, Trevor A.   RANKIN,
BOLTON, Ian R.   JENKINS, Ross A.   Andrew G.
BOOTH, Dennis   JOSLYN,   SHERWOOD,
CASSELLS, Keith B.   Roger D. W.   Stephen
DOWNES, Robert D.   MERCER, Keith   SIMS, Steven F.
GARNER, Alan H.   POLLARD, Brian E.   STIRK, John
HARRISON,   PRITCHETT,   TRAIN, Raymond
    Steven J.   Keith B.

LEAGUE APPEARANCES: Blissett, L. L. 40(1); Bolton, I. R. 43; Booth,
D. 37; Cassells, K. B. –(3); Downes, R. D. 34(3); Ellis, S. 3(3); Garner,
A. H. 42; Harrison, S. J. 23; Jenkins, R. A. 46; Joslyn, R. D. W. 44(1);
Mayes, A. K. 5(8); Mercer, K. 9(5); Pollard, B. E. 33(1); Pritchett, K. B.
22; Rankin, A. G. 30; Sherwood, S. 16; Sims, S. F. 13(1); Stirk, J. 46;
Train, R. 20(1).
GOALS—League (83): Jenkins 29, Blissett 21 (1 pen.), Bolton 9 (4 pens.),
    Joslyn 8, Garner and Pollard 4, Downes 2, Mercer 2, Pritchett 2
    (2 pens.), Sims 1, Train 1.
    F.A. Cup (4): Jenkins 4.
    League Cup (17): Blissett 7, Jenkins 4, Downes 2, Bolton, Joslyn,
        Mayes, Pritchett (pen.).
Ground: Vicarage Road, Watford WD1 8ER. (Watford 49747/9.)
Nearest station: Watford Junction.
Team Manager: Graham Taylor. General Secretary: R. E. Rollitt, F.A.A.I.
Colours: Gold shirts with black/red stripe, black shorts.
Record home gate: 34,099 v. Manchester Utd., February, 1969 (F.A. Cup).
Honours—Champions: Div. 3: 1968–69. Div. 4: 1977–78.
    F.A. Cup Winners: Nil.

WEST BROMWICH ALBION   DIV. 1

ANDERSON, John   DANKS, Philip P.   PAGE, Robert F.
ARTHUR, David R.   EVANS, Paul E.   REGIS, Cyrille
BATSON, Brendon M.   GODDEN,   ROBERTSON,
BENNETT, Martyn   Anthony L.   Alistair
BROWN, Alistair   GREW, Mark S.   ROBSON, Bryan
BROWN, Anthony   HODGSON,   STATHAM, Derek J.
CANTELLO,   Vernon G.   STEWART, David S.
    Leonard   LEWIS, Nicholas A.   SUMMERFIELD,
COWDRILL, Barry   LOVERIDGE, John   Kevin
CROSS,   MILLS, David J.   TREWICK, John
    Nicholas J. R.   MONAGHAN,   WILE, John D.
CUNNINGHAM,   Derek J.
    Lawrence P.   MOSES, Remi M.

65

LEAGUE APPEARANCES: Batson, B. M. 41; Bennett, M. 1; Brown, A. 41; Brown, T. 29(2); Cantello, L. 32; Cunningham, L. P. 39(1); Godden, A. L. 42; Johnston, W. M. 3(4); Martin, M. P. 1; Mills, D. J. 15(3); Regis, C. 38(1); Robertson, A. 39; Robson, B. 41; Statham, D. J. 39; Summerfield, K. –(2); Trewick, J. 19(2); Wile, J. D. 42.

GOALS—League (72): Brown(A.) 18, Regis 15, Brown(T.) 9, Cunningham 9, Robson 7, Cantello 3, Mills 3, Trewick 3, Wile 2, Statham 1, Summerfield 1, Own goal 1.

    F.A. Cup (13): Brown(A.) 5, Cunningham 3, Brown(T.) 2, Batson, Regis, Wile.

    League Cup: Nil.

Ground: The Hawthorns, West Bromwich B71 4LF. (021-553 0095).
Nearest stations: Smethwick Rolfe Street or Birmingham New Street.
Manager: Ron Atkinson. **Secretary:** A. Everiss.
Colours: Navy blue and white striped shirts; white shorts.
Record home gate: 64,815 v. Arsenal, March, 1937 (F.A. Cup).
Honours—Champions: Div. 1: 1919–20. Div. 2: 1901–02, 1910–11.
    F.A. Cup Winners: 1887–88, 1891–92, 1930–31, 1953–54, 1967–68.
    League Cup Winners: 1965–66.

WEST HAM UNITED   DIV. 2

BONDS, William A.	FERGUSON, Robert	MARTIN, Alvin E.
BRIGNULL, Philip A.	HOLLAND,	MORGAN, Nicholas
BROOKING,	Patrick G.	MOSELEY,
Trevor D.	JENNINGS,	Gary J. V.
BRUSH, Paul	William J.	PARKES,
COWIE, George A.	LAMPARD,	Philip B. F.
CROSS, David	Frank R. G.	PIKE, Geoffrey A.
CURBISHLEY,	LANDSDOWNE,	ROBSON, Bryan S.
Llewellyn C.	William	TAYLOR, Alan D.
DAY, Mervyn R.	McDOWELL,	TAYLOR,
DEVONSHIRE,	John A.	Thomas F.
Alan E.		THOMSON, Brian L.

LEAGUE APPEARANCES: Bonds, W. A. 39; Brignull, P. A. –(1); Brooking, T. D. 21; Brush, P. 42; Cross, D. 40; Curbishley, L. C. 26(1); Day, M. R. 13; Devonshire, A. E. 41; Ferguson, R. 11; Holland, P. G. 39; Jennings, W. J. 2(2); Lampard, F. R. G. 28(1); Lansdowne, W. –(1); McDowell, J. A. 26(2); Martin, A. E. 22; Morgan, N. 2; Parkes, P. B. F. 18; Pike, G. A. 10(4); Robson, B. S. 40; Taylor, A. D. 10(3); Taylor, T. F. 32.

GOALS—League (70): Robson 24 (3 pens.), Cross 17, Devonshire 5, Bonds 4, Holland 3, Lampard 3, Taylor (A.) 3, Brooking 2, McDowell 2, Pike 2, Curbishley 1, Martin 1, Own goals 3.

    F.A. Cup (1): Robson.

    League Cup (1): Robson.

Ground: Boleyn Ground, Green Street, Upton Park, E13 (01-472 0704).
Nearest station: Upton Park (District Line).
Team Manager: John Lyall. **Secretary:** Eddie Chapman.
Colours: Claret shirts with blue sleeves; white shorts.
Record home gate: 42,322 v. Tottenham, October, 1970 (League).
Honours—Champions: Div. 2: 1957–58.
    F.A. Cup Winners: 1963–64, 1974–75.
    European Cup-Winners' Cup: 1964–65.

WIGAN ATHLETIC DIV. 4

BROWN, John C.
BROWNBILL,
  Derek A.
CORRIGAN,
  Francis J.
CROMPTON, Alan
DAVIDS, Neil
FRETWELL, David

GILLIBRAND,
  Ian V.
GORE, John T.
HART, Nigel
HINNIGAN,
  Joseph P.
HOUGHTON, Peter
MOORE, Michael

PURDIE, Ian
QUINN, Anthony M.
SMART, Kevin G.
WARD, Noel G.
WILKIE, John C.
WRIGHT,
  Jeffrey K.

LEAGUE APPEARANCES: Brown, J. C. 42; Brownbill, D. A. 20(10); Corrigan, F. J. 45; Crompton, A. 7(6); Curtis, J. 9; Davids, N. 10(2); Fretwell, D. 33; Gay, G. 1; Gillibrand, I. V. 7; Gore, T. 46; Grew, M. S. 4; Hinnigan, J. P. 39; Houghton, P. 23(3); Moore, M. 40(1); Purdie, I. 46; Seddon, I. W. 1; Smart, K. G. 40; Ward, N. G. 44; Wilkie, J. C. 3(1); Worswick, M. A. –(1); Wright, J. K. 46.

GOALS—League (63): Houghton 13, Purdie 11 (3 pens.), Moore 9, Wright 7, Brownbill 6, Hinnigan 5, Corrigan 4, Ward 4, Gore 2, Smart 1, Own goal 1.
  F.A. Cup (3): Gore, Houghton, Moore.
  League Cup (3): Corrigan 2, Gore.
Ground: Springfield Park, Wigan, WNT 7BAS (0942 44433).
Nearest station: Wigan Wallgate, and Wigan North West.
Manager: Ian M. McNeill. Secretary: Derek Welsby.
Colours: Blue and white striped shirts, blue shorts.
Record home gate: 27,500 v. Hereford Utd., December 1953 (F.A. Cup).
Honours—Champions: Northern Premier League 1970–71, 1974–75.
  Northern Premier League Cup: 1972.

WIMBLEDON DIV. 3

BOWGETT, Paul
BRILEY, Leslie
CORK, Alan G.
CUNNINGHAM,
  Thomas E.
DENNY, Paul
DOWNES, Walter J.
DRIVER, Philip

DZIADULEWICZ,
  Mark
EAMES, Terence
GALLIERS, Steven
GODDARD,
  Raymond
HARWOOD, Lee
HAVERSON, Paul

KETTERIDGE,
  Stephen J.
KNOWLES,
  Raymond
LESLIE, John A.
PARSONS, Stephen
PERKINS, Stephen

LEAGUE APPEARANCES: Bowgett, P. 11; Briley, L. 26; Bryant, J. S. 27(3); Connell, R. 2; Cork, A. G. 45; Cowley, F. W. 3(3); Cunningham, T. E. 15; Denny, P. 24(4); Donaldson, D. 23; Downes, W. J. 3; Driver, P. 3(7); Dziadulewicz, M. 1(1); Eames, T. 26; Galliers, S. 44; Galvin, D. 33; Goddard, R. 45; Harwood, L. 1; Haverson, P. 26(1); Ketteridge, S. J. 15(2); Knowles, R. 23(8); Leslie, J. A. 44(1); Parsons, S. 34(3); Perkins, S. 26; Priddy, P. J. 1; Summerill, P. 5(2).

GOALS—League (78): Cork 22, Leslie 19, Parsons 7, Denny 6, Knowles 5, Cunningham 3, Galliers 3, Bryant 2, Galvin 2, Haverson 2 (1 pen.), Briley 1, Downes 1, Driver 1, Eames 1 (pen.), Ketteridge 1, Own goals 2.
  F.A. Cup (4): Cork 2, Denny, Parsons.
  League Cup (4): Cork, Galliers, Galvin, Own goal 1.

Ground: Plough Lane Ground, Durnsford, Wimbledon, S19.
Nearest station: Wimbledon or Haydons Road (BR) South Wimbledon
Tube.
Manager: Dario Gradi. Secretary: Adrian Cook.
Colours: All white with blue trim.
Record home gate: 18,000 v. HMS *Victory*, 1932–33 (F.A. Amateur Cup).
Honours—Champions, Southern League: 1974–75, 1975–76, 1976–77.
Southern League Cup: 1970, 1976.

WOLVERHAMPTON WANDRS. DIV. 1

ARKWRIGHT, Ian
ATKINSON, Hugh A.
BELL, Norman
BERRY, George F.
BLACK, John
BRADSHAW,
Paul W.
BRAZIER, Colin J.
CARR, William M.
CLARKE, Wayne
DALEY, Stephen

DANIEL, Peter W.
EVES, Melvyn J.
FLEMING,
Christopher J.
HAZELL, Robert J.
HIBBITT, Kenneth
HOLLIFIELD,
Michael
HUMPHREY, John
KNOWLES, Peter
McALLE, John E.

MATTHEWS,
Michael
MOSS, Craig A.
MOSS, Paul M.
PALMER, Geoffrey
PARKIN, Derek
PATCHING, Martin
PIERCE, Gary
RAFFERTY,
William H.
RICHARDS, John P.

LEAGUE APPEARANCES: Arkwright, I. 3(1); Bell, N. 17(4); Berry,
G. F. 30; Black, J. 2; Bradshaw, P. W. 39; Brazier, C. J. 6(1); Carr, W. M.
36; Clarke, W. 6(2); Daley, S. 39(1); Daniel, P. W. 40; Eves, M. J. 17(2);
Hazell, R. J. 12(1); Hibbitt, K. 37; McAlle, J. E. 37; Moss, P. M. 1;
Palmer, G. 41; Parkin, D. 42; Patching, M. 11(5); Pierce, G. 3; Rafferty,
W. H. 24(3); Richards, J. P. 19.

GOALS—League (44): Richards 9, Daley 6, Hibbitt 6, Daniel 5 (3 pens.),
Bell 3, Berry 3, Carr 3, Eves 2, Rafferty 2, Clarke 1, Patching 1,
Own goals 3.

F.A. Cup (10): Bell 2, Rafferty 2, Carr, Daley, Daniel (pen.),
Hibbitt, Patching, Own goal 1.

League Cup: Nil.
Ground: Molineux, Wolverhampton WV1 4QR (Wolverhampton 24053/4).
Nearest station: Wolverhampton.
Manager: John Barnwell. Secretary: P. A. Shaw.
Colours: Old gold shirts with black trim; black shorts.
Record home gate: 61,315 v. Liverpool, February, 1939 (F.A. Cup).
Honours—Champions: Div. 1: 1953–54, 1957–58, 1958–59. Div. 2: 1931–
32, 1976–77. Div. 3 (North): 1923–24.
F.A. Cup Winners: 1892–93, 1907–08, 1948–49, 1959–60.
League Cup Winners: 1973–74.

WREXHAM DIV. 2

BUXTON, Stephen C.
CARTWRIGHT,
Leslie
CEGIELSKI, Wayne
DAVIES, William D.
DAVIS, Gareth
DWYER, Alan R.
EVANS, Michael G.

FOX, Stephen D.
GILES, David C.
HILL, Alan G.
JONES, Joseph P.
KENWORTHY,
Stephen
LYONS, John P.
McNEIL, Richard

NIEDZWIECKI,
Edward A.
ROBERTS, John G.
SHINTON,
Robert T.
SUTTON, Melvyn C.
WHITTLE, Graham
WILLIAMS, Peter W.

LEAGUE APPEARANCES: Buxton, S. C. 10(3); Cartwright, L. 23; Cegielski, W. 24(5); Davies, W. D. 36; Davis, G. 22; Dwyer, A. R. 28(1); Evans, M. G. 3(2); Fox, S. D. 21(1); Giles, D. C. 23; Griffiths, A. T. 3(1); Hill, A. G. 15(2); Jones, F. 2; Jones, J. P. 30; Kenworthy, S. 2; Lyons, J. P. 28(7); McNeil, R. 30(1); Niedzwiecki, A. E. 6; Roberts, I. M. –(1); Roberts, J. G. 40; Shinton, R. T. 36; Sutton, M. C. 39(2); Thomas, M. R. 16; Whittle, G. 22(4); Williams, P. W. 3(3).

GOALS—League (45): Lyons 10 (4 pens.), Whittle 7 (1 pen.), Shinton 6, Thomas 6 (1 pen), McNeil 4, Hill 3 (1 pen.), Buxton 2, Jones 2, Fox 1, Giles 1, Williams 1, Own goals 2.

F.A. Cup (11): Lyons 3, (1 pen) McNeil 3, Shinton 2, Cartwright, Cegielski, Davis.

League Cup (5): Cartwright, Davis, McNeil (pen.), Shinton, Whittle.

Ground: The Racecourse, Mold Road, Wrexham LL1 2AN. (Wrexham (0978) 262129.)

Nearest station: Wrexham General.

Manager: Arfon Griffiths, M.B.E. **Secretary:** C. N. Wilson.

Colours: Red shirts with white trimmings; white shorts with red seam.

Record home gate: 34,445 v. Manchester United, January, 1957 (F.A. Cup).

Honours—Champions: Div. 3: 1977–78.

   F.A. Cup Winners: Nil.

YORK CITY   DIV. 4

BROWN, Graham C.	JAMES, Steven R.	STANIFORTH,
BYRNE, John F.	KAY, Robert	Gordon
CLEMENTS,	LOGGIE, David M.	STRONACH, Peter
Andrew P.	McDONALD, Ian C.	WALSH, James T.
FAULKNER,	NEENAN, Joseph P.	WELLINGS, Barry
Stephen A.	PUGH, David	
FORD, Gary	RANDALL, Kevin	

LEAGUE APPEARANCES: Bainbridge, P. E. 2; Brown, G. C. 24; Clements, A. P. 46; Collier, G. 5; Faulkner, S. A. 44; Ford, G. 32(1); Kay, R. 46; Loggie, D. M. 36(2); McDonald, I. C. 43; Neenan, J. P. 22; Pugh, D. 31; Randall, K. 37(5); Scott, P. W. 11; Staniforth, G. 45; Stronach, P. 22(4); Walsh, J. T. 38(1); Warnock, N. 1(3); Wellings, B. 10(5); Young, T. A. 11.

GOALS—League (51): Staniforth 15 (2 pens.), Randall 10, Loggie 8, McDonald 6, Ford 4, Clements 2, Stronach 2, Wellings 2, Faulkner 1, Own goal 1.

F.A. Cup (12): Staniforth 4, Wellings 3, Clements, Faulkner, Ford Pugh, Randall.

League Cup: Nil.

Ground: Bootham Crescent, York YO3 7AQ. (York 24447).

Nearest station: York.

Manager: Charlie Wright. **Secretary:** S. B. Winship.

Colours: Red shirts with blue trim; blue shorts.

Record home gate: 28,123 v. Huddersfield, March, 1938 (F.A. Cup).

Honours—Champions: Nil.

   F.A. Cup Winners: Nil.

HOME TEAM	Arsenal	Aston Villa	Birmingham C.	Bolton W.	Bristol C.	Chelsea	Coventry C.	Derby Co.	Everton
Arsenal	—	1-1	3-1	1-0	2-0	5-2	1-1	2-0	2-2
Aston Villa	5-1	—	1-0	3-0	2-0	2-1	1-1	3-3	1-1
Birmingham C.	0-0	0-1	—	3-0	1-1	1-1	0-0	1-1	1-3
Bolton W.	4-2	0-0	2-2	—	1-2	2-1	0-0	2-1	3-1
Bristol C.	1-3	1-0	2-1	4-1	—	3-1	5-0	1-0	2-2
Chelsea	1-1	0-1	2-1	4-3	0-0	—	1-3	1-1	0-1
Coventry C.	1-1	1-1	2-1	2-2	3-2	3-2	—	4-2	3-2
Derby Co.	2-0	0-0	2-1	3-0	0-1	1-0	0-2	—	0-0
Everton	1-0	1-1	1-0	1-0	4-1	3-2	3-3	2-1	—
Ipswich T.	2-0	0-2	3-0	3-0	0-1	5-1	1-1	2-1	0-1
Leeds U.	0-1	1-0	3-0	5-1	1-1	2-1	1-0	4-0	1-0
Liverpool	3-0	3-0	1-0	3-0	1-0	2-0	1-0	5-0	1-1
Manchester C.	1-1	2-3	3-1	2-1	2-0	2-3	2-0	1-2	0-0
Manchester U.	0-2	1-1	1-0	1-2	1-3	1-1	0-0	0-0	1-1
Middlesbrough	2-3	2-0	2-1	1-1	0-0	7-2	1-2	3-1	1-2
Norwich C.	0-0	1-2	4-0	0-0	3-0	2-0	1-0	3-0	0-1
Nottingham F.	2-1	4-0	1-0	1-1	2-0	6-0	3-0	1-1	0-0
Q.P.R.	1-2	1-0	1-3	1-3	1-0	0-0	5-1	2-2	1-1
Southampton	2-0	2-0	1-0	2-2	2-0	0-0	4-0	1-2	3-0
Tottenham H.	0-5	1-4	1-0	2-0	1-0	2-2	1-1	2-0	1-1
W.B.A.	1-1	1-1	1-0	4-0	3-1	1-0	7-1	2-1	1-0
Wolverhampton	1-0	0-4	2-1	1-1	2-0	0-1	1-1	4-0	1-0

1978-79 Results

Ipswich T.	Leeds U.	Liverpool	Manchester C.	Manchester U.	Middlesbrough	Norwich C.	Nottingham F.	Q.P.R.	Southampton	Tottenham H.	W.B.A.	Wolverhampton
4-1	2-2	1-0	1-1	1-1	0-0	1-1	2-1	5-1	1-0	1-0	1-2	0-1
2-2	2-2	3-1	1-1	2-2	0-2	1-1	1-2	3-1	1-1	2-3	0-1	1-0
1-1	0-1	0-3	1-2	5-1	1-3	1-0	0-2	3-1	2-2	1-0	1-1	1-1
2-3	3-1	1-4	2-2	3-0	0-0	3-2	0-1		2-0	1-3	0-1	3-1
3-1	0-0	1-0	1-1	1-2	1-1	1-1	1-3	2-0	3-1	0-0	1-0	0-1
2-3	0-3	0-0	1-4	0-1	2-1	3-3	1-3	1-3	1-2	1-3	1-3	1-2
2-2	0-0	0-0	0-3	4-3	2-1	4-1	0-0	1-0	4-0	1-3	1-3	3-0
0-1	0-1	0-2	1-1	1-3	0-3	1-1	1-2	2-1	2-1	2-2	3-2	4-1
0-1	1-1	1-0	1-0	3-0	2-0	2-2	1-1	2-1	0-0	1-1	0-2	2-0
—	2-3	0-3	2-1	3-0	2-1	1-1	1-1	2-1	0-0	2-1	0-1	3-1
1-1	—	0-3	1-1	2-3	3-1	2-2	1-2	4-3	4-0	1-2	1-3	3-0
2-0	1-1	—	1-0	2-0	0-0	6-0	2-0	2-1	2-0	7-0	2-1	2-0
1-2	3-0	1-4	—	0-3	1-0	2-2	0-0	3-1	1-2	2-0	2-2	3-1
2-0	4-1	0-3	1-0	—	3-2	1-0	1-1	2-0	1-1	2-0	3-5	3-2
0-0	1-0	0-1	2-0	2-2	—	2-0	1-3	0-2	2-0	1-0	1-1	2-0
0-1	2-2	1-4	1-1	2-2	1-0	—	1-1	1-1	3-1	2-2	1-1	0-0
1-0	0-0	0-0	3-1	1-1	2-2	2-1	—	0-0	1-0	1-1	0-0	3-1
0-4	1-4	1-3	2-1	1-1	1-1	0-0	0-0	—	0-1	2-2	1-1	3-3
1-2	2-2	1-1	0-1	0-1	2-1	2-2	0-1	1-1	—	3-3	1-1	3-2
1-0	1-2	0-0	0-3	1-1	1-2	0-0	1-3	1-1	0-0	—	1-0	1-0
2-1	1-2	1-1	4-0	1-0	2-0	2-2	0-1	2-1	1-0	0-1	—	1-1
1-3	1-1	0-1	1-1	2-4	1-3	1-0	1-0	1-0	2-0	3-2	0-3	—

HOME TEAM	Blackburn R.	Brighton & H.A.	Bristol R.	Burnley	Cambridge U.	Cardiff C.	Charlton Ath.	Crystal Palace	Fulham
Blackburn R.	—	1-1	0-2	1-2	1-0	1-4	1-2	1-1	2-1
Brighton & H.A.	2-1	—	3-0	2-1	0-2	5-0	2-0	0-0	3-0
Bristol R.	4-1	1-2	—	2-0	2-0	4-2	5-5	0-1	3-1
Burnley	2-1	3-0	2-0	—	1-1	0-0	2-1	2-1	5-3
Cambridge U.	0-1	0-0	1-1	2-2	—	5-0	1-1	0-0	1-0
Cardiff C.	2-0	3-1	2-0	1-1	1-0	—	1-4	2-2	2-0
Charlton Ath.	2-0	0-3	3-0	1-1	2-3	1-1	—	1-1	0-0
Crystal Palace	3-0	3-1	0-1	2-0	1-1	2-0	1-0	—	0-1
Fulham	1-2	0-1	3-0	0-0	5-1	2-2	3-1	0-0	—
Leicester C.	1-1	4-1	0-0	2-1	1-1	1-2	0-3	1-1	1-0
Luton T.	2-1	1-1	3-2	4-1	1-1	7-1	3-0	0-1	2-0
Millwall	1-1	1-4	0-3	0-2	2-0	2-0	0-2	0-3	0-0
Newcastle U.	3-1	1-3	3-0	3-1	1-0	3-0	5-3	1-0	0-0
Notts Co.	2-1	1-0	2-1	1-1	1-1	1-0	1-1	0-0	1-1
Oldham Ath.	5-0	1-3	3-1	2-0	4-1	2-1	0-3	0-0	0-2
Orient	2-0	3-3	1-1	2-1	3-0	2-2	2-1	0-1	1-0
Preston N. E.	4-1	1-0	1-1	2-2	0-2	2-1	6-1	2-3	2-2
Sheffield U.	0-1	0-1	1-0	4-0	3-3	2-0	1-1	0-2	1-1
Stoke C.	1-2	2-2	2-0	3-1	1-3	2-0	2-2	1-1	2-0
Sunderland	0-1	2-1	5-0	3-1	0-2	1-2	1-0	1-2	1-1
West Ham U.	4-0	0-0	2-0	3-1	5-0	1-1	2-0	1-1	1-1
Wrexham	2-1	0-0	0-1	0-1	1-2	1-2	1-1	0-0	1-1

1978-79 Results

	Leicester C.	Luton T.	Millwall	Newcastle U.	Notts Co.	Oldham Ath.	Orient	Preston N.E.	Sheff. Utd.	Stoke C.	Sunderland	West Ham U.	Wrexham
	1-1	0-0	1-1	1-3	3-4	0-2	3-0	0-1	2-0	2-2	1-1	1-0	1-1
	3-1	3-1	3-0	2-0	0-0	1-0	2-0	5-1	2-0	1-1	2-0	1-2	2-1
	1-1	2-0	0-3	2-0	2-2	0-0	2-1	0-1	2-1	0-0	0-0	0-1	2-1
	2-2	2-1	0-1	1-0	2-1	1-0	0-1	1-1	1-1	0-3	1-2	3-2	0-0
	1-1	0-0	2-1	0-0	0-1	3-3	3-1	1-0	1-0	0-1	0-2	0-0	1-0
	1-0	2-1	2-1	2-1	2-3	1-3	1-0	2-2	4-0	1-3	1-0	0-0	1-0
	1-0	1-2	2-4	4-1	1-1	2-0	0-2	1-1	3-1	1-4	1-2	0-0	1-1
	3-1	3-1	0-0	1-0	2-0	1-0	1-1	0-0	3-1	1-1	1-1	1-1	1-0
	3-0	1-0	1-0	1-3	1-1	1-0	2-2	5-3	2-0	2-0	2-2	0-0	0-1
	—	3-0	0-0	2-1	0-1	2-0	5-3	1-1	0-1	1-1	1-2	1-2	1-1
	0-1	—	2-2	2-0	6-0	6-1	2-1	1-2	1-1	0-0	0-3	1-4	2-1
	2-0	0-2	—	2-1	0-1	2-3	2-0	0-2	1-1	3-0	0-1	2-1	2-2
	1-0	1-0	1-0	—	1-2	1-1	0-0	4-3	1-3	2-0	4-3	0-3	2-0
	0-1	3-1	1-1	1-2	—	0-0	1-0	0-0	4-1	0-1	1-1	1-0	1-1
	2-1	2-0	4-1	1-3	3-3	—	0-0	2-0	1-1	1-1	0-0	2-2	1-0
	0-1	3-2	2-1	2-0	3-0	0-0	—	2-0	1-1	0-1	3-0	0-2	0-1
	4-0	2-2	0-0	0-0	1-1	1-1	1-1	—	2-2	0-1	3-1	0-0	2-1
	2-2	1-1	0-2	1-0	5-1	4-2	1-2	0-1	—	0-0	3-2	3-0	1-1
	0-0	0-0	2-0	0-0	2-0	4-0	3-1	1-1	2-1	—	0-1	2-0	3-0
	1-1	1-0	3-2	1-1	3-0	3-0	1-0	3-1	6-2	0-1	—	2-1	1-0
	1-1	1-0	3-0	5-0	5-2	3-0	0-2	3-0	1-1	3-3		—	1-1
	0-0	2-0	3-0	0-0	3-1	2-0	3-1	2-1	4-0	0-1	1-2	4-3	—

THE LEAGUE - Division III

HOME TEAM	Blackpool	Brentford	Bury	Carlisle U.	Chester	Chesterfield	Colchester U.	Exeter C.	Gillingham	Hull C.	Lincoln C.
Blackpool	—	0-1	1-2	3-1	3-0	0-0	2-1	1-1	2-0	3-1	2-0
Brentford	3-2	—	0-1	0-0	6-0	0-3	1-0	0-0	0-2	1-0	2-1
Bury	1-3	2-3	—	2-2	1-1	3-1	2-2	4-2	2-2	1-1	2-2
Carlisle U.	1-1	1-0	1-2	—	1-1	1-1	4-0	1-1	1-0	2-2	2-0
Chester	4-2	3-1	1-1	1-2	—	3-0	2-2	3-0	1-1	2-1	5-1
Chesterfield	1-3	0-2	2-1	2-3	3-1	—	2-1	0-1	0-2	1-2	1-3
Colchester	3-1	1-1	0-0	2-1	2-1	0-0	—	2-2	2-2	2-1	2-0
Exeter C.	3-0	2-2	2-1	3-2	0-1	3-1	2-1	—	0-0	3-1	3-2
Gillingham	2-0	0-0	3-3	0-0	1-0	2-1	3-0	2-0	—	2-0	4-2
Hull C.	0-0	1-0	4-1	1-1	1-1	1-0	1-0	1-0	0-1	—	0-0
Lincoln C.	1-2	1-0	1-4	1-1	0-0	0-1	0-0	0-1	2-4	4-2	—
Mansfield T.	1-1	2-1	3-0	1-0	2-0	2-1	1-1	1-1	1-1	0-2	2-0
Oxford U.	1-0	0-1	0-0	5-1	0-0	1-1	2-0	3-2	1-1	1-0	2-1
Peterboro'	1-2	3-1	2-2	0-0	2-1	0-0	1-2	1-1	1-1	3-0	0-1
Plymouth	0-0	2-1	3-0	2-0	2-2	1-1	1-1	4-2	2-1	3-4	2-1
Rotherham	2-1	1-0	2-1	1-3	0-1	1-0	2-1	1-1	2-1	0-2	2-0
Sheffield W.	2-0	1-0	0-0	0-0		4-0	0-0	2-1	2-1	2-3	0-0
Shrewsbury	2-0	1-0	1-0	0-0	1-0	1-1	2-0	4-1	1-1	1-0	2-0
Southend	4-0	1-1	0-0	1-1	0-1	2-0	1-1	0-1	0-1	3-0	2-0
Swansea	1-0	2-1	2-0	0-0	2-2	2-1	4-1	1-0	3-1	5-3	3-0
Swindon T.	0-1	2-0	2-1	0-0	2-0	1-0	1-2	1-1	3-1	2-0	6-0
Tranmere R.	0-2	0-1	0-0	1-1	6-2	1-1	1-5	2-2	1-1	1-3	0-0
Walsall	2-1	2-3	0-1	1-2	2-1	0-1	2-2	2-2	0-1	1-2	4-1
Watford	5-1	2-0	3-3	2-1	1-0	2-0	0-3	1-0	1-0	4-0	2-0

1978-79 Results

	Mansfield T.	Oxford U.	Peterborough U.	Plymouth Arg.	Rotherham U.	Sheffield W.	Shrewsbury T.	Southend U.	Swansea	Swindon T.	Tranmere R.	Walsall	Watford
	2-0	1-0	0-0	0-0	1-2	0-1	5-0	1-2	1-3	5-2	2-0	2-1	1-1
	1-0	3-0	0-0	2-1	1-0	2-1	2-3	3-0	1-0	1-2	2-0	1-0	3-3
	0-0	1-1	1-0	1-2	3-2	0-0	3-0	3-3	0-1	0-1	1-1	1-1	1-2
	1-0	0-1	4-1	1-1	1-1	0-0	1-1	0-0	2-0	2-0	2-0	1-0	1-0
	1-1	4-1	1-1	0-0	0-1	2-2	0-0	0-1	2-0	2-0	1-1	2-1	2-1
	1-0	1-1	3-1	1-3	0-1	3-3	2-1	3-2	2-1	1-1	5-2	0-0	0-2
	1-0	1-1	4-2	2-1	0-0	1-0	1-0	1-1	2-2	3-2	1-0	2-0	0-1
	0-0	2-0	1-0	0-2	2-2	0-0	0-0	2-1	1-2	1-2	3-0	3-1	0-0
	0-0	2-1	1-0	0-0	0-1	2-2	0-1	0-0	2-2	2-2	3-2	3-1	2-3
	3-0	0-1	1-1	2-1	1-0	1-1	1-1	2-0	2-2	1-1	2-1	4-1	4-0
	0-1	2-2	0-1	3-3	3-0	1-2	1-2	1-1	2-1	0-3	2-1	1-1	0-5
	—	1-1	1-1	5-0	0-1	1-1	2-2	1-1	2-2	0-1	0-0	1-3	0-3
	3-2	—	0-2	3-2	1-0	1-1	0-1	0-0	0-2	0-1	0-0	2-1	1-1
	1-2	1-1	—	2-1	1-1	2-0	0-2	0-1	2-0	2-1	1-0	0-3	0-1
	1-4	0-1	3-2	—	2-0	2-0	1-1	1-1	2-2	2-0	2-2	1-0	1-1
	2-0	0-0	1-1	1-0	—	0-1	1-2	2-1	0-1	1-3	3-2	4-1	2-1
	1-2	1-1	3-0	2-3	2-1	—	0-0	3-2	0-0	2-1	1-2	0-2	2-3
	2-2	0-0	2-0	3-1	2-2		—	2-0	3-0	0-0	2-1	1-1	1-1
	1-1	1-1	0-0	2-1	2-1	2-1	0-1	—	0-2	5-3	0-1	1-0	1-0
	3-2	1-1	4-1	2-1	4-4	4-2	1-1	3-2	—	1-2	4-3	2-2	3-2
	1-0	2-0	3-1	1-3	1-0	3-0	2-1	1-0	0-1	—	4-1	4-1	2-0
	1-2	1-0	1-0	2-1	1-1	1-1	2-2	1-2	1-2	1-1	—	0-0	1-1
	1-1	0-1	4-1	2-1	1-0	0-2	1-1	1-1	1-1	4-1	2-0	—	2-4
	1-1	4-2	1-2	2-2	2-2	1-0	2-2	2-0	0-2	2-0	4-0	3-1	—

HOME TEAM	Aldershot	arnsley	Bournemouth	Bradford C.	Crewe Alex.	Darlington	Doncaster R.	Grimsby T.	Halifax T.	Hartlepool U.	Hereford U.
Aldershot ...	—	1-0	1-0	6-0	3-0	1-1	2-1	2-0	1-0	1-1	2-0
Barnsley ...	2-0	—	1-0	0-1	3-1	1-1	3-0	2-1	4-2	1-0	2-1
Bournem'th	0-1	0-2	—	1-0	0-1	2-2	7-1	0-0	1-0	0-1	1-1
Bradford C.	0-2	1-2	2-1	—	6-0	0-0	1-0	1-3	3-0	1-2	2-1
Crewe Alex.	1-1	0-2	1-0	1-2	—	1-1	2-4	0-3	1-0	0-1	0-0
Darlington	2-1	0-0	0-0	1-1	1-1	—	3-2	0-1	2-1	0-0	1-0
Doncaster	1-1	2-2	1-1	2-0	2-0	2-3	—	0-1	1-1	0-0	1-0
Grimsby T.	0-0	2-0	1-0	5-1	2-2	7-2	3-4	—	2-1	0-1	1-1
Halifax T...	1-1	0-2	0-2	2-0	0-0	0-2	2-0	1-2	—	2-4	1-0
Hartlepool	2-2	1-1	0-2	2-2	2-2	0-2	3-4	1-0	3-1	—	2-1
Hereford ...	1-1	1-1	0-0	3-1	6-1	1-0	2-0	0-1	2-2	1-0	—
Huddersfield	0-0	1-0	2-1	0-0	0-0	2-2	1-0	2-0	2-0	2-0	2-3
Newport ...	1-2	1-1	2-0	2-4	1-2	2-1	3-0	1-0	2-0	3-2	4-1
N'thampton	2-3	0-1	4-2	1-0	3-1	4-1	3-0	1-2	2-1	1-1	2-1
Portsmouth	1-1	0-1	1-1	0-1	3-0	3-0	4-0	1-3	3-1	3-0	1-0
Port Vale ...	1-1	3-2	1-2	2-1	2-2	2-0	1-3	1-0	1-1	0-1	0-1
Reading ...	4-0	1-0	1-0	3-0	2-0	1-0	3-0	4-0	1-0	3-1	3-0
Rochdale	1-1	0-3	2-1	1-0	2-1	1-2	2-0	2-5	1-1	1-1	0-2
Scunthorpe	2-0	0-1	1-0	2-1	2-1	0-0	1-0	1-0	1-0	3-1	4-2
Stockport ...	2-2	0-0	1-0	1-0	4-3	3-0	0-1	2-1	1-2	4-0	0-3
Torquay U.	2-1	3-2	0-1	1-2	3-0	1-0	2-1	3-1	2-0	4-1	1-0
Wigan Ath.	3-2	1-1	1-0	1-3	1-0	2-2	1-0	0-3	1-0	2-2	0-0
Wimbledon	3-1	1-1	4-0	2-1	1-1	2-0	3-2	0-1	2-1	3-1	2-0
York C. ...	1-1	0-1	2-1	0-0	1-0	5-2	1-1	0-0	2-0	1-1	1-0

1978-79 Results

Huddersfield T.	Newport Co.	Northampton T.	Portsmouth	Port Vale	Reading	Rochdale	Scunthorpe U.	Stockport Co.	Torquay U.	Wigan Ath.	Wimbledon	York City
1-0	2-3	2-0	0-2	1-1	2-2	1-0	2-0	3-2	1-0	1-0	1-1	1-0
1-0	1-0	1-1	1-1	6-2	3-1	0-3	4-1	4-4	1-2	0-0	3-1	3-0
2-0	3-1	0-0	3-1	3-1	0-0	3-1	0-0	3-1	1-0	2-1	1-2	1-2
1-1	1-3	3-0	2-0	2-3	2-3	1-0	1-1	1-1	3-1	1-1	1-0	2-1
3-3	0-1	2-4	0-0	1-5	0-2	1-2	0-2	2-2	6-2	1-1	1-2	0-1
1-0	1-0	0-0	2-0	4-0	1-2	0-2	2-2	0-1	1-2	1-1	1-1	0-1
0-2	0-0	2-0	2-3	1-3	2-2	1-0	0-0	2-0	1-0	0-1	1-0	1-2
2-1	1-0	4-3	1-0	1-0	1-2	4-0	1-1	2-1	3-0	3-1	2-2	3-0
2-3	1-2	2-2	2-0	0-3	0-0	2-1	2-3	2-1	1-2	1-2	2-1	0-1
2-0	0-0	2-0	1-1	1-2	0-0	5-1	1-1	1-3	3-2	1-1	1-1	1-1
3-0	0-3	4-3	0-1	1-0	0-0	2-2	3-1	1-0	3-1	0-0	0-0	1-0
—	0-1	1-0	2-0	3-2	1-1	1-0	3-2	0-0	1-1	1-1	3-0	1-0
2-1	—	2-1	1-2	1-0	3-2	0-0	2-0	1-2	1-1	2-1	1-3	1-1
2-3	3-1	—	0-2	1-0	2-2	1-0	1-0	2-2	1-2	2-4	1-1	1-0
1-0	2-1	1-0	—	2-0	4-0	1-1	0-0	1-1	1-0	1-1	0-0	1-1
1-0	1-1	2-2	0-0	—	0-3	1-1	2-2	2-1	1-2	2-1	1-0	0-0
1-1	2-1	5-1	2-0	0-0	—	2-0	0-1	3-3	1-0	2-0	1-0	3-0
0-2	1-0	4-1	0-2	0-1	1-0	—	1-0	2-0	1-0	0-2	0-0	1-2
3-1	2-3	0-3	2-2	2-0	0-3	0-4	—	1-0	2-2	0-1	2-0	2-3
3-1	1-1	2-1	4-2	0-0	0-0	3-0	0-2	—	0-1	0-1	0-1	2-0
2-1	2-0	0-1	2-1	2-2	1-1	1-1	0-1	0-0	—	1-1	1-6	3-0
2-1	2-3	2-0	2-0	5-3	3-0	3-0	1-0	2-0	3-1	—	1-2	1-1
2-1	0-0	4-1	2-4	1-0	1-0	3-2	3-1	2-0	5-0	2-1	—	2-1
1-3	1-2	1-0	5-3	4-0	0-1	2-1	1-0	1-0	0-0	0-1	1-4	—

FINAL FOOTBALL LEAGUE TABLES 1978-79

FIRST DIVISION

	P	Home W	D	L	Goals F	A	Away W	D	L	Goals F	A	Pts.
Liverpool	42	19	2	0	51	4	11	6	4	34	12	68
Nottingham F.	42	11	10	0	34	10	10	8	3	27	16	60
W.B.A.	42	13	5	3	38	15	11	6	4	34	20	59
Everton	42	12	7	2	32	17	5	10	6	20	23	51
Leeds U.	42	11	4	6	41	25	7	10	4	29	27	50
Ipswich T.	42	11	4	6	34	21	9	5	7	29	28	49
Arsenal	42	11	8	2	37	18	6	6	9	24	30	48
Aston Villa	42	8	9	4	37	26	7	7	7	22	23	46
Manchester U.	42	9	7	5	29	25	6	8	7	31	38	45
Coventry C.	42	11	7	3	41	29	3	9	9	17	39	44
Tottenham H.	42	7	8	6	19	25	6	7	8	29	36	41
Middlesbrough	42	10	5	6	33	21	5	5	11	24	29	40
Bristol C.	42	11	6	4	34	19	4	4	13	13	32	40
Southampton	42	9	10	2	35	20	3	6	12	12	33	40
Manchester C.	42	9	5	7	34	28	4	8	9	24	28	39
Norwich C.	42	7	10	4	29	19	0	13	8	22	38	37
Bolton W.	42	10	5	6	36	28	2	6	13	18	47	35
Wolverhampton	42	10	4	7	26	26	3	4	14	18	42	34
Derby Co.	42	8	5	8	25	25	2	6	13	19	46	31
Q.P.R.	42	4	9	8	24	33	2	4	15	21	40	25
Birmingham C.	42	5	9	7	24	25	1	1	19	13	39	22
Chelsea	42	3	5	13	23	42	2	5	14	21	50	20

SECOND DIVISION

	P	Home W	D	L	Goals F	A	Away W	D	L	Goals F	A	Pts.
Crystal Pal.	42	12	7	2	30	11	7	12	2	21	13	57
Brighton & H.A.	42	16	3	2	44	11	7	7	7	28	28	56
Stoke C.	42	11	7	3	35	15	9	9	3	23	16	56
Sunderland	42	13	3	5	39	19	9	4	8	31	25	55
West Ham U.	42	12	7	2	46	15	6	7	8	24	24	50
Notts Co.	42	8	10	3	23	15	6	6	9	25	45	44
Newcastle U.	42	13	3	5	35	24	4	5	12	16	31	42
Cardiff C.	42	12	5	4	34	23	4	5	12	22	47	42
Fulham	42	10	7	4	35	19	3	8	10	15	28	41
Preston N.E.	41	7	11	3	36	23	4	7	9	21	34	40
Orient	42	11	5	5	32	18	4	5	12	19	33	40
Cambridge U.	42	7	10	4	22	15	5	6	10	22	37	40
Burnley	42	11	6	4	31	22	3	6	12	20	40	40
Oldham Ath.	42	10	7	4	36	23	4	6	12	16	38	39
Wrexham	42	10	6	5	31	16	2	8	11	14	26	38
Bristol R.	42	10	6	5	34	23	4	4	13	14	37	38
Leicester C.	42	7	8	6	28	23	3	9	9	15	29	37
Luton T.	42	11	5	5	46	24	2	5	14	14	33	36
Charlton Ath.	42	6	8	7	28	28	5	5	11	32	41	35
Sheffield U.	42	9	6	6	34	24	2	6	13	18	45	34
Millwall	41	7	4	9	22	27	4	6	11	20	32	32
Blackburn R.	42	5	8	8	24	29	5	2	14	17	43	30

THIRD DIVISION

		Home			Goals		Away			Goals		
	P	W	D	L	F	A	W	D	L	F	A	Pts.
Shrewsbury T. ...	46	14	9	0	36	11	7	10	6	25	30	61
Watford	46	15	5	3	47	22	9	7	7	36	30	60
Swansea	46	16	6	1	57	32	8	6	9	26	29	60
Gillingham	46	15	7	1	39	15	6	10	7	26	27	59
Swindon T.	46	17	2	4	44	14	8	5	10	30	38	57
Carlisle U.	46	11	10	2	31	13	4	12	7	22	29	52
Colchester U......	46	13	9	1	35	19	4	8	11	25	36	51
Hull C.	46	12	9	2	36	14	7	2	14	30	47	49
Exeter C.	46	14	6	3	38	18	3	9	11	23	38	49
Brentford	46	14	4	5	35	19	5	5	13	18	30	47
Oxford U.	46	10	8	5	27	20	4	10	9	17	30	46
Blackpool	46	12	5	6	38	19	6	4	13	23	40	45
Southend U.	46	11	6	6	30	17	4	9	10	21	32	45
Sheffield W.	46	11	8	4	30	22	4	11	8	23	31	45
Plymouth Arg. ..	46	11	9	3	40	27	4	5	14	27	41	44
Chester	46	11	9	3	42	21	3	7	13	15	40	44
Rotherham U. ...	46	13	3	7	30	23	4	7	12	19	32	44
Bury	46	6	11	6	35	32	5	9	9	24	33	42
Mansfield T.	45	6	11	5	28	23	5	8	10	21	28	41
Chesterfield	45	10	5	8	35	34	3	9	10	15	29	40
Peterborough U.	46	8	7	8	26	24	3	7	13	18	39	36
Walsall	46	7	6	10	34	32	3	6	14	22	39	32
Tranmere R. ...	46	4	12	7	26	31	2	4	17	19	47	28
Lincoln C.	46	5	7	11	26	38	2	4	17	15	50	25

FOURTH DIVISION

		Home			Goals		Away			Goals		
Reading	46	19	3	1	49	8	7	10	6	27	27	65
Grimsby T.	46	15	5	3	51	23	11	4	8	31	26	61
Wimbledon	46	18	3	2	50	20	7	8	8	28	26	61
Barnsley	46	15	5	3	47	23	9	8	6	26	19	61
Aldershot	46	16	5	2	38	14	4	12	7	25	33	57
Wigan Ath.	46	14	5	4	40	24	7	8	8	23	24	55
Portsmouth	46	13	7	3	35	12	7	5	11	27	36	52
Newport Co.	46	12	5	6	39	28	9	5	9	27	27	52
Huddersfield T.	46	13	8	2	32	15	5	3	15	25	38	47
York C.	46	11	6	6	33	24	7	5	11	18	31	47
Torquay U.	46	14	4	5	38	24	5	4	14	20	41	46
Scunthorpe U. ..	46	12	3	8	33	30	5	8	10	21	30	45
Hartlepool U. ...	46	7	12	4	35	28	6	6	11	22	38	44
Hereford U.	46	12	8	3	35	18	3	5	15	18	35	43
Bradford C.	46	11	5	7	38	26	6	4	13	24	42	43
Port Vale	46	8	10	5	29	28	6	4	13	28	42	42
Stockport Co. ...	46	11	5	7	33	21	3	7	13	25	39	40
Bournemouth	46	11	6	6	34	19	3	5	15	13	29	39
Northampton T.	46	12	4	7	40	30	3	5	15	24	46	39
Rochdale	46	11	4	8	25	26	4	5	14	22	38	39
Darlington	46	8	8	7	25	21	3	7	13	24	45	37
Doncaster R.	46	8	8	7	25	22	5	3	15	25	51	37
Halifax T.	46	7	5	11	24	32	2	3	18	15	40	26
Crewe Alex.	46	3	7	13	24	41	3	7	13	19	49	26

FIRST DIVISION

	1978-79	1977-78	1976-77	1975-76	1974-75	1973-74	1972-73	1971-72	1970-71	1969-70	1968-69	1967-68	1966-67	1965-66	1964-65	1963-64	1962-63
Arsenal	7	5	8	17	16	10	2	5	1	12	4	9	7	14	13	8	7
Aston Villa	8	8	4	16	—	—	—	—	—	—	—	—	21	16	16	19	15
Birmingham	21	11	13	19	17	19	10	—	—	—	—	—	—	—	22	20	20
Blackburn	—	—	—	—	—	—	—	—	—	—	—	—	—	22	10	7	11
Blackpool	—	—	—	—	—	—	—	22	—	—	—	—	22	13	17	18	13
Bolton	17	—	—	—	—	—	—	—	—	—	—	—	—	—	—	21	18
Brentford	—	—	—	—	—	—	—	—	—	—	—	—	—	—	—	—	—
Bristol C.	13	17	18	—	—	—	—	—	—	—	—	—	—	—	—	—	—
Burnley	—	—	—	21	10	6	—	—	21	14	14	13	14	3	12	9	3
Cardiff	—	—	—	—	—	—	—	—	—	—	—	—	—	—	—	—	—
Carlisle U.	—	—	—	—	22	—	—	—	—	—	—	—	—	—	—	—	—
Charlton	—	—	—	—	—	—	—	—	—	—	—	—	—	—	—	—	—
Chelsea	22	16	—	—	21	17	12	7	6	3	5	6	9	5	3	5	—
Coventry	10	7	19	14	14	16	19	18	10	6	20	20	—	—	—	—	—
Crystal Palace	—	—	—	—	—	—	21	20	18	20	—	—	—	—	—	—	—
Derby	19	12	15	4	1	3	7	1	9	4	—	—	—	—	—	—	—
Everton	4	3	9	11	4	7	17	15	14	1	3	5	6	11	4	3	1
Fulham	—	—	—	—	—	—	—	—	—	—	—	22	19	20	20	15	16
Grimsby	—	—	—	—	—	—	—	—	—	—	—	—	—	—	—	—	—
Huddersfield	—	—	—	—	—	—	—	22	15	—	—	—	—	—	—	—	—
Ipswich	6	18	3	6	3	4	4	13	19	18	12	—	—	—	—	22	17
Leeds	5	9	10	5	9	1	3	2	2	2	1	4	4	2	2	—	—
Leicester	—	22	11	7	18	9	16	12	—	—	21	12	8	7	18	11	4
Liverpool	1	2	1	1	2	2	1	3	5	5	2	3	5	1	7	1	8
Luton	—	—	—	—	20	—	—	—	—	—	—	—	—	—	—	—	—
Man. City	15	4	2	8	8	14	11	4	10	13	1	15	—	—	—	—	21
Man. United	9	10	6	3	—	21	18	8	8	8	11	2	1	4	1	2	19
Middlesbrough	12	14	12	13	7	—	—	—	—	—	—	—	—	—	—	—	—
Newcastle	—	21	5	15	15	9	11	12	7	9	10	20	15	—	—	—	—
Northampton	—	—	—	—	—	—	—	—	—	—	—	—	—	21	—	—	—
Norwich	16	13	16	10	—	22	20	—	—	—	—	—	—	—	—	—	—
Nottm. Forest	2	1	—	—	—	21	16	15	18	11	2	18	5	13	9	—	—
Orient	—	—	—	—	—	—	—	—	—	—	—	—	—	—	—	—	22
Portsmouth	—	—	—	—	—	—	—	—	—	—	—	—	—	—	—	—	—
Preston	—	—	—	—	—	—	—	—	—	—	—	—	—	—	—	—	—
Q. P. Rangers	20	19	14	2	11	8	—	—	—	—	22	—	—	—	—	—	—
Sheffield Utd.	—	—	22	6	13	14	10	—	—	22	—	21	10	9	19	12	10
Sheffield Wed.	—	—	—	—	—	—	—	—	—	22	15	19	11	17	8	6	6
Southampton	14	—	—	—	20	13	19	7	19	7	15	19	—	—	—	—	—
Stoke	—	21	12	5	5	15	17	13	9	19	18	12	10	11	17	—	—
Sunderland	—	—	20	—	—	—	—	—	—	21	17	16	17	19	15	—	—
Tottenham	11	—	22	9	19	11	8	6	3	11	6	7	3	8	6	4	2
West Brom.	3	6	7	—	—	22	16	17	16	10	8	13	6	14	10	14	—
West Ham	18	20	17	18	13	18	6	14	20	17	8	14	16	12	9	14	12
Wolverh'ton	—	15	—	20	12	12	5	9	4	13	16	17	—	—	21	16	5

LEAGUE POSITIONS (1947-79)

	1961-62	1960-61	1959-60	1958-59	1957-58	1956-57	1955-56	1954-55	1953-54	1952-53	1951-52	1950-51	1949-50	1948-49	1947-48	1946-47
Arsenal	10	11	13	3	12	5	5	9	12	1	3	5	6	—	1	13
Aston Villa	7	9	—	21	14	10	20	6	13	11	6	15	12	10	6	8
Birmingham	17	18	19	9	13	12	6	—	—	—	—	—	22	17	—	—
Blackburn	16	8	17	10	—	—	—	—	—	—	—	—	—	—	21	17
Blackpool	13	20	11	8	7	4	2	19	6	7	9	3	7	16	9	5
Bolton	11	18	6	4	15	9	8	18	5	14	5	8	16	14	17	18
Brentford	—	—	—	—	—	—	—	—	—	—	—	—	—	—	—	21
Bristol C.	—	—	—	—	—	—	—	—	—	—	—	—	—	—	—	—
Burnley	2	4	1	7	6	7	9	12	4	14	10	10	15	3	—	—
Cardiff	21	15	—	—	—	21	17	20	10	12	—	—	—	—	—	—
Carlisle U.	—	—	—	—	—	—	—	—	—	—	—	—	—	—	—	—
Charlton	—	—	—	—	—	22	14	15	9	5	10	17	20	9	13	19
Chelsea	22	12	18	14	11	13	16	1	8	19	19	20	13	13	18	15
Coventry	—	—	—	—	—	—	—	—	—	—	—	—	—	—	—	—
Crystal Palace	—	—	—	—	—	—	—	—	—	—	—	—	—	—	—	—
Derby	—	—	—	—	—	—	—	—	—	22	17	11	11	3	4	14
Everton	4	5	15	16	16	15	11	—	—	22	18	18	14	10	—	—
Fulham	20	17	10	—	—	—	—	—	—	—	22	18	17	—	—	—
Grimsby	—	—	—	—	—	—	—	—	—	—	—	—	—	—	22	16
Huddersfield	—	—	—	—	—	—	21	12	3	—	21	19	15	20	19	20
Ipswich	1	—	—	—	—	—	—	—	—	—	—	—	—	—	—	—
Leeds	—	—	21	15	17	8	—	—	—	—	—	—	—	—	—	22
Leicester	14	6	12	19	18	—	—	21	—	—	—	—	—	—	—	—
Liverpool	—	—	—	—	—	—	—	—	22	17	11	9	8	12	11	1
Luton	—	—	22	17	8	16	10	—	—	—	—	—	—	—	—	—
Man. City	12	13	16	20	5	18	4	7	17	20	15	—	21	7	10	—
Man. United	15	7	7	2	9	1	1	5	4	8	1	2	4	2	2	2
Middlesbrough	—	—	—	—	—	—	—	—	21	13	18	6	9	19	16	11
Newcastle	—	21	8	11	19	17	11	8	15	16	8	4	5	4	—	—
Northampton	—	—	—	—	—	—	—	—	—	—	—	—	—	—	—	—
Norwich	—	—	—	—	—	—	—	—	—	—	—	—	—	—	—	—
Nottm. Forest	19	14	20	13	10	—	—	—	—	—	—	—	—	—	—	—
Orient	—	—	—	—	—	—	—	—	—	—	—	—	—	—	—	—
Portsmouth	—	—	—	22	20	19	12	3	14	15	4	7	1	1	8	12
Preston	—	22	9	12	2	13	19	14	11	2	7	—	—	21	7	7
Q. P. Rangers	—	—	—	—	—	—	—	—	—	—	—	—	—	—	—	—
Sheffield Utd.	5	—	—	—	—	—	22	13	20	—	—	—	—	22	12	6
Sheffield Wed.	6	2	5	—	22	14	22	19	18	—	21	—	—	—	—	—
Southampton	—	—	—	—	—	—	—	—	—	—	—	—	—	—	—	—
Stoke	—	—	—	—	—	—	—	—	—	21	20	13	19	11	15	4
Sunderland	—	—	—	—	21	20	9	4	18	9	12	12	3	8	20	—
Tottenham	3	1	3	18	3	2	18	16	16	10	2	1	—	—	—	—
West Brom.	9	10	4	5	4	11	13	17	2	4	13	16	14	—	—	—
West Ham	8	16	14	6	—	—	—	—	—	—	—	—	—	—	—	—
Wolverhampton	18	3	2	1	1	6	3	2	1	3	16	14	2	6	5	3

SECOND DIVISION

	1978-79	1977-78	1976-77	1975-76	1974-75	1973-74	1972-73	1971-72	1970-71	1969-70	1968-69	1967-68	1966-67	1965-66	1964-65	1963-64	1962-63
Aston Villa	—	—	—	2	14	3	—	—	21	18	17	—	—	—	—	—	—
Barnsley	—	—	—	—	—	—	—	—	—	—	—	—	—	—	—	—	—
Birmingham	—	—	—	—	—	—	2	9	18	7	4	10	10	—	—	—	—
Blackburn	22	5	12	15	—	—	—	21	8	19	9	4	—	—	—	—	—
Blackpool	—	20	5	10	7	5	7	6	—	2	8	3	—	—	—	—	—
Bolton	—	1	4	14	10	11	—	22	16	17	12	9	9	3	—	—	—
Bradford	—	—	—	—	—	—	—	—	—	—	—	—	—	—	—	—	—
Brentford	—	—	—	—	—	—	—	—	—	—	—	—	—	—	—	—	—
Brighton	—	2	4	—	—	—	22	—	—	—	—	—	—	—	—	—	—
Bristol City	—	—	2	5	16	5	8	19	14	16	19	15	5	—	—	—	—
Bristol R.	16	18	15	18	19	—	—	—	—	—	—	—	—	—	—	—	—
Burnley	13	11	16	—	—	1	7	—	—	—	—	—	—	—	—	—	—
Bury	—	—	—	—	—	—	—	—	—	—	21	—	22	19	16	18	8
Cambridge	12	—	—	—	—	—	—	—	—	—	—	—	—	—	—	—	—
Cardiff	9	19	18	—	21	17	20	19	3	7	5	13	20	13	15	10	—
Carlisle	—	—	20	19	—	3	18	10	4	12	12	10	3	14	—	—	—
Charlton	19	17	7	9	—	—	21	20	20	3	15	19	16	18	4	20	—
Chelsea	—	—	2	11	—	—	—	—	—	—	—	—	—	—	—	—	1
Chesterfield	—	—	—	—	—	—	—	—	—	—	—	—	—	—	—	—	—
Coventry	—	—	—	—	—	—	—	—	—	—	—	1	3	10	—	—	—
Crystal Palace	1	9	—	—	—	20	—	—	—	2	11	7	11	7	—	—	—
Derby	—	—	—	—	—	—	—	—	—	—	1	18	17	8	9	13	18
Doncaster	—	—	—	—	—	—	—	—	—	—	—	—	—	—	—	—	—
Everton	—	—	—	—	—	—	—	—	—	—	—	—	—	—	—	—	—
Fulham	10	10	17	12	9	13	9	20	—	—	22	—	—	—	—	—	—
Grimsby	—	—	—	—	—	—	—	—	—	—	—	—	—	—	—	21	19
Hereford U.	—	22	—	—	—	—	—	—	—	—	—	—	—	—	—	—	—
Huddersfield	—	—	—	—	—	21	—	—	1	6	14	6	4	8	12	6	—
Hull	—	22	14	14	8	9	13	12	5	13	11	16	12	—	—	—	—
Ipswich	—	—	—	—	—	—	—	—	—	—	—	1	5	15	5	—	—
Leeds	—	—	—	—	—	—	—	—	—	—	—	—	—	—	—	1	5
Leicester	17	—	—	—	—	—	—	1	3	—	—	—	—	—	—	—	—
Lincoln	—	—	—	—	—	—	—	—	—	—	—	—	—	—	—	—	—
Liverpool	—	—	—	—	—	—	—	—	—	—	—	—	—	—	—	—	—
Luton	18	13	6	7	—	2	12	13	6	—	—	—	—	—	—	—	22

LEAGUE POSITIONS (1947-79)

	1961–62	1960–61	1959–60	1958–59	1957–58	1956–57	1955–56	1954–55	1953–54	1952–53	1951–52	1950–51	1949–50	1948–49	1947–48	1946–47
Aston Villa	—	—	1	—	—	—	—	—	—	—	—	—	—	—	—	—
Barnsley	—	—	—	22	14	19	18	—	—	22	20	15	13	9	12	10
Birmingham	—	—	—	—	—	—	—	1	7	6	3	4	—	—	1	3
Blackburn	—	—	—	2	4	4	6	3	9	14	6	16	44	—	—	—
Blackpool	—	—	—	—	—	—	—	—	—	—	—	—	—	—	—	—
Bolton	—	—	—	—	—	—	—	—	—	—	—	—	—	—	—	—
Bradford	—	—	—	—	—	—	—	—	—	—	—	—	22	17	14	16
Brentford	—	—	—	—	—	—	—	21	17	10	9	9	18	15	—	—
Brighton	22	16	14	12	—	—	—	—	—	—	—	—	—	—	—	—
Bristol City	—	—	22	10	17	13	11	—	—	—	—	—	—	—	—	—
Bristol R.	21	17	9	6	10	9	6	9	9	—	—	—	—	—	—	—
Burnley	—	—	—	—	—	—	—	—	—	—	—	—	—	—	—	2
Bury	18	—	—	—	21	16	13	17	20	17	20	18	12	20	17	—
Cambridge	—	—	—	—	—	—	—	—	—	—	—	—	—	—	—	—
Cardiff	—	—	2	9	15	—	—	—	—	2	3	10	4	5	—	—
Carlisle	—	—	—	—	—	—	—	—	—	—	—	—	—	—	—	—
Charlton	15	10	7	8	3	—	—	—	—	—	—	—	—	—	—	—
Chelsea	—	—	—	—	—	—	—	—	—	—	—	—	—	—	—	—
Chesterfield	—	—	—	—	—	—	—	—	—	—	—	21	14	6	16	4
Coventry	—	—	—	—	—	—	—	—	—	—	21	7	11	16	10	8
Crystal Palace	—	—	—	—	—	—	—	—	—	—	—	—	—	—	—	—
Derby	16	12	18	7	16	—	—	22	18	—	—	—	—	—	—	—
Doncaster	—	—	—	22	14	17	18	12	13	16	11	11	—	—	—	21
Everton	—	—	—	—	—	—	—	—	2	16	7	—	—	—	—	—
Fulham	—	—	2	5	11	9	14	8	8	—	—	—	—	1	11	15
Grimsby	—	21	13	16	—	—	—	—	22	11	11	—	—	—	—	—
Hereford U.	—	—	—	—	—	—	—	—	—	—	—	—	—	—	—	—
Huddersfield	7	20	6	14	9	12	—	—	2	—	—	—	—	—	—	—
Hull	—	21	—	—	22	19	15	18	18	10	7	—	—	—	—	—
Ipswich	1	11	16	8	—	21	—	—	—	—	—	—	—	—	—	—
Leeds	19	14	—	—	2	4	10	10	6	5	5	18	15	18	—	—
Leicester	—	—	—	1	5	—	5	5	14	15	19	9	9	—	—	—
Lincoln	—	22	13	19	20	18	8	16	16	15	—	—	22	—	—	—
Liverpool	1	3	3	4	4	3	11	—	—	—	—	—	—	—	—	—
Luton	3	13	—	—	—	—	—	2	6	3	8	19	17	10	13	13

SECOND DIVISION

	1978–79	1977–78	1976–77	1975–76	1974–75	1973–74	1972–73	1971–72	1970–71	1969–70	1968–69	1967–68	1966–67	1965–66	1964–65	1963–64	1962–63
Man. City	—	—	—	—	—	—	—	—	—	—	—	—	—	1	11	6	—
Man. Utd.	—	—	—	—	1	—	—	—	—	—	—	—	—	—	—	—	—
Mansfield	—	21	—	—	—	—	—	—	—	—	—	—	—	—	—	—	—
Middlesbrough	—	—	—	—	—	1	4	9	7	4	4	6	—	21	17	10	4
Millwall	21	16	10	—	20	12	11	3	8	10	10	7	8	—	—	—	—
Newcastle	8	—	—	—	—	—	—	—	—	—	—	—	—	—	1	8	7
Newport	—	—	—	—	—	—	—	—	—	—	—	—	—	—	—	—	—
Northampton	—	—	—	—	—	—	—	—	—	—	—	—	21	—	2	11	—
Norwich	—	—	—	—	3	—	—	1	10	11	13	8	11	13	6	17	13
Nottm. Forest	—	—	3	8	16	7	14	—	—	—	—	—	—	—	—	—	—
Notts. County	6	15	8	5	14	10	—	—	—	—	—	—	—	—	—	—	—
Oldham	14	8	13	17	18	—	—	—	—	—	—	—	—	—	—	—	—
Orient	11	14	19	13	12	4	15	17	17	—	—	—	—	22	19	16	—
Oxford	—	—	—	20	11	18	8	15	14	15	20	—	—	—	—	—	—
Plymouth	—	—	21	16	—	—	—	—	—	—	—	22	16	18	15	20	12
Portsmouth	—	—	—	22	17	15	17	16	16	17	15	5	14	12	20	9	17
Port Vale	—	—	—	—	—	—	—	—	—	—	—	—	—	—	—	—	—
Preston	7	—	—	—	21	19	18	—	22	14	20	13	17	12	3	16	—
Q.P.R.	—	—	—	—	—	—	2	4	11	9	—	2	—	—	—	—	—
Rotherham	—	—	—	—	—	—	—	—	—	—	—	21	18	7	14	7	14
Scunthorpe	—	—	—	—	—	—	—	—	—	—	—	—	—	—	—	22	9
Sheffield Utd	20	12	11	—	—	—	—	—	2	6	9	—	—	—	—	—	—
Sheffield Wed.	—	—	—	22	19	10	14	15	—	—	—	—	—	—	—	—	—
Southampton	—	2	9	6	13	—	—	—	—	—	—	—	—	2	4	5	11
Stoke	3	7	—	—	—	—	—	—	—	—	—	—	—	—	—	—	1
Sunderland	4	6	—	1	4	6	6	5	13	—	—	—	—	—	—	2	3
Swansea	—	—	—	—	—	—	—	—	—	—	—	—	—	—	22	19	15
Swindon	—	—	—	—	—	22	16	11	12	5	—	—	—	—	21	14	—
Tottenham	—	3	—	—	—	—	—	—	—	—	—	—	—	—	—	—	—
Tranmere	—	—	—	—	—	—	—	—	—	—	—	—	—	—	—	—	—
Walsall	—	—	—	—	—	—	—	—	—	—	—	—	—	—	—	—	21
Watford	—	—	—	—	—	—	—	22	18	19	—	—	—	—	—	—	—
West Brom.	—	—	—	3	6	8	—	—	—	—	—	—	—	—	—	—	—
West Ham	5	—	—	—	—	—	—	—	—	—	—	—	—	—	—	—	—
Wolverh'ton	—	—	1	—	—	—	—	—	—	—	—	—	2	6	—	—	—
Wrexham	15	—	—	—	—	—	—	—	—	—	—	—	—	—	—	—	—
York C.	—	—	—	21	—	—	—	—	—	—	—	—	—	—	—	—	—

1961-62	1960-61	1959-60	1958-59	1957-58	1956-57	1955-56	1954-55	1953-54	1952-53	1951-52	1950-51	1949-50	1948-49	1947-48	1946-47	
—	—	—	—	—	—	—	—	—	—	—	2	—	—	—	1	Man. City
—	—	—	—	—	—	—	—	—	—	—	—	—	—	—	—	Man. United
—	—	—	—	—	—	—	—	—	—	—	—	—	—	—	—	Mansfield
12	5	5	13	7	6	14	12	—	—	—	—	—	—	—	—	Middlesbrough
—	—	—	—	—	—	—	—	—	—	—	—	—	—	22	18	Millwall
11	—	—	—	—	—	—	—	—	—	—	—	—	—	2	5	Newcastle
—	—	—	—	—	—	—	—	—	—	—	—	—	—	22	—	Newport
—	—	—	—	—	—	—	—	—	—	—	—	—	—	—	—	Northampton
17	4	—	—	—	—	—	—	—	—	—	—	—	—	—	—	Norwich
—	—	—	—	—	2	7	15	4	7	4	—	—	21	19	11	Nottm. Forest
—	—	—	21	20	20	7	14	19	15	17	—	—	—	—	—	Notts. County
—	—	—	—	—	—	—	—	—	22	—	—	—	—	—	—	Oldham
2	19	10	17	12	15	—	—	—	—	—	—	—	—	—	—	Orient
—	—	—	—	—	—	—	—	—	—	—	—	—	—	—	—	Oxford
5	11	19	—	—	—	21	20	19	4	—	—	21	20	17	19	Plymouth
—	21	20	—	—	—	—	—	—	—	—	—	—	—	—	—	Portsmouth
—	—	—	—	22	12	17	—	—	—	—	—	—	—	—	—	Port Vale
10	—	—	—	—	—	—	—	—	—	—	1	6	—	—	—	Preston
—	—	—	—	—	—	—	—	—	—	22	16	20	13	—	—	Q.P.R.
9	15	8	20	18	17	19	3	5	12	9	—	—	—	—	—	Rotherham
4	9	15	18	—	—	—	—	—	—	—	—	—	—	—	—	Scunthorpe
—	2	—	6	7	—	—	—	—	1	11	8	3	—	—	—	Sheffield Utd.
—	—	—	1	—	—	1	—	—	—	1	—	—	—	—	—	Sheffield Wed.
6	8	—	—	—	—	—	—	—	21	13	12	4	3	3	14	Southampton
8	18	17	5	11	5	13	5	11	—	—	—	—	—	—	—	Stoke
3	6	16	15	—	—	—	—	—	—	—	—	—	—	—	—	Sunderland
20	7	12	11	19	10	10	10	20	11	19	18	8	—	—	21	Swansea
—	—	—	—	—	—	—	—	—	—	—	—	—	—	—	—	Swindon
—	—	—	—	—	—	—	—	—	—	—	—	1	5	8	6	Tottenham
—	—	—	—	—	—	—	—	—	—	—	—	—	—	—	—	Tranmere
14	—	—	—	—	—	—	—	—	—	—	—	—	—	—	—	Walsall
—	—	—	—	—	—	—	—	—	—	—	—	—	—	—	—	Watford
—	—	—	—	—	—	—	—	—	—	—	—	—	2	7	7	West Brom.
—	—	—	—	1	8	16	8	13	14	12	13	19	7	6	12	West Ham
—	—	—	—	—	—	—	—	—	—	—	—	—	—	—	—	Wolverhampton
—	—	—	—	—	—	—	—	—	—	—	—	—	—	—	—	Wrexham
—	—	—	—	—	—	—	—	—	—	—	—	—	—	—	—	York C.

THIRD DIVISION LEAGUE POSITIONS (1959-79)

Team	1959-60	1960-61	1961-62	1962-63	1963-64	1964-65	1965-66	1966-67	1967-68	1968-69	1969-70	1970-71	1971-72	1972-73	1973-74	1974-75	1975-76	1976-77	1977-78	1978-79
Accrington	24																			
Aldershot															8	20	21			
Aston Villa	17	8										4	1							
Barnsley			22	20	21	24	23	20	13		21	12	24		13					15
Barrow									8	9	7	14	22	3						
Blackburn						1		13	8		10	19		1	13	7	21		3	10
Blackpool													7							
Bolton	12													3	11	1			17	
Bournemouth		10	19	5	21	11	18	20	4	13	21	21	14	7						
Bradford																				
Bradford City		22	23	21	4						10		24	22	11	21				
Brentford	6		17		5	16	23	19	11	4	5	14			19		4		22	
Brighton		19	16	22		5	15		5	8	5	6	16	6	19	2		2	4	
Bristol City						2	16	5			3	2								
Bristol R.	19	6	14	19	12	6	16	5	16	16	3	6	6	5	21	2				
Bury	7						2				2	22	21	19	14	13	4	7	15	19
Cambridge U.																		2		2
Cardiff C.																			13	6
Carlisle					23										11	3	2			
Charlton												23	14	3	14				16	
Chester	20	24			17	23				23	18			16	5	15	17	5	9	
Chesterfield	7	23		18	1			13							16	11	22	18	8	6
Colchester		9	14						23							5			9	9
Coventry	5	15			1															
Crewe						22														
Crystal Palace			15		2									5		5		3		
Darlington								22												
Doncaster					11		23	23					23							22
Exeter								22									17	8		
Fulham	5	7	12	15	10						4	20	2	22	17					
Gillingham			16		24	6	10	11	20	2	17		10	17	11					
Grimsby	4	6	2	18		7								18	3		9	20		
Halifax	15	9	9		20								17	1	18					
Hartlepool														22						

86

Hereford U.	—	—	23	—	1	12	18	—	—	—	—	—	—	—	—	—	—	—	—	—	Hereford U.
Huddersfield T.	—	—	—	—	24	10	—	—	—	—	—	—	—	—	—	—	—	—	—	—	Huddersfield T
Hull	9	—	—	—	—	—	—	—	—	—	—	—	—	1	4	8	10	10	11	—	Hull
Lincoln	24	16	9	—	—	—	—	—	—	1	—	—	—	—	—	—	—	22	—	—	Lincoln
Luton	—	—	—	—	—	—	—	—	—	2	3	—	—	—	21	18	—	—	—	—	Luton
Mansfield	18	—	1	11	—	—	—	21	7	6	15	21	9	19	3	7	—	—	—	22	Mansfield
Middlesbrough	—	—	—	—	—	—	—	—	—	—	—	1	2	—	—	—	—	—	—	—	Middlesbrough
Millwall	—	—	—	3	—	—	—	—	—	—	—	—	—	2	—	21	16	—	—	—	Millwall
Newport	—	—	—	—	—	—	—	—	—	—	—	—	—	—	—	—	—	24	13	13	Newport
Norwich	—	—	—	—	—	—	—	—	—	—	—	—	—	—	—	—	—	—	—	2	Norwich
Northampton	—	—	22	—	—	—	—	—	—	—	21	18	—	—	—	—	1	8	—	—	Northampton
Notts County	—	—	—	—	—	—	2	4	—	—	—	—	—	—	—	24	7	13	5	—	Notts County
Oldham	—	—	—	—	—	1	4	11	—	—	24	17	10	20	20	20	9	—	—	—	Oldham
Orient	—	—	—	—	—	—	—	—	—	1	18	19	14	—	—	—	—	—	—	—	Orient
Oxford	11	18	17	—	—	—	—	—	—	—	—	1	15	14	—	—	—	—	—	—	Oxford
Peterborough	21	4	16	10	7	—	—	—	—	—	—	9*	16	13	8	10	6	5	—	—	Peterborough
Plymouth	15	19	—	—	2	17	8	8	15	17	5	—	—	—	—	—	—	—	—	—	Plymouth
Portsmouth	—	24	20	—	—	—	—	—	—	—	—	—	—	—	—	—	—	1	—	—	Portsmouth
Port Vale	—	21	19	12	6	20	6	15	17	—	—	—	—	22	13	3	12	—	7	14	Port Vale
Preston	—	3	6	8	9	—	—	—	1	—	—	—	—	—	—	—	—	—	—	—	Preston
Q.P.R.	—	—	—	—	—	—	—	—	—	—	—	—	1	3	14	15	13	4	3	8	Q.P.R.
Reading	—	—	21	—	—	—	—	—	21	8	14	5	4	8	13	6	20	7	18	11	Reading
Rochdale	—	—	—	—	—	24	13	18	16	9	—	—	—	—	—	—	—	—	—	—	Rochdale
Rotherham	17	20	4	16	—	—	21	5	8	14	11	—	—	—	—	—	—	—	—	—	Rotherham
Scunthorpe	—	—	—	—	—	—	24	—	—	—	—	24	18	4	18	—	—	—	—	—	Scunthorpe
Sheffield W.	14	14	8	20	—	—	—	—	—	—	—	—	—	—	—	—	—	—	—	—	Sheffield W.
Shrewsbury	1	11	10	9	—	22	15	12	13	15	17	3	6	10	16	11	15	19	10	3	Shrewsbury
Southampton	—	—	—	—	—	—	—	—	—	—	—	—	—	—	—	—	—	—	—	1	Southampton
Southend	13	—	—	23	18	12	14	—	—	—	—	—	—	21	12	14	8	16	20	12	Southend
Southport	—	—	—	—	—	23	—	—	—	22	8	15	—	—	—	—	—	—	—	—	Southport
Stockport	—	—	—	—	—	—	—	—	—	24	9	14	—	—	—	—	—	—	—	—	Stockport
Swansea	3	—	—	—	—	—	23	14	11	—	—	—	21	17	—	—	—	—	—	—	Swansea
Swindon	4	10	11	19	4	—	—	—	—	—	2	10	8	7	—	—	2	9	16	16	Swindon
Torquay	—	—	—	—	—	—	—	23	10	13	6	4	7	—	—	—	—	21	12	—	Torquay
Tranmere	23	12	14	—	22	16	10	20	18	16	7	20	—	—	—	—	—	—	21	10	Tranmere
Walsall	22	6	15	7	8	15	17	9	20	12	13	7	12	9	19	19	—	—	2	—	Walsall
Watford	2	—	—	—	23	7	19	—	—	—	1	6	3	12	9	3	17	17	4	—	Watford
Workington	—	—	—	—	—	—	—	—	—	—	—	—	24	5	15	—	—	—	—	—	Workington
Wrexham	—	24	—	—	3	18	19	—	—	—	—	—	24	—	—	—	—	—	—	21	Wrexham
York	—	5	6	13	4	12	16	9	—	—	—	—	—	23	9	—	—	—	—	23	York

*Relegated by League order.

FOURTH DIVISION LEAGUE POSITIONS (1959-79)

	1959-60	1960-61	1961-62	1962-63	1963-64	1964-65	1965-66	1966-67	1967-68	1968-69	1969-70	1970-71	1971-72	1972-73	1973-74	1974-75	1975-76	1976-77	1977-78	1978-79
Accrington	18	13	R	—	—	—	—	—	—	—	—	—	—	—	—	—	—	—	—	—
Aldershot	—	7	—	9	9	18	—	9	2	15	6	13	17	4	—	—	—	17	5	5
Barnsley	—	10	11	—	—	—	16	10	—	6	15	—	22	—	13	15	—	—	7	6
Barrow	13	22	7	21	24	17	3	2	4	11	13	24	24	—	—	—	—	—	—	—
Bournemouth	18	—	—	—	—	—	—	—	—	—	—	—	—	—	—	—	—	—	17	18
Bradford	15	4	5	23	7	11	23	5	5	11	24	22	16	24	8	10	17	4	—	15
Bradford C.	4	11	—	9	13	—	11	11	14	5	14	2	3	16	8	10	18	2	—	4
Brentford	—	—	5	—	19	—	23	14	—	—	—	14	—	15	19	23	—	7	2	—
Brighton	—	—	—	—	1	—	8	—	—	—	—	—	—	—	—	—	—	—	—	—
Bury	—	—	—	—	—	1	—	—	—	—	—	9	12	—	—	13	1	—	—	—
Cambridge U.	—	—	4	—	2	—	7	19	22	14	5	20	10	3	7	6	13	1	—	2
Carlisle	19	19	23	21	12	—	5	7	15	20	11	—	—	22	—	4	—	—	6	—
Chester	20	24	19	16	16	—	20	15	—	10	6	5	11	21	21	18	12	14	20	23
Chesterfield	—	—	—	3	—	12	4	5	4	20	10	1	6	22	3	7	16	13	21	23
Colchester	—	—	10	—	14	10	14	—	—	23	15	15	24	11	21	18	2	12	14	22
Crewe	14	2	—	—	—	17	—	4	—	—	—	—	—	24	21	21	16	22	13	24
Crystal P.	—	—	—	8	—	—	—	—	—	—	—	—	—	—	—	—	—	—	—	—
Darlington	8	7	13	16	14	2	17	16	5	—	22	12	19	24	20	8	11	11	19	21
Doncaster	—	11	18	16	17	1	—	20	17	18	21	9	22	8	10	17	20	9	22	22
Exeter	—	5	—	18	4	8	—	20	20	17	18	15	15	9	10	9	7	2	—	—
Gateshead	22	15	—	—	—	—	—	—	—	—	—	—	—	—	—	—	—	—	—	—
Gillingham	7	—	20	1	—	—	—	—	23	11	19	13	9	2	1	5	2	—	6	—
Grimsby	—	—	15	5	—	23	15	12	11	16	16	1	19	9	—	—	—	20	21	20
Halifax	—	—	20	—	17	23	20	15	12	23	16	—	13	—	—	23	14	21	18	18
Hartlepool	24	23	19	21	23	15	20	3	8	21	15	18	15	10	11	13	13	23	24	24
Hereford	—	—	—	—	—	—	—	—	—	—	—	—	—	2	—	2	—	21	13	14
Huddersfield	—	—	—	—	—	—	—	—	—	—	—	—	—	—	—	—	5	9	11	10

	Lincoln	Luton	Millwall	Newport	Northampton	Notts County	Oldham	Oxford	Peterborough	Portsmouth	Port Vale	Reading	Rochdale	Rotherham U.	Scunthorpe	Shrewsbury	Southend	Southport	Stockport	Swansea	Torquay	Tranmere	Walsall	Watford	Wigan Ath.	Wimbledon	Workington	Wrexham	York
Lincoln	—	—	—	7	19	—	18	6	20	12	—	14	—	—	2	18	11	3	5	9	—	11	6	1	6	3	9	—	—
Luton	—	—	—	16	10	—	8	24	18	8	23	20	2	10	23	—	5	16	—	22	7	8	13	—	24	13	22	—	—
Mansfield	—	—	—	—	—	—	—	—	—	—	—	—	—	—	—	—	—	—	—	—	—	—	—	—	—	—	—	—	—
Millwall	—	—	1	12	9	5	23	21	7	19	16	—	7	6	—	4	2	11	24	14	16	21	22	15	23	23	3	14	R
Newport	5	12	10	5	21	8	21	8	13	24	22	22	11	22	—	4	14	20	—	—	—	—	7	—	—	—	—	—	—
Northampton	17	6			14	19	7	13	12	17	9	16	15	20	—	18	8	—	—	—	—	—	—	—	—	—	—	—	—
Notts County		3	6		1	7	20	11	3	2	8	13	—	17	23	—	—	—	—	—	—	—	—	—	—	—	—	—	—
Oldham		2			3	19	8	18	4	18	—	2	11	12	21	10	—	—	—	—	—	—	—	—	—	—	—	—	—
Oxford	11	12	23		19	18	9	13	19	17	—	—	—	1	—	—	—	—	—	—	—	—	—	—	—	—	—	—	—
Peterborough	18																												—
Portsmouth	6	8		7	16	4	13	9						1															—
Port Vale	20	8		19	6	13	18		3	19	21	21	6	20	7	12	17												—
Reading	24	18	12	7	17																								—
Rochdale	12	24	18	15	3	15	3	19	21	21	6	20	7	12	17	11													—
Rotherham	14	20	3	18	16	12	16																						—
Scunthorpe		19	2					6	6	10	20	21	13	24	17	16	13												—
Shrewsbury	2	10			17	7	6	1	13																				—
Southend	23	23	11	2	8		10	3		3	11	6	6																—
Southport	18	14	23	16	11	1	15	15		5	13	24	17	8	15														—
Stockport	3	23	20	12	14	23																							—
Swansea	5	21	22	14	18		15	10		3	11	7	6	3															—
Tranmere	9	16	14					4	5	4																			—
Walsall	11	9	16	4	4						7	8	15	6														1	—
Watford	1	7	8																									4	—
Wigan Ath.	6	13				10					3	10	8	8														16	—
Wimbledon	3	13	24	24	23	13			20	12	23	9	9	8	3	10												16	—
Workington																													—
Wrexham	9	22	24	23	23	13		4	13	21	21	22	14	6														5	—
York	—	—	—	—	—	—	—	—	—	—	—	—	—	—	—	—	—	—	—	—	—	—	—	—	—	—	—	—	—

R – Resigned from Football League.

CHAMPIONSHIP HONOURS

THE LEAGUE—Division I

	First	Pts.	Second	Pts.	Third	Pts.
1888-9	aPreston	40	Aston Villa	29	Wolverhampton	28
1889-90	Preston	33	Everton	31	Blackburn R.	27
1890-1	Everton	29	Preston	27	W'hamptonW. } Notts County }	26
1891-2	bSunderland	42	Preston	37	Bolton	36
1892-3	cSunderland	48	Preston	37	Everton	36
1893-4	Aston Villa	44	Sunderland	38	Derby	36
1894-5	Sunderland	47	Everton	42	Aston Villa	39
1895-6	Aston Villa	45	Derby	41	Everton	39
1896-7	Aston Villa	47	Sheffield United	36	Derby	36
1897-8	Sheffield United	42	Sunderland	37	Wolverhampton	35
1898-9	dAston Villa	45	Liverpool	43	Burnley	39
1899-1900	Aston Villa	50	Sheffield United	48	Sunderland	41
1900-1	Liverpool	45	Sunderland	43	Notts County	40
1901-2	Sunderland	44	Everton	41	Newcastle	37
1902-3	Sheffield Wed.	42	Aston Villa	41	Sunderland	41
1903-4	Sheffield Wed.	47	Manchester City	44	Everton	43
1904-5	Newcastle	48	Everton	47	Manchester City	46
1905-6	eLiverpool	51	Preston	47	Sheffield Wed.	44
1906-7	Newcastle	51	Bristol City	38	Everton	45
1907-8	Manchester U.	52	Aston Villa	43	Manchester City	43
1908-9	Newcastle	53	Everton	46	Sunderland	44
1909-10	Aston Villa	53	Liverpool	48	Blackburn R.	45
1910-11	Manchester U.	52	Aston Villa	51	Sunderland	45
1911-12	Blackburn R.	49	Everton	46	Newcastle	44
1912-13	Sunderland	54	Aston Villa	50	Sheffield Wed.	45
1913-14	Blackburn R.	51	Aston Villa	44	Middlesbrough	43
1914-15	Everton	46	Oldham	45	Blackburn R.	43
1919-20	fWest Brom. A.	60	Burnley	51	Chelsea	49
1920-21	Burnley	59	Manchester City	54	Bolton	52
1921-22	Liverpool	57	Tottenham	51	Burnley	49
1922-23	Liverpool	60	Sunderland	54	Huddersfield	53
1923-24	*Huddersfield	57	Cardiff	57	Sunderland	53
1924-25	Huddersfield	58	West Brom. A.	56	Bolton	55
1925-26	Huddersfield	57	Arsenal	52	Sunderland	48
1926-27	Newcastle	56	Huddersfield	51	Sunderland	49
1927-28	Everton	53	Huddersfield	51	Leicester	48
1928-29	Sheffield Wed.	52	Leicester	51	Aston Villa	50
1929-30	Sheffield Wed.	60	Derby	50	Manchester City	47
1930-31	Arsenal	66	Aston Villa	59	Sheffield Wed.	52
1931-32	Everton	56	Arsenal	54	Sheffield Wed.	50
1932-33	Arsenal	58	Aston Villa	54	Sheffield Wed.	51
1933-34	Arsenal	59	Huddersfield	56	Tottenham	49
1934-35	Arsenal	58	Sunderland	54	Sheffield Wed.	49
1935-36	Sunderland	56	Derby	48	Huddersfield	48
1936-37	Manchester City	57	Charlton	54	Arsenal	52
1937-38	Arsenal	52	Wolverhampton	51	Preston	49
1938-39	Everton	59	Wolverhampton	55	Charlton	50
1946-47	Liverpool	57	Manchester U.	56	Wolverhampton	56
1947-48	Arsenal	59	Manchester U.	52	Burnley	52

1948-49	Portsmouth 58	Manchester U. .53	Derby 53
1949-50	*Portsmouth 53	Wolverhampton 53	Sunderland 52
1950-51	Tottenham 60	Manchester U. .56	Blackpool 50
1951-52	Manchester U. .57	Tottenham 53	Arsenal 53
1952-53	*Arsenal 54	Preston 54	Wolverhampton 51
1953-54	Wolverhampton .57	West Brom. A. .53	Huddersfield ..51
1954-55	Chelsea 52	Wolverhampton 48	Portsmouth ...48
1955-56	Manchester U. .60	Blackpool 49	Wolverhampton 49
1956-57	Manchester U. ..64	Tottenham 56	Preston 56
1957-58	Wolverhampton .64	Preston 59	Tottenham ...51
1958-59	Wolverhampton .61	Manchester U. .55	Arsenal 50
1959-60	Burnley 55	Wolverhampton 54	Tottenham ...53
1960-61	Tottenham 66	Sheffield Wed. .58	Wolverhampton 57
1961-62	Ipswich 56	Burnley 53	Tottenham ...52
1962-63	Everton 61	Tottenham 55	Burnley 54
1963-64	Liverpool 57	Manchester U. .53	Everton 52
1964-65	Manchester U. ..61	Leeds 61	Chelsea 56
1965-66	Liverpool 61	Leeds 55	Burnley 55
1966-67	Manchester U. ..60	Nottingham F. .56	Tottenham ...56
1967-68	Manchester C. ..58	Manchester U. .56	Liverpool 55
1968-69	Leeds 67	Liverpool 61	Everton 57
1969-70	Everton 66	Leeds 57	Chelsea 55
1970-71	Arsenal 65	Leeds 64	Tottenham ...52
1971-72	Derby 58	Leeds 57	Liverpool 57
1972-73	Liverpool 60	Arsenal 57	Leeds 53
1973-74	Leeds 62	Liverpool 57	Derby 48
1974-75	Derby 53	Liverpool 51	Ipswich 51
1975-76	Liverpool 60	Q.P.R. 59	Manchester U. .56
1976-77	Liverpool 57	Manchester C. .56	Ipswich 52
1977-78	Nottingham F. ..64	Liverpool 57	Everton 55
1978-79	Liverpool 68	Nottingham F...60	W.B.A. 59

*Won on goal average. Maximum points: a, 44; b, 56; c, 60; d, 58; e, 76; f, 84

THE LEAGUE—Division II

1892-3	aSmall Heath 36	Sheffield U. 35	Darwen 30
1893-4	bLiverpool 50	Small Heath 42	Notts County ..39
1894-5	cBury 48	Notts County ..39	Newton Heath ..38
1895-6	*Liverpool 46	Manchester City 46	Grimsby 42
1896-7	Notts County ...42	Newton Heath .39	Grimsby 38
1897-8	Burnley 48	Newcastle 45	Manchester City 39
1898-9	dManchester City .51	Glossop N.E. ...46	Leicester Fosse .45
1899-1900	Sheffield Wed. .54	Bolton 52	Small Heath ...46
1900-1	Grimsby 49	Small Heath ...48	Burnley 44
1901-2	West Brom. A. ..55	Middlesbrough .51	Preston 42
1902-3	Manchester City .54	Small Heath ...51	W'lwich Arsenal 48
1903-4	Preston 50	W'lwich Arsenal 49	Manchester U. .48
1904-5	Liverpool 58	Bolton 56	Manchester U. .53
1905-6	eBristol City 66	Manchester U. .62	Chelsea 53
1906-7	Nott'm Forest ...60	Chelsea 57	Leicester Fosse .48
1907-8	Bradford City ...54	Leicester Fosse .52	Oldham.......50
1908-9	Bolton 52	Tottenham 51	West Brom. A...51
1909-10	Manchester City..54	Oldham........53	Hull City 53
1910-11	West Brom. A. ..53	Bolton 51	Chelsea 49
1911-12	*Derby 54	Chelsea 54	Burnley 52

91

	First	Pts.	Second	Pts.	Third	Pts.
1912-13	Preston	53	Burnley	50	Birmingham	46
1913-14	Notts County	53	Bradford	49	W'lwich Arsenal	49
1914-15	Derby	53	Preston	50	Barnsley	47
1919-20	ʃTottenham	70	Huddersfield	64	Birmingham	56
1920-21	*Birmingham	58	Cardiff	58	Bristol City	51
1921-22	Nott'm Forest	56	Stoke	52	Barnsley	52
1922-23	Notts County	53	West Ham	51	Leicester City	51
1923-24	Leeds	54	Bury	51	Derby	51
1924-25	Leicester City	59	Manchester U.	57	Derby	55
1925-26	Sheffield Wed.	60	Derby	57	Chelsea	52
1926-27	Middlesbrough	62	Portsmouth	54	Manchester City	54
1927-28	Manchester City	59	Leeds	57	Chelsea	54
1928-29	Middlesbrough	55	Grimsby	53	Bradford	48
1929-30	Blackpool	58	Chelsea	55	Oldham	53
1930-31	Everton	61	West Brom. A.	55	Tottenham	51
1931-32	Wolverhampton	56	Leeds	54	Stoke City	52
1932-33	Stoke City	56	Tottenham	55	Fulham	50
1933-34	Grimsby	59	Preston	52	Bolton	51
1934-35	Brentford	61	Bolton	56	West Ham	56
1935-36	Manchester U.	56	Charlton	55	Sheffield U.	52
1936-37	Leicester City	56	Blackpool	55	Bury	52
1937-38	Aston Villa	57	Manchester U.	53	Sheffield U.	53
1938-39	Blackburn R.	55	Sheffield U.	54	Sheffield Wed.	53
1946-47	Manchester City	62	Burnley	58	Birmingham	55
1947-48	Birmingham	59	Newcastle	56	Southampton	52
1948-49	Fulham	57	West Brom. A.	56	Southampton	55
1949-50	Tottenham	61	Sheffield Wed.	52	Sheffield U.	52
1950-51	Preston	57	Manchester City	52	Cardiff	50
1951-52	Sheffield Wed.	53	Cardiff	51	Birmingham	51
1952-53	Sheffield U.	60	Huddersfield	58	Luton	52
1953-54	Leicester City	56	Everton	56	Blackburn R.	55
1954-55	*Birmingham C.	54	Luton	54	Rotherham	54
1955-56	Sheffield Wed.	55	Leeds	52	Liverpool	48
1956-57	Leicester City	61	Nott'm Forest	54	Liverpool	53
1957-58	West Ham	57	Blackburn	56	Charlton	55
1958-59	Sheffield Wed.	62	Fulham	60	Sheffield U.	53
1959-60	Aston Villa	59	Cardiff	58	Liverpool	50
1960-61	Ipswich	59	Sheffield U.	58	Liverpool	52
1961-62	Liverpool	62	Leyton O.	54	Sunderland	53
1962-63	Stoke	53	Chelsea	52	Sunderland	52
1963-64	Leeds	63	Sunderland	61	Preston	56
1964-65	Newcastle	57	Northampton	56	Bolton	50
1965-66	Manchester City	59	Southampton	54	Coventry	53
1966-67	Coventry	59	Wolverhampton	58	Carlisle	52
1967-68	Ipswich	59	Queen's Park R.	58	Blackpool	58
1968-69	Derby	63	Crystal P.	56	Charlton	50
1969-70	Huddersfield	60	Blackpool	53	Leicester	51
1970-71	Leicester	59	Sheffield U.	56	Cardiff	53
1971-72	Norwich	57	Birmingham	56	Millwall	55
1972-73	Burnley	62	Queen's Park R.	61	Aston Villa	50
1973-74	Middlesbrough	65	Luton	50	Carlisle	49
1974-75	Manchester U.	61	Aston Villa	58	Norwich C.	53

*Won on goal average. Maximum points: a,44; b,56; c,60; d,58; e,76, f,84

	First	Pts.	Second	Pts.	Third	Pts.
1975-76	Sunderland	56	Bristol C.	53	West Brom. A.	53
1976-77	Wolverhampton	57	Chelsea	55	Nott'm Forest	52
1977-78	Bolton W.	58	Southampton	57	Tottenham H.	56
1978-79	Crystal P.	57	Brighton	56	Stoke City	56

THE LEAGUE Division III

	First	Pts.	Second	Pts.	Third	Pts.
1958-59	Plymouth Argyle	62	Hull	61	Brentford	57
1959-60	Southampton	61	Norwich	59	Shrewsbury	52
1960-61	Bury	68	Walsall	62	Queen's Park R.	60
1961-62	Portsmouth	65	Grimsby	62	Bournemouth	59
1962-63	Northampton	62	Swindon	58	Port Vale	54
1963-64	*Coventry	60	Crystal P.	60	Watford	58
1964-65	Carlisle	60	Bristol C.	59	Mansfield	59
1965-66	Hull	69	Millwall	65	Queen's Park R.	57
1966-67	Queen's Park R.	67	Middlesbrough	55	Watford	54
1967-68	Oxford U.	57	Bury	56	Shrewsbury	55
1968-69	*Watford	64	Swindon	64	Luton	61
1969-70	Orient	62	Luton	60	Bristol R.	56
1970-71	Preston	61	Fulham	60	Halifax	56
1971-72	Aston Villa	70	Brighton	65	Bournemouth	62
1972-73	Bolton	61	Notts County	57	Blackburn	55
1973-74	Oldham	62	Bristol R.	61	York C.	61
1974-75	Blackburn R.	60	Plymouth Arg.	59	Charlton Ath.	55
1975-76	Hereford U.	63	Cardiff C.	57	Millwall	56
1976-77	Mansfield T.	64	Brighton	61	Crystal P.	59
1977-78	Wrexham	61	Cambridge U.	58	Preston N.E.	56
1978-79	Shrewsbury T.	61	Watford	60	Swansea	60

*Won on goal average. Maximum points: 92

THE LEAGUE—Division III (Southern Section)

	First	Pts.	Second	Pts.	Third	Pts.
1920-21	aCrystal Palace	59	Southampton	54	Queen's Park R.	53
1921-22	*Southampton	61	Plymouth	53	Portsmouth	53
1922-23	Bristol City	59	Plymouth	53	Swansea	53
1923-24	Portsmouth	59	Plymouth	55	Millwall	54
1924-25	Swansea	57	Plymouth	56	Bristol City	53
1925-26	Reading	57	Plymouth	56	Millwall	53
1926-27	Bristol City	62	Plymouth	60	Millwall	56
1927-28	Millwall	65	Northampton	55	Plymouth	53
1928-29	*Charlton	54	Crystal Palace	54	Northampton	52
1929-30	Plymouth	68	Brentford	61	Queen's Park R.	51
1930-31	Notts County	59	Crystal Palace	51	Brentford	50
1931-32	Fulham	57	Reading	55	Southend	53
1932-33	Brentford	62	Exeter	58	Norwich	57
1933-34	Norwich	61	Coventry	54	Reading	54
1934-35	Charlton	61	Reading	53	Coventry	51
1935-36	Coventry	57	Luton	56	Reading	54
1936-37	Luton	57	Notts County	56	Brighton	53
1937-38	Millwall	56	Bristol City	55	Queen's Park R.	53
1938-39	Newport	55	Crystal Palace	52	Brighton	49
1946-47	Cardiff	66	Queen's Park R.	57	Bristol City	51
1947-48	Queen's Park R.	61	Bournemouth	57	Walsall	51
1948-49	Swansea	62	Reading	55	Bournemouth	52
1949-50	Notts County	58	Northampton	51	Southend	51
1950-51	bNott'm Forest	70	Norwich	64	Reading	57

*Won on goal average. Maximum points: a, 84; b, 92

	First	Pts.	Second	Pts.	Third	Pts.
1951-52	Plymouth	66	Reading	61	Norwich	61
1952-53	Bristol R.	64	Northampton	62	Millwall	62
1953-54	Ipswich	64	Brighton	61	Bristol City	56
1954-55	Bristol City	70	Leyton O.	61	Southampton	59
1955-56	Leyton O.	66	Brighton	65	Ipswich	64
1956-57	*Ipswich	59	Torquay	59	Colchester	58
1957-58	Brighton	60	Brentford	58	Plymouth	58

THE LEAGUE—Division III (Northern Section)

	First	Pts.	Second	Pts.	Third	Pts.
1921-22	aStockport	56	Darlington	50	Grimsby	50
1922-23	Nelson	51	Bradford	47	Walsall	46
1923-24	bWolverhampton	63	Rochdale	62	Chesterfield	54
1924-25	Darlington	58	Nelson	53	New Brighton	53
1925-26	Grimsby	61	Bradford	60	Rochdale	59
1926-27	Stoke City	63	Rochdale	58	Bradford	55
1927-28	Bradford	63	Lincoln	55	Stockport	54
1928-29	Bradford City	63	Stockport	62	Wrexham	52
1929-30	Port Vale	67	Stockport	63	Darlington	50
1930-31	Chesterfield	58	Lincoln	57	Wrexham	54
1931-32	c*Lincoln	57	Gateshead	57	Chester	50
1932-33	bHull	59	Wrexham	57	Stockport	54
1933-34	Barnsley	62	Chesterfield	61	Stockport	59
1934-35	Doncaster	57	Halifax	55	Chester	54
1935-36	Chesterfield	60	Chester	55	Tranmere	55
1936-37	Stockport	60	Lincoln	57	Chester	53
1937-38	Tranmere	56	Doncaster	54	Hull City	53
1938-39	Barnsley	67	Doncaster	56	Bradford City	52
1946-47	Doncaster	72	Rotherham	64	Chester	56
1947-48	Lincoln	60	Rotherham	59	Wrexham	50
1948-49	Hull City	65	Rotherham	62	Doncaster	50
1949-50	Doncaster	55	Gateshead	53	Rochdale	51
1950-51	dRotherham	71	Mansfield	64	Carlisle	62
1951-52	Lincoln	69	Grimsby	66	Stockport	59
1952-53	Oldham	59	Port Vale	58	Wrexham	56
1953-54	Port Vale	69	Barnsley	58	Scunthorpe	57
1954-55	Barnsley	65	Accrington S.	61	Scunthorpe	58
1955-56	Grimsby	68	Derby	63	Accrington S.	59
1956-57	Derby	63	Hartlepool	59	Accrington S.	58
1957-58	Scunthorpe	66	Accrington S.	59	Bradford C.	57

*Won on goal average. Maximum points: a, 70; b, 84; c, 80; d, 90.
No championship during the World Wars.

THE LEAGUE—Division IV

	First	Pts.	Second	Pts.	Third	Pts.
1958-59	Port Vale	64	Coventry	60	York	60
1959-60	Walsall	65	Notts County	60	Torquay	60
1960-61	Peterborough	66	Crystal P.	64	Northampton	60
1961-62	Millwall	56	Colchester	55	Wrexham	53
1962-63	Brentford	62	Oldham	59	Crewe	59
1963-64	*Gillingham	60	Carlisle	60	Workington	59
1964-65	Brighton	63	Millwall	62	York	62
1965-66	*Doncaster	59	Darlington	59	Torquay	58
1966-67	Stockport	64	Southport	59	Barrow	59
1967-68	Luton	66	Barnsley	61	Hartlepool	60
1968-69	Doncaster	59	Halifax	57	Rochdale	56

*Won on goal average. Maximum points 92.

1969-70	Chesterfield	64	Wrexham	61	Swansea	60
1970-71	Notts County	69	Bournemouth	.60	Oldham	59
1971-72	Grimsby	63	Southend	60	Brentford	59
1972-73	Southport	62	Hereford	58	Cambridge U.	..57
1973-74	Peterborough	65	Gillingham	...62	Colchester	60
1974-75	Mansfield T.	68	Shrewsbury T.	..62	Rotherham U.	.59
1975-76	Lincoln C.	74	Northampton	..68	Reading	60
1976-77	Cambridge U.	..65	Exeter C.	62	Colchester	59
1977-78	Watford	71	Southend U.	60	Swansea	56
1978-79	Reading	65	Grimsby T.	61	Wimbledon	61

RELEGATED CLUBS

Since inception of automatic promotion and relegation in 1898-99

Season	Division I to Division II	Division II to Division III
1978-79	Q.P.R., Birmingham, Chelsea	Sheffield U., Millwall, B'burn
1977-78	West Ham, Newcastle, Leicester	Blackpool, Mansfield, Hull C.
1976-77	Sunderland, Stoke, Tottenham	Carlisle, Plymouth, Hereford
1975-76	Wolves, Burnley, Sheff. U.	Oxford, York, Portsmouth
1974-75	Luton, Chelsea, Carlisle	Millwall, Cardiff, Sheff. W.
1973-74	So'ton, Man. U., Norwich	C. Palace, P.N.E., Swindon
1972-73	Crystal Palace and W. Brom. A.	Huddersfield and Brighton
1971-72	Huddersfield and Nott'm F.	Charlton and Watford
1970-71	Burnley and Blackpool	Blackburn and Bolton
1969-70	Sunderland and Sheffield W.	Aston Villa and Preston
1968-69	Leicester and Q.P. Rangers	Bury and Fulham
1967-68	Sheffield U. and Fulham	Rotherham and Plymouth
1966-67	Aston Villa and Blackpool	Northampton and Bury
1965-66	Blackburn and Northampton	Leyton O. and Middlesbrough
1964-65	Birmingham and Wolverh'pton	Swindon and Swansea
1963-64	Bolton and Ipswich	Grimsby and Scunthorpe
1962-63	Manchester C. and Leyton O.	Walsall and Luton
1961-62	Cardiff and Chelsea	Bristol R. and Brighton
1960-61	Newcastle and Preston	Portsmouth and Lincoln
1959-60	Leeds and Luton	Hull and Bristol C.
1958-59	Aston V. and Portsmouth	Grimsby and Barnsley
1957-58	Sunderland and Sheffield W.	Notts. Co. and Doncaster
1956-57	Cardiff and Charlton	Bury and Port Vale
1955-56	Huddersfield and Sheffield U.	Plymouth and Hull
1954-55	Leicester and Sheffield W.	Ipswich and Derby
1953-54	Middlesbrough and Liverpool	Brentford and Oldham
1952-53	Stoke and Derby	Southampton and Barnsley
1951-52	Fulham and Huddersfield	Coventry and Q.P. Rangers
1950-51	Sheffield W. and Everton	Chesterfield and Grimsby
1949-50	Manchester C. and Birmingham	Plymouth and Bradford
1948-49	Preston and Sheffield U.	Lincoln and Nottingham F.
1947-48	Blackburn and Grimsby	Doncaster and Millwall
1946-47	Brentford and Leeds	Swansea and Newport
1938-39	Birmingham and Leicester	Norwich and Tranmere
1937-38	M'chester C. and W. Brom. A.	Barnsley and Stockport
1936-37	M'chester U. and Sheffield W.	Doncaster and Bradford C.
1935-36	Aston Villa and Blackburn	Port Vale and Hull
1934-35	Leicester and Tottenham	Oldham and Notts. Co.

1933-34—Newcastle and Sheffield U.   Millwall and Lincoln
1932-33—Bolton and Blackpool   Chesterfield and Charlton
1931-32—Grimsby and W. Ham   Barnsley and Bristol City
1930-31—Leeds and Manchester U.   Reading and Cardiff
1929-30—Burnley and Everton   Hull and Notts Co.
1928-29—Bury and Cardiff   Port Vale and Clapton O.
1927-28—Tottenham and Middlesbro'   Fulham and South Shields
1926-27—Leeds and W. Brom. A.   Darlington and Bradford C.
1925-26—Manchester C. and Notts Co.   Stoke and Stockport
1924-25—Preston and Nott'm F.   Crystal Palace and Coventry
1923-24—Chelsea and Middlesbro'   Nelson and Bristol City
1922-23—Stoke and Oldham   Rotherham and W'ham'tn
1921-22—Bradford C. and M'chester U.   Bradford and Bristol City
1920-21—Derby and Bradford   Stockport
1919-20—Notts Co. and Sheffield W.
1916-18—During the War the Football League competition was suspended.
            Previously the clubs relegated from Div. I to Div. II were:
1914-15—Tottenham and Chelsea
1913-14—Preston North End and Derby County
1912-13—Notts County and Woolwich Arsenal
1911-12—Preston North End and Bury
1910-11—Bristol City and Nottingham Forest
1909-10—Bolton Wanderers and Chelsea
1908-09—Manchester City and Leicester Fosse
1907-08—Bolton Wanderers and Birmingham
1906-07—Derby County and Stoke
1905-06—Nottingham Forest and Wolverhampton
1904-05   League extended. Bury and Notts County, two bottom clubs in
            First Division, re-elected.
1903-04—Liverpool and West Bromwich Albion
1902-03—Grimsby and Bolton
1901-02—Small Heath and Manchester City
1900-01—Preston North End and West Bromwich
1899-1900—Burnley and Glossop
1898-99—Bolton and Sheffield Wednesday

Season   Relegation from Third to Fourth Division
1978-79—Peterborough, Walsall, Tranmere and Lincoln
1977-78—Port Vale, Bradford, Hereford and Portsmouth
1976-77—Reading, Northampton, Grimsby and York
1975-76—Aldershot, Colchester, Southend U., and Halifax T.
1974-75—Bournemouth, Tranmere, Watford and Hudddersfield
1973-74—Cambridge, Shrewsbury, Southport and Rochdale
1972-73—Rotherham, Brentford, Swansea and Scunthorpe
1971-72—Mansfield, Barnsley, Bradford C. and Torquay
1970-71—Reading, Bury, Doncaster and Gillingham
1969-70—Bournemouth, Southport, Barrow and Stockport
1968-69—Northampton, Hartlepool, Crewe and Oldham
1967-68—Grimsby, Colchester, Scunthorpe and Peterborough*
1966-67—Swansea, Darlington, Workington and Doncaster
1965-66—Southend, Exeter, Brentford and York
1964-65—Luton, Port Vale, Colchester and Barnsley
1963-64—Millwall, Crewe, Wrexham and Notts County
1962-63—Bradford, Brighton, Carlisle and Halifax
1961-62—Torquay, Lincoln, Brentford and Newport

1960-61—Tranmere, Bradford C., Colchester and Chesterfield
1959-60—York, Mansfield, Wrexham and Accrington
1958-59—Stockport, Doncaster, Notts County and Rochdale
   *Expelled to Fourth Division by League

Application for Re-election
to Third Division until 1957-58

SEVEN TIMES: Walsall.

SIX: Exeter, Halifax, Newport.

FIVE: Accrington, Barrow, Gillingham, New Brighton, Southport.

FOUR: Norwich, Rochdale.

THREE: Crewe, Crystal Palace, Darlington, Hartlepool, Merthyr Town, Swindon.

TWO: Aberdare Athletic, Aldershot, Ashington, Bournemouth, Brentford, Chester, Colchester, Millwall, Durham City, Nelson, Queen's Park Rangers, Rotherham, Southend, Tranmere, Watford, Workington.

ONE: Bradford, Bradford City, Brighton, Bristol Rovers, Cardiff, Carlisle, Charlton, Gateshead, Grimsby, Mansfield, Shrewsbury, Thames, Torquay, York.

Application for Re-election
to Fourth Division

NINE TIMES: Hartlepool.

SIX: Barrow and Southport.

FIVE: Lincoln, Workington and York.

FOUR: Bradford, Chester, Crewe, Darlington, Newport and Stockport.

THREE: Doncaster, Halifax, and Rochdale.

TWO: Bradford City, Northampton, and Oldham.

ONE: Aldershot, Colchester, Exeter, Gateshead, Grimsby, Port Vale, Scunthorpe United, Swansea City and Wrexham.

Gateshead not re-elected, their place being taken by Peterborough in the 1960-61 season.

Accrington resigned March 1962, and Oxford United elected to replace them in 1962-63 season.

Bradford not re-elected, their place being taken by Cambridge United in the 1970-71 season

Barrow not re-elected, their place being taken by Hereford United in the 1972-73 season.

Workington not re-elected, their place being taken by Wimbledon in the 1977-78 season.

Southport not re-elected, their place being taken by Wigan in the 1978–79 season.

97

League Title Wins

LEAGUE DIVISION I—11—Liverpool; 8—Arsenal; 7—Everton, Manchester U.; 6—Aston Villa, Sunderland; 4—Newcastle, Sheffield Wed.; 3—Huddersfield, Wolves; 2—Blackburn, Burnley, Derby, Leeds, Manchester City, Portsmouth, Preston, Tottenham; 1—Chelsea, Ipswich, Nottingham Forest, Sheffield United, West Bromwich Albion.

LEAGUE DIVISION II—6—Manchester City; 5—Leicester, Sheffield Wed.; 4—*Birmingham, Liverpool; 3—Derby, Middlesbrough, Notts Co., Preston; 2—Aston Villa, Bolton, Burnley, Grimsby, Ipswich, Leeds, Manchester U., Nottingham Forest, Stoke, Tottenham, West Bromwich, Wolverhampton; 1—Blackburn, Blackpool, Bradford City, Brentford, Bristol City, Bury, Coventry, Crystal Palace, Everton, Fulham, Huddersfield, Newcastle, Norwich, Sheffield United, Sunderland, West Ham.
*Once as Small Heath

LEAGUE DIVISION III—Aston Villa, Blackburn R., Bolton, Bury, Carlisle, Coventry, Hereford U., Hull, Mansfield, Northampton, Oldham Ath., Orient, Oxford Utd., Plymouth, Portsmouth, Preston, Queen's Park Rangers, Shrewsbury T., Southampton, Watford, Wrexham.

LEAGUE DIVISION IV—Doncaster 2, Peterborough 2; Brentford, Brighton, Cambridge, Chesterfield, Gillingham, Grimsby, Lincoln C., Luton, Mansfield T., Millwall, Notts Co., Port Vale, Reading, Southport, Walsall, Watford.

To 1957-58

DIVISION III (SOUTH): Bristol City, three times; Charlton, Ipswich, Millwall, Notts Co., Plymouth, Swansea, twice; Brentford, Brighton, Bristol R., Cardiff, Coventry, Crystal P., Fulham, Leyton Orient, Luton, Newport, Nottingham Forest, Norwich, Portsmouth, Queen's Park Rangers, Reading, Southampton, once.

DIVISION III (NORTH): Barnsley, Doncaster, Lincoln, three times; Chesterfield, Grimsby, Hull, Port Vale, Stockport, twice; Bradford, Bradford City, Darlington, Derby, Nelson, Oldham, Rotherham, Scunthorpe, Stoke, Tranmere, Wolverhampton, once.

TRANSFER TRAIL

(players with British Clubs)

First four-figure transaction:
    Alf Common—Sunderland to Middlesbrough for £1,000 in February, 1905.
First five-figure transaction:
    David Jack—Bolton to Arsenal for £10,340 in October, 1928.
First six-figure transaction:
    Alan Ball—Blackpool to Everton £112,000, August, 1966.
First £200,000 transaction:
    Martin Peters—West Ham to Tottenham £200,000, March, 1970.
First seven-figure transaction :
    Trevor Francis—Birmingham C. to Nottingham Forest £1,000,000, February, 1979.
Phil Parkes—Q.P.R. to West Ham U. £565,000, February, 1979.
David Mills—Middlesbrough to W.B.A. £516,000, January, 1979.
Gerry Francis—Q.P.R., to Crystal Palace £465,000, May, 1979.
Garry Owen—Manchester C. to W.B.A. £450,000, May, 1979.
Brian Talbot—Ipswich T. to Arsenal £450,000, January, 1979.
Gordon McQueen—Leeds U. to Manchester U. £450,000, February, 1978.
Kenny Dalglish—Celtic to Liverpool £440,000, August, 1977.
Alan Curtis—Swansea C. to Leeds U. £400,000, May, 1979.
Charlie George—Derby Co. to Southampton £400,000, December, 1978.
Osvaldo Ardiles—Huracan to Tottenham Hotspur £400,000, July, 1978.
Kevin Hird—Blackburn R. to Leeds U. £360,000, March, 1979.
Graeme Souness—Middlesbrough to Liverpool £352,000, January, 1978.
Ricardo Villa—Racing Club to Tottenham Hotspur £350,000, July, 1978.
Paul Futcher—Luton T. to Manchester C. £350,000, June, 1978.
Joe Jordan—Leeds U. to Manchester U. £350,000, January, 1978.
Bob Latchford—Birmingham to Everton £350,000, February, 1974.
Malcolm Macdonald—Newcastle U. to Arsenal £333,333, August, 1976.
Colin Todd—Derby Co. to Everton £330,000, September, 1978.
Paul Hart—Blackpool to Leeds U. £330,000, March, 1978.
Mick Walsh—Blackpool to Everton £325,000, August, 1978.
Peter Shilton—Leicester to Stoke £325,000, November, 1974.
Frank McGarvey—St. Mirren to Liverpool, £300,000, May, 1979.
Mike Thomas—Wrexham to Manchester U. £300,000, November, 1978.
Alan Kennedy—Newcastle U. to Liverpool £300,000, August, 1978.
Mike Channon—Southampton to Manchester C. £300,000, July, 1977.
Leighton James—Burnley to Derby Co. £300,000, December, 1975.
Martin Dobson—Burnley to Everton £300,000, August, 1974.
Peter Eastoe—Q.P.R. to Everton £280,000, March, 1979.
Mick Walsh—Everton to Q.P.R. £280,000, March, 1979.
Derek Hales—Charlton Ath. to Derby Co. £280,000, December, 1976.

Dave Watson—Sunderland to Manchester C. £280,000, June, 1975.
Steve Wicks—Chelsea to Derby Co. £275,000, January, 1979.
Peter Osgood—Chelsea to Southampton £275,000, March, 1974.
Dennis Tueart—Sunderland to Manchester C. £275,000, March, 1974.
Peter Shilton—Stoke C. to Nottm. Forest £270,000, September, 1977.
Neil McNab—Tottenham Hotspur to Bolton W. £250,000, November, 1978.
Gordon Hill—Manchester U, to Derby Co. £250,000, April, 1978.
Tommy Craig—Newcastle U. to Aston Villa, £250,000, January, 1978.
Asa Hartford—W.B.A. to Manchester C. £250,000, August, 1974.
Tony Currie—Sheffield U. to Leeds U. £245,000, June, 1976.
Alan Sunderland—Wolverhampton W. to Arsenal £240,000, November, 1977.
Larry Lloyd—Liverpool to Coventry £240,000, August, 1974.
Duncan McKenzie—Nottm. Forest to Leeds £240,000, August, 1974.
Alan Hudson—Chelsea to Stoke £240,000, January, 1974.
Alberto Tarantini—Boca Juniors to Birmingham C. £225,000, October 1978.
David Hay—Celtic to Chelsea £225,000, August, 1974.
David Nish—Leicester to Derby Co. £225,000, August, 1972.
Glenn Roeder—Orient to Q.P.R., £220,000, August 1978.
Paul Mariner—Plymouth Arg. to Ipswich T. £220,000, October, 1976.
Alan Ball—Everton to Arsenal £220,000, December, 1971.
Ted MacDougall—Bournemouth to Manchester Utd. £220,000, September, 1972.

Leading League Scorers 1978-79

DIVISION ONE—24: Worthington (Bolton W.); 21: Dalglish (Liverpool); 18: A. Brown (W.B.A.); 17: Stapleton (Arsenal); 16: Johnson (Liverpool), Hawley (Leeds U.); 15: Gowling (Bolton W.), Langley (Chelsea), Regis (W.B.A.), Wallace (Coventry C.); 14: Birtles (Nottingham F.), Burns, (Middlesbrough).

DIVISION TWO—24: Robson (West Ham U.); 21: Bruce (Preston N.E.), Rowell (Sunderland); 20: Biley (Cambridge U.); 18: Randall (Stoke C.) (inc. 13 for Bristol R.); 17: Cross (West Ham U.); 16: Buchanan (Cardiff C.), O'Callaghan (Stoke C.); 15: Robinson (Charlton Ath.). .

DIVISION THREE—29: Jenkins (Watford); 26: Binney (Plymouth Arg.); 24: Edwards (Hull C.); 21: Blissett (Watford); 20: Edwards (Chester), Beamish (Bury) (inc. 4 for Port Vale); 19: Waddle (Swansea C.); 18: Kellow (Blackpool) (inc. 7 for Exeter C.), Kemp (Carlisle U.), Westwood (Gillingham), Austin (Mansfield T.) (inc. 13 for Walsall).

DIVISION FOUR—26: Dungworth (Aldershot); 22: Cork (Wimbledon); 21: Lee (Stockport Co.), Bell (Barnsley) (inc. 3 for Halifax T.); 19: Reilly (Northampton T.), Goddard (Newport C.), Leslie (Wimbledon); 18: Bradd (Stockport Co.).

LEAGUE'S TOP GOALSCORERS SINCE 1952

1978–79	R. Jenkins (Watford)	29
1977–78	A. Curtis (Swansea C.) and S. Phillips (Brentford)	32
1976–77	P. Ward (Brighton & H. A.)	32
1975–76	R. McNeil (Hereford U.)	35
1974–75	R. McNeil (Hereford U.)	31
1973–74	B. Yeo (Gillingham)	31
1972–73	B. Robson (West Ham) and F. Binney (Exeter)	28
1971–72	E. MacDougall (Bournemouth) and A. Wood (Shrewsbury)	35
1970–71	E. MacDougall (Bournemouth)	42
1969–70	G. Jones (Bury) and A. Kinsey (Wrexham)	26
1968–69	J. Greaves (Tottenham)	27
1967–68	G. Best (Manchester Utd.) and R. Davies (Southampton)	28
1966–67	R. Davies (Southampton)	37
1965–66	K. Hector (Bradford)	44
1964–65	A. Jeffrey (Doncaster)	36
1963–64	H. MacIlmoyle (Carlisle)	39
1962–63	J. Greaves (Tottenham)	37
1961–62	R. Hunt (Liverpool) and B. Thomas (Scunthorpe and Newcastle)	41
1960–61	T. Bly (Peterborough)	52
1959–60	C. Holton (Watford)	48
1958–59	B. Clough (Middlesbrough)	43
1957–58	T. Johnston (Blackburn and Leyton O.)	44
1956–57	A. Rowley (Leicester)	44
1955–56	R. Collins (Torquay)	40
1954–55	T. Briggs (Blackburn)	33
1953–54	J. Charles (Leeds)	42
1952–53	G. Rowley (Leicester)	39

Master Gunners

In 1978 Arsenal cruised to Wembley and then lost a timid final, playing poorly. In 1979 it was the other way around. Arsenal had to struggle to reach the final, especially in their first cup match against Sheffield Wednesday, which went to five games before a result. In later rounds, both League Cup finalists had to be overcome, and that meant Forest losing at home for the first time in two years.

Manchester United had a less traumatic journey to the final although things got tough towards the end, when they scraped a draw at White Hart Lane in the quarter-final, going on to win the replay 2–0, and then had to face up to Liverpool, the team in form, in the semis. United almost won this game at the first attempt, but Liverpool made a characteristic late comeback to draw. United allowed no such thing to happen in the replay.

The final will be remembered down the years for an astonishing last four minutes, although it was not a great game. The last 'great' final was probably in 1953, when Stanley Matthews excelled. But the fans at Wembley this year at least had the sunshine, five goals, and a young Irishman called Liam Brady.

After a nervous first 15 minutes, Arsenal opened the scoring when Brady beat a couple of defenders and pushed the ball forward to Price. Price also beat a defender before cutting the ball beyond the reach of the inexperienced Bailey, and Talbot and Sunderland lunged together to put the ball away. Later Talbot was confirmed as the scorer. Another Brady run just before half-time ended in a cross to the far post which Stapleton headed in.

The second half was more exciting, with both sides creating chances, but with four minutes left to play, people were starting to leave the stadium. Then United were awarded a free kick in a harmless spot some way out from goal. The ball floated into a crowded penalty area, was half cleared, Jordan fired it back and McQueen, falling as he struck, scooped the ball home. People started coming back into the stadium. Two minutes later, with two minutes to go, McIlroy made a brilliant run down the right, beating men until he had only Jennings left to pass. He did so emphatically. People started sitting down again – half an hour's extra time seemed certain.

Arsenal kicked off for the second time in two minutes, and now with less than a minute left to play. Straight from the kick-off Brady picked the ball up, took it bewilderingly down the left side of the United midfield, and crossed to the far post again. This time Sunderland was there on his own, and drove the ball home.

FIRST ROUND

Aldershot	1	2	Weymouth	1	0	
Altrincham	4		Southport	3		
Barnet	3 3	0	Woking	3 3	3	
Barnsley	5		Worksop	1		
Blackpool	2		Lincoln	1		
Bournemouth	2		Hitchin	1		
Bradford C.	1		Port Vale	0		
Carlisle U.	1		Halifax T.	0		
Chester	1 5		Runcorn	1 0		

Chorley	0	
Colchester U.	4	
Darlington	1	1
Dartford	1	
Doncaster R.	2	
Exeter C.	1	
Gravesend	0	0
Hartlepool U.	1	
Hereford U.	0	
Hull C.	2	
Leatherhead	2	
Maidstone	1	
Mansfield T.	0	
Nuneaton		
Portsmouth	2	
Reading	0	2
Rochdale		
Rotherham	3	
Scunthorpe U.	1	0
Southend U.	3	
Stockport Co.	5	
Swansea	4	
Swindon T.	2	
Tranmere R.	2	
Walsall	0	
Watford	3	
Wealdstone	0	
Wigan Ath.	2	1
Worcester	2	
Yeovil	0	
York C.	1	5

Scarborough	1	
Oxford U.	2	
Chesterfield	1	0
AP Leamington	2	
Huddersfield T.	1	
Brentford	0	
Wimbledon	0	1
Grimsby T.	1	
Newport Co.	1	
Stafford R.	1	
Merthyr	1	
Wycombe W.	1	
Shrewsbury T.	2	
Crewe Alex.	2	
Northampton T.		
Gillingham	0	1
Droylsden	1	
Workington	0	
Sheffield W.	1	1
Peterborough U.	2	
Morecambe	1	
Hillingdon	1	
March	0	
Boston U.	1	
Torquay	2	
Dagenham	0	
Enfield	5	
Bury	2	4
Plymouth Arg.		
Barking	1	
Blyth Spartans	1	3

SECOND ROUND

Barking	1	
Barnsley	1	1
Bury	3	
Carlisle U.	3	
Crewe Alex.	0	
Darlington	2	
Doncaster R.	0	
Droylsden	0	
AP Leamington	0	
Leatherhead	1	0
Maidstone	1	
Newport Co.	0	2
Portsmouth	0	
Stockport Co.	4	
Swansea	2	5
Swindon T.	3	
Tranmere R.	1	0
Watford	1	0
Wimbledon	1	2
York C.	3	

Aldershot	2	
Rotherham	1	2
Blackpool	1	
Hull C.	0	
Hartlepool U.	1	
Chester	1	
Shrewsbury T.	3	
Altrincham	1	
Torquay	1	
Colchester U.	1	4
Exeter C.	0	
Worcester	0	1
Reading	1	
Bradford C.	2	
Woking	2	3
Enfield	1	
Sheffield W.	1	4
Southend U.	1	1
Bournemouth	1	1
Scarborough	0	

ARSENAL (2) 3
Talbot, Stapleton, Sunderland
At Wembley, attendance 100,000

Third Round	Fourth Round	Fifth Round	Sixth Round	Semi-finals
Middlesbro' 1 0				
Crystal Pal. 1 1	Crystal Pal. 3			
Bristol C. 3	Bristol C. 0	Crystal Pal. 0		
Bolton W. 1				
Newcastle U. 3	Newcastle U. 1 0		Wolver'ton W.1 3	
Torquay 1	Wolver'ton W.1 1	Wolver'ton W. 1		
Br'ton & H.A. 2				
Wolver'ton W. 3				Wolver'ton W. 0
Sheffield U. 0	Aldershot 2			
Aldershot 0 1	Swindon T. 1	Aldershot 2 1		
Swindon T. 0				
Cardiff C. 0			Shrewsbury T. 1 1	
Shrewsbury U. 1	Shrewsbury T. 2			
Cambridge U. 0	Manchester C. 0	Shrewsbury T. 2 3		
Man. C. 2				
Rother'm U. 0				
Hartlepool U. 2	Leeds U. 3 0			
Leeds U. 6	W.B.A. 3 2	W.B.A. 1 1		
Coventry C. 2 0				
W.B.A. 2 4			Southampton 1 0	
Preston N.E. 3	Preston N.E. 0			
Derby Co. 0	Southampton 1	Southampton 1 2		
Wimbledon 0				Arsenal 2
Southampton 2				
Nott'ham F. 0	Nott'ham F. 3			
Aston Villa 0	York C. 1	Nott'ham F. 0		
York C. 2				
Luton T. 0			Arsenal 1 2	
Shef.W. 1 1 2 3	Arsenal 2			
Arsenal 1 1 2 2	Notts Co. 0	Arsenal 1		
Notts Co. 4				
Reading 2				

104

MANCHESTER U. (0) 2
McQueen, McIlroy
Receipts £500,000

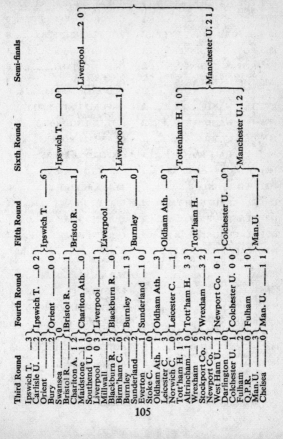

Third Round	Fourth Round	Fifth Round	Sixth Round	Semi-finals
Ipswich T. ——3				
Carlisle U. ——1	Ipswich T. ——0 2			
Orient ——3		Ipswich T. ——6		
Bury ——2	Orient ——0 0			
Swansea ——0			Ipswich T. ——0	
Bristol R. ——1	1Bristol R. ——1			
Charlton A. ——1 2		Bristol R. ——1		
Maidstone ——1 0	Charlton Ath. ——0			Liverpool ——2 0
Southend U. ——0 0				
Liverpool ——1 0 3	Liverpool ——1			
Millwall ——1		Liverpool ——3		
Blackburn R. ——2	Blackburn R. ——0			
Birm'ham C. ——0			Liverpool ——1	
Burnley ——1 3	Burnley ——1			
Sunderland ——1 0		Burnley ——0		
Everton ——1	Sunderland ——1 0			
Stoke C. ——0				
Oldham Ath. ——3	Oldham Ath. ——3			
Leicester C. ——1		Oldham Ath. ——0		
Norwich C. ——1	Leicester C. ——1			
Tott'ham H. ——1 3			Tottenham H. ——1 0	
Altrincham ——0	Tott'ham H. ——3 3			Manchester U. 2 1
Wrexham ——6		Tott'ham H. ——1		
Stockport Co. ——3	Wrexham ——3 2			
Newport Co. ——1				
West Ham U. ——1	Newport Co. ——0 1			
Darlington ——1				
Colchester U. ——1	Colchester U. ——0 0	Colchester U. ——0		
Fulham ——2			Manchester U.1 2	
Q.P.R. ——0	Fulham ——1 0			
Man. U. ——3		Man.U. ——1		
Chelsea ——0	Man. U. ——1 1			

FA CUP FINALS 1872-1979

Some goalscorers are not available in the early years

Year	Winner	Score	Loser	Score
1872	THE WANDERERS	1	ROYAL ENGINEERS	0
	Betts			
1873	THE WANDERERS	2	OXFORD UNIVERSITY	0
	Kinnaird, Wollaston			
1874	OXFORD UNIVERSITY	2	ROYAL ENGINEERS	0
	Mackarness, Patton			
1875	ROYAL ENGINEERS	1	OLD ETONIANS	1
	Unknown		*Unknown*	
	ROYAL ENGINEERS	2	OLD ETONIANS	0
	Scorers in replay: Renny-Tailyour and one from a rush			
1876	THE WANDERERS	0	OLD ETONIANS	0
	THE WANDERERS	3	OLD ETONIANS	0
	Wollaston, Hughes 2			
1877	THE WANDERERS	2	OXFORD UNIVERSITY	0
	Kenrick, Lindsay		*(After extra time)*	
1878	THE WANDERERS	3	ROYAL ENGINEERS	1
	Kenrick 2, unknown		*Unknown*	
1879	OLD ETONIANS	1	CLAPHAM ROVERS	0
	Clerke			
1880	CLAPHAM ROVERS	1	OXFORD UNIVERSITY	0
	Lloyd-Jones			
1881	OLD CARTHUSIANS	3	OLD ETONIANS	0
	Page, Wynyard, Tod			
1882	OLD ETONIANS	1	BLACKBURN R.	0
	Anderson			
1883	BLACKBURN OLYMPIC	2	OLD ETONIANS	1
	Costley, unknown		*Goodhart (After extra time)*	
1884	BLACKBURN R.	2	QUEEN'S PARK	1
	Forrest, Brown		*Christie*	
1885	BLACKBURN R.	2	QUEEN'S PARK	0
	Forrest, Brown			
1886	BLACKBURN R.	0	W.B.A.	0
	BLACKBURN R.	2	W.B.A.	0
	Brown, Sowerbutts			
1887	ASTON VILLA	2	W.B.A.	0
	Hunter, Hodgetts			
1888	W.B.A.	2	PRESTON N.E.	1
	Woodall, Bayliss		*Goodall*	
1889	PRESTON N.E.	3	WOLVERHAMPTON W.	0
	Ross, Dewhurst, Thomson			
1890	BLACKBURN R.	6	SHEFFIELD W.	1
	Dewar, Lofthouse, John, Townley 3		*Bennett*	
1891	BLACKBURN R.	3	NOTTS CO.	1
	Dewar, John, Townley		*Oswald*	
1892	W.B.A.	3	ASTON VILLA	0
	Reynolds, Nicholls, Geddes			
1893	WOLVERHAMPTON W.	1	EVERTON	0
	Allen			
1894	NOTTS CO.	4	BOLTON W.	1
	Watson, Logan 3		*Cassidy*	

1895	ASTON VILLA ....1 *Unknown*	W.B.A. 0	
1896	SHEFFIELD W. ....2 *Spiksley* 2	WOLVERHAMPTON W. ...1 *Black*	
1897	ASTON VILLA ....3 *Crabtree, Campbell, Wheldon*	EVERTON ....2 *Boyle, Bell*	
1898	NOTTINGHAM F. ....3 *McPherson, Capes* 2	DERBY CO. ....1 *Bloomer*	
1899	SHEFFIELD U. ....4 *Bennett, Beer, Almond, Priest*	DERBY CO. ....1 *Boag*	
1900	BURY ....4 *Wood, McLuckie* 2, *Plant*	SOUTHAMPTON..............0	
1901	TOTTENHAM H. ....2 *Brown* 2	SHEFFIELD U. ....2 *Bennett, Priest*	
	TOTTENHAM H. ....3 *Cameron, Smith, Brown*	SHEFFIELD U. ....1 *Priest*	
1902	SHEFFIELD U. ....1 *Common*	SOUTHAMPTON..............1 *Brown*	
	SHEFFIELD U. ....2 *Hedley, Barnes*	SOUTHAMPTON..............1 *Brown*	
1903	BURY ....6 *Wood, Sagar, Ross, Plant, Leeming* 2	DERBY CO. 0	
1904	MANCHESTER C.............1 *Meredith*	BOLTON W. 0	
1905	ASTON VILLA ....2 *Hampton* 2	NEWCASTLE U. 0	
1906	EVERTON ....1 *Young*	NEWCASTLE U. 0	
1907	SHEFFIELD W. ....2 *Stewart, Simpson*	EVERTON ....1 *Sharp*	
1908	WOLVERHAMPTON W....3 *Hunt, Harrison, Hedley*	NEWCASTLE U. ....1 *Howie*	
1909	MANCHESTER U. ....1 *A. Tyrnbull*	BRISTOL C. 0	
1910	NEWCASTLE U. ....1 *Rutherford*	BARNSLEY ....1 *Tuffnell*	
	NEWCASTLE U. ....2 *Shepherd* 2 (1 *pen.*)	BARNSLEY 0	
1911	BRADFORD C. 0	NEWCASTLE U. 0	
	BRADFORD C. ....1 *Spiers*	NEWCASTLE U. 0	
1912	BARNSLEY ....2 *Tuffnell* 2	W.B.A. ....0 (*After extra time*)	
1913	ASTON VILLA ....1 *Barber*	SUNDERLAND 0	
1914	BURNLEY ....1 *Freeman*	LIVERPOOL 0	
1915	SHEFFIELD U. ....3 *Simmons, Fazackerley, Kitchen*	CHELSEA 0	
1920	ASTON VILLA ....1 *Kirton*	HUDDERSFIELD T. 0	
1921	TOTTENHAM H. ....1 *Dimmock*	WOLVERHAMPTON W. ...0	

Year	Winner	Score	Runner-up	Score
1922	HUDDERSFIELD T.	1	PRESTON N.E.	0
	Smith(pen)			
1923	BOLTON W.	2	WEST HAM U.	0
	Jack, J. R. Smith			
1924	NEWCASTLE U.	2	ASTON VILLA	0
	Harris, Seymour			
1925	SHEFFIELD U.	1	CARDIFF C.	0
	Tunstall			
1926	BOLTON W.	1	MANCHESTER C.	0
	Jack			
1927	CARDIFF C.	1	ARSENAL	0
	Ferguson			
1928	BLACKBURN R.	3	HUDDERSFIELD T.	1
	Roscamp 2, M'Lean		A. Jackson	
1929	BOLTON W.	2	PORTSMOUTH	0
	Butler, Blackmore			
1930	ARSENAL	2	HUDDERSFIELD T.	0
	Lambert, James			
1931	W.B.A.	2	BIRMINGHAM C.	1
	W. G. Richardson 2		Bradford	
1932	NEWCASTLE U.	2	ARSENAL	1
	Allen 2		John	
1933	EVERTON	3	MANCHESTER C.	0
	Dunn, Dean, Stein			
1934	MANCHESTER C.	2	PORTSMOUTH	1
	Tilson 2		Rutherford	
1935	SHEFFIELD W.	4	W.B.A.	2
	Hooper, Palethorpe, Rimmer 2		Sandford, Boyes	
1936	ARSENAL	1	SHEFFIELD U.	0
	Drake			
1937	SUNDERLAND	3	PRESTON N.E.	1
	Carter, Gurney, Burbanks		F. O'Donnell	
1938	PRESTON N.E.	1	HUDDERSFIELD T.	0
	Mutch(pen)			
1939	PORTSMOUTH	4	WOLVERHAMPTON W.	1
	Anderson, Barlow, Parker 2		Dorsett	
1946	DERBY CO.	4	CHARLTON ATH.	1
	H. Turner (o.g.), Stamps 2, Doherty		H. Turner (After extra time)	
1947	CHARLTON ATH.	1	BURNLEY	0
	Duffy			
1948	MANCHESTER U.	4	BLACKPOOL	2
	Anderson, Rowley 2, Pearson		Shimwell(pen), Mortensen	
1949	WOLVERHAMPTON W.	3	LEICESTER C.	1
	Smyth, Pye 2		Griffiths	
1950	ARSENAL	2	LIVERPOOL	0
	Lewis 2			
1951	NEWCASTLE U.	2	BLACKPOOL	0
	Milburn 2			
1952	NEWCASTLE U.	1	ARSENAL	0
	G. Robledo			
1953	BLACKPOOL	4	BOLTON W.	3
	Mortensen 3, Perry		Bell, Moir, Lofthouse	

1954	W.B.A. 3	PRESTON N.E. 2	
	Griffin, Allen 2	*Wayman, Morrison*	
1955	NEWCASTLE U. 3	MANCHESTER C. 1	
	Milburn, Hannah, Mitchell	*Johnstone*	
1956	MANCHESTER C............3	BIRMINGHAM C. 1	
	Johnstone, Hayes, Dyson	*Kinsey*	
1957	ASTON VILLA 2	MANCHESTER U. 1	
	McParland 2	*T. Taylor*	
1958	BOLTON W.....................2	MANCHESTER U. 0	
	Lofthouse 2		
1959	NOTTINGHAM F. 2	LUTON T. 1	
	Dwight, Wilson	*Pacey*	
1960	WOLVERHAMPTON W. ...3	BLACKBURN R. 0	
	Deeley 2, McGrath (o.g.)		
1961	TOTTENHAM H. 2	LEICESTER C. 0	
	Smith, Dyson		
1962	TOTTENHAM H. 3	BURNLEY 1	
	Blanchflower (p), Smith, Greaves	*Robson*	
1963	MANCHESTER U. 3	LEICESTER C. 1	
	Herd 2, Law	*Keyworth*	
1964	WEST HAM U. 3	PRESTON N.E. 2	
	Boyce, Hurst, Sissons	*Dawson, Holden*	
1965	LIVERPOOL 2	LEEDS U. 1	
	Hunt, St John	*Bremner*	
1966	EVERTON 3	SHEFFIELD W. 2	
	Trebilcock 2, Temple	*McCalliog, Ford*	
1967	TOTTENHAM H. 2	CHELSEA 1	
	Robertson, Saul	*Tambling*	
1968	W.B.A. 1	EVERTON 0	
	Astle		
1969	MANCHESTER C. 1	LEICESTER C. 0	
	Young		
1970	CHELSEA 2	LEEDS U. 2	
	Houseman, Hutchinson	*Charlton, Jones*	
	CHELSEA 2	LEEDS U. 1	
	Webb, Osgood	*Jones (After extra time)*	
1971	ARSENAL 2	LIVERPOOL 1	
	Kelly, George	*Heighway (After extra time)*	
1972	LEEDS U. 1	ARSENAL 0	
	Clarke		
1973	SUNDERLAND 1	LEEDS U. 0	
	Porterfield		
1974	LIVERPOOL 3	NEWCASTLE U. 0	
	Keegan 2, Heighway		
1975	WEST HAM U. 2	FULHAM 0	
	A. Taylor 2		
1976	SOUTHAMPTON 1	MANCHESTER U. 0	
	Stokes		
1977	MANCHESTER U. 2	LIVERPOOL 1	
	Pearson, J. Greenhoff	*Case*	
1978	IPSWICH T.......................1	ARSENAL 0	
	Osborne		
1979	ARSENAL 3	MANCHESTER U. 2	
	Talbot, Stapleton, Sunderland	*McQueen, McIlroy*	

SUMMARY OF CUP WINNERS FROM 1871

Aston Villa 7	West Ham 2
Blackburn Rovers 6	Barnsley 1
Newcastle 6	Blackburn Olympic 1
Arsenal 5	Blackpool 1
Tottenham 5	Bradford City 1
Wanderers 5	Burnley 1
West Bromwich Albion 5	Cardiff 1
Bolton 4	Charlton 1
Manchester City 4	Chelsea 1
Manchester United 4	Clapham Rovers 1
Sheffield United 4	Derby 1
Wolverhampton 4	Huddersfield 1
Everton 3	Ipswich Town 1
Sheffield Wednesday 3	Leeds..................................1
Bury 2	Notts County 1
Liverpool 2	Old Carthusians 1
Nottingham Forest 2	Oxford University 1
Old Etonians 2	Portsmouth 1
Preston 2	Royal Engineers 1
Sunderland 2	Southampton 1

APPEARANCES IN FINAL

Newcastle 11	Sheffield Wednesday 5	Barnsley 2
Arsenal 10	Tottenham 5	Birmingham 2
West Brom. Albion ...10	Wanderers 5	Bury 2
Aston Villa 9	Derby 4	Cardiff 2
Blackburn Rovers 8	Leeds....................4	Charlton 2
Manchester United ...8	Leicester City 4	Clapham Rovers ..2
Wolverhampton 8	Oxford University ..4	Nottingham Forest ...2
Bolton 7	Royal Engineers ..4	Notts County 2
Everton 7	Blackpool 3	Queen's Pk. (G'gow) 2
Manchester City 7	Burnley 3	Blackburn Olympic...1
Preston 7	Chelsea 3	Bradford City ...1
Liverpool................6	Portsmouth 3	Bristol City 1
Old Etonians 6	Southampton 3	Fulham 1
Sheffield United 6	Sunderland 3	Ipswich Town 1
Huddersfield 5	West Ham 3	Luton 1
		Old Carthusians 1

LEAGUE CUP FINALS 1961-78

Played as two legs up to 1966

1961	ROTHERHAM U. 2	ASTON VILLA 0	
	Webster, Kirkman		
	ASTON VILLA 3	ROTHERHAM U. 0	
	O'Neill, Burrows, McParland		
1962	ROCHDALE 0	NORWICH C. 3	
		Lythgoe 2, Punton	
	NORWICH C. 1	ROCHDALE 0	
	Hill		
1963	BIRMINGHAM C. 3	ASTON VILLA 1	
	Leek 2, Bloomfield	*Thomson*	
	ASTON VILLA 0	BIRMINGHAM C. 0	
1964	STOKE C. 1	LEICESTER C. 1	
	Bebbington	*Gibson*	
	LEICESTER C. 3	STOKE C. 2	
	Stringfellow, Gibson, Riley	*Viollett, Kinnell*	
1965	CHELSEA 3	LEICESTER C. 2	
	Tambling, Venables (pen),	*Appleton, Goodfellow*	
	McCreadie		
	LEICESTER C. 0	CHELSEA 0	
1966	WEST HAM U. 2	W.B.A. 1	
	Moore, Byrne	*Astle*	
	W.B.A. 4	WEST HAM U. 1	
	Kaye, Brown, Clark, Williams	*Peters*	
1967	Q.P.R. 3	W.B.A. 2	
	Morgan R., Marsh, Lazarus	*Clark C. 2*	
1968	LEEDS U. 1	ARSENAL 0	
	Cooper		
1969	SWINDON T. 3	ARSENAL 1	
	Smart, Rogers 2	*Gould*	
1970	MANCHESTER C. 2	W.B.A. 1	
	Doyle, Pardoe	*Astle*	
1971	ASTON VILLA 0	TOTTENHAM H. 2	
		Chivers 2	
1972	CHELSEA 1	STOKE C. 2	
	Osgood	*Conroy, Eastham*	
1973	TOTTENHAM H. 1	NORWICH C. 0	
	Coates		
1974	WOLVERHAMPTON W. 2	MANCHESTER C. 1	
	Hibbitt, Richards	*Bell*	
1975	ASTON VILLA 1	NORWICH C. 0	
	Graydon		
1976	MANCHESTER C. 2	NEWCASTLE U. 1	
	Barnes, Tueart	*Gowling*	
1977	ASTON VILLA 0	EVERTON 0	
Replay	ASTON VILLA 1	EVERTON 1	
	Kenyon (o.g.)	*Latchford*	
Replay	ASTON VILLA 3	EVERTON 2	
	Little 2, Nicholl	*Latchford, Lyons*	
1978	NOTTINGHAM F. 1	LIVERPOOL 0	
	Robertson (pen)		

Forest, again

Nottingham Forest in defeating Southampton by three goals to two became the first club successfully to defend the Football League Cup. The match, whilst never an epic, will be remembered for a long while by many people for different reasons.

Off the field Nottingham and Southampton both managed to catch the headlines. Brian Clough showed everyone just how much Peter Taylor means in Nottingham's success by leaving it to him to lead the team out at Wembley. This was the first time a club manager had foregone the honour of leading his team out. Two days before the final Alan Ball for Southampton, with the lack of psychological understanding that some of our leading players seem to specialise in, accused Forest of being a negative team. If the Forest players were in need of motivation then this was like a gift from the gods.

The season's unusual wintry weather had left its mark on the hallowed turf and the heavy and lumpy surface was hardly conducive to making the game a classic. It was, however, a good match with Southampton in complete control for the first 25 minutes.

After 16 minutes came the first goal. Boyer on the left passed to Ball, he pushed it on to Peach who dribbled across the goal and gave it back to Ball, who, whilst Peach rushed through the centre of the defence, was engineering a superb chip to land exactly at Peach's feet. Shilton dived at his feet, but Peach checked, waltzed around him and Southampton were in the lead. Shilton and Clark remained overworked for the next 14 minutes, and really the Saints should have put the match out of Forest's reach.

Two-thirds of the way through the first half Ball began to lose control of the midfield to Gemmill, and so the match slowly began to change as Forest took control.

Five minutes into the second half and Birtles had levelled the score. It was a surprising goal. Chris Nicholl appeared to be standing on the ball as though he was unsure whether to pass it back to his goalkeeper, who was having a bad game. Perhaps it is best described by Birtles who said, 'I saw Chris Nicholl day dreaming so I nipped in and whacked it home'.

Forest's second goal was again scored by Birtles who dribbled all the way from the centre then rounded the keeper and slotted it in. Five minutes later Gemmill played a perfect diagonal pass into the penalty area, Woodcock collected it, turned superbly and the ball was in the net.

With eight minutes to go Forest were leading 3–1 and it stayed that way for the next six minutes, when Holmes scored the best goal of the match. The ball came to him on the left edge of the penalty area and he volleyed home a terrific shot which left Shilton with no chance.

Forest players, their wives and girl-friends went back to Nottingham to a private disco at the Club. Brian Clough, different as ever, went off home. He stopped and bought fish and chips for all his family 'stuck the Cup on top of the telly and watched Match of the Day' – surely another first.

FIRST ROUND

Aldershot	0 0	Millwall	1 1
Barnsley	1 0	Chesterfield	2 0
Bournemouth	0 1	Exeter C.	1 1
Bradford C.	2 1	Lincoln C.	0 1
Bristol R.	2 0	Hereford U.	1 4
Cambridge U.	2 1	Northampton T.	2 2
Cardiff C.	1 1	Oxford U.	2 2
Carlisle U.	2 1	Blackpool	2 2
Colchester U.	2 0	Charlton Ath.	2 0
Crewe Alex.	1 4	Rochdale	0 2
Doncaster R.	0 1 0	Sheffield W.	1 0 1
Grimsby T.	2 3	York C.	0 0
Hull C.	0 2 0	Peterborough U.	1 1 1
Mansfield T.	0 2	Darlington	1 2
Newport Co.	2 0	Swansea C.	1 5
Plymouth Arg.	1 2	Torquay U.	1 1
Portsmouth	0 2	Swindon T.	0 4
Port Vale	0 1	Chester	3 1
Preston N.E.	3 2	Huddersfield T.	0 2
Reading	3 2	Gillingham	1 1
Rotherham U.	5 1	Hartlepool U.	0 1
Scunthorpe U.	0 0	Notts. Co.	1 3
Southend U.	1 1	Wimbledon	0 4
Tranmere R.	1 1	Wigan Ath.	1 2
Walsall	2 2	Halifax	1 0
Watford	4 3	Brentford	0 1
Wrexham	2 2	Bury	0 1
Shrewsbury	1 1	Stockport	0 3

First team mentioned in each pair played first leg at home

113

NOTTINGHAM FOREST (0) 3

Birtles 2, Woodcock
At Wembley, attendance 100,000

Nott'gham F. 3 0   **Watford 1 0**

Second Round

Everton	8
Wimbledon	2
Fulham	0
Darlington	2
Oxford U.	1
Plymouth A.	1
Oldham Ath.	0
Nott'gham F.0	4
Burnley	1
Bradford C.	1
Br'ton & H.A.	0
Millwall	0
Middlesbro'	0
Peterboro'	0 1
West Ham U.	0 1
Swindon T.	2
Orient	2
Chesterfield	2
Walsall	1
Charlton A.	1
North'pton	0 1
Hereford U.	0 0
Sunderland	0
Stoke C.	2
Exeter C.	1
Blackburn	2
Bolton W.	1
Chelsea	2
Stockport	1
Manchester U.	3
Watford	2
Newcastle U.	1

Third Round

Everton	1
Darlington	0
Oxford U.	0
Nott'gham F.	5
Burnley	1
Br'ton & H.A.	3
Peterboro'	1 2
Swindon T.	1 0
Chesterfield	4
Charlton A.	5
North'pton T.	1
Stoke C.	3
Exeter C.	2
Bolton W.	1
Manchester U.	1
Watford	2

Fourth Round

Everton	2
Nottingham F.	3
Br'ton & H.A.	1
Peterboro'	0
Charlton A.	2
Stoke C.	3
Exeter C.	0
Watford	2

Fifth Round

Nottingham F.	3
Br'ton & H.A.	1
Stoke C.	0 1
Watford	0 3

Semi-finals

Nott'gham F.	3 0
Watford	1 0

SOUTHAMPTON (1) 2

Peach, Holmes
Receipts £422,000

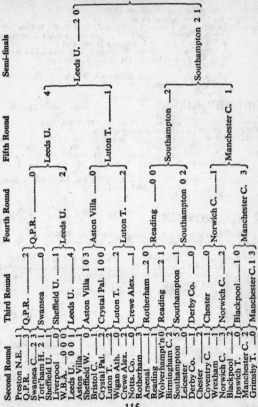

Semi-finals

Leeds U. — 2 0

Southampton 2 1

Fifth Round

Leeds U. — 4

Luton T. — 1

Southampton — 2

Manchester C. — 1

Fourth Round

Q.P.R. — 0

Leeds U. — 2

Aston Villa — 0

Luton T. — 2

Reading — 0 0

Southampton 0 2

Norwich C. — 1

Manchester C. — 3

Third Round

Q.P.R. — 2

Swansea — 0

Sheffield U. — 1

Leeds U. — 4

Aston Villa 1 0 3

Crystal Pal. 1 0 0

Luton T. — 2

Crewe Alex. — 1

Rotherham — 2 0

Reading — 2 1

Southampton — 1

Derby Co. — 0

Chester — 0

Norwich C. — 2

Blackpool — 1 0

Manchester C. 1 3

Second Round

Preston N.E. — 1

Q.P.R. — 3

Swansea C. — 2 3

Tott'ham H. 2 1

Sheffield U. — 1

Liverpool — 0 0

W.B.A. — 0 0

Leeds U. — 0 1

Aston Villa — 1

Sheffield W. — 0

Bristol C. — 1

Crystal Pal. — 2

Luton T. — 2

Wigan Ath. — 0

Crewe Alex. — 0

Notts. Co. — 3

Rotherham — 1

Arsenal — 1

Wolverhampt'n 0

Birmingham C. 2

Southampton — 5

Leicester — 1

Chester — 0

Coventry C. — 1

Wrexham — 3

Norwich C. — 2

Blackpool — 0

Ipswich T. — 0

Manchester C. 2

Grimsby T. — 0

115

SCOTTISH CLUBS

ABERDEEN PREM. DIV.

Ground: Pittodrie Stadium, Aberdeen. (Aberdeen 21428).
Colours: Scarlet shirts; scarlet shorts.
GOALS—League (59): Harper 19 (4 pens.), Archibald 13, Strachan 5
(1 pen.), Jarvie 4, McGhee 4, Sullivan 4, McMaster 3, Davidson
2, Scanlon 2, Cooper 1, Fleming 1, McLeish 1.
League Cup (25): Harper 9 (2 pens.), Archibald 3, Kennedy 3,
Sullivan 3, Scanlon 2, Davidson 1, Fleming 1, Jarvie 1,
McLellard 1, Rougrie 1.
Cup (12): Archibald 4, Harper 3, Scanlon 2, Davidson 1,
McMaster 1, Miller 1.

AIRDRIEONIANS DIV. 1

Ground: Broomfield Park, Gatlea Road, Aidrie. (Aidrie 62067).
Colours: White shirts with red diamond; white shorts.
GOALS—League (72): Clark 23 (2 pens.), Goldthorp 16 (1 pen.), Mc-
Guire 8 (1 pen.), Lapsley 6 (5 pens.), McVeigh 4, March 4 (2
pens.), McCann 2, Jonquin 1, Kirkland 1, McCormack 1,
McCulloch 1, McKeown 1, Short 1, Smith 1, Walker 1, own
goal 1.
League Cup (10): Clark 2, Goldthorp 2, Lapsley 2 (2 pens.),
Walker 2, Jonquin 1, McCann 1.
Cup (1): Clark 1.

ALBION ROVERS DIV. 2

Ground: Clifton Hill Park, Coatbridge. (Coatbridge 21865).
Colours: Yellow shirts with white sleeves; white shorts with red stripes
on side.
GOALS—League (57): Cleland 24 (4 pens.), Hart 7, Hill 5, Leishman 5,
Franchetti 4, Shields 3, Loughran 2, Main 2, Allan 1, Coyle 1,
Gillespie 1, McGillivray 1, Robertson J. 1.
League Cup (0).
Cup (4): Loughran 2, Cleland 1, Main 1.

ALLOA DIV. 2

Ground: Recreation Park, Alloa. (Alloa 2695).
Colours: Gold shirts with black trim; black shorts.
GOALS—League (57): Irvine 13, Kelly 7 (1 pen.), Cochrane 6, Miller 6
(4 pens.), Morrison 6, Hamilton 5, Carberry 3, McIntosh 2,
McLeod 2, Muir 2, Donald 1, Henderson 1, Holt 1, Steele 1,
Wallace 1.
League Cup (6): Miller 2 (1 pen.), Morrison 2, Cochrane 1,
Steele 1.
Cup (2): Holt 1, Morrison 1.

116

ARBROATH
DIV. 1

Ground: Gayfield Park, Arbroath. (Arbroath 2157).
Colours: Maroon shirts; white shorts.
GOALS—League (50): Mylles 9, Yule 9, Kidd A. 8 (1 pen.), Gavine 7,
Fletcher 5 (1 pen.), Wilson 4, Carson 2, Kydd L. 2, Cargill 1,
McKenzie 1, Mitchell 1, own goal 1.
League Cup (6): McKenzie 2, Cargill 1, Fletcher 1, Gavine 1,
Yule 1.
Cup (0).

AYR UNITED
DIV. 1

Ground: Somerset Park, Ayr. (Ayr 63435).
Colours: White shirts with black trimmings; black shorts.
GOALS—League (71): McLaughlin 19 (7 pens.), Phillips 14, Christie 6,
McCall 6, McCutcheon 5, McSherry 5, Masterson 5, Cramond
4, Wells 2, McAllister 1, McLelland 1, Reilly 1, own goals 2.
League Cup (11): McLaughlin 4 (1 pen.), McLelland 3,
Cramond 2, McCall 2.
Cup (6): McLaughlin 3 (1 pen.), Phillips 2, McLelland 1.

BERWICK RANGERS
DIV. 1

Ground: Shielfield Park, Berwick-on-Tweed. (Berwick 7424).
Colours: Black and gold striped shirts; black shorts.
GOALS—League (82): Morton 20 (6 pens.), Tait 12, Davidson 9, McLean
9, Smith G. 8, McLeod 5, Georgeson 3, Jobson 3 (1 pen.),
Smith D. 3 (2 pens.), Wheatley 3, Moyes 2, Brown 1, McDowell
1, Rutherford 1, Smith I. 1, own goal 1.
League Cup (4): McLean 3, Rutherford 1.
Cup 3): Smith G. 2, Jobson 1.

BRECHIN CITY
DIV. 2

Ground: Glebe Park, Brechin. (Brechin 2856).
Colours: Red shirts; red shorts.
GOALS—League (49): Campbell I. 16, Gillespie 10, Cairns 4, Robb 4,
Watt 3 (3 pens.), Glover 2, Johnston 2, Campbell R. 1, Elvin 1,
Grant 1, Kyles 1, Laing 1, Reid 1, own goals 2.
League Cup (1): Campbell R. 1.
Cup (1): own goal 1.

CELTIC
PREM. DIV.

Ground: Celtic Park, Glasgow. (041-554 2710).
Colours: Green and white hooped shirts; white shorts.
GOALS—League (61): Lynch 7 (5 pens.), McAdam 7, Conn 6, Aitken 5,
McCluskey 5, Conroy 4, Lennox 4, Proven 4, Burns 3, Glavin 3,
(1 pen.), McGrain 3, MacLeod 3, Doyle 2, McDonald 2,
Davidson 1, Edvaldsson 1, own goal 1.

League Cup (20): McAdam 6, Doyle 3, Lynch 3 (2 pens.), Glavin 2 (1 pen.), Aitken 1, Conn 1, Conroy 1, Edvaldsson 1, Lennox 1, McDonald 1.
Cup (9): McCluskey 3, Lynch 2 (2 pens.), Burns 1, Doyle 1, Lennox 1, own goal 1.

CLYDE   DIV. 1

Ground: Shawfield Stadium, Glasgow. (041-647 6329).
Colours: White shirts with red trimmings; black shorts.
GOALS—League (54): Ward 10, Ahern 8 (3 pens.), Grant 8, Hood 7, Marshall 7, O'Neill 4, McCabe 3, Kean 2, Anderson 1, Brogan 1, Ferris 1, own goals 2.
League Cup (3): Ahern 1 (pen.), O'Neill 1, Ward 1.
Cup (1): Ahern 1 (pen.).

CLYDEBANK   DIV. 1

Ground: KilbowiePark, Clydebank. (041-952 2887).
Colours: Red shirts with broad white vertical stripe on front; black shorts.
GOALS—League 78): Miller 28, McDougall 25, McCormick 10 (2 pens.), Given 3, Hall 3, Colgan 2, Honston 2, Brown 1, Fallon 1, Fanning 1, McIntyre 1, McLaughlin 1.
League Cup (5): McCormack 2 (1 pen.), Miller 2, McDougall 1.
Cup (5): McDougall 2, Miller 2, McCormack 1.

COWDENBEATH   DIV. 2

Ground: Central Park, Cowdenbeath. (Cowdenbeath 511205).
Colours: Royal blue shirts with white stripes; white shorts.
GOALS—League (63): Steele 20, Harley 8, Caithness 6, Liddle 5, Marshall 4, Purdie 4, Ferrier 3, Hunter 3, Markey 3 (3 pens.), Milne 3, Davies 1, Fair 1, Paterson 1, Russell 1.
League Cup (3): Harley 2, Steele 1 (pen.).
Cup (3): Hunter 1, Liddle 1, Markey 1.

DUMBARTON   DIV. 1

Ground: Boghead Park, Dumbarton. (Dumbarton 2569).
Colours: White with gold horizontal band between two black bands; white shorts.
GOALS—League (58): Blair 9, Gallagher B. 8, Fyfe 7, Whiteford D. 7, Brown 4, Whiteford, J. 4, McCluskey 3 (3 pens.), McNeil 3, Coyle J. 2, McLean 2, Muir 2, Sinclair 2, Findlay 1, MacLeod A. 1, MacLeod M. 1, Sharp 1, own goal 1.
League Cup (0).
Cup (4): Sharp 2, Blair 1, Gallagher B. 1.

DUNDEE

Ground: Dens Park, Dundee. (Dundee 86104).
Colours: White shirts; dark blue shorts.
GOALS—League (68): Pirie 19 (4 pens.), Redford 16, Sinclair 10, Shirra 5,
    McLaren 4, Williamson 4, Lamb 2, McGhee 2, Murphy 2,
    Barr 1, Caldwell 1, Glennie 1, McDougall 1, Phillip 1,
    Schaedler 1, own goal 1.
    League Cup (1): Sinclair 1.
    Cup (8): McLaren 2, Pirie 2 (2 pens.), Sinclair 2, Lamb 1,
    Shirra 1.

DUNDEE UNITED

Ground: Tannadice Park, Dundee. (Dundee 86289).
Colours: Tangerine shirts with black facings; tangerine shorts, black
  trimmings.
GOALS—League (56): Dodds 10, Kirkwood 9, Sturrock 6, Hegarty 5,
    Narey 5 (1 pen.), Stewart 4 (2 pens.), Addison 3, Fleming 3,
    Holt 3, Payne 3, Kopel 2, Frye 1, Stark 1, own goal 1.
    League Cup (2): Fleming 1, Sturrock 1.
    Cup (0).

DUNFERMLINE ATHLETIC

Ground: East End Park, Dunfermline. (Dunfermline 24295).
Colours: Black candy stripe; black shorts.
GOALS—League (66): Leonard 20, Mullin 12, Hegarty 7, Rolland 6
    (5 pens.), Dickson 5, Sharp 4, Salton 3, Borthwick 2, McLaren
    2, Donnelly 1, Dunn 1, Mercer 1, Robertson 1, Thomson 1.
    League Cup (0).
    Cup (8): Leonard 4, McLaren 2, Mullin 1, Rolland 1.

EAST FIFE

Ground: Bayview Park, Methil, Fife. (Leven 2323).
Colours: Old gold jerseys, black trimmings; black shorts.
GOALS—League (64): Mackie 17 (6 pens.), Methven 11, Dickson 9,
    Cairns 4, MacIvor 4, Neilson 4, Clarke 2, Gibson 2, Gillies 2,
    Herd 2, Huskie 2, Wedderburn 2, George 1, Halley 1, own goal
    1.
    League Cup (0).
    Cup (2): Dickson 2.

EAST STIRLINGSHIRE

Ground: Firs Park, Falkirk. (Falkirk 23583).
Colours: Black shirts with white hoops; black shorts.

GOALS—League (61): Docherty 14 (2 pens.), Grant 8, Ashwood 7, McCormack 7, Bennett 5 (3 pens.), Blair 5, Lamont 4, Simpson 4, McCulley 3 (1 pen.), Tempany 2, McCaig 1, Robertson 1.
League Cup (1): Docherty 1.
Cup (4): Docherty 1 (pen.), Lamont 1, McCormack 1, Simpson 1.

FALKIRK   DIV. 2

Ground: Brockville Park, Falkirk, (Falkirk 24121).
Colours: Navy blue shirts with white trimmings; white shorts.
GOAL—League (66): McRoberts 11, McCallan 9, Hay 8 (6 pens.), Perry 6, Thomson 6, Stevenson 5, Granam 3, McDowall 3, Mitchell 3, Oliver 3, Paterson 3, Brown 2, Hamilton 1 (pen.), Hoggan 1, own goals 2.
League Cup (4): McRoberts 2, Hoggan 1, own goal 1.
Cup (6): Brown 2, McCallan 2, McRoberts 1, Perry 1.

FORFAR ATHLETIC   DIV. 2

Ground: Station Park, Forfar, Angus. (Forfar 3576).
Colours: Navy and sky blue vertical striped shirts; sky blue shorts.
GOALS—League (55): Rae 11 (8 pens.), Clark 10, Reid 7, Henderson 6, Kinnear 4, Brash 2, Brown K. 2, Gallacher 2, Hall 2, Henry 2 (1 pen.), Knox 2, Bennett 1, Brown T. 1, McPhee 1, own goals 2.
League Cup (1): Rae 1.
Cup (5): Reid 2, Gallacher 1, Hall 1, Knox 1.

HAMILTON ACADEMICALS   DIV. 1

Ground: Douglas Park, Hamilton. (Hamilton 23108).
Colours: Red and white striped shirts; white shorts.
GOALS—League (62): Graham 18, Fairlie 13 (7 pens.), Howie 10, Glavin 5, Morrison 3, Wright 3, Dempsey 2, McCulloch 2, McManus 2, McDowall 1, McGrogan 1, O'Donnell 1, own goal 1.
League Cup (5): Howie 2, Fairlie 1, Wright 1, own goal 1.
Cup (0).

HEART OF MIDLOTHIAN   DIV. 1

Ground: Tyncastle Park, Gorgie Road, Edinburgh. (031-337 6132).
Colours: White shirts with maroon centre panel at front, maroon trimmings; white shorts.
GOALS—League (39): O'Connor 8, Busby 6, Gibson 6 (2 pens.), Bannon 5 (2 pens.), McQuade 4, Robertson 4, Fraser 3 (1 pen.), Park 1, Shaw 1, own goal 1.
League Cup (2): Bannon 1 (pen.), Shaw 1.
Cup (5): Robertson 2, Busby 1, Gibson 1 (pen.), O'Connor 1.

HIBERNIAN   PREM. DIV.

Ground: Easter Road Park, Edinburgh. (031-661 2159).
Colours: Green shirts with white sleeves and collar; white shorts.
GOALS—League (44): Callachan 9, MacLeod 8 (1 pen.), Rae 7, Bremner
5, Higgins 4, Hutchinson 4, Campbell 3, Duncan 1, Stewart 1,
Temperley 1, own goal 1.
League Cup (10): MacLeod 3 (1 pen.), Callachan 2, Refvik 2,
Rae 1, Smith 1, Stewart 1.
Cup (15): MacLeod 5 (2 pens.), Higgins 3, Callachan 2, Rae 2,
Brazil 1, Duncan 1, Stewart 1.

KILMARNOCK   PREM. DIV.

Ground: Rugby Park, Kilmarnock. (Kilmarnock 25184).
Colours: Royal blue shirts with white trimming stripes; royal blue shorts.
GOALS—League (72): Bourke 21, Maxwell 11 (3 pens.), Cairney 9,
Gibson 9, Street 5, Clark J. 3, Hughes 3, Doherty 2, Jardine 2,
McDicken 2, McDowell 2, Clarke P. 1, Provan 1, own goal 1.
League Cup (7): Cairney 2, McDicken 1, McDowell 1, Maxwell
1, Street 1, Welsh 1.
Cup (6): Bourke 3, Street 2, Gibson 1.

MEADOWBANK THISTLE   DIV. 2

Ground: Meadowbank Stadium, Edinburgh. (031-661 5351).
Colours: Amber, with black trim.
GOALS—League (37): Adair 7, Davidson 6, Small 6, Hancock J. 4,
Downie 3, McKenzie 3, Hancock S. 2, Leetion 2, Conroy 1,
O'Rourke 1, Stewart 1, Wight 1.
League Cup (0).
Cup (8): Johnston 2, McKenzie 2, Conroy 1, Davidson 1,
Hancock J. 1 (pen.), Small 1.

MONTROSE   DIV. 2

Ground: Links Park, Montrose. (Montrose 498).
Colours: Royal blue shirts; royal blue shorts.
GOALS—League (55): Murray 12, Robb 10, Miller 6, Georgeson 5,
Livingstone 5, Lowe 4 (4 pens.), McIntosh 4, Hair 3, Cormack 1,
D'Arcy D. 1, D'Arcy B. 1, Ford 1, Wright 1, own goal 1.
League Cup (15): Livingstone 5, Hair 3, Murray 2, Robb 2,
Georgeson 1, Lowe 1 (pen.), Miller 1.
Cup (2): Miller 1, Murray 1.

MORTON   PREM. DIV.

Ground: Capplehow Park, Greenock. (Greenock 23571).
Colours: Blue and white hooped shirts; white shorts.
GOALS—League (52): Ritchie 22 (6 pens.), Wilson 11, Russell 5, McNeil
4, Scott 3, Tolmie 3, Anderson 1, Hutchison 1, Rooney 1 (pen.),
own goal 1.
League Cup (13): Ritchie 3 (1 pen.), Scott 3, Russell 2,
Thomson 2, Anderson 1, McNeil 1, Orr 1.
Cup (6): Ritchie 4 (2 pens.), Anderson 1, Scott 1.

MOTHERWELL   DIV. 1

Ground: Fir Park, Motherwell. (Motherwell 63229).
Colours: Amber shirts with claret trim; amber shorts with two claret
stripes.
GOALS—League (33): Pettigrew 6, Stevens 6, Clinging 5, Irvine 4,
Larnach 4, Donnelly 2, Lindsay 1 (pen.), McLaren 1, Marinello
1, Millar 1 (pen.), Wilson 1, own goal 1.
League Cup (6): Marinello 3 (1 pen.), Pettigrew 2, Clinging 1.
Cup (1): Clinging 1.

PARTICK THISTLE   PREM. DIV.

Ground: Firhill Park, Glasgow. (041-946 2673).
Colours: Yellow shirts with red trimmings; red shorts.
GOALS—League (42): Somner 11 (3 pens.), Melrose 10, O'Hara 8,
Houston 4, McAdam 4, Park 2, Anderson 1, Sheed 1, own goal
1.
League Cup (2): Craig 1, Gibson 1, own goal 1.
Cup (6): McAdam 2, Somner 2 (2 pens.), Anderson 1, Melrose 1.

QUEEN OF THE SOUTH   DIV. 2

Ground: Palmerston Park, Dumfries. (Dumfries 4853).
Colours: Royal blue shirts with white collar and cuffs; white shorts.
GOALS—League (43): Bryce 12, Conghlin 8, Dempster 6 (2 pens.),
Dickson P. 4, McChesny 3 (2 pens.) Boyd 2, Mitchell 2, Clark.
1, Dickson G. 1, Halley 1, McCann 1, Pollock 1, Shields 1.
League Cup (0).
Cup (0).

QUEEN'S PARK   DIV. 2

Ground: Hampden Park, Glasgow, S.4. (041-632 1275).
Colours: Black and white horizontal striped shirts; white shorts.
GOALS—League (46): Ballantyne 13 (3 pens.), McAloon 9, Nicholson 5,
Wood 4, Reynolds 3, Wilkie 3, Horn 2, Sinclair 2, Greenfield 1,
McDonald 1, McPherson 1, Wylie 1, own goal 1.
League Cup (6): Ballantyne 3, Horn 1, McDonald 1, Wilkie 1.
Cup (6): Ballantyne 2, Edgar 2, McAloon 1, Wood 1.

RAITH ROVERS   DIV. 1.

Ground: Stark's Park, Pratt Street, Kirkcaldy. (Kirkcaldy 3514).
Colours: Royal blue shirts; royal blue shorts.
GOALS—League (47): Wallace 14 (5 pens.), Harrow 10, Forrest 6,
  Duncan 2, McDonough 2, Thomson D. 2, Candlish 1, Ford 1,
  Hunter 1, McComb 1, McFarlane 1, Murray 1, Myles 1,
  Pettie 1, Taylor 1, Thomson R. 1, Urquhart 1.
  League Cup (10): Wallace 5, Harrow 3, Forrest 2.
  Cup (0).

RANGERS   PREM. DIV.

Ground: Ibrox Stadium, Glasgow. (041-427 0159).
Colours: Royal blue shirts; white shorts.
GOALS—League (52): Smith 11, Johnstone 9, Cooper 5, MacDonald 5,
  Forsyth A. 4 (4 pens.), Parlane 4, Russell 4, Urquhart 4,
  Watson 2, Dawson 1, Jackson 1, McLean 1, Robertson 1.
  League Cup (22): Smith 5, Cooper 3, Jackson 2, Johnstone 2,
  Parlane 2, Jardine 1 (pen.), MacDonald 1, McLean 1, Miller 1,
  Russell 1, own goals 3.
  Cup (15): Johnstone 4, Cooper 2, MacDonald 2, Forsyth 1,
  Jackson 1, Jardine 1 (pen.), Russell 1, Smith 1, Urquhart 1,
  own goal 1.

ST. JOHNSTONE   DIV. 1

Ground: Muirton Park, Perth. (Perth 26961).
Colours: Royal blue shirts; white shorts.
GOALS—League (57): Brogan 14, Lawson 11, Rutherford 7 (3 pens.),
  Brannigan 5, Polosi 5, Ward 4, McNeil 3 (1 a pen.), Muir 3,
  Hamilton J. 2, O'Connor 1, Redford 1, Thomas 1.
  League Cup (0):
  Cup (3): Brogan 1, Lawson 1, Thomas 1.

ST. MIRREN   PREM. DIV.

Ground: St. Mirren Park, Paisley. (Paisley 2558).
Colours: White shirts with black vertical stripes; black shorts.
GOALS—League (45): McGarvey 13, Stark 9, Bone 7, Torrance 6,
  Fitzpatrick 3, Abercromby 2, Hyslop 2, Copland 1,
  Richardson 1, Young 1.
  League Cup (12): Bone 3, McGarvey 2, Fitzpatrick 2, Hyslop 2,
  Richardson 1, Stark 1.
  Cup (3): Fitzpatrick 1, Munro 1, Stark 1.

STENHOUSEMUIR DIV. 2

Ground: Ochilview Park, Stenhousemuir. (Larbert 2992).
Colours: Maroon shirts with white trimmings; white shorts.
GOALS—League (54): McNaughton 16 (4 pens.), Sweeney 11, Feeney 6,
Gibb 6, Jenkins 6, Jack 2, Gordon 1, Halliday 1, McCullie 1,
Rose 1, Wilson F. 1 (pen.), own goals 2.
League Cup (2): Gibb 1, Sweeney 1.
Cup (1): Jenkins 1.

STIRLING ALBION DIV. 1

Ground: Annfield, Stirling. (Stirling 3584).
Colours: Red shirts; red shorts.
GOALS—League (43): Steele 7, Armstrong 5 (1 pen.), Heggie 4, McPhee
4, Watson 4, Kennedy A. 3, Gray 2, Kennedy J. 2, Nicol 2,
Brown 1, Browning 1 (pen.), Irving 1, Low 1, McGibbon 1,
Thomson 1 (pen.), own goals 4.
League Cup (1): McPhee 1.
Cup (0).

STRANRAER DIV. 2

Ground: Stair Park, Stranraer. (Stranraer 3271).
Colours: Royal blue shirts; white shorts.
GOALS—League (52): Harvey 11, Hyslop 6 (1 pen.), McDonald 6 (2
pens.), McGuigan 6 (1 pen.), Mills 5, Hay 3 (2 pens.), McCly-
mont 3, McCutcheon 3, Hopkins 2, Robertson 2 (1 pen.),
Steen 2, Tait 2, Milligan 1.
League Cup (1): Robertson 1.
Cup (1): McDonald 1 (pen.).

SCOTTISH LEAGUE - PREMIER DIVISION RESULTS 1978-79

	St. Mirren	Rangers	Partick Th.	Motherwell	Morton	Hibernian	Hearts	Dundee U.	Celtic	Aberdeen
Aberdeen	1-1 1-2	0-2 2-1	2-1 2-1	4-0 8-0	3-1 1-2	4-1 0-0	1-2 5-0	1-0 0-2	4-1 1-1	—
Celtic	2-1 2-1	3-1 4-2	1-0 2-0	2-1 2-1	0-0 3-0	0-1 3-1	4-0 1-0	1-1 2-1	—	0-0 1-0
Dundee U.	1-1 2-0	3-0 1-2	2-0 2-1	2-1 2-1	1-2 4-1	0-0 2-1	3-1 2-1	—	2-1 0-3	1-1 2-2
Hearts	4-0 2-1	5-3 2-0	0-1 3-2	2-2 2-2	1-2 1-1	1-1 1-1	—	3-1 2-1	2-0 0-3	1-4 2-2
Hibernian	1-0 2-3	3-0 1-1	2-1 6-1	2-3 0-3	2-2 3-0	—	1-1 1-2	0-0 2-1	2-2 2-1	2-1 1-1
Morton	1-3 1-0	2-2 0-2	1-0 2-2	1-2 6-0	—	1-1 1-2	1-2 1-1	3-2 3-1	3-1 1-0	2-1 0-1
Motherwell	1-2 0-3	2-0 2-2	0-1 1-1	—	1-1 3-3	2-3 0-3	2-2 2-2	0-1 0-4	0-1 0-4	1-1 1-2
Partick Th.	2-1 3-1	1-0 0-2	—	2-0 0-0	1-0 2-2	0-0 1-0	0-1 1-2	1-1 1-2	1-1 1-2	0-1 2-3
Rangers	0-1 1-0	—	0-0 1-0	4-1 3-0	3-0 1-1	3-0 1-1	0-0 3-2	1-2 3-0	1-1 1-3	1-1 1-2
St. Mirren	—	0-1 1-2	1-0 1-1	0-1 1-0	0-0 3-1	1-0 2-3	4-0 2-1	1-0 2-3	0-2 0-2	2-1 2-2

	Airdrieonians	Arbroath	Ayr United	Clyde	Clydebank	Dumbarton	Dundee	Hamilton A.	Kilmarnock	Montrose	Queen of the South	Raith R.	St. Johnstone	Stirling Albion
Airdrieonians	—	3-3	0-0	2-3	1-1	1-0	1-0	2-0	1-0	2-2	1-3	2-0	0-2	2-1
Arbroath	1-2	—	3-0	1-0	5-2	0-1	0-2	3-0	3-1	3-0	1-1	1-2	1-1	2-1
Ayr U.	2-3	0-5	—	1-4	3-0	2-2	3-1	2-2	3-0	4-6	1-0	0-0	4-2	1-2
Clyde	1-0	5-2	2-2	—	3-0	2-3	3-0	2-1	3-0	2-0	3-0	1-2	1-1	1-2
Clydebank	4-1	2-2	2-0	1-4	—	1-7	0-2	1-1	2-3	2-1	3-0	1-2	1-1	2-0
Dumbarton	1-0	0-2	2-2	2-3	1-2	—	2-0	2-0	2-1	1-0	2-2	1-2	1-0	2-2
Dundee	2-0	3-0	2-1	2-1	5-1	5-0	—	1-1	3-1	2-4	0-2	2-3	2-2	1-0
Hamilton A.	2-0	3-1	2-1	3-0	2-1	0-0	2-0	—	4-0	1-1	2-1	2-0	0-0	0-0
Kilmarnock	1-0	3-1	0-3	2-1	1-1	2-2	3-3	2-0	—	0-4	2-1	1-3	0-0	1-0
Montrose	2-2	3-0	4-6	2-3	2-3	0-1	2-2	4-0	2-3	—	3-1	3-1	3-4	0-1
Queen of the South	1-3	1-1	0-1	2-0	3-2	2-1	1-2	1-4	2-1	1-3	—	4-0	5-2	4-1
Raith R.	1-5	2-2	0-0	1-2	4-2	1-2	2-4	2-3	2-1	3-1	2-2	—	3-1	3-0
St. Johnstone	0-2	1-1	2-2	1-1	1-1	0-0	2-2	2-0	2-3	3-1	3-3	1-0	—	1-5
Stirling A.	1-2	2-1	2-1	1-1	1-1	2-3	2-2	2-2	1-3	2-1	0-0	1-2	1-3	—

126

SCOTTISH LEAGUE — Division II Results 1978-79

	Albion Rovers	Alloa	Berwick	Brechin City	Cowdenbeath	Dunfermline Ath.	East Fife	E. Stirling	Falkirk	Forfar Athletic	Meadowbank	Queens Park	Stenhousemuir	Stranraer
Albion R.		2-6	2-1	3-2	1-1	1-1	0-2	1-2	1-1	1-1	2-0	2-0	3-2	1-1
Alloa	2-1		2-1	1-1	2-4	2-3	3-3	2-1	0-2	2-0	0-1	1-1	2-3	1-1
Berwick	2-1	4-1		2-0	1-1	0-1	3-1	2-1	0-1	2-1	0-1	2-1	1-1	1-1
Brechin C.	1-2	2-2	1-2		1-1	0-1	1-1	2-1	1-0	1-1	4-2	3-1	1-1	1-1
Cowdenbeath	0-2	3-1	2-1	0-0		1-0	1-1	5-0	1-1	1-1	2-1	3-2	1-1	2-0
Dunfermline	3-1	1-0	3-1	2-1	3-0		1-1	2-1	1-1	2-2	1-1	2-2	2-0	1-1
East Fife	0-2	3-0	2-4	0-2	0-0	2-1		4-1	1-1	1-1	2-2	2-2	1-1	3-0
E. Stirling	1-1	2-1	2-1	3-1	4-4	2-1	2-1		2-2	1-1	2-2	1-1	1-1	0-3
Falkirk	2-1	3-1	0-1	2-2	2-2	1-1	3-0	1-1		2-2	1-1	2-1	1-1	2-1
Forfar	1-1	2-0	0-0	3-0	4-2	0-1	2-1	2-2	2-2		3-1	2-2	1-1	0-3
Meadowbank	2-0	2-0	0-1	1-1	1-1	2-1	2-1	1-1	1-1	3-0		1-1	3-0	2-2
Queen's Park	2-0	1-1	4-2	0-0	1-1	0-1	2-1	1-0	2-1	2-2	2-3		1-1	2-2
Stenhousemuir	3-1	2-1	3-0	4-2	1-2	1-0	2-1	2-1	1-1	1-1	1-1	1-1		1-0
Stranraer	0-1	4-0	0-2	1-1	2-0	1-2	2-4	2-1	2-1	0-3	1-1	1-1	1-1	

127

Note: In the Scottish League Divisions I and II, each team plays each other team once and then subsequent to a draw being made at the beginning of the season, half of the fixtures are repeated.

SCOTTISH FOOTBALL LEAGUE
Final Tables 1978-79

PREMIER DIVISION

	P	Home W	D	L	Goals F	A	Away W	D	L	Goals F	A	Pts.
Celtic	36	13	3	2	32	12	8	3	7	29	28	45
Rangers	36	12	5	1	32	10	6	4	8	20	25	45
Dundee Utd.	36	12	4	2	33	16	6	4	8	23	21	44
Aberdeen	36	9	5	4	39	16	4	9	5	20	20	40
Hibernian	36	7	9	2	23	16	5	4	9	21	32	37
St. Mirren	36	8	3	7	23	20	7	3	8	22	21	36
Morton	36	9	4	5	34	23	3	8	7	18	30	36
Partick Th.	36	10	2	6	31	21	3	6	9	11	18	34
Hearts	36	5	5	8	19	25	3	2	13	20	46	23
Motherwell	36	2	5	11	20	38	3	2	13	13	48	17

FIRST DIVISION

	P	Home W	D	L	Goals F	A	Away W	D	L	Goals F	A	Pts.
Dundee	39	13	5	1	36	12	11	2	7	32	24	55
Kilmarnock	39	13	5	1	41	14	9	5	6	31	21	54
Clydebank	39	15	3	2	48	23	6	4	10	30	27	54
Ayr	39	12	3	5	39	19	9	2	8	32	33	47
Hamilton	39	13	4	2	39	17	4	5	11	23	43	43
Airdrie	39	9	4	7	44	33	7	4	8	28	28	40
Dumbarton	39	9	3	8	30	21	5	8	6	28	28	39
Stirling Alb.	39	6	4	9	23	29	5	3	11	20	26	35
Clyde	39	8	3	8	30	29	5	5	10	24	36	34
Arbroath	39	8	6	6	33	26	3	1	15	17	35	33
Raith R.	39	8	3	8	29	21	4	5	11	18	34	32
St. Johnstone	39	6	8	6	32	28	4	3	12	25	38	31
Montrose	39	4	6	9	31	37	4	3	13	24	55	25
Queen of the Sth.	39	8	4	8	31	35	0	4	15	12	58	24

SECOND DIVISION

	P	Home W	D	L	Goals F	A	Away W	D	L	Goals F	A	Pts.
Berwick R.	39	11	4	4	45	22	11	4	4	37	22	54
Dunfermline Ath.	39	13	6	1	41	19	6	8	5	25	21	52
Falkirk	39	13	4	3	39	16	6	8	5	27	21	50
East Fife	39	10	7	3	33	22	7	7	6	31	31	43
Cowdenbeath	39	10	4	5	37	22	6	5	9	26	36	42
Alloa Ath.	39	10	3	6	36	26	6	2	11	21	36	41
Albion R.	39	9	6	4	28	17	6	4	10	29	39	40
Forfar Ath.	39	9	7	4	35	25	4	5	12	20	27	38
Stranraer	39	11	1	7	32	27	7	1	12	20	39	38
Stenhousemuir	39	6	4	10	34	30	6	4	9	20	28	32
Brechin City	39	8	7	5	31	33	1	7	11	18	32	32
E. Stirling	39	10	4	5	42	31	2	4	14	19	56	32
Queen's Park	39	4	7	8	19	19	4	5	11	27	38	28
Meadowbank	39	5	3	11	17	31	3	5	11	20	43	24

SCOTTISH LEAGUE HONOURS LIST

PREMIER DIVISION

	First	Pts.	Second	Pts.	Third	Pts.
1975–76	Rangers	54	Celtic	48	Hibernian	43
1976–77	Celtic	55	Rangers	46	Aberdeen	43
1977–78	Rangers	55	Aberdeen	53	Dundee U.	40
1978–79	Celtic	48	Rangers	45	Dundee U.	44

Maximum points: 72

FIRST DIVISION

	First	Pts.	Second	Pts.	Third	Pts.
1975–76	Partick T.	41	Kilmarnock	35	Montrose	30

Maximum points: 52

1976–77	St. Mirren	62	Clydebank	58	Dundee	51
1977–78	*Morton	58	Hearts	58	Dundee	57
1978–79	Dundee	55	Kilmarnock	54	Clydebank	54

Maximum points: 78

SECOND DIVISION

	First	Pts.	Second	Pts.	Third	Pts.
1975–76	*Clydebank	40	Raith R.	40	Alloa	35

Maximum points: 52

1976–77	Stirling A	55	Alloa	51	Dunfermline	50
1977–78	*Clyde	53	Raith R.	53	Dunfermline	48
1978–79	Berwick	54	Dunfermline	52	Falkirk	50

Maximum points: 78

FIRST DIVISION to 1974–75

	First	Pts.	Second	Pts.	Third	Pts.
1890–1	a††Dumbarton	29	Rangers	29	Celtic	24
1891–2	bDumbarton	37	Celtic	35	Hearts	30
1892–3	aCeltic	29	Rangers	28	St. Mirren	23
1893–4	aCeltic	29	Hearts	26	St. Bernards	22
1894–5	aHearts	31	Celtic	26	Rangers	21
1895–6	aCeltic	30	Rangers	26	Hibernian	24
1896–7	aHearts	28	Hibernian	26	Rangers	25
1897–8	aCeltic	33	Rangers	29	Hibernian	22
1898–9	aRangers	36	Hearts	26	Celtic	24
1899–1900	aRangers	32	Celtic	25	Hibernian	24
1900–1	cRangers	35	Celtic	29	Hibernian	25
1901–2	aRangers	28	Celtic	26	Hearts	22
1902–3	bHibernian	37	Dundee	31	Rangers	29
1903–4	dThird Lanark	43	Hearts	39	*Rangers	38
1904–5	d‡Celtic	41	Rangers	41	Third Lanark	35
1905–6	eCeltic	49	Hearts	43	Airdrieonians	38
1906–7	fCeltic	55	Dundee	48	Rangers	45
1907–8	fCeltic	55	Falkirk	51	Rangers	50
1908–9	fCeltic	51	Dundee	50	Clyde	48
1909–10	fCeltic	54	Falkirk	52	Rangers	46
1910–11	fRangers	52	Aberdeen	48	Falkirk	44
1911–12	fRangers	51	Celtic	45	Clyde	42
1912–13	fRangers	53	Celtic	49	*Hearts	41
1913–14	gCeltic	65	Rangers	59	*Hearts	54
1914–15	gCeltic	65	Hearts	61	Rangers	50
1915–16	gCeltic	67	Rangers	56	Morton	51

1916–17	gCeltic	64	Morton	54	Rangers	53
1917–18	fRangers	56	Celtic	55	Kilmarnock	43
1918–19	fCeltic	58	Rangers	57	Morton	47
1919–20	hRangers	71	Celtic	68	Motherwell	57
1920–21	hRangers	76	Celtic	66	Hearts	56
1921–22	hCeltic	67	Rangers	66	Raith R.	56
1922–23	gRangers	55	Airdrieonians	50	Celtic	46
1923–24	gRangers	59	Airdrieonians	50	Celtic	41
1924–25	gRangers	60	Airdrieonians	57	Hibernian	52
1925–26	gCeltic	58	*Airdrieonians	50	Hearts	50
1926–27	gRangers	56	Motherwell	51	Celtic	49
1927–28	gRangers	60	*Celtic	55	Motherwell	55
1928–29	gRangers	67	Celtic	51	Motherwell	50
1929–30	gRangers	60	Motherwell	55	Aberdeen	53
1930–31	gRangers	60	Celtic	58	Motherwell	56
1931–32	gMotherwell	66	Rangers	61	Celtic	48
1932–33	gRangers	62	Motherwell	59	Hearts	50
1933–34	gRangers	66	Motherwell	62	Celtic	47
1934–35	gRangers	55	Celtic	52	Hearts	50
1935–36	gCeltic	66	*Rangers	61	Aberdeen	61
1936–37	gRangers	61	Aberdeen	54	Celtic	52
1937–38	gCeltic	61	Hearts	58	Rangers	49
1938–39	gRangers	59	Celtic	48	Aberdeen	46
1946–47	fRangers	46	Hibernian	44	Aberdeen	39
1947–48	jHibernian	48	Rangers	46	Partick T.	36
1948–49	jRangers	46	Dundee	45	Hibernian	39
1949–50	jRangers	50	Hibernian	49	Hearts	43
1950–51	jHibernian	48	*Rangers	38	Dundee	38
1951–52	jHibernian	45	Rangers	41	East Fife	37
1952–53	j*Rangers	43	Hibernian	43	East Fife	39
1953–54	jCeltic	43	Hearts	38	Partick T.	35
1954–55	jAberdeen	49	Celtic	46	Rangers	41
1955–56	fRangers	52	Aberdeen	46	*Hearts	45
1956–57	fRangers	55	Hearts	53	Kilmarnock	42
1957–58	fHearts	62	Rangers	49	Celtic	46
1958–59	fRangers	50	Hearts	48	Motherwell	44
1959–60	fHearts	54	Kilmarnock	50	*Rangers	42
1960–61	fRangers	51	Kilmarnock	50	Third Lanark	42
1961–62	fDundee	54	Rangers	51	Celtic	46
1962–63	fRangers	57	Kilmarnock	48	Partick T.	46
1963–64	fRangers	55	Kilmarnock	49	*Celtic	47
1964–65	f*Kilmarnock	50	Hearts	50	Dunfermline Ath.	49
1965–66	fCeltic	57	Rangers	55	Kilmarnock	45
1966–67	fCeltic	58	Rangers	55	Clyde	46
1967–68	fCeltic	63	Rangers	61	Hibernian	45
1968–69	fCeltic	54	Rangers	49	Dunfermline Ath.	45
1969–70	fCeltic	57	Rangers	45	Hibernian	44
1970–71	fCeltic	56	Aberdeen	54	St. Johnstone	44
1971–72	fCeltic	60	Aberdeen	50	Rangers	44
1972–73	fCeltic	57	Rangers	56	Hibernian	45
1973–74	fCeltic	53	Hibernian	49	Rangers	48
1974–75	fRangers	56	Hibernian	49	Celtic	45

Maximum points: a, 36; b, 44; c, 40; d, 52; e, 60; f, 68; g, 76; h, 84; j, 60.

SECOND DIVISION to 1974–75

	First	Pts	Second	Pts	Third	Pts
1921–22	a†Alloa	60	Cowdenbeath	47	Armadale	48
1922–23	aQueen's Park	57	Clydebank	¶50	St. Johnstone	¶45
1923–24	aSt. Johnstone	56	Cowdenbeath	55	Bathgate	44
1924–25	aDundee U.	50	Clydebank	48	Clyde	47
1925–26	aDunfr'line A.	59	Clyde	53	Ayr U.	52
1926–27	aBo'ness	56	Raith R.	49	Clydebank	45
1927–28	aAyr U.	54	Third Lanark	45	King's Park	44
1928–29	bDundee U.	51	Morton	50	Arbroath	47
1929–30	a*Leith Ath.	57	East Fife	57	Albion R.	54
1930–31	aThird Lanark	61	Dundee U.	50	Dunfermline A.	47
1931–32	a*East Stirling	55	St. Johnstone	55	*Raith Rovers	46
1932–33	cHibernian	54	Queen of the S.	49	DunfermlineA.	47
1933–34	cAlbion R.	45	*Dunfermline A.	44	Arbroath	44
1934–35	cThird Lanark	52	Arbroath	50	St. Bernard's	47
1935–36	cFalkirk	59	St. Mirren	52	Morton	48
1936–37	cAyr U.	54	Morton	51	St. Bernard's	48
1937–38	cRaith R.	59	Albion R.	48	Airdrieonians	47
1938–39	cCowdenbeath	60	*Alloa	48	East Fife	48
1946–47	dDundee	45	Airdrieonians	42	East Fife	31
1947–48	eEast Fife	53	Albion R.	42	Hamilton A.	40
1948–49	e*Raith R.	42	Stirling Albion	42	*Airdrieonians	41
1949–50	eMorton	47	Airdrieonians	44	*St. Johnstone	36
1950–51	e*Q. of the S.	45	Stirling Albion	45	Ayr U.	36
1951–52	eClyde	43	Falkirk	33	Ayr U.	39
1952–53	eStirling Albion	44	Hamilton A.	43	Queen's Park	37
1953–54	eMotherwell	45	Kilmarnock	42	*Third Lanark	36
1954–55	eAirdrieonians	46	Dunfermline A.	42	Hamilton A.	39
1955–56	bQueen's Park	54	Ayr U.	51	St. Johnstone	49
1956–57	bClyde	64	Third Lanark	51	Cowdenbeath	45
1957–58	bStirling Albion	55	Dunfermline A.	53	Arbroath	47
1958–59	bAyr U.	60	Arbroath	51	Stenhousemuir	46
1959–60	bSt. Johnstone	53	Dundee U.	50	Queen of the S.	49
1960–61	bStirling Albion	55	Falkirk	54	Stenhousemuir	50
1961–62	bClyde	54	Queen of the S.	53	Morton	44
1962–63	bSt. Johnstone	55	East Stirling	49	Morton	48
1963–64	bMorton	67	Clyde	53	Arbroath	46
1964–65	bStirling Albion	59	Hamilton A.	50	Queen of the S.	45
1965–66	bAyr U.	53	Airdrieonians	50	Queen of the S.	49
1966–67	bMorton	69	Raith R.	58	Arbroath	57
1967–68	bSt. Mirren	62	Arbroath	53	East Fife	40
1968–69	bMotherwell	64	Ayr U.	53	*East Fife	47
1969–70	bFalkirk	56	Cowdenbeath	55	Queen of the S.	58
1970–71	bPartick Thistle	56	East Fife	51	Arbroath	46
1971–72	b†Dumbarton	52	Arbroath	52	Stirling Albion	50
1972–73	bClyde	56	Dunfermline A.	52	*Raith R.	47
1973–74	bAirdrieonians	60	Kilmarnock	58	Hamilton A.	55
1974–75	bFalkirk	54	*Queen of the S.	53	Montrose	53

Maximum points: a, 76; b, 72; c, 68; d, 52; e, 60.
*On goal average. †Held jointly after indecisive play-off. ‡Won on deciding match. ††Held jointly. ¶Two points deducted for fielding ineligible player.
Competition suspended 1940–45 during war.

131

RELEGATED CLUBS

FROM PREMIER DIVISION

1975–76—Dundee, St. Johnstone   1977–78—Ayr U., Clydebank
1976–77—Hearts, Kilmarnock   1978–79—Hearts, Motherwell

FROM DIVISION 1

1975–76—Dunfermline Ath, Clyde   1977–78—Alloa, East Fife
1976–77—Raith R., Falkirk   1978–79—Montrose, Queen of the S.

RELEGATED FROM DIVISION 1 to 1973-74

1921–22*—Queen's Park, Dumbarton, Clydebank
1922–23—Albion R., Alloa
1923–24—Clyde, Clydebank
1924–25—Third Lanark, Ayr U.
1925–26—Raith R., Clydebank
1926–27—Morton, Dundee U.
1927–28—Dunfermline Ath., Bo'ness
1928–29—Third Lanark, Raith R.
1929–30—St. Johnstone, Dundee U.
1930–31—Hibernian, East Fife
1931–32—Dundee U., Leith Ath.
1932–33—Morton, East Stirling
1933–34—Third Lanark, Cowdenbeath
1934–35—St. Mirren, Falkirk
1935–36—Airdrieonians, Ayr U.
1936–37—Dunfermline Ath., Albion R.
1937–38—Dundee, Morton
1938–39—Queen's Park, Raith R.
1946–47—Kilmarnock, Hamilton A.
1947–48—Airdrieonians, Queen's Park
1948–49—Morton, Albion R.
1949–50—Queen of the S., Stirling Albion
1950–51—Clyde, Falkirk
1951–52—Morton, Stirling Albion
1952–53—Motherwell, Third Lanark

1953–54—Airdrieonians, Hamilton A.
1954–55—No clubs relegated
1955–56—Stirling Albion, Clyde
1956–57—Dunfermline Ath., Ayr U.
1957–58—East Fife, Queen's Park
1958–59—Queen of the S., Falkirk
1959–60—Arbroath, Stirling Albion
1960–61—Ayr U., Clyde
1961–62—St. Johnstone, Stirling Albion
1962–63—Clyde, Raith R.
1963–64—Queen of the S., East Stirling
1964–65—Airdrieonians, Third Lanark
1965–66—Morton, Hamilton A.
1966–67—St. Mirren, Ayr U.
1967–68—Motherwell, Stirling Albion
1968–69—Falkirk, Arbroath
1969–70—Raith, R., Partick T.
1970–71—St. Mirren, Cowdenbeath
1971–72—Clyde, Dunfermline Ath.
1972–73—Kilmarnock, Airdrieonians
1973–74—East Fife, Falkirk
1974–75—League re-organised at end of season

*Season 1921–22—only 1 club promoted, 3 clubs relegated.

RANGERS TAKE THE SCOTTISH CUP

Third Round	Fourth Round	Quarter-finals	Semi-finals	Final
Dumbarton 1	Dumbarton 1 3	Dumbarton 0	Partick 0	Rangers 0 0 3
Alloa 0	Clydebank 4 1	Partick Th. 1	Rangers 0	Hibernian ...0 0 2
Clydebank 3 0	Partick Th. 3	Rangers 6	Aberdeen 1	
Queen's Park ...3 0	Airdrie 0	Dundee 3	Hibernian 2	
Stirling 3 0	Rangers 1 1	Aberdeen 1 2		
Partick Th. 2	Kilmarnock 1 0	Celtic 1 1		
Arbroath 0	Dundee 4	Hibernian 2		
Airdrie 1	St. Mirren 1	Hearts 1		
Rangers 3	Aberdeen 2			
Motherwell 1	Ayr U. 2			
Clyde 1 1	Celtic 4			
Kilmarnock 5 0	Berwick 0			
Dundee 0	Meadowbank Th. ..2			
Falkirk 4	Hibernian 0			
Dundee U. 2	Hearts 1 1			
St. Mirren 1	Morton 1 0			
Hamilton A. 2				
Aberdeen 6				
Ayr U. 4				
Queen of the S. .2				
Montrose 2				
Celtic 3				
East Fife 0				
Berwick R. 2				
Meadowbank Th. ..2				
Spartans 1				
Dunfermline 0				
Hibernian 6				
Raith 1 1				
Hearts 1 0				
Morton 4				
t Johnstone 2				

SCOTTISH F.A. CUP FINALS 1874-1978

1874	Queens Park	2	Clydesdale	0
1875	Queens Park	3	Renton	0
1876	Queens Park	1 2	Third Lanark	1 0
1877	Vale of Leven	0 1 3	Rangers	0 1 2
1878	Vale of Leven	1	Third Lanark	0
1879	Vale of Leven	1	Rangers	1

Vale of Leven awarded cup, Rangers did not appear for replay

1880	Queens Park	3	Thornlibank	0
1881	Queens Park	2 3	Dumbarton	1 1

Replayed because of protest

1882	Queens Park	2 4	Dumbarton	2 1
1883	Dumbarton	2 2	Vale of Leven	2 1
1884	*Queens Park awarded cup when Vale of Leven did not appear for the final*			

1885	Renton	0 3	Vale of Leven	0 1
1886	Queens Park	3	Renton	1
1887	Hibernian	2	Dumbarton	1
1888	Renton	6	Cambuslang	1
1889	Third Lanark	3 2	Celtic	0 1

Replayed because of protest

1890	Queens Park	1 2	Vale of Leven	1 1
1891	Hearts	1	Dumbarton	0
1892	Celtic	1 5	Queens Park	0 1

Replayed because of protest

1893	Queens Park	0	Celtic	1
1894	Rangers	3	Celtic	1
1895	St. Bernards	2	Renton	1
1896	Hearts	3	Hibernian	1
1897	Rangers	5	Dumbarton	1
1898	Rangers	2	Kilmarnock	0
1899	Celtic	2	Rangers	0
1900	Celtic	4	Queens Park	3
1901	Hearts	4	Celtic	3
1902	Hibernian	1	Celtic	0
1903	Rangers	1 0 2	Hearts	1 0 0
1904	Celtic	3	Rangers	2
1905	Third Lanark	0 3	Rangers	0 1
1906	Hearts	1	Third Lanark	0
1907	Celtic	3	Hearts	0
1908	Celtic	5	St Mirren	1
1909	*After two drawn games between Celtic and Rangers, 2–2–, 1–1, there was a riot and the cup was withheld*			

1910	Dundee	2 0 2	Clyde	2 0 1
1911	Celtic	0 2	Hamilton	0 0
1912	Celtic	2	Clyde	0
1913	Falkirk	2	Raith R.	0
1914	Celtic	0 4	Hibernian	0 1
1920	Kilmarnock	3	Albion R.	2
1921	Partick T.	1	Rangers	0

1922	Morton	1	Rangers	0
1923	Celtic	1	Hibernian	0
1924	Airdrieonians	2	Hibernian	0
1925	Celtic	2	Dundee	1
1926	St Mirren	2	Celtic	0
1927	Celtic	3	East Fife	1
1928	Rangers	4	Celtic	0
1929	Kilmarnock	2	Rangers	0
1930	Rangers	0 2	Partick T.	0 1
1931	Celtic	2 4	Motherwell	2 2
1932	Rangers	1 3	Kilmarnock	1 0
1933	Celtic	1	Motherwell	0
1934	Rangers	5	St Mirren	0
1935	Rangers	2	Hamilton A.	1
1936	Rangers	1	Third Lanark	0
1937	Celtic	2	Aberdeen	1
1938	East Fife	1 4	Kilmarnock	1 2
1939	Clyde	4	Motherwell	0
1947	Aberdeen	2	Hibernian	1
1948	Rangers	1 1	Morton	1 0
1949	Rangers	4	Clyde	1
1950	Rangers	3	East Fife	0
1951	Celtic	1	Motherwell	0
1952	Motherwell	4	Dundee	0
1953	Rangers	1 1	Aberdeen	1 0
1954	Celtic	2	Aberdeen	1
1955	Clyde	1 1	Celtic	1 0
1956	Hearts	3	Celtic	1
1957	Falkirk	1 2	Kilmarnock	1 1
1958	Clyde	1	Hibernian	0
1959	St Mirren	3	Aberdeen	1
1960	Rangers	2	Kilmarnock	0
1961	Dunfermline A.	0 2	Celtic	0 0
1962	Rangers	2	St. Mirren	0
1963	Rangers	1 3	Celtic	1 0
1964	Rangers	3	Dundee	1
1965	Celtic	3	Dunfermline A.	2
1966	Rangers	0 1	Celtic	0 0
1967	Celtic	2	Aberdeen	0
1968	Dunfermline A.	3	Hearts	1
1969	Celtic	4	Rangers	0
1970	Aberdeen	3	Celtic	1
1971	Celtic	1 2	Rangers	1 1
1972	Celtic	6	Hibernian	1
1973	Rangers	3	Celtic	2
1974	Celtic	3	Dundee U.	0
1975	Celtic	3	Airdrieonians	1
1976	Rangers	3	Hearts	1
1977	Celtic	1	Rangers	0
1978	Rangers	2	Aberdeen	1

SCOTTISH LEAGUE CUP 1978-79

Quarter-finals		Semi-finals		Final	
Rangers	1 2	Rangers	3		
Arbroath	0 1			Rangers	2
Montrose	1 1	Celtic	2		
Celtic	1 3			*At Hampden Park Attendance 60,600*	

Ayr U.	3 1	Aberdeen	1		
Aberdeen	3 3			Aberdeen	1
Morton	1 1	Hibernian	0		
Hibernian	0 2				

PAST SCOTTISH LEAGUE CUP FINALS

1946–47	Hampden Park	Rangers	4	Aberdeen	0
1947–48	Hampden Park	East Fife	4	Falkirk	1
		(After draw 1–1)			
1948–49	Hampden Park	Rangers	2	Raith Rovers	0
1949–50	Hampden Park	East Fife	3	Dunfermline	0
1950–51	Hampden Park	Motherwell	3	Hibernian	0
1951–52	Hampden Park	Dundee	3	Rangers	2
1952–53	Hampden Park	Dundee	2	Kilmarnock	0
1953–54	Hampden Park	East Fife	3	Partick Thistle	2
1954–55	Hampden Park	Hearts	4	Motherwell	2
1955–56	Hampden Park	Aberdeen	2	St Mirren	1
1956–57	Hampden Park	Celtic	3	Partick Thistle	0
		(After draw 0–0)			
1957–58	Hampden Park	Celtic	7	Rangers	1
1958–59	Hampden Park	Hearts	5	Partick Thistle	1
1959–60	Hampden Park	Hearts	2	Third Lanark	1
1960–61	Hampden Park	Rangers	2	Kilmarnock	0
1961–62	Hampden Park	Rangers	3	Hearts	1
		(After draw 1–1)			
1962–63	Hampden Park	Hearts	1	Kilmarnock	0
1963–64	Hampden Park	Rangers	5	Morton	0
1964–65	Hampden Park	Rangers	2	Celtic	1
1965–66	Hampden Park	Celtic	2	Rangers	1
1966–67	Hampden Park	Celtic	1	Rangers	0
1967–68	Hampden Park	Celtic	5	Dundee	3
1968–69	Hampden Park	Celtic	6	Hibernian	2
1969–70	Hampden Park	Celtic	1	St. Johnstone	0
1970–71	Hampden Park	Rangers	1	Celtic	0
1971–72	Hampden Park	Partick Thistle	4	Celtic	1
1972–73	Hampden Park	Hibernian	2	Celtic	1
1973–74	Hampden Park	Dundee	1	Celtic	0
1974–75	Hampden Park	Celtic	6	Hibernian	3
1975–76	Hampden Park	Rangers	1	Celtic	0
1976–77	Hampden Park	Aberdeen	2	Celtic	1
1977–78	Hampden Park	Rangers	2	Celtic	1

136

Gates down slightly

Attendances at Football League matches in 1978–79 were down slightly overall, with only the Third Division showing a small increase over the previous season. Once again Manchester United were the best supported club, although they were only a little way ahead of Liverpool, and the Old Trafford crowds were down by an average of over 5,000 compared with 1977–78. Swansea City showed the most improvement, with an average gate increase of 5,638. The Divisional totals, with last year's figures in brackets, were:

Division I—12,704,549 (13,255,677)
Division II—6,153,223 (6,474,763)
Division III—3,374,558 (3,332,042)
Division IV—2,308,297 (2,330,390)

FIRST DIVISION

	League position	Average 1978–79	Average 1977–78	Difference
Arsenal	7	36,371	35,466	+905
Aston Villa	8	32,838	35,464	−2,626
Birmingham C.	21	20,164	23,911	−3,747
Bolton W.	17	24,772	22,877	+1,895
Bristol C.	13	22,306	23,357	−1,051
Chelsea	22	24,782	28,734	−3,952
Coventry C.	10	22,637	23,353	−716
Derby Co.	19	21,555	23,345	−1,790
Everton	4	35,456	39,513	−4,057
Ipswich T.	6	21,673	23,586	−1,913
Leeds U.	5	27,633	29,186	−1,553
Liverpool	1	46,406	45,546	+860
Manchester C.	15	36,203	41,687	−5,484
Manchester U.	9	46,430	51,860	−5,430
Middlesbrough	12	18,459	19,874	−1,415
Norwich C.	16	17,874	19,366	−1,492
Nottingham F.	2	29,587	32,501	−2,914
Queen's Park R.	20	16,287	19,940	−3,653
Southampton	14	21,330	21,167	+163
Tottenham H.	11	34,902	33,417	+1,485
West Bromwich A.	3	26,517	24,126	+2,391
Wolverhampton W.	18	20,796	22,325	−1,529

SECOND DIVISION

	League position	Average 1978–79	Average 1977–78	Difference
Blackburn R.	22	8,640	12,227	—3,587
Brighton & H. A.	2	22,145	25,265	—3,120
Bristol R.	16	7,593	8,108	—515
Burnley	13	10,748	11,581	—833
Cambridge U.	12	6,849	5,633	+1,216
Cardiff C.	8	9,246	8,365	+881
Charlton A.	19	9,563	11,307	—1,744
Crystal Pal.	1	23,294	19,636	+3,658
Fulham	9	10,135	10,550	—415
Leicester C.	17	14,187	17,768	—3,581
Luton T.	18	8,792	9,252	—460
Millwall	21	7,002	8,197	—1,195
Newcastle U.	7	20,834	24,729	—3,895
Notts Co.	6	9,281	9,268	+13
Oldham Ath.	14	7,045	9,583	—2,538
Orient	11	7,232	8,785	—1,462
Preston N. E.	10	12,117	8,799	+3,318
Sheffield U.	20	16,339	15,489	+850
Stoke C.	3	19,125	15,037	+4,088
Sunderland	4	25,454	22,276	+3,178
West Ham U.	5	25,778	25,620	+158
Wrexham	15	11,519	11,650	—131

THIRD DIVISION

	League position	Average 1978–79	Average 1977–78	Difference
Blackpool	12	5,647	10,118	—4,471
Brentford	10	7,455	8,578	—1,123
Bury	18	3,782	4,979	—1,197
Carlisle U.	6	5,204	5,319	—115
Chester	16	4,052	4,165	—113
Chesterfield	20	4,822	4,866	—44
Colchester U.	7	3,419	4,572	—1,153
Exeter C.	9	4,408	4,887	—479
Gillingham	4	7,143	7,167	—24
Hull C.	8	5,238	6,835	—1,597
Lincoln C.	24	3,168	4,878	—1,710
Mansfield T.	19	5,151	8,982	—3,831
Oxford U.	11	4,647	4,972	—325
Peterborough U.	21	4,635	5,974	—1,339
Plymouth Arg.	15	7,526	6,887	+639
Rotherham U.	17	4,466	4,913	—447
Sheffield Wed.	14	10,860	11,592	—732
Shrewsbury T.	1	6,098	3,378	+2,720
Southend U.	13	6,610	7,287	—677
Swansea C.	3	13,746	8,108	+5,638
Swindon T.	5	7,975	7,367	+608
Tranmere R.	23	2,179	3,926	—1,747
Walsall	22	4,047	5,317	—1,270
Watford	2	14,435	11,352	+3,083

FOURTH DIVISION

	League position	Average 1978–79	Average 1977–78	Difference
A.F.C. Bournemouth	18	3,759	3,348	+411
Aldershot	5	4,163	4,347	—184
Barnsley	4	11,048	5,659	+5,389
Bradford C.	15	3,924	5,103	—1,179
Crewe Alex.	24	1,995	2,290	—295
Darlington	21	1,807	1,993	—186
Doncaster R.	22	2,999	3,228	—229
Grimsby T.	2	6,528	4,696	+1,832
Halifax T.	23	1,821	2,199	—378
Hartlepool U.	13	2,997	2,833	+164
Hereford U.	14	3,369	4,900	—1,531
Huddersfield T.	9	3,649	4,508	—859
Newport C.	8	3,731	4,074	—343
Northampton T.	19	2,895	3,517	—622
Portsmouth	7	10,123	9,687	+436
Port Vale	16	3,287	3,947	—660
Reading	1	7,616	4,567	+3,049
Rochdale	20	1,767	1,275	+492
Scunthorpe U.	12	2,721	3,281	—560
Stockport C.	17	4,142	4,010	+132
Torquay U.	11	2,669	2,878	—209
Wigan Ath.	6	6,701	—	—
Wimbledon	3	3,712	3,135	+577
York C.	10	2,936	2,284	+652

WELSH F.A. CUP WINNERS (Since 1901)

1900–1 Oswestry	1927–28 Cardiff	1956–57 Wrexham
1901–2 Wellington	1928–29 Connah's Quay	1957–58 Wrexham
1902–3 Wrexham	1929–30 Cardiff	1958–59 Cardiff
1903–4 Druids	1930–31 Wrexham	1959–60 Wrexham
1904–5 Swansea	1931–32 Swansea	1960–61 Swansea
1905–6 Wellington	1932–33 Chester	1961–62 Bangor
1906–7 Oswestry	1933–34 Bristol City	1962–63 Borough Utd
1907–8 Chester	1934–35 Tranmere	1963–64 Cardiff
1908–9 Wrexham	1935–36 Crewe	1964–65 Cardiff
1909–10 Wrexham	1936–37 Crewe	1965–66 Swansea
1910–11 Wrexham	1937–38 Shrewsbury	1966–67 Cardiff
1911–12 Cardiff	1938–39 S. Liverpool	1967–68 Cardiff
1912–13 Swansea	1939–40 Wellington	1968–69 Cardiff
1913–14 Wrexham	1940–46 No contest	1969–70 Cardiff
1914–15 Wrexham	1946–47 Chester	1970–71 Cardiff
1915–16 Abandoned	1947–48 Lovell's Ath.	1971–72 Wrexham
1919–20 Cardiff	1948–49 Merthyr Tydfil	1972–73 Cardiff
1920–21 Wrexham	1949–50 Swansea	1973–74 Cardiff
1921–22 Cardiff	1950–51 Merthyr Tydfil	1974–75 Wrexham
1922–23 Cardiff	1951–52 Rhyl	1975–76 Cardiff
1923–24 Wrexham	1952–53 Rhyl	1976–77 Shrewsbury
1924–25 Wrexham	1953–54 Flint	1977–78 Wrexham
1925–26 Ebbw Vale	1954–55 Bury	1978–79 Shrewsbury
1926–27 Cardiff	1955–56 Cardiff	

NORTHERN IRISH CUP FINALS 1881-1978

1880–81	Moyola Park	1	Cliftonville	0
1881–82	Queen's Island	2	Cliftonville	1
1882–83	Cliftonville	5	Ulster	0
1883–84	Distillery	5	Wellington Park	0
1884–85	Distillery	2	Limavady	0
1885–86	Distillery	1	Limavady	0
1886–87	Ulster	3	Cliftonville	1
1887–88	Cliftonville	2	Distillery	1
1888–89	Distillery	5	Y.M.C.A.	4
1889–90	Gordon Highlanders	3	Cliftonville	1
1890–91	Linfield	4	Ulster	2
1891–92	Linfield	7	The Black Watch	0
1892–93	Linfield	5	Cliftonville	1
1893–94	Distillery	3	Linfield	2
1894–95	Linfield	10	Bohemians	1
1895–96	Distillery	3	Glentoran	1
1896–97	Cliftonville	3	Sherwood Foresters	1
1897–98	Linfield	2	St. Columb's Hall Celtic	0
1898–99	Linfield	2	Glentoran	1
1899–1900	Cliftonville	2	Bohemians	1
1900–1	Cliftonville	1	Freebooters	0
1901–2	Linfield	5	Distillery	1
1902–3	Distillery	3	Bohemians	1
1903–4	Linfield	5	Derry Celtic	1
1904–5	Distillery	3	Shelbourne	0
1905–6	Shelbourne	2	Belfast Celtic	1
1906–7	Cliftonville	1	Shelbourne	0
1907–8	Bohemians	3	Shelbourne	1
1908–9	Cliftonville	2	Bohemians	1
1909–10	Distillery	1	Cliftonville	0
1910–11	Shelbourne	2	Bohemians	1
1911–12	Linfield were awarded Cup. Final not played.			
1912–13	Linfield	2	Glentoran	0
1913–14	Glentoran	3	Linfield	1
1914–15	Linfield	1	Belfast Celtic	0
1915–16	Linfield	1	Glentoran	0
1916–17	Glentoran	2	Belfast Celtic	0
1917–18	Belfast Celtic	2	Linfield	0
1918–19	Linfield	2	Glentoran	1
1919–20	Cup awarded to Shelbourne.			
1920–21	Glentoran	2	Glenavon	0
1921–22	Linfield	2	Glenavon	0
1922–23	Linfield	2	Glentoran	0
1923–24	Queen's Island	1	Willowfield	0
1924–25	Distillery	2	Glentoran	1
1925–26	Belfast Celtic	3	Linfield	2
1926–27	Ards	3	Cliftonville	2
1927–28	Willowfield	1	Larne	0
1928–29	Ballymena	2	Belfast Celtic	1
1929–30	Linfield	4	Ballymena	3
1930–31	Linfield	3	Ballymena	0
1931–32	Glentoran	2	Linfield	1

1932–33	Glentoran 3	Distillery 1	
1933–34	Linfield 5	Cliftonville 0	
1934–35	Glentoran 1	Larne 0	
1935–36	Linfield 2	Derry City 1	
1936–37	Belfast Celtic 3	Linfield 0	
1937–38	Belfast Celtic 2	Bangor 0	
1938–39	Linfield 2	Ballymena 0	
1939–40	Ballymena 2	Glenavon 0	
1940–41	Belfast Celtic 1	Linfield 0	
1941–42	Linfield 3	Glentoran 1	
1942–43	Belfast Celtic 1	Glentoran 0	
1943–44	Belfast Celtic 2	Linfield 1	
1944–45	Linfield 4	Glentoran 2	
1945–46	Linfield 3	Distillery 0	
1946–47	Belfast Celtic 1	Glentoran 0	
1947–48	Linfield 3	Coleraine 0	
1948–49	Derry City 3	Glentoran 1	
1949–50	Linfield 2	Distillery 1	
1950–51	Glentoran 3	Ballymena United 1	
1951–52	Ards 1	Glentoran 0	
1952–53	Linfield 5	Coleraine 0	
1953–54	Derry City 3	Glentoran 0	
1954–55	Dundela 3	Glenavon 0	
1955–56	Distillery....................1	Glentoran 0	
1956–57	Glenavon...................2	Derry City 0	
1957–58	Ballymena United 2	Linfield 0	
1958–59	Glenavon 2	Ballymena United 0	
1959–60	Linfield 5	Ards 1	
1960–61	Glenavon 5	Linfield 1	
1961–62	Linfield 4	Portadown 0	
1962–63	Linfield 2	Distillery 1	
1963–64	Derry City 2	Glentoran 0	
1964–65	Coleraine 2	Glenavon 1	
1965–66	Glentoran 2	Linfield 0	
1966–67	Crusaders 3	Glentoran 1	
1967–68	Crusaders 2	Linfield 0	
1968–69	Ards 4	Distillery 2	
1969–70	Linfield 2	Ballymena United 1	
1970–71	Distillery....................3	Derry City 0	
1971–72	Coleraine 2	Portadown 1	
1972–73	Glentoran 3	Linfield 2	
1973–74	Ards 2	Ballymena 1	
1974–75	Coleraine 1	Linfield 0	
	(After 1–1 and 0–0 draws)		
1975–76	Carrick Rangers 2	Linfield 1	
1976–77	Coleraine 4	Linfield 1	
1977–78	Linfield 3	Ballymena United 1	

Clough proves his point

Nottingham Forest won the European Cup at their first attempt (it took Liverpool 12 years) and of course the triumph was as much a tribute to the skills of Brian Clough and Peter Taylor as it was to the team. On the domestic front they had already won the League Cup for the second year running, and were runners-up in the League, so the game in Munich, although not memorable in itself, set the seal on another wonderful season for the dazzling duo of British soccer management.

Forest's most difficult tie was probably their first, against holders Liverpool, although they did have to visit Cologne after a 3–3 first leg in the semi-finals, and some people wrote them off at that point, but they gained a 1–0 away win to go through to the final, where 'golden boy' Trevor Francis repaid some of his ridiculously high fee by scoring the only goal of a dull game.

So the European Cup has come to England for the third year running, which emulates the feats of West Germany (Bayern), Holland (Ajax), Italy (AC and Inter) but not yet reaching the heights of Real Madrid so early in the competition's history when they won the trophy for the first five years. It took us a long time to get round to it, but now we're up there with the greats.

The Cup-Winners' Cup produced a much more exciting final, with Barcelona running out 4–3 winners after extra time against Fortuna of Dusseldorf, although some of the tackling was a little grim from both sides at times.

Barcelona had accounted for our entry, Ipswich, in the quarter-finals.

In the UEFA Cup, Borussia Munchengladbach, having knocked Manchester City out in the quarter-finals, went on to beat Red Star of Belgrade – one of the most consistently good sides never to win a European club trophy – in the two-leg final.

142

EUROPEAN CHAMPIONS' CUP 1978-79

Second Round	Quarter-finals	Semi-finals	Final
Austria Vienna (A) 4 0	Austria Vienna ...3 0	Austria Vienna 0 0	Malmoe 0
Lillestroem (NO) 0 0	Dynamo Dresden 1 1		*In Munich*
Bohemians (E) 0 0	Wisla Krakow ..2 1	Malmoe 0 1	
Dynamo Dresden (EG) 0 6	Malmoe 1 4		
Zbrojovka Brno (CZ) 2 1	Nottingham F. ..4 1	Nottingham F. 3 1	Nottingham F. 1
Wisla Krakow (PO)* 2 1	Grasshoppers ...1 1		*Francis*
Dynamo Kiev (USSR) 0 0	FC Cologne 1 1	Cologne 3 0	
Malmoe (SW) 0 2	Cologne 3 0		
AEK Athens (G) 1 1			
Nottingham Forest 2 5			
Real Madrid (SP) 3 0			
Grasshoppers (S)* 1 2			
Lokomotiv Sofia (B) 0 0			
Cologne (WG) 1 4			
Rangers 0 3			
PSV Eindhoven (N) 0 1			

Key: A—Austria; B—Bulgaria; BE—Belgium; CY—Cyprus; CZ—Czechoslovakia; D—Denmark; E—Eire; EG—East Germany; FI—Finland; F—France; G—Greece; H—Hungary; I—Italy; IC—Iceland; L—Luxembourg; N—Netherlands; NI—Northern Ireland; NO—Norway; PO—Poland; P—Portugal; R—Rumania; S—Switzerland; SP—Spain; SW—Sweden; T—Turkey; WG—West Germany; Y—Yugoslavia.

*Won on away goals rule. **After extra time. †Aggregate score—two-leg final. ‡Won on penalties. §One-leg final.

143

EUROPEAN CUP-WINNERS' CUP 1978-79

Second Round	Quarter-finals	Semi-finals	Final

Fortuna Dusseldorf (WG) 3 0
Aberdeen 0 2
→ Fortuna* 0 1
Servette Geneva (S) 2 2
Nancy (F).........................1 1
→ Servette Geneva 0 1
Fortuna 3 1
→ Fortuna 3

FC Magdeburg (EG)* 1 1
Ferencvaros (H) 0 2
→ FC Magdeburg ...2 2
Banik Ostrava (CZ) 3 3
Shamrock R. (E) 0 1
→ Banik Ostrava 1 4
Banik Ostrava...1 2

Ipswich Town 0 2
SW Innsbruck (A) 1 0
→ Ipswich Town 2 0
Anderlecht (BE) 3 0
Barcelona (SP)‡ 0 3
→ Barcelona* 1 1
Barcelona 1 1
→ Barcelona 4
(After extra time)

Inter Milan (I) 5 2
Bodo Glimt (NO) 0 1
→ Inter Milan 0 0
Rijeka (Y) 0 0
SK Beveren (BE) 0 2
→ SK Beveren 0 1
SK Beveren 0 0

144

UEFA CUP 1978-79

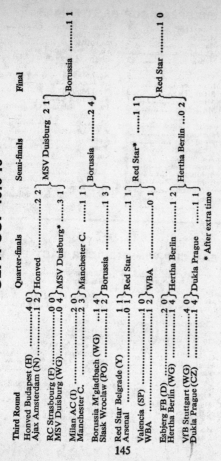

Third Round	Quarter-finals	Semi-finals	Final
Honved Budapest (H) ....4 0 } Ajax Amsterdam (N).........1 2 } Honved ....2 2 } 	MSV Duisburg* ....3 1 } MSV Duisburg 2 1 } RC Strasbourg (F).........0 0 } MSV Duisburg (WG).........0 4 }		Borussia 1 1
Milan AC (I).........2 0 } Manchester C. ....2 3 } Manchester C. ....1 1 } Borussia M'gladbach (WG) ...1 4 } Slask Wroclaw (PO).........1 2 } Borussia ....3 }	Borussia 2 4		
Red Star Belgrade (Y).........1 1 } Arsenal ....0 1 } Red Star ....1 1 } Valencia (SP) ....1 0 } WBA ....1 2 } Red Star* ....1 1 } 	Red Star* ....1 1 }		Red Star 1 0
Esbjerg FB (D).........2 0 } Hertha Berlin (WG).........1 4 } Hertha Berlin ....1 2 } VfB Stuttgart (WG).........4 0 } Dukla Prague (CZ).........1 4 } Dukla Prague ....1 1 }	Hertha Berlin ...0 2 }		

145

* After extra time

EUROPEAN CUP PAST FINALS

Year	Winner		Runner-up	
1956	Real Madrid (SP)	4	Stade de Rheims (F)	3
1957	Real Madrid	2	Florentina (I)	0
1958	Real Madrid	3	AC Milan (I)	2**
1959	Real Madrid	2	Stade de Rheims (F)	0
1960	Real Madrid	7	Eintracht Frankfurt (WG)	3
1961	SL Benfica	3	Barcelona (SP)	2
1962	SL Benfica	5	Real Madrid	3
1963	AC Milan	2	SL Benfica	1
1964	Inter Milan (I)	3	Real Madrid	1
1965	Inter Milan	1	SL Benfica	0
1966	Real Madrid	2	Partizan Belgrade (Y)	1
1967	Celtic	2	Inter Milan	1
1968	Manchester United	4	SL Benfica	1
1969	AC Milan	4	Ajax Amsterdam (N)	1
1970	Feyenoord (N)	2	Celtic	1**
1971	Ajax Amsterdam	2	Panathinaikos (G)	0
1972	Ajax Amsterdam	2	Inter Milan	0
1973	Ajax Amsterdam	1	Juventus (I)	0
1974	Bayern Munich	1 4	Atlético Madrid	1 0
1975	Bayern Munich	2	Leeds United	0
1976	Bayern Munich	1	St. Etienne	0
1977	Liverpool	3	Borussia Munchengladbach	1
1978	Liverpool	1	FC Bruges	0

EUROPEAN CUP-WINNERS' CUP PAST FINALS

Year	Winner		Runner-up	
1961	Florentina (I)	4	Rangers	1†
1962	Atlético Madrid (SP)	3	Florentina	1
	(After 1-1 *draw*)			
1963	Tottenham Hotspur	5	Atlético Madrid (SP)	1
1964	Sporting Lisbon (P)	1	MTK Budapest (H)	0
	(After 3-3 *draw*)			
1965	West Ham United	2	Munich 1860 (WG)	0
1966	Borussia Dortmund (WG)	2	Liverpool	1**
1967	Bayern Munich (WG)	1	Rangers	0**
1968	AC Milan (I)	2	SV Hamburg (WG)	0
1969	Slovan Bratislava (CZ)	3	Barcelona (SP)	2
1970	Manchester City	2	Gornik Zabrze (PO)	1
1971	Chelsea	2	Real Madrid (SP)	1
	(After 1-1 *draw*)			
1972	Rangers	3	Dynamo Moscow (USSR)	2
1973	AC Milan (I)	1	Leeds United	0
1974	FC Magdeburg (EG)	2	AC Milan	0
1975	Dynamo Kiev	3	Ferencvaros (H)	0
1976	RSC Anderlecht	4	West Ham United	2
1977	SV Hamburg	2	Anderlecht	0
1978	RSC Anderlecht	4	Austria Wien	0

FAIRS CUP PAST FINALS (Aggregate Scores)

1958	Barcelona (SP)..............8	London 2
1960	Barcelona (SP)..............4	Birmingham City 1
1961	AS Roma (I) 4	Birmingham City 2
1962	Valencia (SP) 7	Barcelona (SP)............3
1963	Valencia (SP) 4	Dynamo Zagreb (Y) 1
1964	Real Zaragoza (SP) 2	Valencia (SP) ....1¶
1965	Ferencvaros (H) 1	Juventus (I) ....0¶
1966	Barcelona (SP)..............4	Real Zaragoza (SP) 3**
1967	Dynamo Zagreb (Y) 2	Leeds United 0
1968	Leeds United 1	Ferencvaros (H) 0
1969	Newcastle United 6	Ujpest Dozsa (H) 2
1970	Arsenal 4	Anderlecht (BE) 3
1971	Leeds United 3*	Juventus (I) 3

UEFA CUP PAST FINALS

1972	Tottenham H. 3	Wolverhampton W. 2
1973	Liverpool 3	Borussia Munchengladbach ...2
1974	Feyenoord (N)...............4	Tottenham H. 2
1975	Borussia Munchengladbach 5	Twente Enschede (N) 1
1976	Liverpool 4	FC Bruges 3
1977	Juventus 2	Atletico Bilbao ....2‡
1978	P.S.V. Eindhoven 3	S.E.C. Bastia 0

England unconvincing

With the European Championships looming on the horizon, England took the 1979 British Championship easily enough in the end, but their overall performance was less than convincing. They started with a 2–0 victory against the weakest team in the tournament, in Belfast, but both goals came early in the game, which then degenerated into forgettable mediocrity. Meanwhile, Wales were thumping the Scots 3–0 in Cardiff, thanks to a hat-trick by veteran striker John Toshack, now player-manager at Swansea.

Even the Scots managed a narrow 1–0 victory over Northern Ireland on the Tuesday evening, to keep their hopes alive, and on the following evening Wales held England to a frustrating draw at Wembley, putting one in mind of many England games in the past where midfield superiority has not been turned into goals. This match, in particular, did not bode well for Rome.

Luckily for England, within the context of this Championship, Wales could surprisingly only draw with Northern Ireland on the Friday evening, and so England had only to worry about beating the Scots – goal difference, which had been introduced to the Championship for the first time, no longer mattered. The superiority of the Scots in the first half was almost unbelievable, and they took the lead through Wark in the 21st minute. Just before half-time a Scottish lunatic ran on the pitch and held play up for so long that the referee added time on to the end of the half. During this time, England equalised with a goal by Barnes, presented to him by another in the long line of heart-breaking goalkeeping errors which seem to have plagued Scotland at Wembley for so long.

148

England settled down in the second half and ran out 3–1 winners, the last goal, from Keegan, making up for much which had gone before, but you couldn't help wondering where England stood in the world, or even the European league. Higher than a year ago, no doubt, but there's still some way to go.

British International Championship 1978-79

NORTHERN IRELAND 0, ENGLAND 2
at Windsor Park, Belfast, May 19, 1979, 35,000
NORTHERN IRELAND: Jennings; Rice, J. Nicholl, C. Nicholl, Nelson, Moreland (McGrath), Hamilton, McIlroy, Armstrong, Caskey, Cochrane (Spence).
ENGLAND: Clemence; Neal, Thompson, Watson, Mills, Wilkins, McDermott, Currie, Coppell, Latchford, Barnes.
SCORERS: England: Watson, Coppell.

WALES 3, SCOTLAND 0
at Ninian Park, Cardiff, May 19, 1979, 20,371
WALES: Davies, Stevenson, Jones, Mahoney, Dwyer, Phillips, Yorath, Flynn, James, Toshack, Curtis.
SCOTLAND: Rough; Burley, F. Gray, Wark, Hegarty, Hansen, Dalglish, Souness, Wallace (Jordan), Hartford, Graham.
SCORER: Wales: Toshack 3.

SCOTLAND 1, NORTHERN IRELAND 0
at Hampden Park, Glasgow, May 22, 1979, 28,529
SCOTLAND: Wood; Burley, Gray, Wark, McQueen, Hegarty, Dalglish, Souness, Jordan, Hartford, Graham.
NORTHERN IRELAND: Jennings; Rice, Nelson, Nicholl J., Hunter Hamilton, Moreland, Sloan, Armstrong, Spence, McIlroy.
SCORER: Scotland: Graham.

ENGLAND 0, WALES 0
at Wembley, May 23, 1979, 70,220
ENGLAND: Corrigan; Cherry, Sansom, Currie, Watson, Hughes, Keegan, Wilkins, Latchford, McDermott, Cunningham.
WALES: Davies; Stevenson, Jones, Mahoney, Dwyer, Phillips, Yorath, Flynn, James, Toshack, Curtis.

NORTHERN IRELAND 1, WALES 1
at Windsor Park, Belfast, May 25, 1979, 6,500
NORTHERN IRELAND: Jennings; Rice, Nicholl C., Hunter, Nelson, Hamilton, Nicholl J., McCreery, McIlroy, Spence, Armstrong.
WALES: Davies; Stevenson, Dwyer, Phillips, Jones, Mahoney, Yorath, Flynn, James, Toshack, Curtis.
SCORERS: N. Ireland: Spence. Wales: James.

ENGLAND 3, SCOTLAND 1
at Wembley, May 26, 1979, 100,000
ENGLAND: Clemence; Neal, Mills, Thompson, Watson, Wilkins, Coppell, Keegan, Latchford, Brooking, Barnes.
SCOTLAND: Wood; Burley, Gray, Wark, McQueen, Hegarty, Dalglish, Souness, Jordan, Hartford, Graham.
SCORERS: England: Barnes, Coppell, Keegan. Scotland: Wark.

FINAL TABLE

	P	W	D	L	F	A	Pts.
England	3	2	1	0	5	1	5
Wales	3	1	2	0	4	1	4
Scotland	3	1	0	2	2	6	2
N. Ireland	3	0	1	2	1	4	1

THE WORLD CUP FINALS
URUGUAY 1930

Uruguay 4, Argentina 2 (1–2).
Uruguay: Ballesteros; Nasazzi (capt.), Mascheroni, Andrade, Fernandez, Gestido, Dorado, Scarone, Castro, Cea, Iriarte.
Argentina: Botasso; Della Torre, Paternoster, Evaristo, J., Monti, Suarez, Peucelle, Varallo, Stabile, Ferreira (capt.), Evaristo M.
Scorers: Dorado, Cea, Iriarte, Castro for Uruguay; Peucelle, Stabile for Argentina.
Leading Scorers Stabile (Argentina) 8.

ITALY 1934

Italy 2, Czechoslovakia 1 (0–0) (1–1) after extra time. *Rome*
Italy: Combi (capt.), Monzeglio, Allemandi, Ferraris IV, Monti, Bertolini Guaita, Meazza, Schiavio, Ferrari, Orsi.
Czechoslovakia: Planicka (capt.), Zenisek, Ctyroky, Kostalek, Cambal, Krcil, Junek, Svoboda, Sobotka, Nejedly, Puc.
Scorers: Orsi, Schiavio for Italy, Puc for Czechoslovakia.
Leading Scorers: Schiavio (Italy), Nejedly (Czechoslovakia), Conen (Germany) each 4.

FRANCE 1938

Italy 4, Hungary 2 (3–1). *Paris*
Italy: Olivieri; Foni, Rava, Serantoni, Andreolo, Locatelli, Biavati, Meazza (capt.), Piola, Ferrari, Colaussi.
Hungary: Szabo; Polgar, Biro, Szalay, Szucs, Luzar, Sas, Vincze, Sarosi, (capt.), Szengeller, Titkos.
Scorers: Colaussi (2), Piola (2) for Italy, Titkos, Sarosi for Hungary.
Leading Scorer: Leonidas (Brazil) 8.

BRAZIL 1950

Final pool replaced knock-out system.
FINAL POOL

Uruguay 2, Spain 2   Brazil 6, Spain 1
Brazil 7, Sweden 1   Sweden 3, Spain 1
Uruguay 3, Sweden 2   Uruguay 2, Brazil 1

FINAL POSITIONS

	P	W	D	L	F	A	Pts.
Uruguay	3	2	1	0	7	5	5
Brazil	3	2	0	1	14	4	4
Sweden	3	1	0	2	6	11	2
Spain	3	0	1	2	4	11	1

Leading Scorers: Ademir (Brazil) 7, Schiaffino (Uruguay), Basora (Spain) 5.

SWITZERLAND 1954

West Germany 3, Hungary 2.
West Germany: Turek; Posipal, Kohlmeyer, Eckel, Liebrich, Mai, Rahn, Morlock, Walter, O., Walter, F. (capt.), Schaefer.
Hungary: Grosics; Buzansky, Lantos, Boszik, Lorant, Zakarias, Czibor, Kocsis, Hidegkuti, Puskas (capt.), Toth, J.
Scorers: Morlock, Rahn (2) for Germany, Puskas, Czibor for Hungary.
Leading Scorer: Kocsis (Hungary) 11.

SWEDEN 1958

Brazil 5, Sweden 2 (2–1). *Stockholm.*
Brazil: Gilmar; Santos, D., Santos, N., Zito, Bellini, Orlando, Garrincha, Didi, Vava, Pele, Zagalo.
Sweden: Svensson; Bergmark, Axbom, Boerjesson, Gustavsson, Parling, Hamrin, Gren, Simonsson, Liedholm, Skoglund.
Scorers: Vava (2), Pele (2), Zagalo for Brazil, Liedholm, Simonsson for Sweden.
Leading Scorer: Fontaine 13 (present record total).

CHILE 1962

Brazil 3, Czechoslovakia 1 (1–1). *Santiago.*
Brazil: Gilmar; Santos, D., Mauro, Zozimo, Santos, N., Zito, Didi, Garrincha, Vava, Amarildo, Zagalo.
Czechoslovakia: Schroiff; Tichy, Novak, Pluskal, Popluhar, Masopust, Pospichal, Scherer, Kvasniak, Kadraba, Jelinek.
Scorers: Amarildo, Zito, Vava for Brazil, Masopust for Czechoslovakia.
Leading Scorers: Albert (Hungary), Ivanov (Russia), Sanchez, L. (Chile), Garrincha, Vava (Brazil), Jerkovic (Yugoslavia) each 4.

ENGLAND 1966

England 4, West Germany 2 (1–1) (2–2) after extra time. *Wembley.*
England: Banks; Cohen, Wilson, Stiles, Charlton, J., Moore, Ball, Hurst, Hunt, Charlton, R., Peters.
West Germany: Tilkowski; Hottges, Schulz, Weber, Schnellinger, Haller, Beckenbauer, Overath, Seller, Held, Emmerich.
Scorers: Hurst 3, Peters for England, Haller, Weber for Germany.
Leading Scorer: Eusebio (Portugal) 9.

MEXICO 1970

Brazil 4, Italy 1. *Mexico City.*
Brazil: Felix; Carlos, Alberto, Brito, Piazza, Everaldo, Gerson, Clodoaldo, Jairzinho, Pele, Tostao, Rivelino. No subs.
Italy: Albertosi, Burgnich, Cera, Rosato, Facchetti, Bertini, Riva, Domenghini, Mazzola, De Sisti, Boninsegna, Subs: Juliano for Bertini, Rivera for Boninsegna.
Scorers: Pele, Gerson, Jairzinho, Carlos Alberto for Brazil, Boninsegna for Italy.

WEST GERMANY 1974

West Germany 2, Holland 1 (2–1). *Munich.*
West Germany: Maier; Vogts, Schwarzenbeck, Beckenbauer, Breitner, Bonhof, Hoeness, Overath, Grabowski, Muller, Holzenbein.
Holland: Jongbloed; Suurbier, Rijsbergen (De Jong), Haan, Krol, Jansen, Van Hanegem, Neeskens, Rep, Cruyff, Rensenbrink (Van der Kerkhof, R.).
Scorers: Breitner (*pen*), Muller for West Germany, Neeskens (*pen*) for Holland.

ARGENTINA 1978

Argentina 3, Holland 1 (after extra time). *Buenos Aires.*
Argentina: Fillol; Olguin, Passarella, Galvan, Tarantini, Ardiles, (Larossa), Gallego, Ortiz (Houseman), Bertoni, Luque, Kempes.
Holland: Jongbloed; Poortvliet, Brandts, Krol, Jansen (Suurbier), Neeskens, W. Van der Kerkhof, R. Van der Kerkhof, Haan, Rep (Nanninga), Rensenbrink.
Scorers: Kempes 2, Bertoni for Argentina, Nanninga for Holland.

OTHER INTERNATIONALS

ENGLAND (0) 1, CZECHOSLOVAKIA (0) 0
at Wembley, November 29, 1978, 92,000

ENGLAND: Shilton; Anderson, Cherry, Thompson, Watson, Wilkins, Keegan, Coppell, Woodcock (Latchford), Currie, Barnes.
CZECHOSLOVAKIA: Michakik; Barmos, Vojacek, Jurkemik, Gogh, Stambacher, Kozak, Gajdusek, Jarusek (Panenka), Masny, Nehoda.
SCORER: England: Coppell.

SWEDEN (0) 0   ENGLAND (0) 0
at Stockholm, June 10, 1979, 35,691

SWEDEN: Moller; Arvidsson, Aman, Erlandsson, Borg, Torstensson, Linderoth, Nilsson, Gronhagen, Cervin, Johansson.
ENGLAND: Shilton; Anderson, Cherry, McDermott (Wilkins), Watson (Thompson), Hughes, Keegan, Francis, Woodcock, Currie (Brooking), Cunningham.

AUSTRIA (3) 4, ENGLAND (1) 3
at Vienna, June 13, 1979, 33,000

AUSTRIA: Koncilia; Sara, Obermayer, Pezzey, Baumeister, Hattenberger, Prohaska, Jara, Welzl (Schachner), Kreuz, Jurtin.
ENGLAND: Shilton (Clemence); Neal, Thompson, Watson, Mills, Wilkins, Brooking, Coppell, Keegan, Latchford (Francis), Barnes (Cunningham).
SCORERS: Austria: Pezzey 2, Welzl 2. England: Keegan, Coppell, Wilkins.

EIRE (1) 1, WEST GERMANY (1) 3
at Dublin, May 22, 1979, 20,000

EIRE: Paynton; Gregg, Martin, O'Leary, Mulligan, Grealish, Giles, Brady, Stapleton, Givens, Ryan.
WEST GERMANY: Maier (Burdenski); Kaltz, Cullmann, K-H. Foerster, B. Foerster, Schuster, Rummenigge (Memering), Zimmermann (Hartweg) Hoeness, Alloffs, Mueller (Kelsche).
SCORERS: Eire: Ryan. West Germany: Rummenigge, Kelsche, Hoeness.

SCOTLAND (0) 1, ARGENTINA (1) 3
at Hampden Park, June 2, 1979, 61,918

SCOTLAND: Rough (Wood); Burley, Munro, Narey, Hegarty, Hansen McGarvey, Wark, Dalglish, Hartford (Gray), Graham.
ARGENTINA: Fillol; Villaverde (Trossero), Tarantini, Olguin, Gailego Pasarella, Houseman (Outes), Barbas, Luque, Maradona, Valencia.
SCORERS: Scotland: Graham. Argentina: Luque 2, Maradona.

154

EUROPEAN CHAMPIONSHIPS
PAST FINALS

1958-60 Paris, July 10, 1960
USSR 2, Yugoslavia 1 (*after extra time*)
USSR: Yachin; Tchekeli, Kroutikov, Voinov, Maslenkin, Netto, Metreveli, Ivanov, Ponedelnik, Bubukin, Meshki.
Yugoslavia: Vidinic; Durkovic, Jusufi, Zanetic, Miladinovic, Perusic, Sekularac, Jerkovic, Galic, Matus, Kostic.
Scorers: *USSR*—Metreveli, Ponedelnik; *Yugoslavia*—Netto o.g.

1962-64 Madrid, June 21, 1964
SPAIN 2, USSR 1
Spain: Iribar; Rivilla, Calleja, Fuste, Olivella, Zoco, Amancio, Pereda, Marcellino, Suarez, Lapetra.
USSR: Yachin; Chustikov, Mudrik, Voronin, Shesternjev, Anitchkin, Chislenko, Ivanov, Ponedelnik, Kornaev, Khusainov.
Scorers: *Spain*—Pereda, Marcellino; *USSR*—Khusainov.

1966-68 Rome, June 8, 1968
ITALY 1, YUGOSLAVIA 1
Italy: Zoff; Burgnich, Facchetti, Ferrini, Guarneri, Castano, Domenghini, Juliano, Anastasi, Lodetti, Prati.
Yugoslavia: Pantelic; Fazlagic, Damjanovic, Pavlovic, Paunovic, Holcer, Petkovic, Acimovic, Musemic, Trivic, Dzajic.
Scorers: *Italy*—Domenghini, *Yugoslavia*—Dzajic.

Replay: Rome, June 10, 1968
ITALY 2, YUGOSLAVIA 0
Italy: Zoff; Burgnich, Facchetti, Rosato, Guarneri, Salvadore, Domenghini, Mazzola, Anastasi, De Sisti, Riva.
Yugoslavia: Pantelic; Fazlagic, Damjanovic, Pavlovic, Paunovic, Holcer, Hosic, Acimovic, Musemic, Trivic, Dzajic.
Scorers: *Italy*—Riva, Anastasi.

1970-72 Brussels, June 18, 1972
WEST GERMANY 3, USSR 0
West Germany: Maier; Hottges, Schwarzenbeck, Beckenbauer, Breitner, Hoeness, Wimmer, Netzer, Heynckes, Muller, Kremers.
USSR: Rudakov; Dzodzuashvili, Khurtislava, Kaplichny, Istomin, Troshkin, Kolotov, Baidachini, Konkov (Dolmatov), Banishevski (Kozinkievits), Onishenko.
Scorers: *West Germany*—Muller 2, Wimmer.

1974-76 Belgrade, June 20, 1976
CZECHOSLOVAKIA 2, WEST GERMANY 2 (*after extra time*)
Czechoslovakia: Viktor; Dobias (Vesely, F.), Pivarnik, Ondrus, Capkovic, Gogh, Moder, Panenka, Svehlik (Jurkemik), Masny, Nehoda.
West Germany: Maier; Vogts, Beckenbauer, Schwarzenbeck, Dietz, Bonhof, Wimmer (Flohe), Muller, D., Beer (Bongartz), Hoeness, Holzenbein.
Scorers: *Czechoslovakia*—Svehlik, Dobias; *West Germany*— Muller, Holzenbein.
Czechoslovakia won 5-3 on penalties.

THE EUROPEAN CHAMPIONSHIP
1978-80
The Qualifying Tournament

No fewer than 32 teams have entered the fourth European Football Championship for the Henri Delaunay Cup. Thirty-one of the entrants are divided into seven groups of between four and five teams, and the winner of each group will progress to the quarter-final stages. The eighth quarter-finalist will be Italy, who plays host to the group winners in a two-week period in the summer of 1980, and thus qualifies automatically. Here are the qualifying match fixtures, with results so far:

GROUP ONE
England, *Northern Ireland, Republic of Ireland, Denmark, Bulgaria.*

DENMARK (1) 3, EIRE (2) 3   May 24 1978
DENMARK: Jensen B.; Hensen, Rontved, Jensen H. M., Lerby, Olsen (Hujiland), Neilsen, Nygaard (Armefen), Sorensen, Jensen H., Kristensen.
EIRE: Kearns; Mulligan, Holmes (Gregg), Lawrenson, O'Leary, Grealish, Daly, Stapleton, Heighway, Giles, Givens (McGee).
SCORERS: Denmark: Jensen H. 2, Lerby. Eire: Stapleton, Grealish, Daly.

EIRE (0) 0, NORTHERN IRELAND (0) 0   September 20 1978
EIRE: Kearns; Grealish, Holmes, Lawrenson, Synott, Brady, Daly, Stapleton (Walsh), Heighway (Givens), Giles, McGee.
NORTHERN IRELAND: Jennings; Rice, Nelson, C. Nicholl, Hunter (Hamilton), J. Nicholl, O'Neill, McCreery, Armstrong, McIlroy, Spence (Cochrane).

DENMARK (2) 3, ENGLAND (2) 4   September 20 1978
DENMARK: Jensen; F. Neilsen, Munk Jensen, Rontved, Lerby, Arnesen, C. Neilsen, Lund, Simonsen, B. Neilsen, (A. Hansen), Kristensen.
ENGLAND: Clemence; Neal, Watson, Mills, Hughes, Wilkins, Keegan, Coppell, Brooking, Latchford, Barnes.
SCORERS: Denmark: Simonsen (pen), Arnesen, Rontved. England: Keegan 2, Latchford, Neal.

DENMARK (1) 2, BULGARIA (1) 2   October 11 1978
EIRE (1) 1, ENGLAND (1) 1   October 25 1978
EIRE: Kearns; Mulligan, Holmes, Lawrenson, O'Leary (Gregg), Brady, Daly, Grealish, McGee, (Stapleton), Ryan, Givens.
ENGLAND: Clemence; Neal, Mills, Wilkins, Watson (Thompson), Keegan, Coppell, Latchford, Brooking, Barnes (Woodcock).
SCORERS: Eire: Daly. England: Latchford.

NORTHERN IRELAND (0) 2, DENMARK (0) 1   October 25 1978
NORTHERN IRELAND: Jennings; Rice, Nicholl J., Hunter, McCreery, Nelson, McIlroy, O'Neill, Armstrong, Morgan (Spence) (Anderson), Cochrane.

156

DENMARK: Kjaer; Neilsen F., Rontved, Larsen, Andersen, Rasmussen, C. Nielsen, Berg, Agerbeck, (Sorensen), Jensen, Kristensen.
SCORERS: Northern Ireland: Spence, Anderson, Denmark: Jensen.

BULGARIA (0) 0, NORTHERN IRELAND (1) 2   November 29 1978
BULGARIA: Goranov; Grancharov, P. Stankov, Karakolev, Dimitrov, Stretkov, Gochev, Slavkov, Mladenov (Dzevizov), Panov, A. Stankov (Svetkov).

NORTHERN IRELAND: Jennings; Hamilton, J. Nicholl, C. Nicholl, Nelson, O'Neill, McCreery, McIlroy (Moreland), Cochrane (McGrath), Armstrong, Caskey.
SCORERS: Northern Ireland: Armstrong, Caskey.

ENGLAND (1) 4, NORTHERN IRELAND (0) 0   February 7 1979
ENGLAND: Clemence; Neal, Mills, Currie, Watson, Hughes, Keegan, Coppell, Latchford, Brooking, Barnes.

NORTHERN IRELAND: Jennings; Rice, Nelson, J. Nicholl, C. Nicholl, McCreery, O'Neill, McIlroy, Armstrong, Caskey (Spence), Cochrane (McGrath).
SCORERS: England: Keegan, Latchford 2, Watson.

EIRE (1) 2, DENMARK (0) 0   May 2 1979
EIRE: Paynton; Gregg, Mulligan, Martin, Holmes, Daly, Giles, Brady, Stapleton, Hayes, Givens.

DENMARK: Kjar; F. Neilsen, Rontved, Larsson, Lerby, Lunn, Arnesen, Olsen, Simonsen, B. Neilsen, Elkjer.
SCORERS: Eire: Daly, Givens.

NORTHERN IRELAND (2) 2, BULGARIA (0) 0   May 2 1979
NORTHERN IRELAND: Jennings; Hamilton, Nelson, J. Nicholl, C. Nicholl, McCreery, O'Neill, McIlroy, Armstrong, Casey, Cochrane.
BULGARIA: Stojanov; Vassilev, Ivkov, Bonnev, Kolev, Rainov, Zdravkov, Stedkov, Dzevizov, Panov, Zvetkov.
SCORERS: Northern Ireland: C. Nicholl, Armstrong.

BULGARIA (0) 1, EIRE (0) 0   May 19 1979
BULGARIA: Filipov; Vassilev, Ivkov, Bozev, Iliev, Zdravkov, Voynov, Borissov, Zhelvazkov, Penov, Tsvetkov.

EIRE: Peyton; Gregg, O'Leary, Martin, Holmes (Mulligan), Daly, Giles, Brady, Walsh (McGee), Givens, Heighway.
SCORER: Bulgaria: Tsvetkov.

BULGARIA (0) 0, ENGLAND (1) 3   June 6 1979
BULGARIA: Filipov; Grantcharov, Ivkov, Bonev, Iliev, Zdravkov (Barzov), Voinov (Gotschev), Borisov, Zeliazkov, Panov, Zvetkov.

ENGLAND: Clemence; Neal, Thompson, Watson, Mills, Wilkins, Keegan, Brooking, Coppell, Latchford (Francis), Barnes (Woodcock).
SCORERS: England: Keegan, Watson, Barnes.

DENMARK (2) 4, NORTHERN IRELAND (0) 0   June 6 1979
DENMARK: Kjaer; Hojgaard, Ziegler, Busk, Andersen, Olsen, Arnesen, Lerby, Norregaard, Simonsen, Elkjaer.

NORTHERN IRELAND: Jennings; Rice, Nelson, Nicholl, Hunter McCreery, O'Neill, McIlroy, Armstrong, Spence, Hamilton.
SCORERS: Denmark: Elkjaer 3, Simonsen.

157

	September 12 1979
ENGLAND v DENMARK	September 12 1979
EIRE v BULGARIA	October 17 1979
NORTHERN IRELAND v ENGLAND	October 17 1979
BULGARIA v DENMARK	October 31 1979
ENGLAND v BULGARIA	November 21 1979
NORTHERN IRELAND v EIRE	November 21 1979
ENGLAND v EIRE	February 6 1980

Table so far:

	P	W	D	L	F	A	Pts.
England	4	3	1	0	12	4	7
Northern Ireland	6	3	1	2	6	9	7
Eire	5	1	3	1	6	5	5
Denmark	6	1	2	3	13	13	4
Bulgaria	5	1	1	3	3	9	3

GROUP TWO

Portugal, *Austria, Belgium, Scotland, Norway.*

NORWAY (0) 0, AUSTRIA (2) 2 — August 30 1978

BELGIUM (0) 1, NORWAY (1) 1 — September 20 1978

AUSTRIA (1) 3, SCOTLAND (0) 2 — September 20 1978
AUSTRIA: Fuchsbichler; Sara, Obermayer, Pezzey, Strasser, Prohaska (Oberacher), Weber, Jara, Schachner, Kreuz, Krankl.

SCOTLAND: Rough; Kennedy, McQueen, Buchan, Donachie, Gemmill, Hartford, Souness, Jordan (Graham), Gray, Dalglish.
SCORERS: Austria: Pezzey, Schachner, Kreuz. Scotland: McQueen, Gray.

PORTUGAL (1) 1, BELGIUM (1) 1 — October 11 1978

SCOTLAND (1) 3, NORWAY (1) 2 — October 25 1978
SCOTLAND: Stewart; Donachie, F. Gray, Souness, McQueen, Buchan, Dalglish, Gemmill, A. Gray, Hartford, Graham.

NORWAY: T. R. Jacobsen; Pedersen, Kordahl, Birkelund, Grondalen, Aas, Johansen, T. Jacobsen, Thoresen, Okland, Mathisen.
SCORERS: Scotland: Dalglish 2, Gemmill (pen). Norway: Aas, Okland.

AUSTRIA (0) 1, PORTUGAL (1) 2 — November 15 1978

PORTUGAL (1) 1, SCOTLAND (0) 0 — November 29 1978
PORTUGAL: Bento; Artur, Humberto, Alhinho, Alberto, Pietra, Alves, Oliveira (Eurico), Costa (Sheu), Gomes, Nene.

SCOTLAND: Rough; Kennedy, McQueen, Buchan, F. Gray (Donachie), Narey, Gemmill, Hartford, Dalglish, Jordan (Wallace), Robertson.
SCORER: Portugal: Alberto.

BELGIUM (1) 1, AUSTRIA (0) 1 — March 28 1979

AUSTRIA (0) 0, BELGIUM (0) 0 — May 2 1979

NORWAY (0) 0, PORTUGAL (1) 1 — May 9 1979

NORWAY (0) 0, SCOTLAND (3) 4 — June 7 1979

NORWAY: Jacobsen; Karlsen, Kordahl, Grondalen, Pedersen, Aas, Albertsen, Thunderg, Thoresen, Mathisen, Okland.

SCOTLAND: Rough; Burley, Munro, Burns, McQueen, Gemmill, Graham, Dalglish, Jordan, Hartford, Robertson.

SCORERS: Scotland: Jordan, Dalglish, Robertson, McQueen.

AUSTRIA v NORWAY	August 20 1979
NORWAY v BELGIUM	September 12 1979
BELGIUM v PORTUGAL	October 17 1979
SCOTLAND v AUSTRIA	October 17 1979
PORTUGAL v NORWAY	November 1 1979
BELGIUM v SCOTLAND	November 21 1979
PORTUGAL v AUSTRIA	November 21 1979
SCOTLAND v PORTUGAL	February 6 1980
SCOTLAND v BELGIUM	To be announced

Table so far:

	P	W	D	L	F	A	Pts.
Portugal	4	3	1	0	5	2	7
Austria	5	2	2	1	7	5	6
Scotland	4	2	0	2	9	6	4
Belgium	4	0	4	0	3	3	4
Norway	5	0	1	4	3	11	1

GROUP THREE

Spain, *Rumania, Yugoslavia, Cyprus*

YUGOSLAVIA (1) 1, SPAIN (2) 2	October 4 1978
RUMANIA (0) 3, YUGOSLAVIA (1) 2	October 25 1978
SPAIN (1) 1, RUMANIA (0) 0	November 15 1978
SPAIN (2) 5, CYPRUS (0) 0	December 13 1978
CYPRUS (0) 0, YUGOSLAVIA (1) 3	April 1 1979
RUMANIA (0) 2, SPAIN (0) 2	April 4 1979
CYPRUS (1) 1, RUMANIA (1) 1	May 13 1979
SPAIN v YUGOSLAVIA	October 10 1979
YUGOSLAVIA v RUMANIA	October 31 1979
YUGOSLAVIA v CYPRUS	November 14 1979
RUMANIA v CYPRUS	November 18 1979
CYPRUS v SPAIN	December 9 1979

Table so far:

	P	W	D	L	F	A	Pts.
Spain	4	3	1	0	10	3	7
Rumania	4	1	2	1	6	6	4
Yugoslavia	3	1	0	2	6	5	2
Cyprus	3	0	1	2	1	9	1

GROUP FOUR

Netherlands, *Poland, East Germany, Iceland, Switzerland.*

ICELAND (0) 0, POLAND (1) 2	September 6 1978
NETHERLANDS (1) 3, ICELAND (0) 0	September 20 1978
EAST GERMANY (2) 3, ICELAND (1) 1	October 4 1978
SWITZERLAND (1) 1, NETHERLANDS (1) 3	October 11 1978

159

NETHERLANDS (1) 3, EAST GERMANY (0) 0   November 15 1978
POLAND (1) 2, SWITZERLAND (0) 0   November 15 1978
NETHERLANDS (0) 3, SWITZERLAND (0) 0   March 28 1979
EAST GERMANY (0) 2, POLAND (1) 1   April 18 1979
POLAND (1) 2, NETHERLANDS (0) 0   May 2 1979
SWITZERLAND (0) 0, EAST GERMANY (1) 2   May 5 1979
SWITZERLAND (1) 2, ICELAND (0) 0   May 22 1979
ICELAND (0) 1, SWITZERLAND (1) 2   June 9 1979
ICELAND v NETHERLANDS   September 5 1979
ICELAND v EAST GERMANY   September 12 1979
SWITZERLAND v POLAND   September 12 1979
POLAND v EAST GERMANY   September 26 1979
POLAND v ICELAND   October 10 1979
EAST GERMANY v SWITZERLAND   October 13 1979
NETHERLANDS v POLAND   October 17 1979
EAST GERMANY v NETHERLANDS   November 21 1979

Table so far:

	P	W	D	L	F	A	Pts.
Netherlands	5	4	0	1	12	3	8
Poland	4	3	0	1	7	2	6
East Germany	4	3	0	1	7	5	6
Switzerland	6	2	0	4	5	11	4
Iceland	5	0	0	5	2	12	0

GROUP FIVE
Czechoslovakia, *France, Sweden, Luxembourg.*

FRANCE (0) 2, SWEDEN (0) 2   September 1 1978
SWEDEN (1) 1, CZECHOSLOVAKIA (1) 3   October 4 1978
LUXEMBOURG (1) 1, FRANCE (0) 3   October 7 1978
FRANCE (1) 3, LUXEMBOURG (0) 0   February 25 1979
CZECHOSLOVAKIA (0) 2, FRANCE (0) 0   April 4 1979
LUXEMBOURG (0) 0, CZECHOSLOVAKIA (1) 3   May 1 1979
SWEDEN (2) 3, LUXEMBOURG (0) 0   June 7 1979
SWEDEN v FRANCE   September 5 1979
CZECHOSLOVAKIA v SWEDEN   October 10 1979
LUXEMBOURG v SWEDEN   October 23 1979
FRANCE v CZECHOSLOVAKIA   November 17 1979
CZECHOSLOVAKIA v LUXEMBOURG   November 24 1979

Table so far:

	P	W	D	L	F	A	Pts.
Czechoslovakia	3	3	0	0	8	1	6
France	4	2	1	1	8	5	5
Sweden	3	1	1	1	6	5	3
Luxembourg	4	0	0	4	1	12	0

GROUP SIX
Greece, *Finland, Hungary, USSR.*

FINLAND (1) 3, GREECE (0) 0	May 25 1978
FINLAND (1) 2, HUNGARY (0) 1	September 20 1978
USSR (1) 2, GREECE (0) 0	September 20 1978
HUNGARY (1) 2, USSR (0) 0	October 11 1978
GREECE (5) 8, FINLAND (0) 1	October 11 1978
GREECE (0) 4, HUNGARY (0) 1	October 29 1978
HUNGARY (0) 0, GREECE (0) 0	May 2 1979
USSR (1) 2, HUNGARY (1) 2	May 19 1979
FINLAND v USSR	July 4 1979
GREECE v USSR	September 12 1979
HUNGARY v FINLAND	October 17 1979
USSR v FINLAND	October 31 1979

Table so far:

	P	W	D	L	F	A	Pts.
Greece	5	2	1	2	12	7	5
Hungary	5	1	2	2	6	8	4
Finland	3	2	0	1	6	9	4
USSR	3	1	1	1	4	4	3

GROUP SEVEN
Wales, *West Germany, Turkey, Malta.*

WALES (3) 7, MALTA (0) 0   October 25 1978
WALES: Davies; Stevenson, Jones, Phillips, Page, Thomas, Harris,
Flynn, Edwards, James, Cartwright (O'Sullivan).

MALTA: Gatti; Ciantar, Farrugia (Consiglio), Toretell, Schembri,
Holland, Magro, Aquilina (Spiteri-Gonzi), Xuereb G., Xuereb R.,
Sychell.

SCORERS: Wales: Edwards 4, O'Sullivan, Thomas, Flynn.

WALES (0) 1, TURKEY (0) 0   November 29 1978
WALES: Davies; Stevenson, Jones, Phillips, Yorath, Thomas, Harris,
Flynn, Deacy, Dwyer, James.

TURKEY: Senol; Turgay, Erdoan, Cem, Necati, Fatih, Necdet,
Mehmeteski, Sedat, Onder, Ahmet.

SCORER: Wales: Deacy.

MALTA (0) 0, WEST GERMANY (0) 0   February 25 1979
TURKEY (1) 2, MALTA (0) 1   March 18 1979
TURKEY (0) 0, WEST GERMANY (0) 0   April 1 1979
WALES (0) 0, WEST GERMANY (1) 2   May 2 1979
WALES: Davies; Page, Jones, Mahoney, Phillips, Berry, Harris, Thomas,
Yorath, Edwards, Curtis.

WEST GERMANY: Maier; Kaltz, Stielke, Foerster, Dietz, Bonhof,
Cullmann, Zimmermann, Fischer, Rummenigge, Alloffs.

SCORERS: West Germany: Zimmermann, Fischer.

161

MALTA (0) 0, WALES (1) 2   June 2 1979
MALTA: Sciberras; Buckingham, Ed Farrugia, Holland, Buttigieg, Em
   Farrugia, Magro, Xuereb J., Spitteri-Gonzi, Xuereb R., Xuereb G.

WALES: Davies; Stevenson, Jones, Mahoney, Nicholas, Phillips, Harris,
   Flynn, James, Toshack, Curtis.
SCORERS: Wales: Nicholas, Flynn.

WEST GERMANY v WALES	October 17 1979
MALTA v TURKEY	October 28 1979
TURKEY v WALES	November 21 1979
WEST GERMANY v TURKEY	December 22 1979
WEST GERMANY v MALTA	February 27 1980

Table so far:

	P	W	D	L	F	A	Pts.
Wales	4	3	0	1	10	2	6
West Germany	3	1	2	0	2	0	4
Turkey	3	1	1	1	2	2	3
Malta	4	0	1	3	1	11	1

INTERNATIONAL GOALSCORERS
1946-79
Up to June 13 1979
ENGLAND

Charlton,R.	49	Edwards	5	Perry	2
Greaves	44	Hitchens	5	Tueart	2
Finney	30	Latchford	5	Pointer	2
Lofthouse	30	Pearson, Stan	5	Taylor,P.	2
Hurst	24	Pearson, Stuart	5	Wignall	2
Mortensen	23	Pickering	5	Worthington	2
Channon	21	Barnes	4	A'Court	1
Peters	21	Hassall	4	Astall	1
Haynes	18	Revie	4	Beattie	1
Hunt	18	Robson	4	Bowles	1
Lawton	16	Baker	3	Bradford	1
Taylor,T.	16	Currie	3	Bridges	1
Keegan	15	Elliott	3	Brooking	1
Chivers	13	Francis, G.	3	Crawford	1
Smith,R.	13	Grainger	3	Hughes	1
Douglas	11	Johnson	3	Kay	1
Mannion	11	Kennedy	3	Kidd	1
Clarke	10	Matthews	3	Langton	1
Flowers	10	Morris	3	Lawler	1
Lee,F.	10	Neal	3	Lee,J.	1
Milburn	10	O'Grady	3	Mariner	1
Wilshaw	10	Peacock	3	Marsh	1
Bell	9	Ramsey	3	Medley	1
Bentley	9	Sewell	3	Melia	1
Ball	8	Watson	3	Mullery	1
Broadis	8	Wright	3	Nicholls	1
Byrne,J.	8	Allen, R.	2	Nicholson	1
Kevan	8	Bradley	2	Parry	1
Connelly	7	Broadbent	2	Shackleton	1
Paine	7	Brooks	2	Stiles	1
Charlton,J.	6	Eastham	2	Summerbee	1
Macdonald	6	Francis, T.	2	Tambling	1
Mullen	6	Froggatt, J.	2	Thomson	1
Rowley,J.	6	Froggatt, R.	2	Viollet	1
Atyeo	5	Haines	2	Weller	1
Baily	5	Hancocks	2	Wilkins	1
Carter	5	Hunter	2		
Coppell	5	Moore	2		
		Royle	2		
		Own Goals	8		

NORTHERN IRELAND

Crossan	10	Simpson	4	McGarry	1
McIlroy, J.	10	Armstrong	4	Ferris	1
Best	9	Harvey	3	D'Arcy	1
Bingham	9	Lockhart	3	Walker	1
Irvine	9	McMordie	3	Blanchflower, J.	1
McParland	9	Morgan	3	Elder	1
Dougan	8	Spence	3	Johnston	1
Wilson	7	Doherty	2	Nelson	1
Cush	7	Clements	2	Ferguson	1
McAdams	7	Finney	2	Jones	1
McLaughlin	6	Tully	2	McCrory	1
Nicholson	6	Peacock	2	Barr	1
Smyth	5	Casey	2	Humphries	1
Walsh	5	Nicholl, C.	2	Hunter	1
Anderson	4	Harkin	2	Welsh	1
McMorran	4	Blanchflower, D.	2	Campbell	1
O'Neill	4	McIlroy, S.	2	O'Kane	1
Hamilton	4	Neill	2	Cassidy	1
McGrath	4	Stevenson	1	Caskey	1
		Brennan	1		
		Own Goals	2		

SCOTLAND

Law	30	McLaren	4	Houliston	2
Dalglish	22	Lorimer	4	Graham, A.	2
Reilly	22	Mason	4	Johnstone, D.	2
Steel	13	Hamilton	4	McMillan	2
Gilzean	12	Johnstone, J.	4	Harper	2
Stein	11	Smith	3	Fleming	2
Collins	10	Caldow	3	Ring	2
Johnstone, R.	10	Bremner	3	Robertson	2
Mudie	9	Mackay	3	Baird	2
Jordan	9	Gray, A.	3	Hewie	2
St. John	9	Hartford	3	Holton	2
Wilson	9	Herd	3	Gemmell	1
Brand	8	MacDougall	3	Combe	1
Leggat	8	McNeill	3	Duncan	1
Brown	6	Morris	3	Herd	1
Gemmill	6	McPhail	3	Howie	1
Liddell	6	Baxter	3	Linwood	1
Waddell	6	White	3	Mitchell	1
Rioch	6	Gibson	3	Orr	1
Scott	5	Lennox	3	Thornton	1
Young	5	Greig	3	Henderson	1
Macari	5	Chalmers	3	McKenzie	1
McQueen	5	Gray, E.	3	Ormond	1
Murdoch	5	Graham, A.	3	Davidson	1
Henderson	5	Bauld	2	Buckley	1
Masson	5	Pettigrew	2	Docherty	1
O'Hare	5	Flavell	2	Curran	1

Conn	1	Mulhall	1	Morgan	1
Fernie	1	Hunter	1	Bone	1
Hutchison	1	McLintock	1	Jardine	1
Burns	1	McCalliog	1	Craig	1
Jackson	1	McKinnon	1	Wallace	1
Parlane	1	Hughes	1	Wark	1
Quinn	1	McLean	1	Robertson, J.	1
Weir	1	Johnstone	1		
Murray	1	Campbell	1		
		Own Goals	8		

WALES

Ford	23	Rees	3	Bowen	1
Allchurch	22	England	3	Moore	1
Jones, C.	16	Woosnam	3	Hewitt	1
Charles, J.	15	Lowrie	2	Powell	1
Toshack	12	Edwards	2	Kryzwicki	1
Davies, R.	8	Griffiths, M.	2	Williams	1
Vernon	8	Godfrey	2	Hockey	1
James, L.	8	Jones, Bryn	2	Smallman	1
Medwin	6	Jones, Barrie	2	Roberts	1
Griffiths, A.	6	Dwyer	2	Yorath	1
Charles, M.	6	Reece	2	Mahoney	1
Clarke	5	Durban	2	Curtis	1
Leek	5	Paul	2	Evans	1
Deacy	5	Powell	1	Jones D.	1
Tapscott	4	Burgess	1	Thomas	1
Palmer	3	Foulkes	1	O'Sullivan	1
Flynn	3	Barnes	1	Nicholas	1
		Own Goals	1		

POST-WAR INTERNATIONAL APPEARANCES

(as at June 14, 1979)

Abbreviations A—Albania; Arg—Argentina; Aust—Austria; Bel—Belgium; Braz—Brazil; Bulg—Bulgaria; Ch—Chile; Czecho—Czechoslovakia; Co—Colombia; C—Cyprus; D—Denmark; Ec—Ecuador; E—England; E/Germ—East Germany; F—France; FIFA—Federation of International Associations; Fin—Finland; G—West Germany; Gr—Greece; H—Hungary; Holl—Holland; I—N. Ireland; Ic—Iceland; Ir—Iran; Isr—Israel; It—Italy; K—Kuwait; Lux—Luxembourg; M—Malta; Mex—Mexico; N—Norway; Par—Paraguay; Per—Peru; Pol—Poland; Port—Portugal; Ru—Rumania; Rus—Russia; S—Scotland; Sp—Spain; Swdn—Sweden; Switz—Switzerland; T—Turkey; U—Uruguay; U.K.—Rest of United Kingdom; U.S.—United States of America; W—Wales; Y—Yugoslavia; Z—Zaire.

ENGLAND

A'COURT A. (5) (Liverpool) 1957/8 v. I, Braz, Aust, Rus; 1958/9 v. W.

ALLEN, R. (5) (West Bromwich) 1951/2 v. Switz; 1953/4 v. S, Y; 1954/5 v. W, G.

ALLEN, T. (3) (Stoke) 1959/60 v. W. Swdn, I.

ANDERSON, S. (2) (Sunderland) 1961/2 v. Aust, S.

ANDERSON, V. (2) (Nottingham F.) 1978/9 v. Czecho, Swdn.

ANGUS, J. (I) (Burnley) 1960/I v. Aust.

ARMFIELD, J. (43) (Blackpool) 1958/9 v. Braz, Per, Mex, U.S.; 1959/60 v. S, Y, Sp, H; 1960/I v. I, Lux, Sp, W, S, Mex, Port, It, Aust; 1961/2 v Lux, W, Port, I, Aust, S, Switz, Per, H, Arg, Bulg, Braz; 1962/3 v. F, I, W, F, S, Braz, E/Germ, Switz; 1963/4 v. W, FIFA, I, S; 1965/6 v. Y, Fin.

ARMSTRONG, K. (I) (Chelsea) 1954/5 v. S.

ASTALL, G. (2) (Birmingham) 1955/6 v. Fin, G.

ASTLE, J. (5) (West Bromwich) 1968/9 v. W; 1969/70 v. Port, S, Braz, Czecho.

ASTON, J. (17) (Manchester United) 1948/9 v. W, S, D, Switz, Swdn, N, F; 1949/50 v. W, I, S, Eire, It, Port, Bel, Ch, U.S.; 1950/I v. I.

ATYEO, J. (6) (Bristol City) 1955/6 v. Sp, Braz, Swdn; 1956/7 v. Eire, D, Eire.

BAILEY, M. (2) (Charlton) 1963/4 v. U.S.; 1964/5 v. W.

BAILY, E. (9) (Tottenham) 1949/50 v. Sp; 1950/I v. I, W, Y; 1951/2 v. W, Aust (2), Switz; 1952/3 v. I.

BAKER, J. (8) (Hibernian) 1959/60 v. I, S, Y, Sp, H; 1965/6 (Arsenal) v. i, Sp, Pol.

ALL, A. (72) (Blackpool) 1964/5 v. Y, G, Swdn; 1965/6 v. Sp, Pol, G, S, Fin, D, Pol, U, Arg, Port, G; 1966/7 (Everton) v. I, Czecho, W, S, Sp, Aust; 1967/8 v. W, Rus, S, Sp (2), G, Y; 1968/9 v. Ru (2), I, W, S, Mex, U, Braz; 1969/70 v. Port, Bel, W, S, Co, Ec, Ru, Braz, Czecho, G; 1970/I v. E/Germ, M, Gr, M, I, S; 1971/2 v. Switz, Gr (Arsenal) G, (2), S; 1972/3 v. Y, W (2), S, I, W, S, Czecho, Pol; 1973/4 v. Port; 1974/5 v. G, C (2), I, W, S.

BANKS, G. (73) (Leicester) 1962/3 v. S, Braz, Czecho, E/Germ; 1963/4 v. W, FIFA, I, S, U, Port, U.S., Port, Arg; 1964/5 v. I, S, H, Y, G, Swdn; 1965/6 v. I, Sp, Pol, G, S, Y, Fin, Pol, Y, Mex, F, Arg, Port, G; 1966/7 v. I, Czecho, W, S; 1967/8 (Stoke) v. W, I, Rus, S, Sp, G, Y, Rus; 1968/9 v. Ru (2), F, I, S, U, Braz; 1969/70 v. Holl, Bel, W, S, Co, Ec, Ru, Braz, Czecho; 1970/I v. M, Gr, M, I, S; 1971/2 v. Switz, Gr, G (2), W, S,

166

BANKS, T. (6) (Bolton) 1957/8 v. Rus (2), Braz, Aust, Rus; 1958/9 v. I.
BARLOW, R. (l) (West Bromwich) 1954/5 v. I.
BARNES, P. (14) (Manchester C.) 1977/8 v. It, G, Braz, W, S, H; 1978/9 v. D, Eire, Czecho, I, I, S, Bulg, Aust.
BARRASS, M. (3) (Bolton) 1951/2 v. W, I; 1952/3 v. S.
BAYNHAM, R. (3) (Luton) 1955/6 v. D, I, Sp.
BEATTIE, T. K. (9) (Ipswich T.) 1974/5 v. C (2), S; 1975/6 v. Switz, Port; 1976/7 v. Fin, It, Holl; 1977/8 v. Lux.
BELL, C. (48) (Manchester City) 1967/8 v. Swdn, G; 1968/9 v. Bulg, F, W, U, Braz; 1969/70 v. Holl, Port, Holl, I, Braz, Czecho, G; 1971/2 v. Gr, G (2), W, I, S; 1972/3 v. Y, W (2), S, I, W, S, Czecho, Pol; 1973/4 v. Pol, It, W, I, S, Arg, Aust, E/Germ, Bulg, Y; 1974/5 v. Czecho, Port, G, C (2), I, S; 1975/6 v. Switz, Czecho.
BENTLEY, R. (12) (Chelsea) 1948/9 v. Swdn; 1949/50 v. S, Port, Bel, Ch, U.S.; 1952/3 v. W, Bel; 1954/5 v. W, G, Sp, Port.
BERRY, J. (4) (Manchester United) 1952/3 v. Arg, Ch, U; 1955/6 v. Swdn.
BLOCKLEY, J. (1) (Arsenal) 1972/3 v. Y.
BLUNSTONE, F. (5) (Chelsea) 1954/5 v. W, S, F, Port; 1956/7 v. Y.
BONETTI, P. (7) (Chelsea) 1965/6 v. D,; 1966/7 v. Sp. Aust; 1967/8 v. Sp; 1969/70 v. Holl, Port, G.
BOWLES, S. (5) (Q.P.R.) 1973/4 v. Port, W, I; 1976/7 v. It, Holl.
BOYER, P. (1) (Norwich C.) 1975/6 v. W.
BRABROOK, P. (3) (Chelsea) 1957/8 v. Rus; 1959/60 v. I, Sp.
BRADFORD, G. (1) (Bristol R.) 1955/6 v. D.
BRADLEY, W. (3) (Manchester United) 1958/9 v. It, Mex, U.S.
BRIDGES, B. (4) (Chelsea) 1964/5 v. S, H, Y; 1965/6 v. Aust.
BROADBENT, P. (7) (Wolverhampton) 1957/8 v. Rus; 1958/9 v. I, W, S, It, Braz; 1959/60 v. S.
BROADIS, I. (14) (Manchester City) 1951/2 v. Aust, S, It; 1952/3 v. S, Arg, Ch, U, U.S. (Newcastle); 1953/4 v. S, Y, H, Bel, Switz, U.
BROOKING, T. (30) (West Ham) 1973/4 v. Port, Arg, E/Germ, Bulg, Y; 1974/5 v. Czecho, Port; 1975/6 v. W, Port, Braz, It, Fin; 1976/7 v. Eire, Fin, It, Holl, I, W; 1977/8 v. It, G, W, S, H; 1978/9 v. D, Eire, I, S, Bulg, Swdn, Aust.
BROOKS, J. (3) (Tottenham) 1956/7 v. W, Y, D.
BROWN, Tony (1) (West Bromwich) 1970/1 v. W.
BROWN, K. (1) (West Ham) 1959/60 v. I.
BYRNE, G. (2) (Liverpool) 1962/3 v. S; 1965/6 v. N.
BYRNE, J. (11) (Crystal Palace) 1961/2 v. I; 1962/3 (West Ham) v. Switz; 1963/4 v. S, U, Port, Eire, Braz, Arg; 1964/5 v. W, S.
BYRNE, R. (33) (Manchester United) 1953/4 v. S, Y, H, Bel, Switz, U; 1954/5 v. I, W, G, S, F, Sp, Port; 1955/6 v. D, W, I, Sp, Braz, Swdn, Fin, G; 1956/7 v. I, W, Y, D, S, Eire; 1957/8 v. W, I, F.

CALLAGHAN, I. (4) (Liverpool) 1965/6 v. Fin, F; 1977/8 v. Switz, Lux.
CARTER, H. (7) (Derby) 1946/7 v. I, W, S, Eire, Holl, F, Switz.
CHANNON, M. (46) (Southampton) 1972/3 v. Y, S, I, W, S, Czecho, Rus, It. 1973/4 v. Pol, It, Port, W, I, S, Arg, Aust, E/Germ, Bulg, Y; 1974/5 v. Czecho, Port, G, C (2), I, W, S; 1975/6 v. Switz, Czecho; Port, W, I, S, Braz, It, Fin; 1976/7 v. Fin, It, Lux, I, W, S, Braz, Arg, U; 1977/8 v. Switz.
CHARLTON, J. (35) (Leeds) 1964/5 v. S, H, Y, G, Swdn; 1965/6 v. N, Aust. I, Sp, Pol, G, S, Y, Fin, D, Pol, U, Mex, F, Arg, Port, G; 1966/7 v. I, Czecho, W, S; 1967/8 v. W, Sp; 1968/9 v. Ru, F, W; 1969/70 v. Holl, Port, Holl, Czecho.

167

CHARLTON, R. (106) (Manchester United) 1957/8 v. S, Port, Y; 1958/9
v. I, Rus, W, S, It, Braz, Per, Mex, U.S.; 1959/60 v. W, Swdn, S, Y, Sp, H;
1960/1 v. I, Lux, Sp, W, S, Mex, Port, It, Aust; 1961/2 v. Lux, W, Port, I,
Aust, S, Switz, Per, H, Arg, Bulg, Braz; 1962/3 v. F, S, Braz, Czecho,
E/Germ, Switz; 1963/4 v. W, FIFA, I, S, U, Port, Eire, U.S., Braz, Arg;
1964/5 v. I, Holl, S; 1965/6 v. W, Aust, I, G, S, Sp, Y, Fin, N, Pol, U, Mex, F,
Arg, Port, G; 1966/7 v. I, Czecho, W, S; 1967/8 v. W, I, Rus, S, Sp (2),
Swdn, Y, Rus; 1968/9 v. Ru, Bulg, Ru, I, W, S, Mex, Braz; 1969/70 v. Holl,
Port, Holl, W, I, Co, Ec, Ru, Braz, Czecho, G.
CHARNLEY, R. (1) (Blackpool) 1961/2 v. F.
CHERRY, T. (20) (Leeds U.) 1975/6 v. W, S, Braz, Fin; 1976/7 v. Eire, It,
Lux, I, S, Braz, Arg, U; 1977/8 v. Switz, Lux, It, Braz, W; 1978/9 v. Czecho,
W, Swdn.
CHILTON, A. (2) (Manchester United) 1950/1 v. I; 1951/2 v. F.
CHIVERS, M. (24) (Tottenham) 1970/1 v. M, Gr, M, I, S; 1971/2 v. Switz (2),
Gr, G (2), S; 1972/3 v. W (2), S, I, W, S, Czecho, Pol, Rus, It; 1973/4 v. Pol,
Aust.
CLAMP, E. (4) (Wolverhampton) 1957/8 v. Rus. (2), Braz, Aust.
CLAPTON, D. (1) (Arsenal) 1958/9 v. W.
CLARKE, A. (19) (Leeds) 1969/70 v. Czecho; 1970/1 v. E/Germ, M, I, W, S;
1972/3 v. S, W, S, Czecho, Pol, Rus, It; 1973/4 v. Pol, It, Aust; 1974/5 v.
Port; 1975/6 v. Czecho, Port.
CLARKE, H. (1) (Tottenham) 1953/4 v. S.
CLAYTON, R. (35) (Blackburn) 1955/6 v. I, Sp, Braz, Swdn, Fin, G; 1956/7
v. I, W, Y, D, S, Eire; 1957/8 v. W, I, F, S, Port, Y, Rus; 1958/9 v. I, Rus, W,
S, It, Braz, Per, Mex, U.S.; 1959/60 v. W, Swdn, I, S, Y.
CLEMENCE, R. (43) (Liverpool) 1972/3 v. W (2); 1973/4 v. E/Germ, Bulg, Y;
1974/5 v. Czecho, Port, G, C, I, W, S; 1975/6 v. Switz, Czecho, Port, U (2),
I, S, Braz, Fin; 1976/7 v. Eire, Fin, It, Holl, Lux, S, Braz, Arg, U; 1977/8
v. Switz, Lux, It, G, I, S; 1978/9 v. D, Eire, I, I, S, Bulg, Aust.
CLEMENT, D. (5) (Q.P.R.) 1975/6 v. W (2); 1976/7 v. It, Holl.
CLOUGH, B. (2) (Middlesbrough) 1959/60 v. W, Swdn.
COATES, R. (4) (Burnley) 1969/70 v. I; 1970/1 v. Gr, (Tottenham) M, W.
COCKBURN, H. (13) (Manchester United) 1946/7 v. I, W, Eire; 1947/8 v. S,
It; 1948/9 v. I, S, D, Switz; 1950/1 v. Arg, Port; 1951/2 v. F.
COHEN, G. (37) (Fulham) 1963/4 v. U, Port, Eire, U.S., Braz; 1964/5 v.
I, Bel, W, Holl, S, H, Y, G, Swdn; 1965/6 v. W, Aust, I, Sp, Pol, G, S, N, D,
Pol, U, Mex, F, Arg, Port, G; 1966/7 v. I, Czecho, W, S, Sp; 1967/8 v. W, I.
COMPTON, L. (2) (Arsenal) 1950/1 v. W, Y.
CONNELLY, J. (20) (Burnley) 1959/60 v. W, Swdn, I, S; 1961/2 v. W, Port,
Aust, Switz; 1962/3 v. W, F; 1964/5 (Manchester United) v. H, Y, Swdn;
1965/6 v. W, Aust, I, S, N, D, U.
COOPER, T. (20) (Leeds) 1968/9 v. F, W, S, Mex; 1969/70 v. Holl, Bel, Co,
Ec, Ru, Braz, Czecho, G; 1970/1 v. E/Germ, M, I, W, S; 1971/2 v. Switz (2);
1974/5 v. Port.
COPPELL, S. (15) (Manchester U.) 1977/8 v. It, G, Braz, W, I, S, H; 1978/9 v.
D, Eire, Czecho, I, I, S, Bulg, Aust.
CORRIGAN, J. (3) (Manchester City) 1975/6 v. It; 1977/8 v. Braz; 1978/9 v. W
CRAWFORD, R. (2) (Ipswich) 1961/2 v. I, Aust.
CROWE, C. (1) (Wolverhampton) 1962/3 v. F.
CUNNINGHAM, L. (3) (W.B.A.) 1978/9 v. W, Swdn, Aust.
CURRIE, A. (17) (Sheffield United) 1971/2 v. I; 1972/3 v. Rus, It; 1973/4 v. Pol,
It, Aust; 1975/6 v. Switz; (Leeds U.) 1977/8 v. Braz, W, I, S, H; 1978/9 v.
Czecho, I, I, W, Swdn.

168

DEELEY, N. (2) (Wolverhampton) 1958/9 v. Braz, Per.
DICKINSON, J. (48) (Portsmouth) 1948/9 v. N, F; 1949/50 v. W, S, Eire,
Port, Bel, Ch, U.S., Sp; 1950/1 v. I, W, Y; 1951/2 v. W, I, Aust (2), S, It,
Switz; 1952/3 v. I, W, Bel, S, Arg, Ch, U, U.S.; 1953/4 v. W, FIFA, I, H (2),
S, Y, Bel, Switz, U; 1954/5 v. Sp, Port; 1955/6 v. D, W, I, Sp, S; 1956/7 v.
W, Y, D.
DITCHBURN, E. (6) (Tottenham) 1948/9 v. Switz, Swdn; 1952/3 v. U.S.;
1956/7 v. W, Y, D.
DOBSON, M. (5) (Burnley) 1973/4 v. Port, E/Germ, Bulg, Y; 1974/5
(Everton) v. Czecho.
DOUGLAS, B. (36) (Blackburn) 1957/8 v. W, I, F, S, Port, Y, Rus (2), Braz,
Aust; 1958/9 v. Rus, S.; 1959/60 v. Y, H; 1960/1 v. I, Lux, Sp, W, S, Mex,
Port, It, Aust; 1961/2 v. Lux, W, Port, I, S, Per, H, Arg, Bulg, Braz; 1962/3
v. S, Braz, Switz.
DOYLE, M. (5) (Manchester C.) 1975/6 v. W, S, Braz, It; 1976/7 v. Holl.

EASTHAM, G. (19) (Arsenal) 1962/3 v. Braz, Czecho, E/Germ; 1963/4 v.
W, FIFA, I, S, U, Port, Eire, U.S., Braz, Arg; 1964/5 v. H, G, Swdn; 1965/6
v. Sp, Pol, D.
ECKERSLEY, W. (17) (Blackburn) 1949/50 v. Sp; 1950/1 v. Y, S, Arg, Port;
1951/2 v. Aust (2), Switz; 1952/3 v. I, Arg, Ch, U, U.S.; 1953/4 v. W, FIFA,
I, H.
EDWARDS, D. (18) (Manchester United) 1954/5 v. S, F, Sp, Port; 1955/6
v. S, Braz, Swdn, Fin, G; 1956/7 v. I, D, S, Eire, D, Eire; 1957/8 v. W, I, F.
ELLERINGTON, W. (2) (Southampton) 1948/9 v. N, F.
ELLIOTT, W. H. (5) (Burnley) 1951/2 v. It, Aust; 1952/3 v. I, W, Bel.

FANTHAM, J. (1) (Sheffield Wednesday) 1961/2 v. Lux.
FINNEY, T. (76) (Preston) 1946/7 v. I, Eire Holl, F, Port; 1947/8 v. W,
I, S, Bel, Swdn, It; 1948/9 v. I, W, S, Swdn, N, F; 1949/50 v. W, I, S, Eire,
It, Port, Bel, Ch, U.S., Sp; 1950/1 v. W, S, Arg, Port; 1951/2 v. F, W, I, S,
It, Aust, Switz; 1952/3 v. I, W, Bel, S, Arg, Ch, U, U.S.; 1953/4 v. D, S, Y,
H, Bel, Switz, U; 1954/5 v. G; 1955/6 v. D, W, I, Sp, S; 1956/7 v. W, Y,
D, S, Eire, D, Eire; 1957/8 v. W, F, S, Port, Y, Rus (2); 1958/9 v. I, Rus.
FLOWERS, R. (49) (Wolverhampton) 1954/5 v. F; 1958/9 v. W, S, It, Braz,
Per, Mex, U.S.; 1959/60 v. W, S, Y, Sp, H, Swdn, I; 1960/1 v. Lux, Sp, W,
S, Mex, Port, It, Aust; 1961/2 v. Lux, W, Port, I, Aust, S, Switz, Per, H,
Arg, Bulg, Braz; 1962/3 v. F, I, W, F, S, Switz; 1963/4 v. Eire, U.S., Port;
1964/5 v. W, Holl, G; 1965/6 v. N.
FOULKES, W. (1) (Manchester United) 1954/5 v. I.
FRANCIS, G. (12) (Q.P.R.) 1974/5 v. Czecho, Port, W, S; 1975/6 v. Switz,
Czecho, Port, W, I, S, Braz, Fin.
FRANCIS, T. (15) (Birmingham) 1976/7 v. Holl, Lux, S, Braz; 1977/8 v.
Switz, Lux, It, G, Braz, W, S, H; 1978/9 v. Bulg, Swdn, Aust.
FRANKLIN, N. (27) (Stoke) 1946/7 v. I, W, S, Eire, Holl, F, Switz, Port;
1947/8 v. W, I, S, Bel, Swdn, It; 1948/9 v. I, W, S, D, Switz, Swdn, N, F;
1949/50 v. W, I, S, Eire, It.
FROGGATT, J. (13) (Portsmouth) 1949/50 v. I, It; 1950/1 v. S; 1951/2 v.
Aust (2), S, It, Switz; 1952/3 v. I, W, Bel, S, U.S.
FROGGATT, R. (4) (Sheffield Wednesday) 1952/3 v. W, Bel, S, U.S.

GARRETT, T. (3) (Blackpool) 1951/2 v. S, It; 1953/4 v. W.
GEORGE, F. C. (1) (Derby) 1976/7 v. Eire.
GIDMAN, J. (1) (Aston Villa) 1976/7 v. Lux.

GILLARD, I. (3) (Q.P.R.) 1974/5 v. G, W; 1975/6 v. Czecho.
GRAINGER, C. (7) (Sheffield United) 1955/6 v. Braz, Swdn, Fin, G; 1956/7 v. I, W, (Sunderland) S.
GREAVES, J. (57) (Chelsea) 1958/9 v. Per, Mex, U.S.; 1959/60 v. W, Swdn, Y, Sp; 1960/1 v. I, Lux, Sp, W, S, Port, It, Aust; 1961/2 (Tottenham) v. S, Switz, Per, H, Arg, Bulg, Braz; 1962/3 v. F, I, W, F, S, Braz, Czecho, Switz; 1963/4 v. W, FIFA, I, U, Port, Eire, Braz, Port, Arg; 1964/5 v. I, Bel, Holl, S, H, Y; 1965/6 v. W, Aust, Y, N, D, Pol, U, Mex, F; 1966/7 v. S, Sp, Aust.
GREENHOFF, B. (17) (Manchester U.) 1975/6 v. W, I; 1976/7 v. Eire, Fin, It, Holl, I, W, S, Braz, Arg, U; 1977/8 v. Braz, W, I, S, H.
HAGAN, J. (1) (Sheffield United) 1948/9 v. D.
HAINES, J. (1) (West Bromwich) 1948/9 v. Switz.
HALL, J. (17) (Birmingham) 1955/6 v. D, I, W, Sp, S, Braz, Swdn, Fin, G; 1956/7 v. I, W, Y, D, S, Eire, D, Eire.
HANCOCKS, J. (3) (Wolverhampton) 1948/9 v. Switz; 1949/50 v. W; 1950/1 v. Y.
HARDWICK, G. (13) (Middlesbrough) 1946/7 v. I, W, S, Eire, Holl, F, Switz, Port; 1947/8 v. W, I, S, Bel, Swdn.
HARRIS, G. (1) (Burnley) 1965/6 v. Pol.
HARRIS, P. (2) (Portsmouth) 1949/50 v. Eire; 1953/4 v. H.
HARVEY, C. (1) (Everton) 1970/1 v. M.
HASSALL, H. (5) (Huddersfield) 1950/1 v. S, Arg, Port; 1951/2 v. F (Bolton); 1953/4 v. I.
HAYNES, J. (56) (Fulham) 1954/5 v. I; 1955/6 v. I, Sp, S, Swdn, Fin, G; 1956/7 v. W, Y, Eire, D, Eire; 1957/8 v. W, I, F, S, Port, Y, Rus (2), Braz, Aust, Rus; 1958/9 v. I, Rus, S, It, Braz, Per, Mex, U.S.; 1959/60 v. I, Y, Sp, H; 1960/1 v. I, Lux, Sp, W, S, Mex, Port, It, Aust; 1961/2 v. W, Port, I, Aust, S, Switz, H, Per, Arg, Bulg, Braz.
HECTOR, K. (2) (Derby) 1973/4 v. Pol, It.
HELLAWELL, M. (2) (Birmingham) 1962/3 v. F, I.
HENRY, R. (1) (Tottenham) 1962/3 v. F.
HILL, F. (2) (Bolton) 1962/3 v. I. W.
HILL, G. (6) (Manchester United) 1975/6 v. It; 1976/7 v. Eire, Fin, Lux; 1977/8 v. Switz, Lux.
HINTON, A. (3) (Wolverhampton) 1962/3 v. F; 1964/5 (Nottingham Forest) v. Bel, W.
HITCHENS, G. (7) (Aston Villa) 1960/1 v. Mex, It, Aust (Inter Milan); 1961/2 v. Switz, Per, H, Braz.
HODGKINSON, A. (5) (Sheffield United) 1956/7 v. S, Eire, D, Eire; 1960/1 v. W.
HOLDEN, D. (5) (Bolton) 1958/9 v. S, It, Braz, Per, Mex.
HOLLIDAY, E. (3) (Middlesbrough) 1959/60 v. W, Swdn, I.
HOLLINS, J. (1) (Chelsea) 1966/7 v. Sp.
HOPKINSON, E. (14) (Bolton) 1957/8 v. W, I, F, S, Port, Y; 1958/9 v. S, It, Braz, Per, Mex, U.S.; 1959/60 v. W, Swdn.
HOWE, D. (23) (West Bromwich) 1957/8 v. W, I, F, S, Port, Y, Rus (2), Braz, Aust, Rus; 1958/9 v. I, Rus, W, S, It, Braz, Per, Mex, U.S.; 1959/60 v. W, Swdn, I.
HOWE, J. (3) (Derby) 1947/8 v. It; 1948/9 v. I, S.
HUDSON, A. (2) (Stoke C.) 1974/5 v. G, C.
HUGHES, E. (58) (Liverpool) 1969/70 v. Holl, Port, Bel, W, I, S; 1970/1 v. E/Germ, M, Gr, M, W; 1971/2 v. Switz, Gr, G (2), W, I, S; 1972/3 v. W (2), S, W, S, Pol, Rus, It; 1973/4 v. Pol, It, W, I, S, Arg, Aust, E/Germ, Bulg, Y;

1974/5 v. Czecho, Port, C, I; 1976/7 v. It, Lux, W, S, Braz, Arg, U; 1977/8 v. Switz, Lux, It, G, I, S, H; 1978/9 v. D, I, W, Swdn.

HUGHES, L. (3) (Liverpool) 1949/50 v. Ch, U.S., Sp.

HUNT, R. (34) (Liverpool) 1961/2 v. Aust; 1962/3 v. E/Germ; 1963/4 v. S (2), U.S., Port; 1964/5 v. W; 1965/6 v. Sp, Pol, G, S, Fin, N, Pol, U, Mex, F, Arg, Port, G; 1966/7 v. I, Czecho, W, Sp, Aust; 1967/8 v. W, I, Rus, Sp (2), Swdn, Y, Rus; 1968/9 v. Ru (2).

HUNTER, N. (28) (Leeds) 1965/6 v. Sp, G, Y, Fin; 1966/7 v. Aust; 1967/8 v. Sp, Swdn, G, Y, Rus; 1968/9 v. Ru, W; 1969/70 v. Holl, G; 1970/1 v. M; 1971/2 v. G (2), W, I, S; 1972/3 v. W (2), Rus; 1973/4 v. Pol, I, S, Aust; 1974/5 v. Czecho.

HURST, G. (49) (West Ham) 1965/6 v. G, S, Y, Fin, D, Arg, Port, G; 1966/7 v. I, Czecho, W, S, Sp, Aust; 1967/8 v. W, I, Rus, S, Swdn, G, Rus; 1968/9 v. Ru, Bulg, Ru, F, I, S, Mex, U, Braz; 1969/70 v. Holl (2), Bel, W, I, S, Co, Ec, Ru, Braz, G; 1970/1 v. E/Germ, Gr, W, S; 1971/2 v. Switz (2), Gr, G.

JEZZARD, B. (2) (Fulham) 1953/4 v. H; 1955/6 v. I.

JOHNSON, D. (3) (Ipswich) 1974/5 v. W, S; 1975/6 v. Switz.

JOHNSTON, H. (10) (Blackpool) 1946/7 v. S, Holl; 1950/1 v. S; 1952/3 v. Arg, Ch, U, U.S.; 1953/4 v. W, I, H.

JONES, M. (3) (Sheffield United) 1964/5 v. G, Swdn (Leeds); 1969/70 v. Holl.

JONES, W. H. (2) (Liverpool) 1949/50 v. Port, Bel.

KAY, A. (1) (Everton) 1962/3 v. Switz.

KEEGAN, K. (46) (Liverpool) 1972/3 v. W (2); 1973/4 v. W, I, Arg, E/Germ, Bulg, Y; 1974/5 v. Czecho, G, C (2), I, S; 1975/6 v. Switz, Czecho, Port, W (2), I, S, Braz, Fin; 1976/7 v. Eire, Fin, It, Holl, Lux, (SV Hamburg), W, Braz, Arg, U; 1977/8 v. Switz, It, G, Braz, H; 1978/9 v. D, Eire, Czecho, I, W, S, Bulg, Swdn, Aust.

KENNEDY, R. (11) (Liverpool) 1975/6 v. W (2), I, S; 1976/7 v. Lux, W, S, Braz, Arg; 1977/8 v. Switz, Lux.

KEVAN, D. (14) (West Bromwich) 1956/7 v. S; 1957/8 v. W, I, S, Port, Y, Rus (2), Braz, Aust, Rus; 1958/9 v. Mex, U.S.; 1960/1 v. Mex.

KIDD, B. (2) (Manchester United) 1969/70 v. I, Ec.

KNOWLES, C. (4) (Tottenham) 1967/8 v. Rus, Sp, Swdn, G.

LABONE, B. (26) (Everton) 1962/3 v. I, W, F; 1966/7 v. Sp, Aust; 1967/8 v. S, Sp, Swdn, G, Y, Rus; 1968/9 v. Ru, Bulg, I, S, Mex, U, Braz; 1969/70 v. Bel, W, S, Co, Ec, Ru, Braz, G.

LAMPARD, F. (1) (West Ham) 1972/3 v. Y.

LANGLEY, J. (3) (Fulham) 1957/8 v. S, Port, Y.

LANGTON, R. (11) (Blackburn) 1946/7 v. I, W, Eire, Holl, F, Switz; 1947/8 v. Swdn; 1948/9 (Preston) v. D, Swdn; 1949/50 (Bolton) v. S; 1950/1 v. I.

LATCHFORD, R. (12) (Everton) 1977/8 v. It, Braz, W; 1978/9 v. D, Eire, Czecho, I, I, W, S, Bulg, Aust.

LAWLER, C. (4) (Liverpool) 1970/1 v. M, W, S; 1971/2 v. Switz.

LAWTON, T. (15) (Chelsea) 1946/7 v. I, W, S, Eire, Holl, F, Switz, Port; 1947/8 v. W, I (Notts Co), S, Bel, Swdn, It; 1948/9 v. D.

LEE, F. (27) (Manchester City) 1968/9 v. Bulg, F, I, W, S, Mex, U; 1969/70 v. Holl, Port, Holl, Bel, W, Co, Ec, Ru, Braz, G; 1970/1 v. E/Germ, Gr, M, I, W, S; 1971/2 v. Switz (2), Gr, G.

LEE, J. (1) (Derby) 1950/1 v. I.

LINDSAY, A. (4) (Liverpool) 1973/4 v. Arg, E/Germ, Bulg, Y.

LITTLE, B. (1) (Aston Villa) 1974/5 v. W.
LLOYD, L. (3) (Liverpool) 1970/1 v. W; 1971/2 v. Switz, I.
LOFTHOUSE, N. (33) (Bolton) 1950/1 v. Y; 1951/2 v. W, I, Aust (2), It,
    Switz; 1952/3 v. I, W, Bel, S, Arg, Ch, U, U.S.; 1953/4 v. W, FIFA, I, Bel,
    U; 1954/5 v. I, S, F, Sp, Port; 1955/6 v. D, W, Sp, S, Fin; 1958/9 v. Rus, W.
LOWE, E. (3) (Aston Villa) 1946/7 v. F, Switz, Port.

MACDONALD, M. (14) (Newcastle) 1971/2 v. W, I, S; 1972/3 v. Rus; 1973/4
    v. Port, S, Y; 1974/5 v. G, C (2), I; 1975/6 v. Switz, Czecho, Port.
MADELEY, P. (24) (Leeds) 1970/1 v. I; 1971/2 v. Switz (2), Gr, G (2), W, S;
    1972/3 v. S, Czecho, Pol, Rus, It; 1973/4 v. Pol, It, Aust; 1974/5 v. Czecho,
    Port, C; 1975/6 v. Czecho, Port, Fin; 1976/7 v. Eire, Holl.
MANNION, W. (26) (Middlesbrough) 1946/7 v. I, W, S, Eire, Holl, F, Switz,
    Port; 1947/8 v. W, I, Bel, Swdn, It; 1948/9 v. N, F; 1949/50 v. S, Eire, Port,
    Bel, Ch, U.S.; 1950/1 v. I, W, Y, S; 1951/2 v. F.
MARINER, P. (5) (Ipswich) 1976/7 v. Lux, I; 1977/8 v. Lux, W, S.
MARSH, R. (9) (Q.P.R.) 1971/2 v. Switz, (Manchester City), G (2), W, I, S;
    1972/3 v. Y, W (2).
MATTHEWS, R. (5) (Coventry) 1955/6 v. S, Braz, Swdn, G; 1956/7 v. I,
    (Chelsea).
MATTHEWS, S. (37) (Stoke) 1946/7 v. S (Blackpool), Switz, Port; 1947/8
    v. W, I, S, Bel, It; 1948/9 v. I, W, S, D, Switz; 1949/50 v. Sp; 1950/1 v. I, S;
    1953/4 v. FIFA, I, H, Bel, U; 1954/5 v. I, W, G, S, F, Sp, Port; 1955/6 v.
    W, Braz; 1956/7 v. I, W, Y, D, S, Eire, D.
McDERMOTT, T. (5) (Liverpool) 1977/8 v. Switz, Lux; 1978/9 v. I, W, Swdn.
McDONALD, C. (8) (Burnley) 1957/8 v. Rus (2), Braz, Aust, Rus; 1958/9 v.
    I, Rus, W.
McFARLAND, R. (28) (Derby) 1970/1 v. M, Gr, M, I, S; 1971/2 v. Switz, Gr,
    G, W, S; 1972/3 v. W, D (2), I, W, S, Czecho, Pol, Rus, It; 1973/4 v. Pol, It,
    W, I, Aust; 1975/6 v. Czecho, S; 1976/7 v. Eire, It.
McGARRY, W. (4) (Huddersfield) 1953/4 v. Switz, U; 1955/6 v. D, W.
McGUINNESS, W. (2) (Manchester United) 1958/9 v. I, Mex.
McNAB, R. (4) (Arsenal) 1968/9 v. Ru, Bulg, Ru, I.
McNEIL, M. (9) (Middlesbrough) 1960/1 v. I, Lux, Sp, W, Mex, Port, It;
    1961/2 v. Lux.
MEADOWS, J. (1) (Manchester C) 1954/5 v. S.
MEDLEY, L. (6) (Tottenham) 1950/1 v. W, Y; 1951/2 v. F, W, I, Aust.
MELIA, J. (2) (Liverpool) 1962/3 v. S, Switz.
MERRICK, G. (23) (Birmingham) 1951/2 v. I, Aust (2), S, It, Switz; 1952/3 v"
    I, W, Bel, S, Arg, Ch, U; 1953/4 v. W, FIFA, I, H (2), S, Y, Bel, Switz, U.
METCALFE, V. (2) (Huddersfield) 1950/1 v. Arg, Port.
MILBURN, J. (13) (Newcastle) 1948/9 v. I, W, S, Switz; 1949/50 v. W, Port,
    Bel, Sp; 1950/1 v. W, Arg, Port; 1951/2 v. F; 1955/6 v. D.
MILLER, B. (1) (Burnley) 1960/1 v. Aust.
MILLS, M. (26) (Ipswich) 1972/3 v. Y; 1975/6 v. W (2), I, S, Braz, It, Fin;
    1976/7 v. Fin, It, I, W, S; 1977/8 v. G, Braz, W, I, S, H; 1978/9 v. D, Eire, I, I,
    S, Bulg, Aust.
MILNE, G. (14) (Liverpool) 1962/3 v. Braz, Czecho, E/Germ; 1963/4 v. W,
    FIFA, I, S, U, Port, Eire, Braz, Arg; 1964/5 v. I, Bel.
MILTON, C. A. (1) (Arsenal) 1951/2 v. Aust.
MOORE, I. (1) (Nottingham Forest) 1969/70 v. Holl.
MOORE, R. (108) (West Ham) 1961/2 v. Per, H, Arg, Bulg, Braz; 1962/3 v.
    F, I, W, F, S, Braz, Czecho, E/Germ, Switz; 1963/4 v. W, FIFA, I, S, U, Port,
    Eire, Braz, Port, Arg; 1964/5 v. I, Bel, S, H, Y, G, Swdn; 1965/6 v. W,

172

Aust, I, Sp, Pol, G, S, N, D, Pol, U, Mex, F, Arg, Port, G; 1966/7 v. I, Czecho, W, S, Sp, Aust; 1967/8 v. W, I, Rus, S, Sp (2), Swdn, G, Y, Rus; 1968/9 v. Ru, Bulg, F, I, W, S, Mex, U, Braz; 1969/70 v. Holl, Port, Bel, W, I, S, Co, Ec, Ru, Braz, Czecho, G; 1970/1 v. E/Germ, Gr, M, I, S; 1971/2 v. Switz (2), Gr, G (2), W, S; 1972/3 v. Y, W (3), S (2), I, Czecho, Pol, Rus, It; 1973/4 v. It.

MORRIS, J. (3) (Derby) 1948/9 v. N, F; 1949/50 v. Eire.

MORTENSEN, S. (25) (Blackpool) 1946/7 v. Port; 1947/8 v. W, I, S, Bel, Swdn, It; 1948/9 v. I, W, S, Swdn, N; 1949/50 v. W, I, S, It, Port, Bel, Ch, U.S., Sp; 1950/1 v. S, Arg; 1953/4 v. FIFA, H.

MOZLEY, B. (3) (Derby) 1949/50 v. W, I, Eire.

MULLEN, J. (12) (Wolverhampton) 1946/7 v. S; 1948/9 v. N, F; 1949/50 v. Bel, Ch, U.S.; 1953/4 v. W, FIFA, I, S, Y, Switz.

MULLERY, A. (35) (Tottenham) 1964/5 v. Holl; 1966/7 v. Sp, Aust; 1967/8 v. W, I, Rus, S, Sp (2), Swdn, Y; 1968/9 v. Ru, Bulg, F, I, S, Mex, U, Braz; 1969/70 v. Holl, Port, Holl, W, I, S, Co, Ec, Ru, Braz, Czecho, G; 1970/1 v. E/Germ, M, Gr; 1971/2 v. Switz.

NEAL, P. (20) (Liverpool) 1975/6 v. W, It; 1976/7 v. W, S, Braz, Arg, U; 1977/8 v. Switz, It, G, I, S, H; 1978/9 v. D, Eire, I, I, S, Bulg, Aust.

NEWTON, K. (27) (Blackburn) 1965/6 v. G, S; 1966/7 v. Sp, Aust; 1967/8 v. W, S, Sp, Swdn, G, Y; 1968/9 v. Ru, Bulg, F, I, W, S, Mex, U, Braz; 1969/70 (Everton) v. Holl, I, S, Co, Ec, Ru, Czecho, G.

NICHOLLS, J. (2) (West Bromwich) 1953/4 v. S, Y.

NICHOLSON, W. (1) (Tottenham) 1950/1 v. Port.

NISH, D. (5) (Derby) 1972/3 v. I; 1973/4 v. Port, W, I, S.

NORMAN, M. (23) (Tottenham) 1961/2 v. Per, H, Arg, Bulg, Braz; 1962/3 v. F, S, Braz, Czecho, E/Germ; 1963/4 v. W, FIFA, I, S, U, Port, U.S., Braz, Port, Arg; 1964/5 v. I, Bel, Holl.

OWEN, S. (3) (Luton) 1953/4 v. H, Bel.

O'GRADY, M. (2) (Huddersfield) 1962/3 v. I; 1968/9 (Leeds) v. F.

OSGOOD, P. (4) (Chelsea) 1969/70 v. Bel, Ru, Czecho; 1973/4 v. It.

PAINE, T. (19) (Southampton) 1962/3 v. Czecho, E/Germ; 1963/4 v. W, FIFA, I, S, U, U.S., Port; 1964/5 v. I, H, Y, G, Swdn; 1965/6 v. W, Aust, Y, N, Mex.

PARKES, P. (1) (Q.P.R.) 1973/4 v. Port.

PARRY, R. (2) (Bolton) 1959/60 v. I, S.

PEACOCK, A. (6) (Middlesbrough) 1961/2 v. Arg, Bulg; 1962/3 v. I, W; 1965/6 (Leeds) v. W, I.

PEARSON, Stan (8) (Manchester United) 1947/8 v. S; 1948/9 v. I, S; 1949/50 v. I, It; 1950/1 v. Port; 1951/2 v. S, It.

PEARSON, Stuart (15) (Manchester United) 1975/6 v. W, I, S, Braz, Fin; 1976/7 v. Eire, Holl, W, S, Braz, Arg, U; 1977/8 v. It, G, I.

PEGG, D. (1) (Manchester United) 1956/7 v. Eire.

PEJIC, M. (4) (Stoke) 1973/4 v. Port, W, I, S.

PERRY, W. (3) (Blackpool) 1955/6 v. I, Sp, S.

PETERS, M. (67) (West Ham) 1965/6 v. Y, Fin, Pol, Mex, F, Arg, Port, G; 1966/7 v. I, Czecho, W, S; 1967/8 v. W, I, Rus, S, Sp (2), Swdn, Y, Rus; 1968/9 v. Ru, Bulg, F, I, S, Mex, U, Braz; 1969/70 v. Holl, Port, Holl, Bel, (Tottenham) W, I, S, Co, Ec, Ru, Braz, Czecho, G; 1970/1 v. E/Germ, M, Gr, M, I, W, S; 1971/2 v. Switz, Gr, G (2), I; 1972/3 v. S, I, W, S, Czecho, Pol, Rus, It; 1973/4 v. Pol, It, Port, S, Aust.

PHILLIPS, L. (3) (Portsmouth) 1951/2 v. I; 1954/5 v. W, G.
PICKERING, F. (3) (Everton) 1963/4 v. U.S.; 1964/5 v. I, Bel.
PILKINGTON, B. (1) (Burnley) 1954/5 v. I.
POINTER, R. (3) (Burnley) 1961/2 v. Lux, W, Port.
PYE, J. (1) (Wolverhampton) 1949/50 v. Eire.

QUIXALL, A. (5) (Sheffield Wednesday) 1953/4 v. W, FIFA, I; 1954/5 v. Sp, Port.

RADFORD, J. (2) (Arsenal) 1968/9 v. Ru; 1971/2 v. Switz.
RAMSEY, A. (32) (Southampton) 1948/9 v. Switz; 1949/50 (Tottenham) v. S, It, Port, Bel, Ch, U.S., Sp; 1950/1 v. I, W, Y, S, Arg, Port; 1951/2 v. F, W, I, Aust (2), S, It, Switz; 1952/3 v. I, W, Bel, S, Arg, Ch, U, U.S.; 1953/4 v. FIFA, H.
REANEY, P. (3) (Leeds) 1968/9 v. Bulg; 1969/70 v. Port; 1970/1 v. M.
REVIE, D. (6) (Manchester City) 1954/5 v. I, S, F; 1955/6 v. D, W; 1956/7 v. I.
RICHARDS, J. (1) (Wolverhampton) 1972/3 v. I.
RICKABY, S. (1) (West Bromwich) 1953/4 v. I.
RIMMER, J. (1) (Arsenal) 1975/6 v. It.
ROBB, G. (1) (Tottenham) 1953/4 v. H.
ROBSON, R. (20) (West Bromwich) 1957/8 v. F, Rus (2), Braz, Aust; 1959/60 v. Sp, H; 1960/1 v. I, Lux, Sp, W, S, Mex, Port, It; 1961/2 v. Lux, W, Port, I, Switz.
ROWLEY, J. (6) (Manchester United) 1948/9 v. Switz, Swdn, F; 1949/50 v. I, It; 1951/2 v. S.
ROYLE, J. (6) (Everton) 1970/1 v. M; 1972/3 v. Y; (Manchester City) 1975/6 v. I, It; 1976/7 v. Fin, Lux.

SADLER, D. (4) (Manchester United) 1967/8 v. I, Rus; 1969/70 v. Ec; 1970/1 v. E/Germ.
SANSOM, K. (1) (Crystal Palace) 1978/9 v. W.
SCOTT, L. (17) (Arsenal) 1946/7 v. I, W, S, Eire, Holl, F, Switz, Port; 1947/8 v. W, I, S, Bel, Swdn, It; 1948/9 v. I, W, D.
SEWELL, J. (6) (Sheffield Wednesday) 1951/2 v. I, Aust, Switz; 1952/3 v. I; 1953/4 v. H (2).
SHACKLETON, L. (5) (Sunderland) 1948/9 v. W, D; 1949/50 v. W; 1954/5 v. W, G.
SHAW, G. (5) (Sheffield United) 1958/9 v. Rus, W, S, It; 1962/3 v. W.
SHELLITO, K. (1) (Chelsea) 1962/3 v. Czecho.
SHILTON, P. (28) (Leicester) 1970/1 v. E/Germ, W; 1971/2 v. Switz, It; 1972/3 v. Y, S, I, W, S, Czecho, Pol, Rus, It; 1973/4 v. Pol, It, W, I, S, Arg, Aust; 1974/5 (Stoke) v. C; 1976/7 v. I, W; (Nottingham F.) 1977/8 v. W, H; 1978/9 v. Czecho, Swdn, Aust.
SHIMWELL, E. (1) (Blackpool) 1948/9 v. Swdn.
SILLETT, P. (3) (Chelsea) 1954/5 v. F, Sp, Port.
SLATER, W. (12) (Wolverhampton) 1954/5 v. W, G; 1957/8 v. S, Port, Y, Rus (2), Braz, Aust, Rus; 1958/9 v. Rus; 1959/60 v. S.
SMITH, L. (6) (Arsenal) 1950/1 v. W; 1951/2 v. W, I; 1952/3 v. W, Bel, S.
SMITH, Trevor (1) (Birmingham) 1959/60 v. W.
SMITH, Tom (1) (Liverpool) 1970/1 v. W.
SMITH, R. (15) (Tottenham) 1960/1 v. I, Lux, Sp, W, S, Port; 1961/2 v. S; 1962/3 v. F, S, Braz, Czecho, E/Germ; 1963/4 v. W, FIFA, I.
SPRINGETT, R. (33) (Sheffield Wednesday) 1959/60 v. I, S, Y, Sp, H; 1960/1 v. I, Lux, Sp, Mex, Port, It, Aust; 1961/2 v. Lux, W, Port, I, Aust, S, Switz,

174

Per, H, Arg, Bulg, Braz; 1962/3 v. F, I, W, F, Switz; 1965/6 v. W, Aust, N.

STANIFORTH, R. (8) (Huddersfield) 1953/4 v. S, Y, H, Bel, Switz, U; 1954/5 v. W, G.

STEPNEY, A. (1) (Manchester United) 1967/8 v. Swdn.

STILES, N. (28) (Manchester United) 1964/5 v. S, H, Y, Swdn; 1965/6 v. W, Aust, I, Sp, Pol, G, S, N, D, Pol, U, Mex, F, Arg, Port, G; 1966/7 v. I, Czecho, W, S; 1967/8 v. Rus; 1968/9 v. Ru; 1969/70 v. I, S.

STOREY, P. (19) (Arsenal) 1970/1 v. Gr, I, S; 1971/2 v. Switz, G, W, I, S; 1972/3 v. Y, W (2), S, I, W, S, Czecho, Pol, Rus, It.

STRETEN, B. (1) (Luton) 1949/50 v. I.

SUMMERBEE, M. (8) (Manchester City) 1967/8 v. S, Sp, G; 1971/2 v. Switz, G, W, I; 1972/3 v. Rus.

SWAN, P. (19) (Sheffield Wednesday) 1959/60 v. Y. Sp; 1960/1 v. I, Lux, Sp, W, S, Mex, Port, It, Aust; 1961/2 v. Lux, W, Port, I, Aust, S, Switz.

SWIFT, F. (19) (Manchester City) 1946/7 v. I, W, S, Eire, Holl, F, Switz, Port; 1947/8 v. W, I, S, Bel, Swdn, It; 1948/9 v. I, W, S, D, N.

TALBOT, B. (5) (Ipswich) 1976/7 v. I, S, Braz, Arg, U.

TAMBLING, R. (3) (Chelsea) 1962/3 v. W, F; 1965/6 v. Y.

TAYLOR, E. (1) (Blackpool) 1953/4 v. H.

TAYLOR, J. (2) (Fulham) 1950/1 v. Arg, Port.

TAYLOR, P. (3) (Liverpool) 1947/8 v. W, I, Swdn.

TAYLOR, P. (4) (Crystal Palace) 1975/6 v. W (2), I, S.

TAYLOR, T. (19) (Manchester United) 1952/3 v. Arg, Ch, U; 1953/4 v. Bel, Switz; 1955/6 v. S, Braz, Swdn, Fin, G; 1956/7 v. I, Y, D, Eire, D, Eire; 1958/9 v. W, I, F.

TEMPLE, D. (1) (Everton) 1964/5 v. G.

THOMAS, D. (8) (Q.P.R.) 1974/5 v. Czecho, Port, C (2), W, S; 1975/6 v. Czecho, Port.

THOMSON, R. (8) (Wolverhampton) 1963/4 v. I, U.S., Port, Arg; 1964/5 v. I, Bel, W, Holl.

THOMPSON, P. (16) (Liverpool) 1963/4 v. Port, Eire, U.S., Braz, Port, Arg; 1964/5 v. I, Bel, W, Holl, S; 1965/6 v. I; 1967/8 v. I, G; 1969/70 v. Holl, S.

THOMPSON, P. (15) (Liverpool) 1975/6 v. W (2), I, S, Braz, It, Fin; 1976/7 v. Fin; 1978/9 v. Eire, Czecho, I, S, Bulg, Swdn, Aust.

THOMPSON, T. (2) (Aston Villa) 1951/2 v. W (Preston); 1956/7 v. S.

TODD, C. (27) (Derby) 1971/2 v. I; 1973/4 v. Port, W, I, S, Arg, E/Germ, Bulg, Y; 1974/5 v. Port, G, C (2), I, W, S; 1975/6 v. Switz, Czecho, Port, I, S, Braz, Fin; 1976/7 v. Eire, Fin, Holl, I.

TOWERS, T. (2) (Sunderland) 1975/6 v. W, It.

TUEART, D. (6) (Manchester City) 1974/5 v. C, I; 1976/7 v. Fin, I, W, S.

UFTON, D. (1) (Charlton) 1953/4 v. FIFA.

VENABLES, T. (2) (Chelsea) 1964/5 v. Bel, Holl.

VILJOEN, C. (2) (Ipswich T.) 1974/5 v. I, W.

VIOLLET, D. (2) (Manchester United) 1959/60 v. H; 1961/2 v. Lux.

WAITERS, A. (5) (Blackpool) 1963/4 v. Eire, Braz; 1964/5 v. Bel, W, Holl.

WARD, T. (2) (Derby) 1947/8 v. Bel; 1948/9 v. W.

WATSON, D. (44) (Sunderland) 1973/4 v. Port, S, Arg, E/Germ, Bulg, Y; 1974/5 v. Czecho, Port, G, C (2), I, W, S; 1975/6 (Manchester City) v. Switz, Czecho, Port; 1976/7 v. Holl, Lux, I, W, S, Braz, Arg, U; 1977/8

175

v. Switz, Lux, It, G, Braz, W, I, S, H; 1978/9 v. D, Eire, Czecho, I, I, W, S,
Bulg, Swdn, Aust.

WATSON, W. (4) (Sunderland) 1949/50 v. I, It; 1950/I v. W, Y.

WELLER, K. (4) (Leicester) 1973/4 v. W, I, S, Arg.

WEST, G. (3) (Everton) 1968/9 v. Bulg, W, Mex.

WHEELER, J. (I) (Bolton) 1954/5 v. I.

WHITWORTH, S. (7) (Leicester) 1974/5 v. G, C, I, W, S; 1975/6 v. Switz,
Port.

WHYMARK, T. (I) (Ipswich) 1977/8 v. Lux.

WIGNALL, F. (2) (Nottingham Forest) 1964/5 v. W, Holl.

WILKINS, R. (24) (Chelsea) 1975/6 v. It; 1976/7 v. Eire, Fin, I, Braz, Arg, U;
1977/8 v. Switz, Lux, It, G, W, I, S, H; 1978/9 v. D, Eire, Czecho, I, I, W, S,
Bulg, Swdn, Aust.

WILLIAMS, B. (24) (Wolverhampton) 1948/9 v. F; 1949/50 v. W, S, Eire, It,
Port, Bel, Ch, U.S., Sp; 1950/I v. I, W, Y, S, Arg, Port; 1951/2 v. F, W;
1954/5 v. G, S, F, Sp, Port; 1955/6 v. W.

WILLIS, A. (I) (Tottenham) 1951/2 v. F.

WILSHAW, D. (12) (Wolverhampton) 1953/4 v. W, Switz, U; 1954/5 v. S,
F, Sp, Port; 1955/6 v. W, I, Fin, G; 1956/7 v. I.

WILSON, R. (63) (Huddersfield) 1959/60 v. S, Y, Sp, H; 1961/2 v. W, Port,
I, Aust, S, Switz, Per, H, Aust, Bulg, Braz; 1962/3 v. F, I, Braz, Czecho,
E/Germ, Switz; 1963/4 v. W, FIFA, S, U, Port, Eire, Braz, Port, Arg;
1964/5 (Everton) S, H, Y, G, Swdn; 1965/6 v. W, Aust, I, Sp, Pol, G,
Y, Fin, D, Pol, U, Mex, F, Arg, Port, G; 1966/7 v. I, Czecho, W, S, Aust;
1967/8 v. I, Rus, S, Sp(2), Y, Rus.

WOOD, R. (3) (Manchester United) 1954/5 v. I, W; 1955/6 v. Fin.

WOODCOCK, A. (5) (Nottingham F.) 1977/8 v. I; 1978/9 v. Eire, Czecho,
Bulg, Swdn.

WORTHINGTON, F. (8) (Leicester) 1973/4 v. I, S, Arg, E/Germ, Bulg, Y;
1974/5 v. Czecho, Port.

WRIGHT, T. (11) (Everton) 1967/8 v. Rus; 1968/9 v. Ru (2), Mex, U, Braz;
1969/70 v. Holl, Bel, W, Ru, Braz.

WRIGHT, W. (105) (Wolverhampton) 1946/7 v. I, W, S, Eire, Holl, Switz,
Port; 1947/8 v. W, I, S, Bel, Swdn, It; 1948/9 v. I, W, S, D, Switz, Swdn,
N, F; 1949/50 v. W, I, S, Eire, It, Port, Bel, Ch, U.S., Sp; 1950/I v. I, S, Arg;
1951/2 v. F, W, I, Aust (2), S, It, Switz; 1952/3 v. I, W, Bel, S, Arg, Ch, U,
U.S.; 1953/4 v. W, FIFA, I, H (2), S, Y, Bel, Arg, Y; 1954/5 v. I, W, G, S,
F, Sp, Port; 1955/6 v. D, W, I, Sp, Braz, Swdn, Fin, G; 1956/7 v. I, W,
Y, D, S, Eire, D, Eire; 1957/8 v. W, I, F, S, Port, Y, Rus (2), Braz, Aust, Rus;
1958/9 v. Rus, W, S, It, Braz, Per, Mex, U.S.

YOUNG, G. (I) (Sheffield Wednesday) 1964/5 v. W.

NORTHERN IRELAND

AHERNE, T. (4) (Belfast Celtic) 1946/7 v. E; 1947/8 v. S; 1948/9 v. W;
1949/50 (Luton) v. W.

ANDERSON, T. (22) (Manchester United) 1972/3 v. C, E, S, W; 1973/4 v.
Bulg, Port; 1974/5 (Swindon T.) v. S; 1975/6 v. Isr; 1976/7 v. Hol. G, Bel,
E, S, W, Ic; 1977/8 v. Ic, Holl, Bel, S, E, W; 1978/9 v. D.

ARMSTRONG, G. (17) (Tottenham) 1977/8 v. G, E, W, Ic; 1977/8 v. Bel, S,
E, W; 1978/9 v. Eire, D, Bulg, E, Bulg, E, S, W, D.

BARR, H. (3) (Linfield) 1961/2 v. E; 1962/3 (Coventry) v. Pol, E.

176

BEST, G. (37) (Manchester United) 1963/4 v. W, U; 1964/5 v. E, Switz (2), S, Holl (2, A); 1965/6 v. S, E, A; 1966/7 v. E; 1967/8 v. S; 1968/9 v. T, E, S, W; 1969/70 v. Rus, S, E, W; 1970/1 v. Sp, C (2), E, S, W; 1971/2 v. Rus, Sp; 1972/3 v. Bulg; 1973/4 v. Port; 1976/7 v. Holl, G. Bel; (Fulham) 1977/8 v. Ic, Holl.

BINGHAM, W. (56) (Sunderland) 1950/1 v. F; 1951/2 v. S, E, W; 1952/3 v. E, S, F, W; 1953/4 v. S, E, W; 1954/5 v. E, S, W; 1955/6 v. S, E, W; 1956/7 v. E, S, W, It, Port (2); 1957/8 v. S, E, It, W, Czecho, Arg, G, It, Czecho, F; 1958/9 (Luton) v. E, S, W, Sp; 1959/60 v. S, E, W; 1960/1 (Everton) v. E, G, S, It, Gr, G; 1961/2 v. Gr, E; 1962/3 v. Pol, E, S, Pol, Sp; 1963/4 (Port Vale) v. S, Sp, E.

BLAIR, R. (5) (Oldham Ath.) 1974/5 v. Swdn, S, W; 1975/6 v. Swdn, Isr.

BLANCHFLOWER, D. (54) (Barnsley) 1949/50 v. S, W; 1950/1 v. E, S, F; 1951/2 (Aston Villa) v. W; 1952/3 v. E, S, F, W; 1953/4 v. S, E, W; 1954/5 v. E, S (Tottenham), W; 1955/6 v. S, E, W; 1956/7 v. E, S, W, It, Port; 1957/8 v. S, E, It (2), W, Czecho, Arg, Czecho, F; 1958/9 v. E, S, W, Sp; 1959/60 v. S, E, W; 1960/1 v. F, G, S, W, G; 1961/2 v. S, Gr, E, W, Holl; 1962/3 v. Pol, E, S, Pol.

BLANCHFLOWER, J. (11) (Manchester United) 1953/4 v. W; 1954/5 v. E, S; 1955/6 v. S, W; 1956/7 v. E, S; 1957/8 v. S, E, It (2).

BOWLER, G. (4) (Hull) 1949/50 v. S, E, W, G.

BRAITHWAITE, R. (10) (Linfield) 1961/2 v. W; 1962/3 v. Pol, Sp (Middlesbrough) 1963/4 v. W, U; 1964/5 v. E, Switz (2), S, Holl.

BRENNAN, R. (5) (Luton) 1948/9 v. W; 1949/50 (Birmingham) v. S, E, W, (Fulham); 1950/1 v. E.

BRIGGS, R. (2) (Manchester United) 1961/2 v. W; 1964/5 (Swansea) v. Holl.

BRUCE, W. (2) (Glentoran) 1960/1 v. S; 1966/7 v. W.

CAMPBELL, J. (2) (Fulham) 1950/1 v. E, S.

CAMPBELL, R. (2) (Crusaders) 1962/3 v. W; 1964/5 v. Switz.

CAMPBELL, W. (6) (Dundee) 1967/8 v. S. E; 1968/9 v. T; 1969/70 v. Rus, S, W.

CAREY, J. (7) (Manchester United) 1946/7 v. E, S, W; 1947/8 v. E; 1948/9 v. E, S, W.

CASEY, T. (11) (Newcastle) 1954/5 v. W; 1955/6 v. W; 1956/7 v. E, S, W, It, Port; 1957/8 v. G, F; 1958/9 (Portsmouth) v. E, Sp.

CASKEY, A. (4) (Derby) 1978/9 v. Bulg, E, Bulg, E.

CASSIDY, T. (11) (Newcastle) 1970/1 v. E; 1971/2 v. Rus; 1973/4 v. Bulg, S, E, W; 1974/5 v. N; 1975/6 v. S, E, W; 1976/7 v. G.

CLEMENTS, D. (48) (Coventry) 1964/5 v. Holl, W; 1965/6 v. Mex; 1966/7 v. S, W; 1967/8 v. S, E; 1968/9 v. T (2), S, W; 1969/70 v. Rus (2), S, E, W; 1970/1 v. Sp, C, E, S, W; 1971/2 (Sheffield Wednesday) v. Rus (2), Sp, S, E, W; 1972/3 v. Bulg, C, Port, C, E, S, W; (Everton) 1973/4 v. Bulg, Port, S, E, W; 1974/5 v. N, Y, E, S, W; 1975/6 v. Swdn, Y, E, W.

COCHRANE, A. (8) (Coleraine) 1975/6 v. N; 1977/8 v. S; (Burnley) 1978/9 v. Eire, D, Bulg, E, Bulg, (Middlesbrough) v. N.

COCHRANE, D. (10) (Leeds) 1946/7 v. E, S, W; 1947/8 v. S, E, W; 1948/9 v. S, W; 1949/50 v. S, E.

COWAN, J. (1) (Newcastle) 1969/70 v. E.

COYLE, F. (3) (Coleraine) 1955/6 v. S, E; 1957/8 (Nottingham Forest) v. Arg.

COYLE, R. (3) (Sheffield Wednesday) 1972/3 v. Port, W; 1973/4 v. Bulg.

CRAIG, D. (25) (Newcastle) 1966/7 v. W; 1967/8 v. W; 1968/9 v. T (2), E, S, W; 1969/70 v. Rus, S, E, W; 1970/1 v. Sp, C (2), S; 1971/2 v. Rus, Sp; 1972/3 v. C (2), E, S, W; 1973/4 v. Bulg, Port; 1974/5 v. N.

CROSSAN, E. (3) (Blackburn) 1949/50 v. S; 1950/1 v. E; 1954/5 v. W.
CROSSAN, J. (23) (Rotterdam Sparta) 1959/60 v. E; 1962/3 (Sunderland) v.
Pol, W, Sp; 1963/4 v. S, Sp, E, W, U; 1964/5 v. E, Switz (2), S, Holl (2),
W; 1965/6 (Manchester C.) v. S, E, A, G; 1966/7 v. E, S; 1967/8 (Middles-
brough) v. S.
CUNNINGHAM, W. (29) (St. Mirren) 1950/1 v. W; 1952/3 v. E; 1953/4 v.
S; 1954/5 v. S; 1955/6 v. S, E, W; 1956/7 (Leicester) v. E, S, W, It, Port;
1957/8 v. S, It, W, Czecho, Arg, G, Czecho, F; 1958/9 v. E, S, W; 1959/60
v. S, E, W; 1960/1 v. W; 1961/2 (Dunfermline) v. W, Holl.
CUSH, W. (25) (Glentoran) 1950/1 v. E, S; 1953/4 v. S, E; 1956/7 v. W, It,
Port; 1957/8 v. It (Leeds), W, Czecho, Arg, F, Czecho, It, F; 1958/9 v. E, S,
W, Sp; 1959/60 v. S, E, W; 1960/1 (Portadown) v. Gr, G; 1961/2 v. Gr.

D'ARCY, S. (5) (Chelsea) 1951/2 v. W; 1952/3 v. E, (Brentford), S, F, W.
DICKSON, D. (2) (Coleraine) 1972/3 v. C, Port.
DICKSON, T. (1) (Linfield) 1956/7 v. S.
DICKSON, W. (12) (Chelsea) 1950/1 v. W, F; 1951/2 v. S, E, W; 1952/3 v. E,
S, F, W; (Arsenal) 1953/4 v. E, W; 1954/5 v. E.
DIXON, D. (2) (Coleraine) 1969/70 v. S, W.
DOHERTY, P. (6) (Derby County) 1946/7 v. E (Huddersfield Town), W;
1947/8 v. E, W; 1948/9 v. S; 1950/1 v. S.
DOUGAN, D. (41) (Portsmouth) 1957/8 v. Czecho; 1959/60 (Blackburn)
v. S; 1960/1 v. W, It, Gr; 1962/3 (Aston Villa) v. Pol, S, Pol; 1965/6
Leicester v. S, E, A, W, G, Mex; 1966/7 v. E (Wolverhampton), W;
1967/8 v. S, W; 1968/9 v. Isr, T, T, E, S, W; 1969/70 v. Rus (2), S, E; 1970/1
v. Sp, C (2), E, S, W; 1971/2 v. Rus (2), S, E, W; 1972/3 v. Bulg, C.
DOUGLAS, S. (1) (Belfast Celtic) 1946/7 v. E.
DOWD, D. (3) (Glentoran) 1972/3 v. W; 1974/5 (Sheffield W.) v. N, Swdn.

EGLINGTON, T. (6) (Everton) 1946/7 v. S, W; 1947/8 v. S, E, W; 1948/9 v. S.
ELDER, A. (39) (Burnley) 1959/60 v. W; 1960/1 v. E, G, S, W, Gr; 1961/2
v. S, Gr, E; 1962/3 v. Pol, E, S, Pol, W, Sp; 1963/4 v. W, U; 1964/5 v. W,
Switz (2), S, Holl (2), W; 1965/6 v. S, E, A, W, Mex; 1966/7 v. E, S, W;
(Stoke) 1967/8 v. E, W; 1968/9 v. E, S, W; 1969/70 v. Rus.

FARRELL, P. (7) (Everton) 1946/7 v. S, W; 1947/8 v. S, E, W; 1948/9 v. E, W.
FEENEY, A. (1) (Glentoran) 1975/6 v. Isr.
FEENEY, J. (2) (Linfield) 1946/7 v. S (Swansea); 1949/50 v. E.
FERGUSON, W. (2) (Linfield) 1965/6 v. Mex; 1966/7 v. E.
FERRIS, R. (3) (Birmingham) 1949/50 v. S; 1950/1 v. F; 1951/2 v. S.
FINNEY, T. (7) (Sunderland) 1974/5 v. N, E, S, W; 1975/6 v. N, Y, S.
FORDE, T. (4) (Ards) 1958/9 v. Sp; 1960/1 v. E, G, S.

GASTON, R. (1) (Coleraine) 1968/9 v. Isr.
GALLOGLY, C. (2) (Huddersfield) 1950/1 v. E, S.
GORMAN, W. (4) (Brentford) 1946/7 v. E, S, W; 1947/8 v. W.
GRAHAM, R. (13) (Doncaster) 1950/1 v. W, F; 1951/2 v. S, E, W; 1952/3
v. S, F; 1953/4 v. E, W; 1954/5 v. S, W; 1955/6 v. E; 1958/9 v. E.
GREGG, H. (24) (Doncaster) 1953/4 v. W; 1956/7 v. E, S, W, It, Port;
1957/8 v. E (Manchester United) W, Czecho, Arg, G, F, It; 1958/9 v.
E, W; 1959/60 v. S, E, W; 1960/1 v. E, S; 1961/2 v. S, Gr; 1963/4 v. S, E.

HAMILTON, B. (48) (Linfield) 1968/9 v. T; 1970/1 v. C (2), E, S, W; 1971/2
(Ipswich) v. Rus (2), Sp; 1972/3 v. Bulg, C, Port, C, E, S, W; 1973/4 v. Bulg,
S, E, W; 1974/5 v. N, Swdn, Y, E; 1975/6 v. Swdn, N, Y, (Everton) Isr, S,

178

E, W; 1976/7 v. Holl, G, Bel, E, S, W, Ic; 1977/8 v. S, E, W; (Millwall) 1978/9 v. Eire, Bulg, Bulg, (Swindon) E, S, W, D.

HAMILTON, W. (1) (Q.P.R.) 1977/8 v. S.

HARKIN, T. (5) (Southport) 1967/8 v. W; 1968/9 v. T, W; 1969/70 v. Rus. 1970/1 v. Sp.

HARVEY, M. (34) (Sunderland) 1960/1 v. It; 1961/2 v. Holl; 1962/3 v. W, Sp; 1963/4 v. S, Sp, E, W, U; 1964/5 v. W, Switz (2), E, S, Holl (2), A; 1965/6 v. S, E, A, W, G, Mex; 1966/7 v. E, S; 1967/8 v. E, W; 1968/9 v. Isr, T, T, E; 1969/70 v. Rus; 1970/1 v. C, W.

HATTON, S. (2) (Linfield) 1962/3 v. Pol, S.

HEGAN, D. (7) (West Bromwich) 1969/70 v. Rus; 1971/2 (Wolverhampton) v. Rus, S, E, W; 1972/3 v. Bulg, C.

HILL, J. (6) (Norwich) 1958/9 v. W; 1959/60 v. W; 1960/1 v. G (Everton); 1963/4 v. S, Sp, E.

HINTON, E. (7) (Fulham) 1946/7 v. S, W; 1947/8 v. S, E, W (Millwall) 1950/1 v. W, F.

HUGHES, W. (1) (Bolton) 1950/1 v. W.

HUMPHRIES, W. (13) (Ards) 1961/2 v. W (Coventry) Holl; 1962/3 v. Pol, E, S, W, Sp; 1963/4 v. S, Sp, E; 1964/5 v. S, Holl, W.

HUNTER, A. (51) (Blackburn) 1969/70 v. Rus; 1970/1 v. C (2), E, S, W; 1971/2 (Ipswich) v. Rus (2), Sp, S, E, W; 1972/3 v. Bulg, C, Port, C, E, S, W; 1973/4 v. Bulg, S, E, W; 1974/5 v. N, Swdn, Y, E, S, W; 1975/6 v. Swdn, N, Y, Isr, S, E, W; 1976/7 v. Holl, G, Bel, E, S, W, Ic; 1977/8 v. Ic, Holl, Bel; 1978/9 v. Eire, D, S, W, D.

IRVINE, R. (8) (Linfield) 1961/2 v. Holl; 1962/3 v. Pol, E, S, Pol, W, Sp; (Stoke) 1964/5 v. W.

IRVINE, W. (22) (Burnley) 1962/3 v. W, Sp; 1964/5 v. Switz, S, Holl (2), W; 1965/6 v. S, E, A, W, Mex; 1966/7 v. E, S; 1967/8 v. E, W; 1968/9 (Preston) v. Isr, T, E; (Brighton) 1971/2 v. S, E, W.

JACKSON, T. (35) (Everton) 1968/9 v. Isr, E, S, W; 1969/70 v. Rus (2); 1970/1 (Nottingham Forest) v. Sp; 1971/2 c. S, E, W; 1972/3 v. C, E, S, W; 1973/4 v. Bulg, Port, S, E, W; 1974/5 v. N, Swdn, Y, E, S, W; 1975/6 v. Swdn, N, Y; 1976/7 v. Holl, G, Bel, E, S, W, Ic.

JAMISON, A. (1) (Glentoran) 1975/6 v. N.

JENNINGS, P. (80) (Watford) 1963/4 v. W, U; 1964/5 (Tottenham) v. E, Switz (2), S, Holl, A; 1965/6 v. S, E, A, W, G; 1966/7 v. E, S; 1967/8 v. S, E, W; 1968/9 v. Isr, T (2), E, S; 1969/70 v. Rus (2), S, E; 1970/1 v. C (2), E, S, W; 1971/2 v. Rus, Sp, S, E, W; 1972/3 v. Bulg, C, Port, E, S, W; 1973/4 v. Port, S, E, W; 1974/5 v. N, Swdn, Y, E, S, W; 1975/6 v. Swdn, N, Y, Isr, S, E, W; 1976/7 v. Holl, G, Bel, E, S, W, Ic; (Arsenal) 1977/8 v. Ic, Holl, Bel; 1978/9 v. Eire, D, Bulg, E, Bulg, E, S, W, D.

JOHNSTON, W. (1) (Glentoran) 1961/2 v. W.

JOHNSTON, W. (1) (Oldham) 1965/6 v. Mex.

JONES, J. (4) (Glenavon) 1955/6 v. W; 1956/7 v. E, S, W.

KEANE, T. (1) (Swansea) 1948/9 v. S.

KEITH, R. (23) (Newcastle) 1957/8 v. E, W, Czecho, Arg, G, Czecho, F; 1958/9 v. It, E, S, W, Sp; 1959/60 v. S, E; 1960/1 v. E, G, S, W, It, Gr, G; 1961/2 v. W, Holl.

KELLY, H. (4) (Fulham) 1949/50 v. E, W (Southampton); 1950/1 v. E, S.

KELLY, P. (1) (Barnsley) 1949/50 v. S.

LAWTHER, I. (4) (Sunderland) 1959/60 v. W; 1960/1 v. It; 1961/2 (Blackburn Rovers) v. S, Holl.

LOCKHART, N. (8) (Linfield) 1946/7 v. E; 1949/50 (Coventry) v. W; 1950/1.
v. W; 1951/2 v. W; 1953/4 (Aston Villa) v. S, E; 1954/5 v. W; 1955/6 v. W.
LUTTON, B. (5) (Wolverhampton) 1969/70 v. S, E; 1972/3 (West Ham) v.
S, W; 1973/4 v. Port.

MAGILL, E. (25) (Arsenal) 1961/2 v. S, Gr, E; 1962/3 v. Pol, E, S, Pol, W, Sp;
1963/4 v. S, Sp, E, W, U; 1964/5 v. E, Switz (2), S, Holl; 1965/6 v. S, E,
(Brighton) A, W, G, Mex.
MARTIN, C. (5) (Glentoran) 1946/7 v. S; 1947/8 (Leeds) v. S, E, W; 1948/9
(Aston Villa) v. E; 1949/50 v. W.
McADAMS, W. (16) (Manchester City) 1953/4 v. W; 1954/5 v. S; 1956/7
v. E, S; 1957/8 v. S, It; 1960/1 (Bolton) v. E, G, S, W, It, Gr, G; 1961/2
(Leeds) v. Gr, E, Holl.
McALINDEN, J. (2) (Portsmouth) 1946/7 v. E; 1948/9 (Southend) v. E.
McCABE, J. (6) (Leeds) 1948/9 v. S, W; 1949/50 v. E; 1950/1 v. W; 1952/3
v. W; 1953/4 v. S.
McCAVANA, T. (3) (Coleraine) 1954/5 v. S; 1955/6 v. S, E.
McCLEARY, J. W. (1) (Cliftonville) 1954/5 v. W.
McCLELLAND, J. (6) (Arsenal) 1960/1 v. G, W, It, Gr, G; 1965/6 (Fulham)
v. Mex.
McCOURT, F. (6) (Manchester City) 1951/2 v. E, W; 1952/3 v. E, S, F, W.
McCREERY, D. (23) (Manchester U.) 1975/6 v. S, E, W; 1976/7 v. Holl, G,
Bel, E, S, W, Ic; 1977/8 v. Ic, Holl, Bel, S, E, W; 1978/9 v. Eire, D, Bulg, E,
Bulg, W, D.
McCRORY, S. (1) (Southend) 1957/8 v. E.
McCULLOUGH, W. (10) (Arsenal) 1960/1 v. It; 1962/3 v. Sp; 1963/4 v. S,
Sp, E, W, U; 1964/5 v. E, Switz; 1966/7 (Millwall) v. E.
McFAUL, I. (6) (Linfield) 1966/7 v. E; 1969/70 (Newcastle) v. W; 1970/1 v.
Sp; 1971/2 v. Rus; 1972/3 v. C; 1973/4 v. Bulg.
McGARRY, J. K. (3) (Cliftonville) 1950/1 v. S, W, E.
McGRATH, R. (21) (Tottenham) 1973/4 v. S, E, W; 1974/5 v. N; 1975/6 v.
Isr; (Manchester U.) 1976/7 v. Holl, G, Bel, E, S, W, Ic; 1977/8 v. Ic, Holl,
Bel, S, E, W; 1978/9 v. Bulg, E, E.
McILROY, J. (53) (Burnley) 1951/2 v. S, E, W; 1952/3 v. E, S, W; 1953/4 v. S,
E, W; 1954/5 v. E, S, W; 1955/6 v. S, E, W; 1956/7 v. E, S, W, It, Port;
1957/8 v. S, E, It, W, Czecho, Arg, Czecho, F, It; 1958/9 v. E, S, W, Sp;
1959/60 v. S, W, E; 1960/1 v. E, G, W, Gr, G; 1961/2 v. S, Gr, E, Holl;
1962/3 v. Pol, E, S, Pol, W; 1965/6 (Stoke) v. S, E, A.
McILROY, S. (38) (Manchester United) 1971/2 v. Sp, S; 1973/4 v. S, E, W;
1974/5 v. N, Swdn, Y, E, S, W; 1975/6 v. Swdn, N, Y, S, E, W; 1976/7 v.
Holl, Bel, E, S, W, Ic; 1977/8 v. Ic, Holl, Bel, S, E, W; 1978/9 v. Eire, D,
Bulg, E, Bulg, E, S, W, D.
McKEAG, W. (2) (Glentoran) 1967/8 v. S. W.
McKENNA, J. (7) (Huddersfield) 1949/50 v. S, E, W; 1950/1 v. E, S, F;
1951/2 v. E.
McKENZIE, R. (1) (Airdrie) 1966/7 v. W.
McKINNEY, W. (1) (Falkirk) 1965/6 v. W.
McLAUGHLIN, J. (12) (Shrewsbury) 1961/2 v. S, Gr, E, W; 1962/3 v. W,
(Swansea); 1963/4 v. W, U; 1964/5 v. E, Switz (2); 1965/6 v. W.
McMICHAEL, A. (39) (Newcastle) 1949/50 v. S, E; 1950/1 v. E, S, F; 1951/2
v. S, E, W; 1952/3 v. S, E, F, W; 1953/4 v. S, E, W; 1954/5 v. E, W; 1955/6
v. W; 1956/7 v. E, S, W, It, Port; 1957/8 v. E, S, It, W, Czecho, Arg, G,
Czecho, F, It; 1958/9 v. S, W, Sp; 1959/60 v. S.
McMILLAN, S. (2) (Manchester United) 1962/3 v. E, S.

180

McMORDIE, E. (21) (Middlesbrough) 1968/9 v. Isr, T, T, E, S, W; 1969/70 v. Rus, S, E, W; 1970/1 v. C (2) E, S, W; 1971/2 v. Rus, Sp, S, E, W; 1972/3 v. Bulg.

McMORRAN, E. (15) (Belfast Celtic) 1946/7 v. E (Barnsley); 1950/1 v. E, S, W; 1951/2 v. E, S, W; 1952/3 v. E, S, F (Doncaster); 1953/4 v. E; 1955/6 v. W; 1956/7 v. It, Port.

McPARLAND, P. (34) (Aston Villa) 1953/4 v. W; 1954/5 v. E, S; 1955/6 v. S, E; 1956/7 v. E, S, W, Port; 1957/8 v. S, E, It, W, Czecho, Arg, G, Czecho, F, It; 1958/9 v. E, S, W, Sp; 1959/60 v. S, F, W; 1960/1 v. E, G, S, W, It, Gr, G; 1961/2 (Wolverhampton) v. Holl.

MONTGOMERY, F. (1) (Coleraine) 1954/5 v. E.

MOORE, C. (1) (Glentoran) 1948/9 v. W.

MORELAND, A. (3) (Derby) 1978/9 v. Bulg, E, S.

MORGAN, S. (18) (Port Vale) 1971/2 v. Sp; 1972/3 v. Bulg, Port, C, E, S, W; 1973/4 (Aston Villa) v. Bulg, Port, S, E; 1974/5 v. Swdn; 1975/6 v. Swdn, N, Y (Brighton), S, W; 1978/9 v. D.

NAPIER, R. (1) (Bolton) 1965/6 v. G.

NEILL, T. (58) (Arsenal) 1960/1 v. It, Gr, G; 1961/2 v. S, Gr, E, W; 1962/3 v. E, Pol, W, Sp; 1963/4 v. S, Sp, E, W, U; 1964/5 v. E, Switz, S, Holl (2), W; 1965/6 v. S, E, A, W, G, Mex; 1966/7 v. S, W; 1967/8 v. S, E; 1968/9 v. Isr, T, T, E, S, W; 1969/70 v. Rus (2), S, E, W; 1970/1 v. Sp, C; 1971/2 (Hull) v. Rus (2), Sp, S, E, W; 1972/3 v. Bulg, C, Port, C, E, S, W.

NELSON, S. (40) (Arsenal) 1969/70 v. E, W; 1970/1 v. Sp, C, E, S, W; 1971/2 v. Rus (2), Sp, S, E, W; 1972/3 v. Bulg, C, Port; 1973/4 v. S, E; 1974/5 v. Swdn, Y; 1975/6 v. Swdn, N, Isr, E; 1976/7 v. G, Bel, W, Ic; 1977/8 v. Ic, Holl, Bel; 1978/9 v. Eire, D, Bulg, E, Bulg, E, S, W, D.

NICHOLL, C. (22) (Aston Villa) 1974/5 v. Swdn, Y, E, S, W; 1975/6 v. Swdn, N, Y, S, E, W; 1976/7 v. W; 1977/8 v. Bel, S, E, W (Southampton); 1978/9 v. Eire, Bulg, E, Bulg, E, W.

NICHOLL, J. (23) (Manchester United) 1975/6 v. Isr, W; 1976/7 v. Holl, Bel, E, S, W, Ic; 1977/8 v. Ic, Holl, Bel, S, E, W; 1978/9 v. Eire, D, Bulg, E, Bulg, E, S, W, D.

NICHOLSON, J. (40) (Manchester United) 1960/1 v. S, W; 1961/2 v. Gr, E, W, Holl; 1962/3 v. Pol, E, S, Pol; 1964/5 (Huddersfield) v. Holl (2), W; 1965/6 v. S, E, A, W, Mex; 1966/7 v. S, W; 1967/8 v. S, E, W; 1968/9 v. T, T, E, S, W; 1969/70 v. Rus (2), S, E, W; 1970/1 v. C (2), E, S, W; 1971/2 v. Rus (2).

O'DOHERTY, A. (3) (Coleraine) 1969/70 v. S, E, W.

O'DRISCOLL, J. (3) (Swansea) 1948/9 v. E, S, W.

O'KANE, L. (20) (Nottingham Forest) 1969/70 v. E, W, S; 1970/1 v. Sp, E, S, W; 1971/2 v. Rus (2); 1972/3 v. Port, C; 1973/4 v. Bulg, Port, S, E, W; 1974/5 v. N, Swdn, E, S.

O'NEILL, J. (1) (Sunderland) 1961/2 v. W.

O'NEILL, M. (30) (Distillery) 1971/2 v. Rus, (Nottingham Forest), Sp, W; 1972/3 v. Port, C, E, S, W; 1973/4 v. Bulg, Port, S, E, W; 1974/5 v. Swdn, Y, E, S; 1975/6 v. Y; 1976/7 v. E, S, W; 1977/8 v. Ic, Holl, S, E, W; 1978/9 v. Eire, D, Bulg, E, Bulg, D.

PARKE, J. (13) (Hibernian) 1963/4 v. S, Sp E; 1964/5 (Sunderland) v. Switz, S, Holl (2), W; 1965/6 v. G; 1966/7 v. E, S; 1967/8 v. S, E.

PEACOCK, R. (31) (Glasgow Celtic) 1951/2 v. S; 1952/3 v. F; 1953/4 v. W; 1954/5 v. E, S; 1955/6 v. S, E; 1956/7 v. W, It, Port; 1957/8 v. S, E, It,

W, Czecho, Arg, G, Czecho, It; 1958/9 v. E, S, W; 1959/60 v. S, E; 1960/1 v. E, G, S, It, Gr, G; 1961/2 v. S.
PLATT, J. (4) (Middlesbrough) 1975/6 v. Isr; 1977/8 v. S, E, W.

RICE, P. (48) (Arsenal) 1968/9 v. Isr; 1969/70 v. Rus; 1970/1 v. E, S, W; 1971/2 v. Rus, Sp, S, E, W; 1972/3 v. Bulg, C, E, S, W; 1973/4 v. Bulg, Port, S, E, W; 1974/5 v. N, Y, E, S, W; 1975/6 v. Swdn, N, Y, Isr, S, E, W; 1976/7 v. Holl, G, Bel, E, S, Ic; 1977/8 v. Ic, Holl, Bel; 1978/9 v. Eire, D, E, E, S, W, D.
ROSS, E. (1) (Newcastle) 1968/9 v. Isr.
RUSSELL, A. (1) (Linfield) 1946/7 v. E.
RYAN, R. (1) (West Bromwich) 1949/50 v. W.

SCOTT, J. (2) (Grimsby) 1957/8 v. Czecho, F.
SCOTT, P. (8) (Everton) 1974/5 v. W; 1975/6 (York C.) v. Y, Isr, S, W; 1977/8 v. S, E, W.
SHARKEY, P. (1) (Ipswich) 1975/6 v. S.
SHIELDS, J. (1) (Southampton) 1956/7 v. S.
SIMPSON, W. (12) (Glasgow Rangers) 1950/1 v. W, F; 1953/4 v. S, E; 1954/5 v. E; 1956/7 v. It, Port; 1957/8 v. S, E, It, W; 1958/9 v. S.
SLOAN, A. (1) (Manchester United) 1970/1 v. S.
SLOAN, D. (2) (Oxford) 1968/9 v. Isr; 1970/1 v. Sp.
SLOAN, W. (1) (Arsenal) 1946/7 v. W.
SMYTH, S. (9) (Wolverhampton) 1947/8 v. S, E, W; 1948/9 v. S, W; 1949/50 v. S, E, W (Stoke); 1951/2 v. E.
SMYTH, W. (4) (Distillery) 1948/9 v. E, S; 1953/4 v. S, E.
SPENCE, D. (22) (Bury) 1974/5 v. Y, E, S, W; 1975/6 v. Swdn, Isr, E, W, S; (Blackpool) 1976/7 v. Holl, G, E, S, W, Ic; 1978/9 v. Eire, D, E, E, S, W, D.
STEVENSON, A. (3) (Everton) 1946/7 v. S, W; 1947/8 v. S.
STEWART, A. (6) (Glentoran) 1966/7 v. W; 1967/8 v. S, E, (Derby) W; 1968/9 v. Isr, T.
STEWART, P. (1) (Linfield) 1960/1 v. W.
STEWART, D. (1) (Hull) 1977/8 v. Bel.

TODD, S. (9) (Burnley) 1966/7 v. E; 1967/8 v. W; 1968/9 v. E, S, W; 1969/70 v. Rus, S; 1970/1 v. Sp (Sheffield Wednesday), C (2).
TRAINOR, D. (1) (Crusaders) 1966/7 v. W.
TULLEY, C. (10) (Glasgow Celtic) 1948/9 v. E; 1949/50 v. E; 1951/2 v. S; 1952/3 v. E, S, F, W; 1953/4 v. S; 1955/6 v. E; 1958/9 v. Sp.

UPRICHARD, N. (18) (Swindon) 1951/2 v. S, E, W; 1952/3 v. E, S, (Portsmouth) F, W; 1954/5 v. E, S, W; 1955/6 v. S, E, W; 1957/8 v. S, It, Czecho; 1958/9 v. S, Sp.

SCOTLAND

AIRD, J. (4) (Burnley) 1953/4 v. N (2), Aust, U.
AITKEN, G. (8) (East Fife) 1948/9 v. E, F; 1949/50 v. I, W, Switz; 1952/3 (Sunderland) v. W, I; 1953/4 v. E.
ALLAN, T. (2) (Dundee) 1973/4 v. G, N.
ANDERSON, J. (1) (Leicester) 1953/4 v. Fin.
AULD, B. (3) (Celtic) 1958/9 v. Holl, Port; 1959/60 v. W.

BAIRD, H. (1) (Airdrieonians) 1955/6 v. Aust.
BAIRD, S. (7) (Rangers) 1956/7 v. Y, Sp, Switz, G, Sp; 1957/8 v. I, F.
BAULD, W. (3) (Hearts) 1949/50 v, E, Switz, Port.
BAXTER, J. (34) (Rangers) 1960/1 v. I, Eire (2), Czecho; 1961/2 v. Czecho, I,
    W, Czecho, E, U; 1962/3 v. W, I, E, Aust, N, Eire, Sp; 1963/4 v. N, W, E,
    G; 1964/5 v. W, Fin, I (Sunderland); 1965/6 v. I, It, W, E, Port, Braz;
    1966/7 v. W, E, Rus; 1967/8 v. W.
BELL, W. (2) (Leeds) 1965/6 v. Port, Braz.
BLACK, I. (1) (Southampton) 1947/8 v. E.
BLACKLAW, A. (3) (Burnley) 1962/3 v. N, Sp; 1965/6 v. It.
BLACKLEY, J. (7) (Hibernian) 1973/4 v. Czecho, E, Bel, Z; 1975/6 v. Switz;
    1976/7 v. W, Swdn.
BLAIR, J. (1) (Blackpool) 1946/7 v. W.
BLYTH, J. (2) (Coventry C.) 1977/8 v. Bulg, W.
BONE, J. (1) (Norwich) 1972/3 v. D.
BRAND, R. (8) (Rangers) 1960/1 v. I, Eire (2), Czecho; 1961/2 v. I, W,
    Czecho, U.
BREMNER, D. (1) (Hibernian) 1975/6 v. Switz.
BREMNER, W. (54) (Leeds) 1964/5 v. Sp; 1965/6 v. Pol, It (2) E, Port, Braz;
    1966/7 v. W, I, E; 1967/8 v. W, E; 1968/9 v. D, C, Aust, G, W, I, E, C;
    1969/70 v. Eire, G, Aust; 1970/1 v. W, E; 1971/2 v. Port, Bel, Holl, I, W,
    E, Y, Czecho, Braz; 1972/3 v. D (2), E, I, E, Switz, Braz; 1973/4 v. Czecho,
    G, I, W, E, Bel, N, Z, Braz, Y; 1974/5 v. Sp (2); 1975/6 v. D.
BRENNAN, F. (7) (Newcastle) 1946/7 v. W, I; 1952/3 v. W, I, E; 1963/4 v.
    I, E.
BROGAN, J. (4) (Celtic) 1970/1 v. Port, W, I, E.
BROWN, A. (14) (East Fife) 1949/50 v. Switz, Port, F; (Blackpool) 1951/2 v.
    U.S., D, Swdn; 1952/3 v. W; 1953/4 v. W, E, N (2), Fin, Aust, U.
BROWN, H. (3) (Partick) 1946/7 v. W, Bel, Lux.
BROWN, J. (1) (Sheffield U.) 1974/5 v. Rus.
BROWN, R. (3) (Rangers) 1946/7 v. I; 1948/9 v. I; 1951/2 v. E.
BROWN, W. (28) (Dundee) 1957/8 v. F; 1958/9 v. W, I, E; 1959/60 (Totten-
    ham) v. I, N, Pol, Aust, H, T; 1961/2 v. Czecho, I, W, E; 1962/3 v. W, I, E,
    Aust; 1963/4 v. I, N, W; 1964/5 v. E, Sp, Pol, Fin; 1965/6 v. I, Pol, It.
BROWNLIE, J. (7) (Hibernian) 1970/1 v. Rus; 1971/2 v. Per, I, E; 1972/3 v.
    D (2); 1975/6 v. Ru.
BUCHAN, M. (34) (Aberdeen) 1971/2 v. Bel (Manchester United) W, Y,
    Port, Czecho, Braz; 1972/3 v. D (2), E; 1973/4 v. G, I, W, N, Braz, Y;
    1974/5 v. E/Germ, Sp, Port; 1975/6 v. D, Ru; 1976/7 v. Fin, Czecho, Ch,
    Arg, Braz; 1977/8 v. E/Germ, W, I; 1978/9 v. Per, Ir, Holl, Aust, N, Port.
BUCKLEY, P. (3) (Aberdeen) 1953/4 v. N; 1954/5 v. W, I.
BURLEY, G. (5) (Ipswich) 1978/9 v. W, I, E, N, Arg.
BURNS, F. (1) (Manchester United) 1969/70 v. Aust.
BURNS, K. (14) (Birmingham) 1973/4 v. G; 1974/5 v. E/Germ, Sp (2); 1976/7
    v. Czecho, W, Swdn, W; (Nottingham F.) 1977/8 v. I, W, E; 1978/9 v. Per,
    Ir, N.

CALDOW, E. (40) (Rangers) 1956/7 v. E, Sp, Switz, G, Sp; 1957/8 v. I,
    Switz, W, H, Pol, Y, Per, F; 1958/9 v. W, I, E, G, Holl, Port; 1959/60 v. I,
    W, E, Aust, H, T; 1960/1 v. W, I, E, Eire (2), Czecho; 1961/2 v. Czecho, I,
    W, Czecho, E, U; 1962/3 v. W, I, E.
CALLAGHAN, T. (2) (Dunfermline) 1969/70 v. Eire, W.
CAMPBELL, R. (3) (Chelsea) 1949/50 v. Switz, Port, F.

183

CAMPBELL, W. (7) (Morton) 1946/7 v. I, Bel, Lux; 1947/8 v. E, Bel, Switz, F.
CARR, W. (6) (Coventry) 1969/70 v. I, W, E; 1970/1 v. D; 1971/2 v. Per; 1972/3 v. D.
CHALMERS, S. (5) (Celtic) 1964/5 v. W, Fin; 1965/6 v. Port, Braz; 1966/7 v. I.
CLARK, J. (4) (Celtic) 1965/6 v. Braz; 1966/7 v. W, I, Rus.
CLARK, R. (16) (Aberdeen), 1967/8 v. W, Holl; 1969/70 v. I; 1970/1 v. Port, W, I, E, D, Rus; 1971/2 v. Bel, I, W, E, Czecho, Braz; 1972/3 v D, E.
COLLINS, R. (31) (Celtic) 1950/1 v. W, I, Aust; 1954/5 v. Y, Aust, H; 1955/6 v. I, W; 1956/7 v. W, E, Sp, Switz, G, Sp; 1957/8 v. I, Switz, W, H, Pol, Y, Par, F; 1958/9 (Everton) v. W, I, E, G, Holl, Port; 1964/5 (Leeds) v. E, Sp, Pol.
COLQUHOUN, E. (9) (Sheffield United) 1971/2 v. Port, Holl, Per, Y, Czecho, Braz; 1972/3 v. D (2), E.
COMBE, R. (3) (Hibernian) 1947/8 v. E, Bel, Switz.
CONN, A. (1) (Hearts) 1955/6 v. Aust.
CONN, A. (2) (Tottenham H.) 1974/5 v. I, E.
CONNACHAN, E. (2) (Dunfermline) 1961/2 v. Czecho, U.
CONNELLY, G. (2) (Celtic) 1973/4 v. Czecho, G.
CONNOLLY, J. (1) (Everton) 1972/3 v. Switz.
COOKE, C. (16) (Dundee) 1965/6 v. W, It, Port, Braz (Chelsea); 1967/8 v. E, Holl; 1968/9 v. C, Aust, G, W, I, C; 1969/70 v. Aust; 1970/1 v. Bel; 1974/5 v. Sp, Port.
CORMACK, P. (9) (Hibernian) 1965/6 v. Braz; 1969/70 v. Eire, G, Aust; (Nottingham Forest) 1970/1 v. D, Port, W, E; 1971/2 v. Holl.
COWAN, J.(25) (Morton) 1947/8 v. Bel, Switz, F.;1948/9 v. W, E, F; 1949/50 v. I, W, E, Switz, Port, F; 1950/1 v. W, I, Aust (2), E, D, F, Bel; 1951/2 v. I, W, U.S., D, Swdn.
COWIE, D. (20) (Dundee) 1952/3 v. E, Swdn; 1953/4 v. I, W, N, Fin, Aust, U; 1954/5 v. W, I, Aust, H; 1955/6 v. W, Aust; 1956/7 v. I, W; 1957/8 v. H, Pol, Y, Par.
COX, S. (25) (Rangers) 1947/8 v. F; 1948/9 v. E, F; 1949/50 v. I, W, E, Switz, Port, F; 1950/1 v. E (2), F, Bel, Aust; 1951/2 v. I, W, U.S., D, Swdn; 1952/3 v. W, I, E; 1953/4 v. I, W, E.
CRAIG, J. (1) (Celtic) 1967/8 v. W.
CRAIG, J. (1) (Celtic) 1976/7 v. Swdn.
CRAIG, T. (1) (Newcastle U.) 1975/6 v. Switz.
CRERAND, P. (16) (Celtic) 1960/1 v. Eire (2), Czecho; 1961/2 v. Czecho, I, W, Czecho, E, W; 1962/3 v. W, I; 1963/4 v. I; 1964/5 (Manchester United) v. E, Pol, Fin; 1965/6 v. Pol.
CROPLEY, A. (2) (Hibernian) 1971/2 v. Port, Bel.
CRUICKSHANK, J. (6) (Hearts) 1963/4 v. G; 1969/70 v. W, E; 1970/1 v. D, Bel; 1975/6 v. Ru.
CULLEN, M. (1) (Luton) 1955/6 v. Aust.
CUMMING, J. (9) (Hearts) 1954/5 v. H, E, Port, Y; 1959/60 v. E, Pol, Aust, H, T.
CUNNINGHAM, W. (8) (Preston) 1953/4 v. N (2), Fin, Aust, U; 1954/5 v. W, H, E.
CURRAN, H. (5) (Wolverhampton) 1969/70 v. Aust; 1970/1 v. I, E, D, Rus.

DALGLISH, K. (65) (Celtic) 1971/2 v. Bel, Holl; 1972/3 v. D (2), E, W, I, E, Switz, Braz; 1973/4 v. Czecho (2), G (2), I, W, E, Bel, N, Z, Braz, Y; 1974/5 v. E/Germ, Sp (2), Swdn, Port, W, I, E, Ru; 1975/6 v. D (2), Ru, Switz, I, E; 1976/7 v. Fin, Czecho, W, Swdn, W, I, E, Ch, Arg, Braz; (Liver-

184

pool) 1977/8 v. /EGerm, Czecho, W (2), Bulg, I, E; 1978/9 v. Per, Ir, Holl, Aust, N, Port, W, I, E, N, Arg.

DAVIDSON, J. (8) (Partick) 1953/4 v. N (2), Aust, U; 1954/5 v. W, I, H, E.

DEANS, D. (2) (Celtic) 1974/5 v. E/Germ, Sp.

DELANEY, J. (4) (Manchester United) 1946/7 v. E; 1947/8 v. I, W, E.

DICK, J. (1) (West Ham) 1958/9 v. E.

DICKSON, A. (5) (Kilmarnock) 1969/70 v. I, W, E; 1970/1 v. D, Rus.

DOCHERTY, T. (25) (Preston) 1951/2 v. W; 1952/3 v. E, Swdn; 1953/4 v. N (2), Aust, U; 1954/5 v. W, H (2), F, Aust; 1956/7 v. E, Sp, Switz, G, Sp; 1957/8 v. I, Switz, W, E; 1958/9 (Arsenal) v. W, I, E.

DONACHIE, W. (35) (Manchester City) 1971/2 v. Per, I, E, Y, Czecho, Braz; 1972/3 v. D, E, W, I; 1973/4 v. I; 1975/6 v. Ru, I, W, E; 1976/7 v. Fin, Czecho, W, Swdn, W, I, E, Ch, Arg, Braz; 1977/8 v. E/Germ, W (2), Bulg, E; 1978/9 v. Ir, Holl, Aust, N, Port.

DOUGALL, C. (1) (Birmingham) 1946/7 v. W.

DOUGAN, R.(1) (Hearts) 1949/50 v. Switz.

DOYLE, J. (1) (Ayr U.) 1975/6 v. Ru.

DUNCAN, A. (6) (Hibernian) 1974/5 v. Port, W, I, E, Ru; 1975/6 v. D.

DUNCAN, D. (3) (East Fife) 1947/8 v. Bel, Switz, F.

DUNCANSON, J. (1) (Rangers) 1946/7 v. I.

EVANS, R. (48) (Celtic) 1948/9 v. W, I, E, F; 1949/50 v. I, W, Switz, Port; 1950/1 v. Aust, E; 1951/2 v. I; 1952/3 v. Swdn; 1953/4 v. I, W, E, N, Fin; 1954/5 v. I, Port, Y, Aust, H; 1955/6 v. I, W, E, Aust; 1956/7 v. G, Sp; 1957/8 v. I, Switz, W, E, H, Pol, Y, Par, F; 1958/9 v. E, G, Holl, Port; 1959/60 v. I, W, E, (Chelsea) Pol, Aust, H, T.

EWING, T. (2) (Partick) 1957/8 v. W, E.

FARM, G. (10) (Blackpool) 1952/3 v. W, I, E, Swdn; 1953/4 v. I, W, E; 1958/9 v. G, Holl, Port.

FERGUSON, R. (7) (Kilmarnock) 1965/6 v. W, E, Holl, Port, Braz; 1966/7 v. W, I.

FERNIE, W. (11) (Celtic) 1953/4 v. Fin, Aust, U; 1954/5 v. W, I; 1956/7 v. Y, W, E; 1957/8 v. Switz, W, Par.

FLAVELL, R. (2) (Airdrieonians) 1946/7 v. Bel, Lux.

FLEMING, C. (1) (East Fife) 1953/4 v. I.

FORBES, A. (14) (Sheffield United) 1946/7 v. E, Bel, Lux; 1947/8 v. I, W, (Arsenal) 1949/50 v. E, Port, F; 1950/1 v. W, I, Aust; 1951/2 v. W, D, Swdn.

FORD, D. (3) (Hearts) 1973/4 v. Czecho, G, W.

FORREST, J. (1) (Motherwell) 1957/8 v. E.

FORREST, J. (2) (Rangers) 1965/6 v. W, It.

FORREST, J. (3) (Aberdeen) 1970/1 v. Bel, D, Rus.

FORSYTH, A. (18) (Partick) 1971/2 v. Y, Czecho, Braz; 1972/3 v. D, (Manchester United), E; 1974/5 v. E/Germ, Sp, I, Ru; 1975/6 v. D; 1977/8 v. Czecho, W (2), I, E; 1978/9 v. Per, Ir, Holl.

FORSYTH, C. (3) (Kilmarnock) 1963/4 v. E; 1964/5 v. W, Fin.

FORSYTH, T. (14) (Motherwell) 1970/1 v. D (Rangers) 1973/4 v. Czecho; 1975/6 v. Switz, I, W, E; 1976/7 v. Fin, Swdn, W, I, E, Ch, Arg, Braz.

FRASER, D. (2) (West Bromwich) 1967/8 v. Holl; 1968/9 v. C.

FRASER, W. (2) (Sunderland) 1954/5 v. D, I.

GABRIEL, J. (1) (Everton) 1960/1 v. W.

GARDINER, W. (1) (Motherwell) 1957/8 v. W

185

GEMMELL, T. (2) (St. Mirren) 1954/5 v. Port, Y.
GEMMELL, T. (18) (Celtic) 1965/6 v. E; 1966/7 v. W, I, E, Rus; 1967/8 v. I,
E; 1968/9 v. Aust, D, G, W, I, E, C; 1969/70 v. Eire, G, E; 1970/1 v. Bel.
GEMMILL, A. (33) (Derby) 1970/1 v. Bel; 1971/2 v. Port, Holl, Per, I, W, E;
1975/6 v. D, Ru,I, W, E; 1976/7 v. Fin, Czecho, W (2), I, E, Ch, Arg, Braz;
1977/8 v. E/Germ, Bulg, I, W, E; 1978/9 v. Per, Ir, Holl, Aust, N, Port, N.
GIBSON, D. (7) (Leicester) 1962/3 v. Aust, N, Eire, Sp; 1963/4 v. I; 1964/5 v.
W, Fin.
GILZEAN, A. (22) (Dundee) 1963/4 v. N, W, E, G; 1964/5 v. I (Tottenham),
Sp; 1965/6 v. I, Pol, It, W; 1967/8 v. W; 1968/9 v. C, Aust, G, W, E, C;
1969/70 v. G, Aust, I, E; 1970/1 v. Port.
GLAVIN, R. (1) (Celtic) 1976/7 v. Swdn.
GLEN, A. (2) (Aberdeen) 1955/6 v. I, E.
GOVAN, J. (6) (Hibernian) 1947/8 v. W, E, Bel, Switz, F; 1948/9 v. I.
GRAHAM, G. (11) (Arsenal) 1971/2 v. Port, Holl, I, Y, Czecho, Braz;
1972/3 v. D (2), (Manchester United) E, W, I.
GRAHAM, A. (8) (Leeds) 1977/8 v. E/Germ; 1978/9 v. Aust, N, W, I, E, N,
Arg.
GRAY, A. (7) (Aston Villa) 1975/6 v. Ru, Switz; 1976/7 v. Fin, Czecho;
1978/9 v. Aust N, Arg.
GRAY, E. (12) (Leeds U.)1968/9 v. E, C; 1969/70 v. G, Aust; 1970/1 v. W, I;
1971/2 v. Bel, Holl; 1975/6 v. W, E; 1976/7 v. Fin, W.
GRAY, F. (6) (Leeds U.) 1975/6 v. Switz; 1978/9 v. N, Port, W, I, E.
GRANT, J. (2) (Hibernian) 1958/9 v. W, I.
GREEN, A. (16) (Blackpool) 1970/1 v. Bel, Port, I, E; (Newcastle) 1971/2 v.
W, E.
GREIG, J. (44) (Rangers) 1963/4 v. E, G; 1964/5 v. W, Fin, I, E, Sp, Pol, Fin;
1965/6 v. I, Pol, It, W, It, E, Holl, Port, Braz; 1966/7 v. W, I, E; 1967/8 v. I,
W, E, Holl; 1968/9 v. D, C, Aust, G, W, I, E, C; 1969/70 v. Eire, G, Aust,
W, E; 1970/1 v. D, Bel, W, I, E; 1975/6 v. D.

HADDOCK, H. (6) (Clyde) 1954/5 v. H (2), E, Port, Y; 1957/8 v. E.
HAFFEY, H. (2) (Celtic) 1959/60 v. E; 1960/1 v. E.
HAMILTON, A. (24) (Dundee) 1961/2 v. W, Czecho, E, U; 1962/3 v. W, I,
E, Aust, N, I, Eire; 1963/4 v. I, N, W, E, G; 1964/5 v. W, Fin, I, E, Sp, Pol,
Fin; 1965/6 v. I, Pol.
HAMILTON, G. (5) (Aberdeen) 1946/7 v. I; 1950/1 v. Bel, Aust; 1953/4 v.
N (2).
HAMILTON, W. (1) (Hibernian) 1964/5 v. Fin.
HANSEN, A. (2) (Liverpool) 1978/9 v. W, Arg.
HANSEN, J. (1) (Partick) 1971/2 v. Bel.
HARPER, J. (4) (Aberdeen) 1972/3 v. D (2); 1975/6 v. D; 1978/9 v. Ir.
HARTFORD, A. (35) (West Bromwich) 1971/2 v. Per, W, E, Y, Czecho,
Braz; 1975/6 (Manchester C.) v. D, Ru, I; 1976/7 v. Czecho, W, Swdn, W,
I, E, Ch, Arg, Braz; 1977/8 v. E/Germ, Czecho, W (2), Bulg, E; 1978/9 v .
Per, Ir, Holl, Aust, N, Port, W, I, E, N, Arg.
HARVEY, D. (16) (Leeds) 1972/3 v. D; 1973/4 v. Czecho, G, I, W, E, Bel, Z,
Braz, Y; 1974/5 v. E/Germ, Sp (2); 1975/6 v. D (2); 1976/7 v. Fin.
HAUGHNEY, M. (1) (Celtic) 1953/4 v. E.
HAY, D. (27) (Celtic) 1969/70 v. I, W; 1970/1 v. D, Bel, Port, W; 1971/2
v. Port, Bel, Holl; 1972/3 v. W, I, E, Switz, Braz; 1973/4 v. Czecho (2),
G, I, W, E, Bel, N, Z, Braz, Y.
HEGARTY, P. (4) (Dundee U.) 1978/9 v. W, I, E, Arg.

HENDERSON, J. (7) (Portsmouth) 1952/3 v. Swdn; 1953/4 v. I, E, N; 1955/6
    v. W; 1958/9 (Arsenal) v. W, I.
HENDERSON, W. (29) (Rangers) 1962/3 v. W, I, E, Aust, N, Eire, Sp; 1963/4
    v. I, N, W, E, G; 1964/5 v. E, Sp, Pol, Fin; 1965/6 v. I, Pol, It, W, Holl; 1966/7
    v. W, I; 1967/8 v. Holl; 1968/9 v. I, E, C; 1969/70 v. Eire; 1970/1 v. Port.
HERD, D. (5) (Arsenal) 1958/9 v. W, I, E; 1960/1 v. Eire, Czecho.
HERD, G. (5) (Clyde) 1957/8 v. E; 1959/60 v. H, T; 1960/1 v. W, I.
HERRIOT, J. (8) (Birmingham) 1968/9 v. D, C, W, I, E, C; 1969/70 v. Eire, G.
HEWIE, J. (19) (Charlton) 1955/6 v. E, Aust; 1956/7 v. Y, I, W, E, Sp, Switz,
    G, Sp; 1957/8 v. W, Pol, Y, F; 1958/9 v. Holl, Port; 1959/60 v. I, W, Pol.
HOLT, D. (4) (Hearts) 1962/3 v. Aust, N, Eire, Sp.
HOLTON, J. (15) (Manchester United) 1972/3 v. W, I, E, Switz, Braz; 1973/4
    v. Czecho, G, I, W, E, N, Z, Braz, Y; 1974/5 v. E/Germ.
HOPE, R. (2) (West Bromwich) 1967/8 v. Hol; 1968/9 v. D.
HOULISTON, W. (3) (Queen of the South) 1948/9 v. I, E, F.
HOUSTON, S. (1) (Manchester United) 1975/6 v. D.
HOWIE, H. (1) (Hibernian) 1948/9 v. W.
HUGHES, J. (8) (Celtic) 1964/5 v. Sp, Pol; 1965/6 v. I, It (2); 1967/8 v. E;
    1968/9 v. Aust; 1969/70 v. Eire.
HUGHES, W. (1) (Sunderland) 1974/5 v. Swdn.
HUMPHRIES, W. (1) (Motherwell) 1951/2 v. Swdn.
HUNTER, A. (3) (Kilmarnock) 1971/2 v. Per; 1972/3 (Celtic) v. E; 1973/4 v.
    Czecho.
HUNTER, N. (3) (Motherwell) 1959/60 v. H, T; 1960/1 v. W.
HUSBAND, J. (1) (Partick) 1946/7 v. W.
HUTCHISON, T. (17) (Coventry) 1973/4 v. Czecho (2), G (2), I, W, Bel, N,
    Z, Y; 1974/5 v. E/Germ, Sp (2), Port, E, Ru; 1975/6 v. D.

IMLACH, S. (4) (Nottingham Forest) 1957/8 v. H, Pol, Y, F.

JACKSON, C. (8) (Rangers) 1974/5 v. Swdn, Port, W; 1975/6 v. D, Ru, I,
    W, E.
JARDINE, A. (33) (Rangers) 1970/1 v. D; 1971/2 v. Port, Bel, Holl; 1972/3 v.
    E, Switz, Braz; 1973/4 v. Czecho (2), G (2), I, W, E, Bel, N, Z, Braz, Y;
    1974/5 v. E/Germ, Sp (2), Swdn, Port, W, I, E; 1976/7 v. Swdn, Ch; 1977/8
    v. Czecho, W, I; 1978/9 v. Ir.
JARVIE, A. (3) (Airdrie) 1970/1 v. Port, I, E.
JOHNSTON, W. (21) (Rangers) 1965/6 v. Pol, W, E, Holl; 1967/8 v. W, E;
    1968/9 v. I; 1969/70 v. I; 1970/1 v. D; (W.B.A.) 1976/7 v. Swdn, W, I,
    Ch, Arg, Braz; 1977/8 v. E/Germ, Czecho, W (2), E.
JOHNSTONE, D. (14) (Rangers) 1972/3 v. W, I, E, Switz, Braz; 1974/5 v.
    E/Germ, Swdn; 1975/6 v. Switz, I, E; 1977/8 v. Bulg, I, W; 1978/9 v. Per.
JOHNSTONE, J. (23) (Celtic) 1964/5 v. W, Fin; 1965/6 v. E; 1966/7 v. W,
    Rus; 1967/8 v. W; 1968/9 v. Aust, G; 1969/70 v. G, E; 1970/1 v. D, E;
    1971/2 v. Port, Bel, Holl, I, E; 1973/4 v. W, E, Bel, N; 1974/5 v. E/Germ, Sp.
JOHNSTONE, L. (2) (Clyde) 1947/8 v. Bel, Switz.
JOHNSTONE, R. (17) (Hibernian) 1950/1 v. E, D, F; 1951/2 v. I, E; 1952/3
    v. E, Swdn; 1953/4 v. W, E, N, Fin; 1954/5 v. I, H (Manchester City); E;
    1955/6 v. I, W, E.
JORDAN, J. (39) (Leeds) 1972/3 v. E, Switz, Braz; 1973/4 v. Czecho (2), G,
    I, W, E, Bel, N, Z, Braz, Y; 1974/5 v. E/Germ, Sp (2); 1975/6 v. I, W, E;
    1976/7 v. Czecho, W, I, E; (Manchester U.) 1977/8 v. E/Germ, Czecho, W,
    Bulg, I, E; 1978/9 v. Per, Ir, Holl, Aust, Port, W, I, E, N.

187

KELLY, H. (1) (Blackpool) 1951/2 v. U.S.
KELLY, J. (2) (Barnsley) 1948/9 v. W, I.
KENNEDY, J. (6) (Celtic) 1963/4 v. W, E, G; 1964/5 v. W, Fin, I.
KENNEDY, S. (12) (Rangers) 1974/5 v. Swdn, Port, W, I, E; 1977/8 v. Bulg, W, E; 1978/9 v. Per, Holl, Aust, Port.
KERR, A. (2) (Partick) 1954/5 v. Aust, H.

LAW, D. (55) (Huddersfield) 1958/9 v. W, I, Holl, Port; 1959/60 v. I, W, (Manchester City) E, Pol, Aust; 1960/1 v. I, E; 1961/2 (Torino) v. Czecho, (2) E; 1962/3 (Manchester United) v. W, I, E, Aust, N, Eire, Sp; 1963/4 v. N, W, E, G; 1964/5 v. W, Fin, I, E, Sp, Pol, Fin; 1965/6 v. I, Pol, E; 1966/7 v. W, E, Rus; 1967/8 v. I; 1968/9 v. Aust, G, I; 1971/2 v. Per, I, W, E, Y, Czecho, Braz; 1973/4 (Manchester City) v. Czecho (2), G (2), I, Z.
LAWRENCE, T. (3) (Liverpool) 1962/3 v. Eire; 1968/9 v. G, W.
LEGGAT, G. (18) (Aberdeen) 1955/6 v. E; 1956/7 v. W; 1957/8 v. I, H, Pol, Y, Par; 1958/9 (Fulham) v. W, I, E, G, Holl; 1959/60 v. I, W, E, Pol, Aust, H.
LENNOX, R. (10 (Celtic) 1966/7 v. I, E, Rus; 1967/8 v. W, E; 1968/9 v. D, W, Aust, G, C.
LESLIE, L. (5) (Airdrieonians) 1960/I v. W, I, Eire (2), Czecho.
LIDDELL, W. (28) (Liverpool) 1946/7 v. W, I; 1947/8 v. I, W, E; 1949/50 v. W, E, Port, F; 1950/1 v. W, I, Aust, E; 1951/2 v. I, W, E, U.S., D, Swdn; 1952/3 v. W, I, E; 1953/4 v. W; 1954/5 v. Port, Y, Aust, H; 1955/6 v. I.
LINWOOD, A. (1) (Clyde) 1949/50 v. W.
LITTLE, A. (1) (Rangers) 1952/3 v. Swdn.
LOGIE, J. (1) (Arsenal) 1952/3 v. I.
LONG, H. (1) (Clyde) 1946/7 v. I.
LORIMER, P. (21) (Leeds) 1969/70 v. Aust; 1970/1 v. W, I; 1971/2 v. I, W, E; 1972/3 v. D (2), E (2); 1973/4 v. G, E, Bel, N, Z, Braz, Y; 1974/5 v. Sp; 1975/6 v. D (2), Ru.

MACARI, L. (24) (Celtic) 1971/2 v. W, E, Y, Czecho, Braz; 1972/3 v. D, (Manchester United) E, W, I, E; 1974/5 v. Swdn, Port, W, E, Ru; 1976/7 v. I, E, Ch, Arg; 1977/8 v. E/Germ, W, Bulg; 1978/9 v. Per, Ir.
MACAULAY, A. (7) (Brentford) 1946/7 v. E (Arsenal); 1947/8 v. I, W, E, Bel, Switz, F.
MACDOUGALL, E. (7) (Norwich C.) 1974/5 v. Swdn, Port, W, I, E; 1975/6 v. D. Ru.
MACKAY, D. (22) (Hearts) 1956/7 v. Sp; 1957/8 v. F; 1958/9 v. W, I, (Tottenham) E, G; 1959/60 v. I, W, Pol, Aust, H, T; 1960/I v. W, I, E; 1962/3 v. E, Aust, N; 1963/4 v. I, N, W; 1965/6 v. I.
MARTIN, F. (7) (Aberdeen) 1953/4 v. N (2), Aust, U; 1954/5 v. N, E, N.
MARTIN, N. (3) (Hibernian) 1964/5 v. Pol, Fin; 1965/6 (Sunderland) v. It.
MARTIS, J. (1) (Motherwell) 1960/1 v. W.
MASON, J. (7) (Third Lanark) 1948/9 v. W, I, E; 1949/50 v. I; 1950/1 v. I, Bel, Aust.
MASSON, D. (17) (Q.P.R.) 1975/6 v. I. W, E; 1976/7 v. Fin, Czecho, W, I, E, Ch, Arg, Braz; (Derby Co.) 1977/8 v. E/Germ, Czecho, W, I, E; 1978/9 v. Per.
MATHERS, D. (1) (Partick) 1953/4 v. Fin.
McBRIDE, J. (2) (Celtic) 1966/7 v. W, I.
McCALLIOG, J. (5) (Sheffield Wednesday) 1966/7 v. E, Rus; 1967/8 v. I; 1968/9 v. D; 1970/1 (Wolverhampton) v. Port.
McCANN, A. (5) (Motherwell) 1958/9 v. G; 1959/60 v. I, W, E; 1960/1 v. E.
McCLOY, P. (4) (Rangers) 1972/3 v. Switz, Braz, W, I.

McCOLL, I. (14) (Rangers) 1949/50 v. E, F; 1950/1 v. W, I, Bel; 1956/7 v. Y, I, W, E, Sp, Switz, G; 1957/8 v. I, E.

McCREADIE, E. (23) (Chelsea) 1964/5 v. E, Sp, Pol, Fin; 1965/6 v. I, Pol, W, It, Port; 1966/7 v. E, Rus; 1967/8 v. I, W, E, Holl; 1968/9 v. D, C, Aust, G, W, I, E, C.

MacDONALD, A. (1) (Rangers) 1975/6 v. Switz.

MacDONALD, J. (2) (Sunderland) 1955/6 v. I, W.

McFARLANE, W. (1) (Hearts) 1946/7 v. Lux.

McGARR, E. (2) (Aberdeen) 1969/70 v. Eire, Aust.

McGARVEY, A. (1) (St. Mirren) 1978/9 v. Arg.

McGRAIN, D. (34) (Celtic) 1972/3 v. W, I, E, Switz, Braz; 1973/4 v. Czecho (2); G, W, E, Bel, N, Z, Braz, Y; 1974/5 v. Sp, Swdn, Port, W, I, E, Ru; 1975/6 v. D (2), Switz, I, W, E; 1976/7 v. Fin, Czecho, W, Swdn, W, I, E, Ch, Arg, Braz; 1977/8 v. E/Germ, Czecho.

McGRORY, J. (3) (Kilmarnock) 1964/5 v. Fin, I; 1965/6 v. Port.

McKAY, D. (13) (Celtic) 1958/9 v. E, G, Holl, Port; 1959/60 v. E, Pol, Aust, H, T; 1960/1 v. W, I; 1961/2 v. Czecho, I.

McKEAN, R. (1) (Rangers) 1975/6 v. Switz.

McKENZIE, J. (9) (Partick) 1953/4 v. W, E, N, Fin, Aust, U; 1954/5 v. H, E; 1955/6 v. Aust.

McKINNON, R. (28) (Rangers) 1965/6 v. It, W, It, E, Holl, Braz; 1966/7 v. W, I, E; 1967/8 v. I, W, E, Holl; 1968/9 v. D, C, Aust, G; 1969/70 v. Eire, G, Aust, I, W, E; 1970/1 v. D, Bel, Port, D, Rus.

McLAREN, A. (4) (Preston) 1946/7 v. E, Bel, Lux; 1947/8 v. W.

McLEAN, G. (1) (Dundee) 1967/8 v. Holl.

McLEAN, T. (5) (Kilmarnock) 1968/9 v. D, W; 1969/70 v. I, W; 1970/1 (Rangers) v. D.

McLEOD, J. (4) (Hibernian) 1960/1 v. E, Eire (2), Czecho.

McLINTOCK, F. (8) (Leicester) 1962/3 v. Eire, Sp; 1964/5 (Arsenal) v. I; 1966/7 v. Rus; 1969/70 v. I; 1970/1 v. W, I, E.

McMILLAN, I. (6) (Airdrie and Rangers) 1951/2 v. E, U.S., D; 1954/5 v. E; 1955/6 v. E; 1960/1 v. Czecho.

McNAUGHT, W. (5) (Raith) 1950/1 v. W, I, Aust; 1951/2 v. E; 1954/5 v. I.

McNEILL, W. (28) (Celtic) 1960/1 v. E, Eire (2), Czecho; 1961/2 v. Czecho, I, E, U; 1962/3 v. Eire, Sp; 1963/4 v. W, E, G; 1964/5 v. E, Sp, Pol, Fin; 1965/6 v. I, Pol; 1966/7 v. Rus; 1967/8 v. E; 1968/9 v. W, E, C; 1969/70 v. G; 1971/2 v. I, W, E.

McPHAIL, J. (5) (Celtic) 1949/50 v. W; 1950/1 v. W, I, Aust; 1953/4 v. I.

McQUEEN, G. (26) (Leeds) 1973/4 v. Bel; 1974/5 v. Sp (2), Port, W, I, E, Ru; 1975/6 v. D; 1976/7 v. Czecho, W (2), I, E; (Manchester U.) 1977/8 v. E/Germ, Czecho, W (2), Bulg, I; 1978/9 v. Aust, N, Port, I, E, N.

MILLAR, W. (6) (Celtic) 1946/7 v. W, E, Bel, Lux; 1947/8 v. I, W.

MILLER, J. (2) (Rangers) 1962/3 v. Aust, Eire.

MILLER, W. (2) (Aberdeen) 1974/5 2. Ru; 1977/8 v. Bulg.

MITCHELL, R. (2) (Newcastle) 1950/1 v. F, D.

MOCHAN, H. (3) (Celtic) 1953/4 v. N, Aust, U.

MOIR, W. (1) (Bolton) 1949/50 v. E.

MONCUR, R. (16) (Newcastle) 1967/8 v. Hol; 1969/70 v. Eire, I, W, E; 1970/1 v. D, Bel, Port, W, I, E, D; 1971/2 v. Per, I, W, E.

MORGAN, W. (21) (Burnley) 1967/8 v. I; (Manchester United) 1971/2 v. Per, Y, Czecho, Braz; 1972/3 v. D (2), E, W, I, E, Switz, Braz; 1973/4 v. Czecho (2), G (2), I, Bel, Braz, Y.

MORRIS, H. (1) (East Fife) 1949/50 v. I.

189

MUDIE, J. (17) (Blackpool) 1956/7 v. Y, I, W, E, Sp, Switz, G, Sp; 1957/8 v. I, Switz, W, E, H, Pol, Y, Par, F.

MULHALL, G. (3) (Aberdeen) 1959/60 v. I; 1962/3 (Sunderland) v. I; 1963/4 v. I.

MUNRO, F. (9) (Wolverhampton) 1970/I v. I, E, D, Rus; 1974/5 v. Swdn, W, I, E, Ru.

MUNRO, J. (2) (St. Mirren) 1978/9 v. N, Arg.

MURDOCH, R. (12) (Celtic) 1965/6 v. It, W, It, E; 1966/7 v. I; 1967/8 v. I; 1968/9 v. C, G, W, I, E; 1969/70 v. Aust.

MURRAY, J. (5) (Hearts) 1957/8 v. E, H, Pol, Y, F.

MURRAY, S. (I) (Aberdeen) 1971/2 v. Bel.

NAREY, D. (3) (Dundee U.) 1976/7 v. Swdn; 1978/9 v. Port, Arg.

O'HARE, J. (13) (Derby) 1969/70 v. I, W, E; 1970/I v. D, Bel, W, I; 1971/2 v. Port, Bel, Holl, Per, I, W.

ORMOND, W. (6) (Hibernian) 1953/4 v. E, N, Fin, Aust, U; 1958/9 v. E.

ORR, T. (2) (Morton) 1951/2 v. I, W.

PARKER, A. (15) (Falkirk) 1954/5 v. Port, Y, Aust; 1955/6 v. I, W, E, Aust; 1956/7 v. Y, I, W; 1957/8 v. I, Switz, W, E, Par.

PARLANE, D. (13) (Rangers) 1972/3 v. W, Switz, Braz; 1974/5 v. Sp, Swdn, Port, W, I, E, Ru; 1975/6 v. D; 1976/7 v. W, Braz.

PATON, A. (2) (Motherwell) 1951/2 v. D, Swdn.

PEARSON, T. (2) (Newcastle) 1946/7 v. E, Bel.

PENMAN, A. (I) (Dundee) 1965/6 v. Holl.

PETTIGREW, W. (5) (Motherwell) 1975/6 v. Switz, I, W; 1976/7 v W, Swdn.

PLENDERLEITH, J. (I) (Manchester City) 1960/I v. I.

PROVAN, D. (5) (Rangers) 1963/4 v. I, N; 1965/6 v. It (2), Holl.

QUINN, P. (4) (Motherwell) 1960/I v. E, Eire (2); 1961/2 v. U.

REDPATH, W. (9) (Motherwell) 1948/9 v. W, I; 1950/I v. E, D, F, Bel, Aust; 1951/2 v. I, E.

REILLY, L. (38) (Hibernian) 1948/9 v. W, E, F; 1949/50 v. I, W, Switz, F; 1950/I v. W, E, D, F, Bel, Aust; 1951/2 v. I, W, E, U.S., D, Swdn; 1952/3 v. W, I, E, Swdn; 1953/4 v. W; 1954/5 v. H (2), E, Port, Y, Aust; 1955/6 v. I, W, E, Aust; 1956/7 v. Y, I, W, E.

RING, T. (12) (Clyde) 1952/3 v. Swdn; 1954/5 v. W, I, H, E; 1956/7 v. E, Sp, Switz, G, Sp; 1957/8 v. I, Switz.

RIOCH, B. (24) (Derby Co.) 1974/5 v. Port, W, I, E, Ru; 1975/6 v. D (2), Ru, I, W, E; 1976/7 v. Fin, Czecho, W, (Everton) W, I, E, Ch, Braz; (Derby Co.) 1977/8 v. Czecho, I, E; 1978/9 v. Per, Holl.

ROBB, D. (5) (Aberdeen) 1970/I v. Port, W, E, D, Rus.

ROBERTSON, A. (5) (Clyde) 1954/5 v. Port, Aust, H; 1957/8 v. Switz, Par.

ROBERTSON, H. (I) (Dundee) 1961/2 v. Czecho.

ROBERTSON, J. (I) (Tottenham) 1964/5 v. W.

ROBERTSON, J. (4) (Notts F.) 1977/8 v. I; 1978/9 v. Ir, Port, N.

ROBINSON, B. (4) (Dundee) 1973/4 v. G; 1974/5 v. Swdn, I, Ru.

ROUGH, A. (26) (Partick Th.) 1975/6 v. Switz, I, W, E; 1976/7 v. Fin, Czecho, W, Swdn, W, I, E, Ch, Arg, Braz; 1977/8 v. Czecho, W, I, E; 1978/9 v. Per, Ir, Holl, Aust, Port, W, N, Arg.

RUTHERFORD, E. (I) (Rangers) 1947/8 v. F.

SCHAEDLER, E. (1) (Hibernian) 1973/4 v. G.
SCOTT, A. (16) (Rangers) 1956/7 v. Y, I, G; 1957/8 v. Switz, W; 1958/9 v.
Port; 1961/2 v. Czecho, I, W, E, W (Everton); 1963/4 v. N, W; 1964/5 v.
Fin; 1965/6 v. Port, Braz.
SCOTT, A. (1) (Hibernian) 1965/6 v. Holl.
SCOTT, J. (2) (Dundee) 1970/1 v. D, Rus.
SCOULAR, J. (9) (Portsmouth) 1950/1 v. D, I, Aust; 1951/2 v. E, U.S., D,
Swdn; 1952/3 v. W, I.
SHAW, D. (8) (Hibernian) 1946/7 v. W, I; 1947/8 v. E, Bel, Switz, F; 1948/9
v. W, I.
SHAW, J. (4) (Rangers) 1946/7 v. E, Bel, Lux; 1947/8 v. I.
SHEARER, R. (4) (Rangers) 1960/1 v. Eire (2), E, Czecho.
SIMPSON, R. (5) (Celtic) 1966/7 v. E, Rus; 1967/8 v. I, E; 1968/9 v. Aust.
SINCLAIR, J. (1) (Leicester) 1965/6 v. Port.
SMITH, D. (2) (Aberdeen) 1965/6 v. Holl; 1967/8 (Rangers) v. Hol.
SMITH, E. (2) (Celtic) 1958/9 v. Holl, Port.
SMITH, G. (19) (Hibernian) 1946/7 v. I, E; 1947/8 v. W, Bel, Switz, F; 1951/2
v. E, U.S.; 1954/5 v. Port, Y, Aust, H; 1955/6 v. I, E, W; 1956/7 v. E, Sp,
Switz, Sp.
SMITH, J. (4) (Aberdeen) 1967/8 v. Holl; 1973/4 (Newcastle) v. G, I, W.
SOUNESS, G. (12) (Middlesbrough) 1974/5 v. E/Germ, Sp, Swdn; (Liverpool)
1977/8 v. Bulg, W, E; 1978/9 v. Holl, Aust, N, W, I, E.
STANTON, P. (16) (Hibernian) 1965/6 v. Holl; 1968/9 v. I; 1969/70 v. Eire,
Aust; 1970/1 v. D, Bel, Port, D, Rus; 1971/2 v. Port, Bel, Holl, W; 1972/3
v. W, I; 1973/4 v. G.
STEEL, W. (30) (Morton) 1946/7 v. E, Bel, Lux; 1947/8 (Derby) v. I, W, E, F;
1948/9 v. W, I, E, F; 1949/50 v. I, W, E, Switz, Port, F (Dundee); 1950/1 v.
W, I, Aust (2), E, D, F, Bel; 1951/2 v. W; 1952/3 v. W, I, E, Swdn.
STEIN, C. (20) (Rangers) 1968/9 v. D, C, W, I, E, C; 1969/70 v. Eire, G, I, W,
E; 1970/1 v. D, Bel, D, Rus; 1971/2 v. Czecho; (Coventry) E, W, I, E.
STEPHEN, J. (2) (Bradford) 1946/7 v. W; 1947/8 v. W.
STEWART, D. (2) (Leeds U.) 1977/8 v. E/Germ; 1978/9 v. N.
STEWART, J. (1) (Kilmarnock) 1976/7 v. Ch.
ST. JOHN, I. (31) (Motherwell) 1958/9 v. G; 1959/60 v. I, W, E, Pol, Aust;
1960/1 v. E; 1961/2 (Liverpool) v. Czecho, I, W, Czecho, E, W; 1962/3 v.
W, I, E, N, Eire, Sp; 1963/4 v. I; 1964/5 v. E.

TELFER, W. (1) (St. Mirren) 1953/4 v. W.
THORNTON, W. (7) (Rangers) 1946/7 v. W; 1947/8 v. I, E; 1948/9 v. F;
1951/2 v. D, Swdn.
TONER, W. (2) (Kilmarnock) 1958/9 v. W, I.
TURNBULL, E. (8) (Hibernian) 1957/8 v. Bel, Switz; 1950/1 v. Aust; 1957/8
v. H, Pol, Y, Par, F.

URE, I. (11) (Dundee) 1961/2 v. W, Czecho; 1962/3 v. W, I, E, Aust, N, Sp,
(Arsenal); 1963/4 v. I, N; 1967/8 v. I.

WADDELL, W. (17) (Rangers) 1946/7 v. W; 1948/9 v. W, I, E, F; 1949/50 v. I,
E; 1950/1 v. E, D, F, Bel, Aust; 1951/2 v. I, W; 1953/4 v. I; 1954/5 v. W, I.
WALLACE, I. (3) (Coventry C.) 1977/8 v. Bulg; 1978/9 v. Port, W.
WALLACE, W. (7) (Hearts) 1964/5 v. I; 1965/6 v. E, Holl; 1966/7 (Celtic) v.
E, Rus; 1967/8 v. I; 1968/9 v. E.
WARDHAUGH, J. (2) (Hearts) 1954/5 v. H; 1956/7 v. I.
WARK, J. (4) (Ipswich) 1978/9 v. W, I, E, Arg.

191

WATSON, J. (2) (Motherwell) 1947/8 v. I; 1953/4 v. I.
WATSON, R. (I) (Motherwell) 1970/I v. Rus.
WEIR, A. (5) (Motherwell) 1959/60 v. E. Pol, Aust, H, T.
WHITE, J. (22) (Falkirk) 1958/9 v. G, Holl, Port; 1959/60 v. I, (Tottenham)
    W, Pol, Aust, T; 1960/I v. W; 1961/2 v. Czecho, I, W, Czecho, E; 1962/3 v.
    W, I, E; 1963/4 v. I, N, W, E, G.
WILSON, A. (I) (Portsmouth) 1953/4 v. Fin.
WILSON, D. (22) (Rangers) 1960/I v. W, I, E, Eire (2), Czecho; 1961/2 v.
    Czecho, I, W, E, U; 1962/3 v. W, E, Aust, N, Eire, Sp; 1963/4 v. E, G;
    1964/5 v. I, E, Fin.
WILSON, P. (I) (Celtic) 1974/5 v. Sp.
WILSON, R. (2) (Arsenal) 1971/2 v. Port, Holl.
WOOD, G. (3) (Everton) 1978/9 v. I, E, Arg.
WOODBURN, W. (24) (Rangers) 1946/7 v. E, Bel, Lux; 1947/8 v. I, W;
    1948/9 v. Y, E, F; 1949/50 v. I, W, E, Port, F; 1950/I v. W, I, Aust (2), E,
    D, F, Bel; 1951/2 v. I, W, E, U.S.
WRIGHT, T. (2) (Sunderland) 1952/3 v. W, I, E.

YEATS, R. (2) (Liverpool) 1964/5 v. W; 1965/6 v. It.
YORSTON, H. (I) (Aberdeen) 1954/5 v. W.
YOUNG, A. (9) (Hearts) 1959/60 v. F, Aust, H, E, T; 1960/I (Everton) W,
    Eire; 1965/6 v. Port.
YOUNG, G. (53) (Rangers) 1946/7 v. I, E, Bel, Lux; 1947/8 v. I, E, Bel, Switz,
    F; 1948/9 v. W, I, E, F; 1949/50 v. I, W, E, Switz, Port, F; 1950/I v. W, I,
    Aust (2), E, D, F, Bel; 1951/2 v. I, W, E, U.S., D, Swdn; 1952/3 v. W, I, E,
    Swdn; 1953/54 v. I, W; 1954/55 v. W, I, Port Y; 1955/6 v. I, W, E; Aust;
    1956/7 v. Y, I, W, E, Sp, Switz.
YOUNGER, T. (24) (Hibernian) 1954/5 v. Port, Y, Aust, H; 1955/6 v. I, W,
    E, Aust; 1956/7 (Liverpool) v. Y, I, N, E, Sp, Switz, G, Sp; 1957/8 v. I,
    Switz, W, E, H, Pol, W, Par

WALES

ALLCHURCH, I. (68) (Swansea) 1950/I v. E, I, Port, Switz; 1951/2 v. E, S,
    UK, I; 1952/3 v. S, E, I, F, Y; 1953/4 v. E, S, I, Aust; 1954/5 v. Y, S, E, I;
    1955/6 v. E, S, Aust, I; 1956/7 v. S, E; 1957/8 v. Isr (2), I, H, Mex, Swdn, H,
    Braz; 1958/9 (Newcastle) v. S, E, I; 1959/60 v. E, S; 1960/I v. T, Sp (2), H;
    1961/2 v. E, S, Braz (2), Mex; 1962/3 (Cardiff) v. S, H, E, H, I; 1963/4 v.
    E; 1964/5 v. S, E, Gr, I, It, Rus; 1965/6 (Swansea) v. E, Rus, S, D, Braz,
    Braz 'B', Ch.
ALLCHURCH, L. (11) (Swansea) 1954/5 v. I; 1955/6 v. Aust; 1957/8 v.
    E/Germ, S, Isr, I; 1958/9 v. S; 1961/2 (Sheffield United) v. S, I, Braz;
    1963/4 v. E.
ALLEN, B. (2) (Coventry) 1950/I v. S, E.

BAKER, C. (7) (Cardiff) 1957/8 v. Mex; 1959/60 v. S, I; 1960/I v. Eire, S, E;
    1961/2 v. S.
BAKER, W. (I) (Cardiff) 1947/8 v. I.
BARNES, W. (22) (Arsenal) 1947/8 v. E, S, I; 1948/9 v. S, E, I; 1949/50 v.
    E, S, Bel, I; 1950/I v. S, E, I, Port; 1951/2 v. E, S, UK, I; 1953/4 v. E, S;
    1954/5 v. Y, S.

BERRY, G. (1) (Wolverhampton) 1978/9 v. G.
BOWEN, D. (19) (Arsenal) 1954/5 v. Y, S; 1956/7 v. I, Czecho, E/Germ;
    1957/8 v. E/Germ, E, S, Isr (2), I, H, Mex, Swdn, H, Braz; 1958/9 v. S, E, I.
BURGESS, R. (32) (Tottenham) 1946/7 v. S, E, I; 1947/8 v. E, S; 1948/9 v.
    S, E, I, Port, Bel, Switz; 1949/50 v. E, S, Bel, I; 1950/1 v. S, I, Port, Switz;
    1951/2 v. E, S, UK, I; 1952/3 v. S, E, I, F, Y; 1953/4 v. E, S, I, Aust.
BURTON, O. (9) (Norwich) 1962/3 v. H, I, (Newcastle); 1963/4 v. E; 1968/9
    v. It, E/Germ, S, E, I; 1971/2 v. Czecho.

CARTWRIGHT, L. (6) (Coventry) 1973/4 v. E, S, I; 1975/6 v. S; 1976/7 v. G;
    (Wrexham) 1978/9 v. M.
CHARLES, J. (38) (Leeds) 1949/50 v. I; 1950/1 v. Switz; 1952/3 v. I, F, Y;
    1953/4 v. E. S, I, Aust; 1954/5 v. Y, S, E, I; 1955/6 v. E, S, Aust, I; 1956/7
    v. S, E, I, (Juventus Turin) Czecho, E/Germ, Czecho; 1957/8 v. Isr (2), H,
    Mex, Swdn, H; 1959/60 v. S; 1961/2 v. E, Braz (2), Mex; 1962/3 (Leeds)
    v. S, (Cardiff); 1963/4 v. S; 1964/5 v. S, Rus.
CHARLES, M. (31) (Swansea) 1954/5 v. I; 1955/6 v. E, S, Aust; 1956/7 v. E,
    I, Czecho, E/Germ, Czecho; 1957/8 v. E/Germ, E, S, Isr (2), H, Mex, Swdn,
    H, Braz; 1958/9 v. S, E, (Arsenal) 1960/1 v. I, Sp (2), H; 1961/2 v. E, S,
    (Cardiff) I, Braz; 1962/3 v. S, H.
CLARKE, R. (22) (Manchester City) 1948/9 v. E; 1949/50 v. S, Bel, I; 1950/1
    v. S, E, I, Port, Switz; 1951/2 v. E, S, UK, I; 1952/3 v. S, E; 1953/4 v. E, S, I;
    1954/5 v. Y, S, E; 1955/6 v. I.
CROWE, V. (16) (Aston Villa) 1958/9 v. E; 1959/60 v. E, I; 1960/1 v. Eire,
    S, E, I, Sp (2), H; 1961/2 v. E, S, Braz, Mex; 1962/3 v. H.
CURTIS, A. (17) (Swansea) 1975/6 v. E (2), S, I, Y (2); 1976/7 v. G, S, I;
    1977/8 v. G, E, S; 1978/9 v. G, S, E, I, M.

DANIEL, R. (21) (Arsenal) 1950/1 v. E, I, Port; 1951/2 v. E, S, UK, I; 1952/3 v.
    S, E, I, F, Y; 1953/4 (Sunderland) v. . E, S, I; 1954/5 v. E, I; 1956/7 v. S, E, I,
    Czecho.
DAVIES, D. (34) (Everton) 1974/5 v. H, Lux, S, E, I; 1975/6 v. Y (2), E, I;
    1976/7 v. G, S, Czecho, E, I; 1977/8 v. K, S (2), Czecho, G, E, I; (Wrexham)
    1978/9 v. M, T, G, S, E, I, M.
DAVIES, Reg (6) (Newcastle) 1952/3 v. S, E; 1953/4 v. E, S; 1957/8 v. E/Germ,
    E.
DAVIES, Ron (29) (Norwich) 1963/4 v. I; 1964/5 v. E; 1965/6 v. Braz, Braz
    'B', Ch; 1966/7 (Southampton) v. S, E, I; 1967/8 v. I, G; 1968/9 v. It, G,
    S, E, I; 1969/70 v. UK, E, S, I; 1970/1 v. Czecho, S, E, I; 1971/2 v. Ru, E,
    S, I; 1973/4 (Portsmouth) v. E.
DAVIES, R. Wyn (34) (Bolton) 1963/4 v. E; 1964/5 v. S, D, E, Gr, I, Rus;
    1965/6 v. E, Rus, S, D, I, Braz, Braz 'B', Ch; 1966/7 v. S (Newcastle); E;
    1967/8 v. S, I, G; 1968/9 v. It, S, E, I; 1969/70 v. E/Germ; 1970/1 v. Ru,
    Czecho; 1971/2 (Manchester City) v. E, S, I; 1972/3 (Manchester United)
    v. E, S, I; 1973/4 v. Pol.
DAVIS, G. (2) (Wrexham) 1977/8 v. I, E.
DEACY, A. (11) (PSV Eindhoven) 1976/7 v. Czecho, S, E, I; 1977/8 v. K, S (2),
    Czecho, G, I; 1978/9 v. T.
DERRETT, S. (4) (Cardiff) 1968/9 v. G, S; 1969/70 v. It; 1970/1 v. Fin.
DURBAN, A. (26) (Derby) 1966/7 v. I; 1967/8 v. E, S, I, G; 1968/9 v. G,
    E/Germ, S, E, I; 1969/70 v. E/Germ, It, E, S, I; 1970/1 v. Ru, Czecho, S,
    E, I, Fin; 1971/2 v. Fin, Czecho, E, S, I.
DWYER, A. (7) (Wrexham) 1977/8 v. E, S, I; 1978/9 v. T, S, E, I.

EDWARDS, I. (3) (Chester) 1977/8 v. K; 1978/9 v. M, G.
EDWARDS, G. (12) (Birmingham) 1946/7 v. S, E, I; 1947/8 v. E, S, I (Cardiff);
   1948/9 v. I, Port, Bel, Switz; 1949/50 v. E, S.
EDWARDS, T. (2) (Charlton) 1956/7 v. I, E/Germ.
EMANUEL, J. (2) (Bristol City) 1972/3 v. E, I.
ENGLAND, M. (44) (Blackburn) 1961/2 v. I, Braz, Mex; 1962/3 v. H, I; 1963/4
   v. E, S, I; 1964/5 v. D, E, Gr (2), I, It, Rus; 1965/6 v. E, Rus, S, D, I; 1966/7
   (Tottenham) v. S, E; 1967/8 v. E, I, G; 1968/9 v. E/Germ; 1969/70 v.
   UK, E/Germ, It, E, S, I; 1970/1 v. Ru; 1971/2 v. Fin, E, S, I; 1972/3 v. E (2),
   S, E; 1973/4 v. Pol; 1974/5 v. H, Lux.
EVANS, I. (13) (Crystal Palace) 1975/6 v. Aust, E, Y (2), E, I; 1976/7 v. G,
   S (2), Czecho, E, I; 1977/8 v. K.
EVANS, R. (1) (Swansea) 1963/4 v. I.

FLYNN, B. (32) (Burnley) 1974/5 v. Lux (2), H, S, E, I; 1975/ 6v. Aust, E (2),
   Y (2), I; 1976/7 v. G, S, Czecho, S, E, I; 1977/8 v. K (2), S (2), Czecho, G,
   E, I; (Leeds) 1978/9 v. M, T, S, E, I, M.
FORD, T. (38) (Swansea) v   S. (Aston Villa) I; 1947/8 v. S, I; 1948/9
   v. S, E, I, Port, Bel, Switz 1949/50 v. E, S, Bel, I; 1950/51 v. S, (Sunderland,
   E, I, Port, Switz; 1951/2 v. E, S, UK, I; 1952/3 v. S, E, I, F, Y (Cardiff);
   1953/4 v. Aust; 1954/5 v. Y, S, E, I; 1955/6 v. E, S, Aust, I, I; 1956/7 v. S.
FOULKES, W. (11) (Newcastle) 1951/2 v. E, S, UK, I; 1952/3 v. S, E, F, Y;
   1953/4 v. E, S, I.

GODFREY, B. (3) (Preston) 1963/4 v. I; 1964/5 v. D, It.
GREEN, C. (15) (Birmingham) 1964/5 v. It, Rus; 1965/6 v. E, Rus, S, Braz,
   Braz 'B'; 1966/7 v. E; 1967/8 v. E, S, I, G; 1968/9 v. It, S, I.
GRIFFITHS, A. (17) (Wrexham) 1970/1 v. Czecho; 1974/5 v. Aust, H (2), Lux
   (2), E, I; 1975/6 v. Aust, E (2), Y (2), S, I; 1976/7 v. G, S.
GRIFFITHS, H. (1) (Swansea) 1952/3 v. I.
GRIFFITHS, M. (11) (Leicester) 1946/7 v. I; 1948/9 v. Port, Bel; 1949/50
   v. E, S, Bel; 1950/1 v. E, I, Port, Switz; 1953/4 v. Aust.

HARRINGTON, A. (11) (Cardiff) 1955/6 v. I; 1956/7 v. S, E; 1957/8 v. S,
   Isr (2), I; 1960/1 v. S, E; 1961/2 v. E, S.
HARRIS, C. (10) (Leeds U.) 1975/6 v. S, E; 1977/8 v. G, E, S, I; 1978/9 v. M,
   T, G, M.
HARRIS, W. (6) (Middlesbrough) 1953/4 v. Aust; 1956/7 v. E/Germ, Czecho;
   1957/8 v. E/Germ, E, S.
HENNESSEY, T. (39) (Birmingham) 1961/2 v. I, Braz (2); 1962/3 v. S, H, E,
   H; 1963/4 v. E, S; 1964/5 v. S, D, E, Gr, Rus; 1965/6 v. E, Rus, (Nottingham
   Forest), S, D, I, Braz, Braz 'B', Ch; 1966/7 v. S, E; 1967/8 v. E, S, I; 1968/9
   v. G, E/Germ; 1969/70 v. UK, E/Germ (Derby), E, S, I; 1971/2 v. Fin,
   Czecho, E, S; 1972/3 v. E.
HEWITT, R. (5) (Cardiff) 1957/8 v. Isr, I, Swdn, H, Braz.
HILL, M. (2) (Ipswich) 1971/2 v. Czecho, Ru.
HOCKEY, T. (9) (Sheffield United) 1971/2 v. Fin, Ru; 1972/3 v. E (1),
   (Norwich), Pol, S, E, I; 1973/4 (Aston Villa) v. Pol.
HOLE, B. (30) (Cardiff) 1962/3 v. I; 1963/4 v. I; 1964/5 v. S, D, E, Gr (2), I,
   It, Rus; 1965/6 v. E, Rus, S, D, I, Braz 'B', Ch; 1966/7 (Blackburn) v.
   S, E, I; 1967/8 v. E, S, I, G; 1968/9 (Aston Villa) v. It, G, E/Germ; 1969/70
   v. It; (Swansea) 1970/1 v. Ru.
HOLLINS, D. (11) (Newcastle) 1961/2 v. Braz, Mex; 1962/3 v. H, I; 1963/4 v.
   E; 1964/5 v. Gr, I, It; 1965/6 v. S, D, Braz.

194

HOPKINS, M. (34) (Tottenham) 1955/6 v. I; 1956/7 v. S, E, I, Czecho, E/Germ, Czecho; 1957/8 v. E/Germ, E, S, Isr (2), I, H, Mex, Swdn, H, Braz; 1958/9 v. S, E, I; 1959/60 v. E, S; 1960/1 v. I, Sp (2), H; 1961/2 v. I, Braz (2), Mex; 1962/3 v. S, H, I.
HOWELLS, R. (2) (Cardiff) 1953/4 v. E, S.
HUGHES, I. (4) (Luton) 1950/1 v. E, I, Port, Switz.
HUGHES, W. (3) (Birmingham) 1946/7 v. S, E, I.
HUGHES, W. A. (5) (Blackburn) 1948/9 v. E, I, Port, Bel, Switz.
HUMPHREYS, J. (1) (Everton) 1946/7 v. I.

JAMES, G. (9) (Blackpool) 1965/6 v. Braz, Braz 'B', Ch; 1966/7 v. I; 1967/8 v. S; 1970/1 v. Czecho, S, E, I.
JAMES, L. (42) (Burnley) 1971/2 v. Czecho, Rus, S; 1972/3 v. E (2), Pol, S, E, I; 1973/4 v. Pol, E, S, I; 1974/5 v. Aust, H (2), Lux (2), S, E, I; 1975/6 v. Aust, E, S, Y (2), I; (Derby) 1976/7 v. G, S, Czecho, S, E, I; 1977/8 v. K (2) G (Swansea); 1978/9 v. M, T, S, E, I, M.
JARVIS, A. (3) (Hull) 1966/7 v. S, E, I.
JOHNSON, M. (1) (Swansea) 1963/4 v. I.
JONES, Barrie (14) (Swansea) 1962/3 v. S, H, E, I; 1963/4 v. S, I; 1964/5 (Plymouth) v. D; 1968/9 (Cardiff) v. G, E/Germ, S, E, I; 1969/70 v. U.K.
JONES, Bryn (4) (Arsenal) 1946/7 v. S, I; 1947/8 v. E; 1948/9 v. S.
JONES, C. (59) (Swansea) 1953/4 v. Aust; 1955/6 v. E, S, Aust, I; 1956/7 v. S, E, I, Czecho, E/Germ, Czecho; 1957/8 v. E/Germ, E, S, Isr (2), I (Tottenham), I, H, Mex, Swdn, H, Braz; 1958/9 v. I; 1959/60 v. E, S, I; 1960/1 v. Eire, S, E, I, Sp, H; 1961/2 v. E, S, I, Braz (2), Mex; 1962/3 v. S, H, I; 1963/4 v. E, S, I; 1964/5 v. S, D, E, Gr (2), I, It, Rus; 1966/7 v. S, E; 1967/8 v. E, S, G; 1968/9 (Fulham) v. It; 1969/70 v. U.K.
JONES, D. (6) (Norwich C.) 1975/6 v. E, S; 1977/8 v. S, Czecho, G, E.
JONES, E. (4) (Swansea) 1947/8 v. S, E (Tottenham); 1948/9 v. S, E.
JONES, J. (23) (Liverpool) 1975/6 v. Aust, E, S; 1976/7 v. G, S (2), Czecho, E, I; 1977/8 v. K (2), S (2), Czecho, G, E, I; (Wrexham) 1978/9 v. M, T, G, S, E, M.
JONES, K. (1) (Aston Villa) 1949/50 v. S.
JONES, T. G. (13) (Everton) 1946/7 v. S, E; 1947/8 v. E, S, I; 1948/9 v. E, I, Port, Bel, Switz; 1949/50 v. E, S, Bel.
JONES, W. (1) (Bristol R.) 1970/1 v. Fin.

KELSEY, J. (41) (Arsenal) 1953/4 v. I, Aust; 1954/5 v. Y, S, I; 1955/6 v. E, S, Aust, I; 1956/7 v. S, E, I, Czecho, E/Germ, Czecho; 1957/8 v. E, S, Isr (2), I, H, Mex, Swdn, H, Braz; 1958/9 v. S, E; 1959/60 v. E, S, I; 1960/1 v. S, E, I, Sp (2), H; 1961/2 v. E, S, I, Braz (2).
KING, J. (1) (Swansea) 1954/5 v. E.
KINSEY, N. (7) (Norwich) 1950/1 v. I, Port, Switz; 1951/2 v. E; 1953/4 (Birmingham) v. I; 1955/6 v. E, S.
KRZYWICKI, R. (8) (West Bromwich) 1969/70 v. E/Germ, It, (Huddersfield) E, S, I; 1970/1 v. Ru, Fin; 1971/2 v. Czecho.

LAMBERT, R. (5) (Liverpool) 1946/7 v. S; 1947/8 v. E; 1948/9 v. Port, Bel, Switz.
LEA, C. (2) (Ipswich) 1964/5 v. I, It.
LEEK, L. (13) (Leicester) 1960/1 v. S, E, I, Sp (2), H; 1961/2 (Newcastle) v. S, (Birmingham) Braz, Mex; 1962/3 v. E; 1964/5 v. S, Gr (2).
LEVER, A. (1) (Leicester) 1952/3 v. S.
LLOYD, B. (3) (Wrexham) 1975/6 v. Aust, S, E.

LOWRIE, G. (4) (Coventry) 1947/8 v. E, S, I; 1948/9 (Newcastle) v. Port.
LUCAS, M. (4) (Leyton Orient) 1961/2 v. I, Mex; 1962/3 v. S, E.
LUCAS, W. (7) (Swansea) 1948/9 v. S, I, Port, Bel, Switz; 1949/50 v. E;
1950/1 v. E.

MAHONEY, J. (43) (Stoke) 1967/8 v. E; 1968/9 v. E/Germ; 1970/1 v. Czecho;
1972/3 v. E (2), Pol, S, E, I; 1973/4 v. Pol, S, E, I; 1974/5 v. Aust, H (2),
Lux (2), S, E, I; 1975/6 v. Aust, Y (2), E, I; 1976/7 v. G, Czecho, S, E, I;
1977/8 v. K (2), S (2), Czecho, E, I; (Middlesbrough) 1978/9 v. G, S, E, I, M.
MEDWIN, T. (30) (Swansea) 1952/3 v. I, F, Y; 1956/7 (Tottenham) v, S, E.
I, Czecho, E/Germ, Czecho; 1957/8 v. E, S, Isr (2), I, H, Mex, H, Braz;
1958/9 v. S, E, I; 1959/60 v. E, S, I; 1960/I v. Eire, S, E, Sp; 1962/3 v. H, E.
MIELCZAREK, R. (1) (Rotherham) 1970/1 v. Fin.
MILLINGTON, A. (21) (West Bromwich) 1962/3 v. S, H, E; 1964/5 (Crystal
Palace) v. E, Rus; 1965/6 (Peterborough) v. Braz 'B', Ch; 1966/7 v. E, I;
1967/8 v. I, G; 1968/9 v. It, E/Germ; 1969/70 (Swansea) v. E, S, I; 1970/1 v.
Czecho, Fin; 1971/2 v. Fin, Czecho, Ru.
MOORE, G. (21) (Cardiff) 1959/60 v. E, S, I; 1960/1 v. Eire, Sp; 1961/2
(Chelsea) v. Braz; 1962/3 v. H, I; (Manchester United) 1963/4 v. S, I;
(Northampton) 1965/6 v. I, Ch; 1968/9 (Charlton) v. S, E, I; 1969/70 v. UK,
It, E, S, I; 1970/1 v. Ru.
MORRIS, W. (5) (Burnley) 1946/7 v. I; 1948/9 v. E; 1951/2 v. S, UK, I.

NARDIELLO, D. (2) (Coventry C.) 1977/8 v. Czecho, G.
NICHOLAS, P. (1) (Crystal Palace) 1978/9 v. M.
NURSE, M. (12) (Swansea) 1959/60 v. E, I; 1960/1 v. Eire, S, E, I, Sp (2), H;
1962/3 (Middlesbrough) v. H, E; 1963/4 v. S.

O'SULLIVAN, P. (3) (Brighton) 1972/3 v. S; 1975/6 v. S; 1978/9 v. M.

PAGE, M. (27) (Birmingham) 1970/1 v. Fin; 1971/2 v. S, I; 1972/3 v. E (2), I;
1973/4 v. S, I; 1974/5 v. H, Lux, S, E, I; 1975/6 v. E (2), Y (2), I; 1976/7 v.
G, S; 1977/8 v. K (2), G, E, S; 1978/9 v. M, G.
PALMER, D. (3) (Swansea) 1956/7 v. Czecho; 1957/8 v. E/Germ, E.
PARRY, J. (1) (Swansea) 1950/1 v. S.
PAUL, R. (33) (Swansea) 1948/9 v. S, E, I, Port, Switz; 1949/50 v. E, S, Bel, I;
(Manchester City) 1950/1 v. S, E, I, Port, Switz; 1951/2 v. E, S, UK, I;
1952/3 v. S, E, I, F, Y; 1953/4 v. E, S, I; 1954/5 v. Y, S, E; 1955/6 v. E, S,
Aust, I.
PHILLIPS, J. (4) (Chelsea) 1972/3 v. E; 1973/4 v. E; 1974/5 v. H; 1977/8 v. K.
PHILLIPS, L. (44) (Cardiff) 1970/1 v. Czecho, S, E, I; 1971/2 v. Czecho, Ru,
S, I; 1972/3 v. E; 1973/4 v. Pol, I; 1974/5 v. Aust, (Aston Villa) H (2),
Lux (2), S, E, I; 1975/6 v. Aust, E (2), Y (2), I; 1976/7 v. G, S, Czecho, S, E;
1977/8 v. K (2), S (2), Czecho, G, E; 1978/9 v. M, T, G, (Swansea) S, E, I, M.
POWELL, A. (8) (Leeds) 1946/7 v. S; 1947/8 v. E, S, I; 1948/9 (Everton)
v. E; 1949/50 v. Bel; 1950/1 (Birmingham) v. S.
POWELL, D. (11) (Wrexham) 1967/8 v. G; 1968/9 (Sheffield United) v. It,
G, S, E, I; 1969/70 v. E/Germ, E, S, I; 1970/1 v. Ru.
POWELL, J. (8) (Queen's Park Rangers) 1946/7 v. E; 1947/8 v. E, S; 1948/9
(Aston Villa) v. Bel; 1949/50 v. S, Bel; 1950/1 v. S.
PRING, K. (3) (Rotherham) 1965/6 v. D, Ch; 1966/7 v. I.

RANKMORE, F. (1) (Peterborough) 1965/6 v. Ch.

196

REECE, G. (29) (Sheffield United) 1965/6 v. E, Rus, S, I; 1966/7 v. S; 1969/70 v. UK, It; 1970/1 v. S, E, I, Fin; 1971/2 v. Fin, Ru, E, S, I; (Cardiff) 1972/3 v. E, I; 1973/4 v. Pol, E, S, I; 1974/5 v. Aust, H (2), Lux (2), S, I.

REED, W. (2) (Ipswich) 1954/5 v. Y, S.

REES, R. (37) (Coventry) 1964/5 v. S, D, E, Gr (2), I, It, Rus; 1965/6 v. E, Rus, S, D, I, Braz, Braz 'B', Ch; 1966/7 v. E, I; 1967/8 v. E, S, I (West Bromwich), G; 1968/9 v. It, (Nottingham Forest) G, E/Germ, S; 1969/70 v. UK, E/Germ, It, E, S, I; 1970/1 v. Ru, Czecho, Fin; 1971/2 v. Czecho, Ru.

REES, W. (4) (Cardiff) 1948/9 v. I, Bel, Switz, (Tottenham); 1949/50 v. I.

RICHARDS, S. (1) (Cardiff) 1946/7 v. E.

ROBERTS, D. (17) (Oxford United) 1972/3 v. Pol, E, I; 1973/4 v. E, S; 1974/5 v. Aust, (Hull) Lux, I; 1975/6 v. Y, S, I; 1976/7 v. E, I; 1977/8 v. K (2), S, I.

ROBERTS, J. (21) (Arsenal) 1970/1 v. S, E, I, Fin; 1971/2 v. Fin, E, I; 1972/3 (Birmingham) v. E, Pol, S, E, I; 1973/4 v. Pol, E, S, I; 1974/5 v. Aust, H, S, E; 1975/6 v. S.

ROBERTS, J. (1) (Bolton) 1948/9 v. Bel.

ROBERTS, P. (4) (Portsmouth) 1973/4 v. E; 1974/5 v. Aust, H, Lux.

RODRIGUES, P. (40) (Cardiff) 1964/5 v. Gr (2), I; 1965/6 v. E, Rus, S, D, (Leicester) I, Braz, Braz 'B', Ch; 1966/7 v. S; 1967/8 v. E, S, I; 1968/9 v. E/Germ, E, I; 1969/70 v. UK, E/Germ, E, S, I; (Sheffield Wednesday) 1970/1 v. Ru, Czecho, S, E, I; 1971/2 v. Fin, Czecho, Ru, E, I; 1972/3 v. E (2), Pol, S, E, I; 1973/4 v. Pol.

ROUSE, V. (1) (Crystal Palace) 1958/9 v. I.

ROWLEY, T. (1) (Tranmere) 1958/9 v. I.

SAYER, P. (7) (Cardiff) 1976/7 v. Czecho, S, E, I; 1977/8 v. K (2), S.

SCRINE, F. (2) (Swansea) 1949/50 v. E, I.

SEAR, C. (1) (Manchester City) 1962/3 v. E.

SHERWOOD, A. (41) (Cardiff) 1946/7 v. E; 1947/8 v. S, I; 1948/9 v. S, E, I, Port, Switz; 1949/50 v. E, S, Bel, I; 1950/1 v. S, E, I, Port, Switz; 1951/2 v. E, S, UK, I; 1952/3 v. S, E, I, F, Y; 1953/4 v. E, S, I, Aust; 1954/5 v. Y, S, E, I; 1955/6 v. S, E, Aust, I; 1956/7 (Newport) v. S, E.

SHORTT, W. (12) (Plymouth) 1946/7 v. I; 1949/50 v. Bel, I; 1951/2 v. E, S, UK, I; 1952/3 v. S, E, I, F, Y.

HOWERS, D. (2) (Cardiff) 1974/5 v. E, I.

SIDLOW, C. (7) (Liverpool) 1946/7 v. S, E; 1947/8 v. E, S, I; 1948/9 v. S; 1949/50 v. E.

SMALLMAN, D. (7) (Wrexham) 1973/4 v. E, S, I; 1974/5 v. H, E, I; 1975/6 (Everton) v. Aust.

SPRAKE, G. (37) (Leeds) 1963/4 v. S, I; 1964/5 v. S, D, Gr; 1965/6 v. E, Rus, I; 1966/7 v. S; 1967/8 v. E, S; 1968/9 v. G, S, E, I; 1969/70 v. UK, E Germ, It; 1970/1 v. Ru, S, E, I; 1971/2 v. Fin, E, S, I; 1972/3 v. E (2), Pol, S, I; 1973/4 (Birmingham) v. Pol, S, I; 1974/5 v. Aust, H, Lux.

TANSFIELD, G. (1) (Cardiff) 1948/9 v. S.

TEVENSON, B. (7) (Leeds) 1977/8 v. I; 1978/9 v. M, T, S, E, I, M.

STITFALL, R. (2) (Cardiff) 1952/3 v. E; 1956/7 v. Czecho.

SULLIVAN, D. (17) (Cardiff) 1952/3 v. I, F, Y; 1953/4 v. I; 1954/5 v. E, S 1956/7 v. E, S; 1957/8 v. I, H, Swdn, H, Braz; 1958/9 v. S, I; 1959/60 v. E, I.

TAPSCOTT, D. (14) (Arsenal) 1953/4 v. Aust; 1954/5 v. Y, S, E, I; 1955/6 v. E, S, Aust, I; 1956/7 v. I, Czecho, E/Germ; 1958/9 (Cardiff) v. E, I.

THOMAS, D. (2) (Swansea) 1956/7 v. Czecho; 1957/8 v. E/Germ.

197

THOMAS, M. (11) (Wrexham) 1976/7 v. G, S (2), I; 1977/8 v. K, S, Czecho, E;
1978/9 v. M, T, G.
THOMAS, R. (50) (Swindon) 1966/7 v. I; 1967/8 v. G; 1968/9 v. It, G, E, I;
1969/70 v. UK, E/Germ, It, E, S, I; 1970/1 v. Ru, Czecho, S, E, I; 1971/2
v. Fin, Czecho, Ru, E, S, I; 1972/3 v. E (2), Pol, S, E, I; 1973/4 (Derby) v.
Pol, E, S, I; 1974/5 v. H (2), Lux (2), S, E, I; 1975/6 v. Aust, Y, E; 1976/7 v.
S, Czecho, E, I; 1977/8 v. K, S, Czecho.
THOMAS, S. (4) (Fulham) 1947/8 v. E, S, I; 1948/9 v. S.
TOSHACK, J. (38) (Cardiff) 1968/9 v. G, E/Germ, S, E, I; 1969/70 v. UK,
E/Germ, It; 1970/1 v. S, E, I, Fin; 1971/2 (Liverpool) v. Fin, E; 1972/3 v.
E (2), Pol, S, E; 1974/5 v. Aust, H (2), Lux (2), S, E; 1975/6 v. Y (2), E;
1976/7 v. S; 1977/8 v. K (2), S, Czecho; (Swansea) 1978/9 v. S, E, I, M.

VEARNCOMBE, G. (2) (Cardiff) 1957/8 v. E/Germ; 1960/1 v. Eire.
VERNON, R. (32) (Blackburn) 1956/7 v. I, Czecho, E/Germ, Czecho;
1957/8 v. E/Germ, E, S, Swdn; 1958/9 v. S; 1959/60 (Everton) v. I; 1960/1
v. Eire, S, E; 1961/2 v. I, Braz (2), Mex; 1962/3 v. S, H, E; 1963/4 v. E, S;
1964/5 (Stoke) v. Gr, I, It; 1965/6 v. E, Rus, S, D, I; 1966/7 v. I; 1967/8 v. E.
VILLARS, A. (2) (Cardiff) 1973/4 v. E, S.

WALLEY, T. (1) (Watford) 1970/1 v. Czecho.
WARD, D. (2) (Bristol Rovers) 1958/9 v. E; 1961/2 (Cardiff) v. E.
WEBSTER, C. (4) (Manchester United) 1956/7 v. Czecho; 1957/8 v. H, Mex,
Braz.
WILLIAMS, G. (1) (Cardiff) 1950/1 v. Switz.
WILLIAMS, G. E. (26) (West Bromwich) 1959/60 v. I; 1960/1 v. Eire, S, E;
1962/3 v. I; 1963/4 v. H' E, S, I; 1964/5 v. S, D, E, Gr (2), I, It, Rus; 1965/6
v. I, Braz, Braz 'B', Ch; 1966/7 v. S, E, I; 1967/8 v. I; 1968/9 v. It.
WILLIAMS, G. G. (5) (Swansea) 1960/1 v. I, Sp (2), H; 1961/2 v. E.
WILLIAMS, H. (4) (Newport) 1948/9 v. I, Switz (Leeds); 1949/50 v. I; 1950/1
v. S.
WILLIAMS, Herbert (3) (Swansea) 1964/5 v. Gr (2); 1970/1 v. Ru.
WILLIAMS, S. (43) (West Bromwich) 1953/4 v. Aust; 1954/5 v. E, I; 1955/6
v. E, S, Aust; 1957/8 v. E, S, Isr (2), I, H, Mex, Swdn, H, Braz; 1958/9 v.
S, E, I; 1959/60 v. E, S, I; 1960/1 v. Eire, I, Sp (2), H; 1961/2 v. E, S, I,
Braz (2), Mex; 1962/3 (Southampton) v. S, H, E, H; 1963/4 v. E, S; 1964/5
v. S, D, E; 1965/6 v. D.
WITCOMBE, D. (3) (West Bromwich) 1946/7 v. S, E, (Sheffield Wednesday)
v. I.
WOOSNAM, P. (17) (Leyton Orient) 1958/9 v. S, (West Ham), E; 1959/60
v. E, S, I; 1960/1 v. Eire, S, E, I, Sp, H; 1961/2 v. E, S, I, Braz; 1962/3 (Aston
Villa) v. H, I.

YORATH, T. (47) (Leeds) 1969/70 v. It; 1970/1 v. S, E, I; 1971/2 v. Czecho,
E, S, I; 1972/3 v. E, Pol, S; 1973/4 v. Pol, E, S, I; 1974/5 v. Aust, H (2),
Lux (2), S; 1975/6 v. Aust, E (2), Y (2), S, I; (Coventry) 1976/7 v. G, S,
Czecho, S, E, I; 1977/8 v. K (2), S (2), Czecho, G, E, I; 1978/9 v. T, G, S, E, I.

UEFA UNDER-21 CHAMPIONSHIP
1978-79

GROUP ONE
Denmark, *England, Bulgaria*

DENMARK (1) 1, ENGLAND (0) 2   September 19, 1978

DENMARK (1) 2, BULGARIA (0) 0   October 10, 1978

Remaining fixtures: Bulgaria v England 5/6/79; England v Denmark
11/9/79; Bulgaria v Denmark 30/10/79; England v Bulgaria 20/11/79.

Table so far:

	P	W	D	L	F	A	Pts.
Denmark	2	1	0	1	3	2	2
England	1	1	0	0	2	1	2
Bulgaria	1	0	0	1	0	2	0

GROUP TWO
Scotland, *Belgium, Portugal, Norway*

BELGIUM (1) 4, NORWAY (0) 0   September 19, 1978

PORTUGAL (0) 0, BELGIUM (0) 0   October 10, 1978

SCOTLAND (1) 5, NORWAY (0) 1   October 24, 1978

PORTUGAL (0) 0, SCOTLAND (0) 3   November 28, 1978

NORWAY (0) 0, PORTUGAL (0) 0   May 9, 1979

Remaining fixtures: Norway v Scotland 7/6/79; Norway v Belgium 11/9/79;
Belgium v Portugal 16/10/79; Portugal v Norway 31/10/79; Belgium v
Scotland 20/11/79; Scotland v Portugal 5/2/80; Scotland v Belgium (to
be announced).

Table so far:

	P	W	D	L	F	A	Pts.
Scotland	2	2	0	0	8	1	4
Belgium	2	1	1	0	4	0	3
Portugal	3	0	2	1	0	3	2
Norway	3	0	1	2	1	9	1

GROUP THREE
Yugoslavia, *Spain, Cyprus*

SPAIN (0) 0, YUGOSLAVIA (1) 1   October 4, 1978

CYPRUS (0) 0, SPAIN (0) 0   December 10, 1978

YUGOSLAVIA (0) 1, CYPRUS (0) 0   April 1, 1979

Remaining fixtures: Yugoslavia v Spain 10/10/79; Cyprus v Yugoslavia
11/11/79; Spain v Cyprus 9/12/79.

Table so far:

	P	W	D	L	F	A	Pts.
Yugoslavia	2	2	0	0	2	0	4
Spain	2	0	1	1	0	1	1
Cyprus	2	0	1	1	0	1	1

GROUP FOUR

East Germany, *Poland, Netherlands*

EAST GERMANY (0) 2, NETHERLANDS (0) 0	November 14, 1978
POLAND (1) 1, EAST GERMANY (1) 1	April 16, 1979
NETHERLANDS (1) 2, POLAND (2) 3	May 1, 1979

Remaining fixtures: East Germany v Poland 25/9/79; Poland v Netherlands 16/10/79; Netherlands v East Germany 20/11/79.

Table so far:

	P	W	D	L	F	A	Pts.
East Germany	2	1	1	0	3	1	3
Poland	2	1	1	0	4	3	3
Netherlands	2	0	0	2	2	5	0

GROUP FIVE

Czechoslovakia, *France, Sweden*

FRANCE (2) 2, SWEDEN (0) 1	August 31, 1978
SWEDEN (0) 0, CZECHOSLOVAKIA (0) 1	October 3, 1978
CZECHOSLOVAKIA (1) 1, FRANCE (0) 0	April 3, 1979

Remaining fixtures: Sweden v France 4/9/79; Czechoslovakia v Sweden 9/10/79; France v Czechoslovakia 16/11/79.

Table so far:

	P	W	D	L	F	A	Pts.
Czechoslovakia	2	2	0	0	2	0	4
France	2	1	0	1	2	2	2
Sweden	2	0	0	2	1	3	0

GROUP SIX

Greece, *USSR, Finland*

FINLAND (0) 0, GREECE (1) 1	May 24, 1978
GREECE (0) 0, USSR (1) 3	September 20, 1978
GREECE (1) 3, FINLAND (1) 1	October 11, 1978

Remaining fixtures: Finland v USSR 4/7/79; USSR v Greece 12/9/79; USSR v Finland 31/10/79.

Table so far:

	P	W	D	L	F	A	Pts.
Greece	3	2	0	1	4	4	4
USSR	1	1	0	0	3	0	2
Finland	2	0	0	2	1	4	0

GROUP SEVEN

Hungary, *Rumania, Turkey*

TURKEY 0, HUNGARY 3 (won on forfeit)	October 11, 1978
HUNGARY (1) 1, RUMANIA (0) 0	October 25, 1978
RUMANIA 3, TURKEY 0 (won on forfeit)	November 15, 1978
TURKEY (1) 2, RUMANIA (0) 0	April 4, 1979
HUNGARY (2) 5, TURKEY (0) 0	May 2, 1979

Remaining fixture: Rumania v Hungary 17/10/79.

Table so far:

	P	W	D	L	F	A	Pts.
Hungary	3	3	0	0	9	0	6
Rumania...............................	3	1	0	2	3	3	2
Turkey	4	1	0	3	2	11	2

GROUP EIGHT
Switzerland, *Italy, Luxembourg*

LUXEMBOURG (0) 0, SWITZERLAND (1) 3   November 15, 1978
SWITZERLAND (0) 0, ITALY (0) 0   March 29, 1979

Remaining fixtures: Switzerland v Luxembourg 13/10/79; Italy v Switzerland 17/10/79; Luxembourg v Italy 14/11/79; Italy v Luxembourg 23/1/80.

Table so far:

	P	W	D	L	F	A	Pts.
Switzerland	2	1	1	0	3	0	3
Italy.......................................	1	0	1	0	0	0	1
Luxembourg	1	0	0	1	0	3	0

OTHER LEAGUE TABLES

THE NORTHERN PREMIER LEAGUE

	P	W	D	L	F	A	Pts.
Mossley	44	32	5	7	117	48	69
Altrincham	44	25	11	8	93	39	61
Matlock T.	44	24	8	12	100	59	56
Scarborough	44	19	14	11	61	44	52
Southport	44	19	14	11	62	49	52
Boston U.	44	17	18	9	40	33	52
Runcorn	44	21	9	14	79	54	51
Stafford R.	44	18	14	12	67	41	50
Goole T.	44	17	15	12	56	61	49
Northwich Vic	44	18	11	15	64	52	47
Lancaster C.	44	17	12	15	62	54	46
Bangor C.	44	15	14	15	65	66	44
Worksop T.	44	13	14	17	55	67	40
Workington	44	16	7	21	62	74	39
Netherfield	44	13	11	20	39	69	37
Barrow	44	14	9	21	47	78	37
Gainsborough T.	44	12	12	20	52	67	36
Morecambe	44	11	13	20	55	65	35
Frickley Ath.	44	13	9	22	58	70	35
S. Liverpool	44	12	10	22	48	85	34
Gateshead	44	11	11	22	42	63	33
Buxton	44	11	9	24	50	84	31
Macclesfield T.	44	8	10	26	40	92	26

THE SOUTHERN FOOTBALL LEAGUE

Premier Division

	P	W	D	L	F	A	Pts.
Worcester C.	42	27	11	4	92	33	65
Kettering T.	42	27	7	8	109	43	61
Telford U.	42	22	10	10	60	39	54
Maidstone U.	42	18	18	6	55	35	54
Bath C.	42	17	19	6	59	41	53
Weymouth	42	18	15	9	71	51	51
A.P. Leamington	42	19	11	12	65	53	49
Redditch U.	42	19	10	13	70	57	48
Yeovil T.	42	15	16	11	59	49	46
Witney T.	42	17	10	15	53	52	44
Nuneaton Bor.	42	13	17	12	59	50	43
Gravesend & Northfleet	42	15	12	15	56	55	42
Barnet	42	16	10	16	52	64	42
Hillingdon Bor.	42	12	16	14	50	41	40
Wealdstone	42	12	12	18	51	59	36
Atherstone T.	42	9	17	16	46	65	35
Dartford	42	10	14	18	40	56	34
Cheltenham T.	42	11	10	21	38	72	32
Margate	42	10	9	23	44	75	29
Dorchester T.	42	7	11	24	46	86	25
Hastings U.	42	5	13	24	37	85	23
Bridgend T.	42	6	6	30	39	90	18

FIRST DIVISION NORTH

	P	W	D	L	F	A	Pts.
Grantham	38	21	10	7	70	45	52
Merthyr Tydfil	38	22	7	9	90	53	51
Alvechurch	38	20	10	8	70	42	50
Bedford T.	38	19	9	10	74	49	47
King's Lynn	38	17	11	10	57	46	45
Oswestry T.	38	18	8	12	63	43	44
Gloucester C.	38	18	8	12	76	59	44
Burton A.	38	16	10	12	51	40	42
Kidderminster H.	38	13	14	11	70	60	40
Bedworth U.	38	13	14	11	41	34	40
Tamworth	38	15	8	15	47	45	38
Stourbridge	38	15	7	16	64	61	37
Barry T.	38	14	9	15	51	53	37
Enderby T.	38	14	8	16	46	55	36
Banbury U.	38	10	13	15	42	58	33
Wellingborough T.	38	13	6	19	50	71	32
Cambridge C.	38	9	9	20	37	62	27
Bromsgrove R.	38	6	14	18	33	61	26
Milton Keynes C.	38	7	9	22	37	87	23
Corby T.	38	5	6	27	40	85	16

FIRST DIVISION SOUTH

	P	W	D	L	F	A	Pts.
Dover	40	28	9	3	88	20	65
Folkestone & Shepway	40	22	6	12	84	50	50
Gosport Bor.	40	19	11	10	62	47	49
Chelmsford C.	40	20	7	13	65	61	47
Minehead	40	16	13	11	58	39	45
Poole T.	40	15	15	10	48	44	45
Hounslow	40	16	12	12	56	45	44
Waterlooville	40	17	10	13	52	43	44
Trowbridge T.	40	15	12	13	65	61	42
Aylesbury U.	40	16	9	15	54	52	41
Taunton T.	40	16	9	15	53	51	41
Bognor Regis T.	40	17	7	16	58	58	41
Dunstable	40	18	4	18	57	55	40
Tonbridge A.F.C.	40	15	10	15	43	47	40
Salisbury	40	13	10	17	47	51	36
Basingstoke T.	40	12	11	17	49	62	35
Addlestone	40	12	9	19	56	64	33
Andover	40	12	6	22	47	69	30
Ashford T.	40	10	10	20	28	53	30
Crawley T.	40	9	9	22	44	75	27
Canterbury C.	40	6	3	31	31	98	15

THE FOOTBALL COMBINATION

	P	W	D	L	F	A	Pts.
Tottenham H.	42	30	6	6	105	42	66
Ipswich T.	42	29	7	6	94	38	65
Q.P.R.	42	27	8	7	103	57	62
West Ham U.	42	25	11	6	86	43	61
Norwich C.	42	21	13	8	81	45	55
Fulham	42	21	10	11	78	50	52
Chelsea	42	18	14	10	74	54	50
Bristol C.	42	20	8	14	73	68	48
Bristol R.	42	18	10	14	72	72	46
Arsenal	42	13	18	11	55	44	44
Southampton	42	17	9	16	68	63	43
Crystal Palace	42	11	16	15	60	59	38
Plymouth Arg.	42	14	9	19	58	72	37
Cardiff C.	42	13	8	21	54	75	34
Hereford U.	42	10	12	20	54	83	32
Oxford U.	42	11	9	22	68	78	31
Birmingham C.	42	9	12	21	38	61	30
Swindon T.	42	9	12	21	38	76	30
Leicester C.	42	8	11	23	47	72	27
Reading	42	10	6	26	55	117	26
Luton T.	42	9	7	26	37	74	25
Orient	42	9	4	29	45	100	22

THE UNITED COUNTIES LEAGUE
PREMIER DIVISION

	P	W	D	L	F	A	Pts.
Irthlingborough D.	36	25	5	6	88	31	55
Rushden T.	36	22	7	7	72	29	51
Kempton R.	36	20	7	9	55	23	47
Desborough T.	36	20	3	13	82	59	43
Potton U.	36	18	7	11	59	49	43
Wolverton T.	36	17	9	10	61	52	43
Rothwell T.	36	14	12	10	56	50	40
Stamford A.F.C.	36	15	9	12	61	47	39
St Neots T.	36	16	7	13	59	51	39
Wootton Blue Cross	36	15	8	13	77	63	38
Stewart & Lloyds (Corby)	36	16	5	15	48	46	37
Olney T.	36	14	9	13	36	43	37
Buckingham T.	36	10	11	15	46	52	31
Long Buckby A.F.C.	36	12	6	18	41	58	30
Ampthill T.	36	10	5	21	44	74	25
Bourne T.	36	9	6	21	51	86	24
Northampton Spencer OB	36	7	9	20	47	76	23
Holbeach U.	36	9	4	23	51	94	22
Eynesbury R.	36	6	5	25	28	79	17

WEST MIDLANDS (REGIONAL) LEAGUE
PREMIER DIVISION

	P	W	D	L	F	A	Pts.
Willenhall T.	34	23	7	4	82	32	53
Lye T.	34	21	11	2	62	33	53
Dudley T.	34	21	8	5	53	23	50
Hednesford T.	34	19	10	5	59	26	48
Tividale	34	19	6	9	63	40	44
Bilston	34	15	10	9	50	34	40
Brierley Hill All.	34	17	5	12	67	47	39
Brereton Soc.	34	17	5	12	48	40	39
Darlaston	34	15	5	14	52	51	35
Coventry Sp.	34	12	6	16	39	48	30
Hinckley Ath.	34	12	5	17	42	52	29
Ledbury T.	34	10	7	17	57	63	27
VS Rugby	34	9	9	16	29	41	27
Wednesfield Soc.	34	7	12	15	27	45	26
Halesowen T.	34	8	8	18	35	55	24
Armitage	34	7	6	21	44	69	20
Gresley R.	34	4	7	23	27	67	15
Gornal Ath.	34	4	5	25	21	91	13

THE WELSH LEAGUE
PREMIER DIVISION

	P	W	D	L	F	A	Pts.
Pontllanfraith	34	23	7	4	73	37	53
Cardiff Cor.	34	20	4	10	77	45	44
Newport Co.	34	14	13	7	55	25	41
Afan Lido	34	17	7	10	43	37	41
Ton Pentre	34	16	8	10	62	42	40
Swansea C.	34	15	9	10	61	47	39
Ammanford T.	34	14	11	9	47	42	39
Pembroke Bor.	34	16	6	12	63	50	38
Merthyr Tyd.	34	15	7	12	61	58	37
Barry T.	34	12	11	11	54	45	35
Caerau Ath.	34	13	8	13	45	55	34
Sully	34	13	7	14	42	41	33
Milford U.	34	12	8	14	55	45	32
Llanelli	34	11	9	14	41	55	31
Pontlottyn	34	9	10	15	41	57	28
Treharris Ath.	34	9	8	17	43	65	26
Ferndale Ath.	34	3	6	25	36	90	12
Cardiff Col.	34	1	7	26	25	88	9

SOUTH EAST COUNTIES LEAGUE
DIVISION ONE

	P	W	D	L	F	A	Pts.
Tottenham H.	30	19	6	5	80	45	44
Ipswich T.	30	17	6	7	66	38	40
Millwall	30	15	7	8	51	38	37
Arsenal	30	15	6	9	49	32	35
Portsmouth	30	15	5	10	52	51	35
Gillingham	30	15	4	11	54	41	34
Crystal P.	30	14	5	11	58	54	33
West Ham U.	30	11	7	12	52	51	29
Chelsea	30	14	4	12	65	59	28
Orient	30	12	3	15	42	49	27
Charlton Ath.	30	11	3	16	54	62	25
Watford	30	8	6	16	30	48	22
Norwich C.	30	9	6	15	40	62	22
Southend U.	30	9	3	18	48	68	21
Q.P.R.	30	9	3	18	44	68	21
Fulham	30	7	6	17	35	54	20

THE CENTRAL LEAGUE

	P	W	D	L	F	A	Pts.
Liverpool	42	30	7	5	89	34	67
Nottingham F.	42	26	6	10	82	38	58
Stoke C.	42	23	11	8	65	45	57
Manchester C.	42	23	9	10	70	45	55
Wolverhampton W.	42	21	11	10	79	42	53
W.B.A.	42	18	12	12	80	51	48
Coventry C.	42	19	8	15	87	71	46
Sheffield W.	42	19	6	17	74	68	44
Leeds U.	42	14	16	12	50	49	44
Aston Villa	42	16	11	15	67	54	43
Manchester U.	42	17	9	16	66	58	43
Derby Co.	42	17	9	16	67	64	43
Everton	42	18	7	17	50	49	43
Burnley	42	15	9	18	42	56	39
Huddersfield T.	42	13	11	18	52	58	37
Blackburn R.	42	11	13	18	53	69	35
Bolton W.	42	11	13	18	61	83	35
Sheffield U.	42	12	9	21	55	88	33
Newcastle U.	42	12	8	22	44	72	32
Blackpool	42	11	6	25	41	68	28
Bury	42	9	4	29	54	104	22
Preston N. E.	42	6	7	29	46	107	19

BERGER ISTHMIAN LEAGUE
PREMIER DIVISION

	P	W	D	L	F	A	Pts.
Barking	42	28	9	5	92	50	93
Dagenham	42	25	6	11	83	63	81
Enfield	42	22	11	9	69	37	77
Dulwich Hamlet	42	21	13	8	69	39	76
Slough T.	42	20	12	10	61	44	72
Wycombe W.	42	20	9	13	59	44	69
Woking	42	18	14	10	79	59	68
Croydon	42	19	9	14	61	51	66
Hendon	42	16	14	12	55	48	62
Leatherhead	42	17	9	16	57	45	60
Sutton U.	42	17	9	16	62	51	60
Tooting & Mitcham	42	15	14	13	52	52	59
Walthamstow Av.	42	15	6	21	61	69	51
Tilbury	42	13	11	18	60	76	50
Boreham Wood	42	13	10	19	50	67	49
Hitchin T.	42	12	11	19	59	71	47
Carshalton Ath.	42	10	16	16	49	69	46
Hayes	42	9	18	15	45	58	45
Oxford C.	42	12	7	23	50	80	43
Staines T.	42	6	16	20	40	64	34
Leytonstone	42	8	7	27	36	75	31
Kingstonian	42	3	15	24	35	72	24

CHESHIRE COUNTY LEAGUE

	P	W	D	L	F	A	Pts.
Horwich R.M.I.	42	35	2	5	89	45	72
Witton A.	42	30	4	8	114	38	64
Marine	42	29	5	8	104	38	63
Stalybridge Celtic	42	25	5	12	93	47	55
Burscough	42	19	15	8	59	31	53
Winsford U.	42	21	11	10	74	49	53
Chorley	42	21	8	13	66	43	50
Formby	42	20	9	13	73	57	49
Leek T.	42	19	10	13	62	43	48
Droylsden	42	18	9	15	62	61	45
Nantwich T.	42	18	8	16	76	72	44
Fleetwood T.	42	17	10	15	70	68	44
Hyde U.	42	15	12	15	59	57	42
St Helens T.	42	16	9	17	59	57	41
Darwen	42	15	9	18	52	53	39
Rhyl	42	15	8	19	53	60	38
Ashton U.	42	13	5	24	63	94	31
New Mills	42	9	11	22	58	82	29
Rossendale U	42	11	6	25	51	108	28
Radcliffe Bor.	42	4	7	31	37	115	15
New Brighton	42	3	5	34	36	115	11
Middlewich Ath.	42	3	4	35	43	120	10

NORTHERN LEAGUE

	P	W	D	L	F	A	Pts.
Spennymoor U.	38	25	6	7	96	43	81
Bishop Auckland	38	25	5	8	96	38	80
Ashington	38	23	7	8	79	47	76
Crook T.	38	21	10	7	63	38	73
Blyth Spartans	38	19	12	7	81	39	69
Consett	38	21	9	8	84	52	*69
North Shields	38	21	4	13	76	55	67
South Bank	38	16	11	11	58	47	59
Horden Coll.	38	17	8	13	64	56	59
Durham C.	38	15	9	14	63	62	54
Billingham Synth.	38	12	12	14	60	55	48
Tow Law T.	38	12	8	18	54	63	44
Shildon	38	11	10	17	52	69	43
Whitby T.	38	11	12	15	55	68	*42
Whitley Bay	38	9	9	20	54	77	36
West Auckland T.	38	9	9	20	54	87	36
Ferryhill Ath.	38	10	5	23	43	74	35
Willington	38	7	10	21	41	75	31
Penrith	38	8	7	23	35	82	31
Evenwood T.	38	4	5	29	31	112	*14

WESTERN LEAGUE
PREMIER DIVISION

	P	W	D	L	F	A	Pts.
Frome T.	38	21	12	5	60	29	75
Bideford	38	22	8	8	76	39	74
Saltash U.	38	19	10	9	65	39	67
Barnstaple T.	38	18	10	10	65	35	64
Tiverton T.	38	17	9	12	71	60	60
Clandown	38	16	11	11	58	49	59
Weston-super-Mare	38	14	15	9	65	48	57
Falmouth T.	38	15	9	14	51	47	54
Paulton R.	38	15	9	14	40	48	54
Bridport	38	13	13	12	54	50	52
Bridgwater T.	38	14	9	15	57	53	51
Keysham T.	38	13	12	13	47	57	51
Mangotsfield PF	38	15	2	21	53	64	47
Ilminster T.	38	11	12	15	45	55	45
Welton R.	38	11	8	19	44	59	41
Exeter C.	38	12	5	21	48	75	41
Clevedon T.	38	11	7	20	50	64	40
Dawlish	38	10	10	18	43	61	40
Shepton Mallet T.	38	10	10	18	48	74	40
Glastonbury	38	8	9	21	42	76	33

YORKSHIRE LEAGUE
DIVISION ONE

	P	W	D	L	F	A	Pts.
Winterton R.	30	19	5	6	54	21	43
Emley	30	18	5	7	58	31	41
North Ferriby	30	16	9	5	55	31	41
Guiseley	30	11	9	10	35	32	31
Thackley	30	13	5	12	41	39	31
Ossett T.	30	14	2	14	42	37	30
Scarborough	30	10	10	10	34	36	30
Sheffield	30	9	11	10	26	28	29
Leeds Ashley Road	30	10	8	12	34	37	28
Hallam	30	12	4	14	33	42	28
Bridlington T.	30	11	6	13	36	48	28
Frecheville C.A.	30	7	13	10	33	42	27
Tadcaster Al.	30	9	8	13	33	39	26
Bentley V.W.	30	9	7	14	34	38	25
Kiverton Park	30	8	7	15	44	54	23
Lincoln U.	30	5	9	16	28	65	19

LANCASHIRE COMBINATION

	P	W	D	L	F	A	Pts.
Wren R.	28	21	5	2	51	10	47
Leyland Motors	28	18	6	4	63	26	42
Whitworth Valley	28	15	8	5	49	35	38
Colne Dynamoes	28	13	8	7	50	32	34
Bacup Bor.	28	14	6	8	48	36	34
Padiham	28	14	5	9	40	35	33
Lytham	28	11	8	9	41	34	30
Nelson	28	7	10	11	31	33	24
Blackpool Mech.	28	7	10	11	21	33	24
Chorley Res.	28	6	11	11	34	37	23
Wigan R.	28	6	9	13	25	40	21
Barrow Res.	28	6	8	14	25	39	20
Daisey Hill	28	5	10	13	26	45	20
Clitheroe	28	7	5	16	31	46	19
Ashton Ath.	28	3	5	20	17	67	11

THE F.A. CHARITY SHIELD

Year	Winners	Runners-up	Score
1908	Manchester U.	Q.P.R.	4–0 after 1–1 draw
1909	Newcastle U.	Northampton	2–0
1910	Brighton	Aston Villa	1–0
1911	Manchester U.	Swindon T.	8–4
1912	Blackburn R.	Q.P.R.	2–1
1913	Professionals	Amateurs	7–2
1919	W.B.A.	Tottenham H.	2–0
1920	Tottenham H.	Burnley	2–0
1921	Huddersfield	Liverpool	1–0
1922	No Competition		
1923	Professionals	Amateurs	2–0
1924	Professionals	Amateurs	3–1
1925	Amateurs	Professionals	6–1
1926	Amateurs	Professionals	6–3
1927	Cardiff C.	Corinthians	2–1
1928	Everton	Blackburn R.	2–1
1929	Professionals	Amateurs	3–0
1930	Arsenal	Sheffield W.	2–1
1931	Arsenal	W.B.A.	1–0
1932	Everton	Newcastle U.	5–3
1933	Arsenal	Everton	3–0
1934	Arsenal	Manchester C.	4–0
1935	Sheffield W.	Arsenal	1–0
1936	Sunderland	Arsenal	2–1
1937	Manchester C.	Sunderland	2–0
1938	Arsenal	Preston N.E.	2–1
1948	Arsenal	Manchester U.	4–3
1949	Portsmouth	Wolverhampton W.	1–1*
1950	World Cup Team	Canadian Touring Team	4–2
1951	Tottenham H.	Newcastle U.	2–1
1952	Manchester U.	Newcastle U.	4–2
1953	Arsenal	Blackpool	3–1
1954	Wolverhampton W.	W.B.A.	4–4*
1955	Chelsea	Newcastle U.	3–0
1956	Manchester U.	Manchester C.	1–0
1957	Manchester U.	Aston Villa	4–0
1958	Bolton W.	Wolverhampton W.	4–1
1959	Wolverhampton W.	Nottingham F.	3–1
1960	Burnley	Wolverhampton W.	2–2*
1961	Tottenham H.	F.A. XI	3–2
1962	Tottenham H.	Ipswich T.	5–1
1963	Everton	Manchester U.	4–0
1964	Liverpool	West Ham U.	2–2*
1965	Manchester U.	Liverpool	2–2*
1966	Liverpool	Everton	1–0
1967	Manchester U.	Tottenham H.	3–3*
1968	Manchester C.	W.B.A.	6–1
1969	Leeds U.	Manchester C.	2–1
1970	Everton	Chelsea	2–1

1971	Leicester	Liverpool	1–0
1972	Manchester C.	Aston Villa	1–0
1973	Burnley	Manchester C.	1–0
1974	Liverpool†	Leeds	1–1
1975	Derby Co.	West Ham U.	2–0
1976	Liverpool	Southampton	1–0
1977	Liverpool	Manchester U.	0–0*
1978	Nottingham F.	Ipswich T.	5–0

*Each club retained shield for six months.   † won on penalties

WORLD CLUB CHAMPIONSHIP

Played annually up to 1974 between the winners of the European Cup and the winners of the South American Champions Cup—known as the Copa Libertadores de America.

Year	Winners	Runners-up	Score
1960	Real Madrid	Penarol	0–0, 5–1
1961	Penarol	Benfica	0–1, 5–0, 2–1
1962	Santos	Benfica	3–2, 5–2
1963	Santos	AC Milan	2–4, 4–2, 1–0
1964	Inter-Milan	Independiente	0–1, 2–0, 1–0
1965	Inter-Milan	Independiente	3–0, 0–0
1966	Penarol	Real Madrid	2–0, 2–0
1967	Racing Club	Celtic	0–1, 2–1, 1–0
1968	Estudiantes	Manchester United	1–0, 1–1
1969	AC Milan	Estudiantes	3–0, 1–2
1970	Feyenoord	Estudiantes	2–2, 1–0
1971	Nacianal	Panathinaikos	1–1, 2–1
1972	Ajax	Independiente	1–1, 3–0
1973	Independiente	Juventus	1–0
1974	Atlético Madrid	Independiente	0–1, 2–0

STAFFORD RANGERS 2
Wood 2
19th May at Wembley

STAFFORD RANGERS WIN F.A. CHALLENGE TROPHY

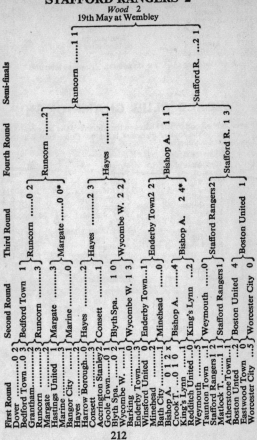

First Round — Second Round — Third Round — Fourth Round — Semi-finals

- Dover 0 2
- Bedford Town ...0 3 — Bedford Town 1
- Grantham..........
- Runcorn ....2 — Runcorn ....3 — Runcorn ......0 2 — Runcorn 2
- Margate............3 — Margate ....3 — Margate 0 0*
- Hastings United ...1
- Marine ....3 — Marine 0
- Bangor City 2
- Hayes ....2 — Hayes ....2 — Hayes ....2 3 — Hayes 1
- Harrow Borough...0
- Consett ....3 — Consett 1
- Accrington Stanley 2
- Goole Town.......0
- Blyth Spa..........0 2 — Blyth Spa. 1 0 — Wycombe W. 2 2
- Wycombe W. 0
- Barking ....3 — Wycombe W. 1 3

Runcorn 1 1

- Enderby Town.....1 — Enderby Town...1 — Enderby Town 2 — Bishop A. 1 1
- Winsford United ...0
- Minehead ....1 — Minehead 0
- Bath City 0
- Bishop A. ..... 0 1 2 x — Bishop A. .....1 — Bishop A. 2 4*
- Crook T.....0 1 0
- King's Lynn ....0 — King's Lynn 2
- Redditch United ...0
- Weymouth ....5 — Weymouth 0
- Taunton Town 0
- Stafford Rangers1..2 — Stafford Rangers1 — Stafford Rangers2 — Stafford R. 1 3
- Matlock T..........1 1
- Atherstone Town...1
- Boston Unted .....2 — Boston United 4 — Boston United 1
- Eastwood Town ...0
- Worcester City ...5 — Worcester City 0

Stafford R. ...2 1

212

KETTERING TOWN 0
attendance 32,000

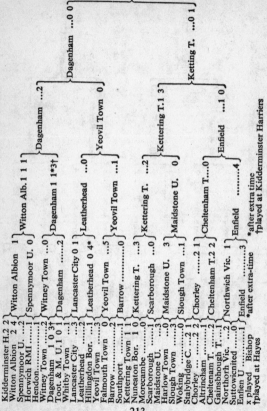

Dagenham ...0 0

Ketting T. ...0 1

Dagenham ...2

Yeovil Town 0

Kettering T.1 3

Enfield ...0

Witton Alb.1 1 1

Dagenham 1 1*3†

Leatherhead ...0

Yeovil Town ...1

Kettering T. ...2

Maidstone U. 0

Cheltenham T....0

Enfield 4

Witton Albion 1

Spennymoor U. 0

Witney Town ...0

Dagenham 2

Lancaster City 0 1

Leatherhead 0 4*

Yeovil Town ...5

Barrow 0

Kettering T. ...3

Scarborough ...0

Slough Town ...1

Chorley 2 1

Cheltenham T.2 2

Northwich Vic. 1

Enfield 3

Kidderminster H.2 2
Witton Albion   2 4
Spennymoor U. ...2
Horwich RMI 1
Hendon...........
Witney Town 2
Dagenham 1 0 3†
Toot. & M. U.1 0 1
Whitby Town 3
Lancaster City ..2
Leatherhead 1
Hillingdon Bor. ..3
Yeovil Town 2
Falmouth Town ...1
Barrow 2
Southport 1
Kettering Town 1 0
Nuneaton Bor. 1 0
Morecambe 0
Scarborough 1
Maidstone U. 3
Harlow Town 0
Slough Town 3
Woking 0
Stalybridge C. ..2 1
Altrincham 2 2
Chorley 2
Cheltenham T. 2
Gainsborough T. ..1
Northorh Vic. 2
Suttowicunited ...0
Enfien U 1

x played Bishop

†played at Hayes

...0 0

Witton Alb. 1 1 1

Spennymoor U. ...2

...2

*after time

†played at Kidderminster Harriers

*after extra time

213

F.A. CHALLENGE VASE - BILLERICAY TOWN'S THIRD WIN

BILLERICAY TOWN 4
Young 3, Clayden
28th April at Wembley

Third Round	Fourth Round	Fifth Round	Sixth Round	Semi-finals
Felixstowe T. ...4 1				
Soham Town R. 4 3	Soham T. R. 1			
Arlesey Town ...2 0		Leyton-W. ...0*0		
Leyton-Wingate...0	Leyton-Wingate...2		Eastbourne U. ...0	
Clanfield 0				
Camberley T. ...2	Camberley T. ...1			
Eastbourne U. ...3		Eastbourne U,0 2		Billericay T.2 0 2 (at home in first leg)
Alma Swanley ...0	Eastbourne U. ...2			
Alton Town 1*				
Worthing 2	Worthing 5			
Peasedown Ath. ...1		Worthing 1		
Ilminster Close ...5	Peasedown Ath. 2		Billericay T. 1	
Epping Town 0				
Billericay Town ..5	Billericay T. 2			
Royston Town ...0		Billericay T. ...2		
Histon 4*	Royston T. 0			
Friar Lane OB...4*				replay at Cambridge City
Sheffield 2	Friar Lane OB ...1			
Hinckley Ath. 1		Friar Lane OB...2		
Wednesfield Soc...1	Hinckley Ath. ...0		Barton Rovers 2*	
Haringey Bor. 1				
Tring Town 2*	Haringey Bor. ...1			
Barton Rovers ...2*		Barton Rovers 4		Shepshed C.0 2 0
Burnham 1	Barton Rovers ...2			
Norton W'seats ...1				
Shepshed C. 1	Shepshed C. 1			
Skegness T. 7		Shepshed C. ...4		
Bourne Town......3	Skegness T. 0		Shepshed C. 3	
Bentley Vic. 2				
Boldon CA........2	Bentley Vic. 0			
Leeds Ashley Rd. 1 2		Winterton R. ..2		
Winterton R. 1 3	Winterton R. ...2			

ALMONDSBURY GREENWAY 1

Price

attendance 17,500

Almondsbury 1 1 (at home in first leg)   Whickham 0 1

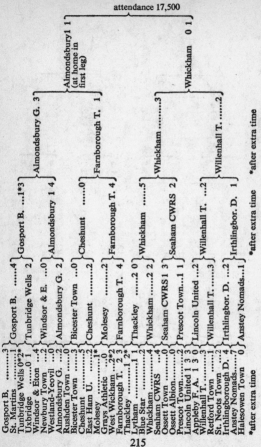

Almondsbury G. 3 — Farnborough T. 1 — Whickham ....3 — Willenhall T. 2

Gosport B. ...1*3 — Almondsbury 1 4 — Cheshunt ......0 — Farnborough T. 4 — Whickham ......5 — Seaham CWRS 2 — Willenhall T. ...2 — Irthlingbor. D. 1

Gosport B. ......4 — Tunbridge Wells 2 — Windsor & E. ...0 — Almondsbury G. 2 — Bicester Town ...0 — Cheshunt ......2 — Molesey ......2 — Farnborough T. 4 — Thackley ......2 0 — Whickham ......2 2 — Seaham CWRS1 3 — Prescot Town...1 1 — Lincoln United ...2 — Willenhall T. ......3 — Irthlingbor. D. ...2 — Anstey Nomads...1

Gosport B. ....3 — St. Martins ....1 — Tunbridge Wells 0*2* — Uxbridge ....0 1 — Windsor & Eton ...4 — Newbury Town ...2 — Westland-Yeovil ...0 — Almondsbury G. ...2 — Rushden Town ...3 — Bicester Town ...5 — Cheshunt ......1* — East Ham U. ....1 — Grays Athletic ...0 — Molesey ....2 — West Wickham ....2*2 — Farnborough T. 2 3 — Thackley ....1 2* — Lytham ......1 1 — Blue Star ....2 — Whickham ....4 — Seaham CWRS ...0 — Ossett Town ......4 — Ossett Albion .....0 — Prescot Town......2 — Lincoln United 1 3 3 — Appleby F. A. 1 3 0 — Willenhall T. ......1 — Retford Town ......1 — St. Neots Town ...3 — Irthlingborough D. 4 — Anstey Nomads...7 — Halesowen Town 0

*after extra time

MILWALL WIN F.A. YOUTH CUP

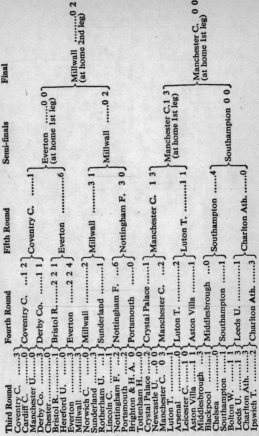

LOBSTER WIN SUNDAY CUP

Third Round	Fourth Round	Fifth Round	Semi-final	Final

Third Round

- Lea Hall RBL 0
- Springfield Soc. 2
- Lobster 3
- Byron Ath. 1
- Lion Rangers 5
- Hallen Sunday 3
- Robin Hood's R. 0
- Counts XI 1
- Piper Club 1
- Magnet 2
- Hull Fruit Trades ...0
- Langley Park 0
- Dingle Rail 4
- Swanfield 1
- Durham Boilers 2
- Hartlepool Lion 0
- Girton Eagles 0
- Clifda 6
- Road Sea 1
- Two-Seven-Nine 4
- Newtown Unity 1
- Corby Kingfisher 1
- Ollis Transport 2
- Colden Common 1
- Troy Ath. 2
- Carlton U. 1
- Sheffield H. R. 4
- Twin Foxes 2
- Arras 0
- Moorgreen 2
- Evergreen 3
- Walmer 0

Fourth Round

- Springfield Soc. 0
- Lobster 3
- Lion Rangers 1
- Counts XI 1
- Magnet 2
- Langley Park 4
- Dingle Rail 0
- Durham Boilers 4
- Clifda 1
- Two-Seven-Nine 0
- Corby Kingfisher 1
- Ollis Transport 1
- Carlton U. 1
- Sheffield H. R. 0
- Moorgreen 1
- Evergreen 3

Fifth Round

- Lobster 2
- Counts XI 1
- Langley Park 2
- Durham Boilers 1
- Clifda 1
- Ollis Transport 0
- Carlton U. 3
- Evergreen 1

Semi-final

- Lobster 1
- Langley Park 0
- Clifda 0
- Carlton U. 1

Final

- Lobster 3
- Carlton U. 2

Winner: Lobster 3

217

FOOTBALL AWARDS 1978-79

FOOTBALLER OF THE YEAR: The Football Writers' Association this year voted Kenny Dalglish (Liverpool) Footballer of the Year. A shrewd buy from Celtic at what now looks like a bargain price of £450,000, Kenny is an integral part of the Liverpool team, and is the fourth Liverpool player to win the award in the past six years.

Past winners: 1947–48—**Stan Mathews** (Blackpool); 1948–49—**Johnie Carey** (Manchester U.); 1949–50—**Joe Mercer** (Arsenal); 1950–51—**Harry Johnston** (Blackpool); 1951–52—**Billy Wright** (Wolverhampton); 1952–53—**Nat Lofthouse** (Bolton); 1953–54—**Tom Finney** (Preston); 1954–55—**Don Revie** (Manchester C.); 1955–56—**Bert Trautmann** (Manchester C.); 1956–57—**Tom Finney** (Preston); 1957–58—**Danny Blanchflower** (Tottenham); 1958–59—**Sid Owen** (Luton); 1959–60—**Bill Slater** (Wolverhampton); 1960–61—**Danny Blanchflower** (Tottenham); 1961–62—**Jimmy Adamson** (Burnley); 1962–63—**Stan Matthews** (Stoke); 1963–64—**Bobby Moore** (West Ham); 1964–65—**Bobby Collins** (Leeds); 1965–66—**Bobby Charlton** (Manchester U.); 1966–67—**Jackie Charlton** (Leeds); 1967–68—**George Best** (Manchester U.); 1968–69—**Dave Mackay** (Derby); **Tony Book** (Manchester C.); 1969–70—**Billy Bremner** (Leeds); 1970–71—**Frank McLintock** (Arsenal); 1971–72—**Gordon Banks** (Stoke); 1972–73—**Pat Jennings** (Tottenham); 1973–74—**Ian Callaghan** (Liverpool); 1974–75—**Alan Mullery** (Fulham); 1975–76—**Kevin Keegan** (Liverpool); 1976–77—**Emlyn Hughes** (Liverpool); 1977–78—**Kenny Burns** (Nottingham F.).

P.F.A. PLAYER OF THE YEAR: The Professional Footballers' Association this year chose Liam Brady (Arsenal) as their Player of the Year. A brilliantly gifted player who came up through the youth ranks at Highbury, Brady went on to win a Cup-winner's medal with Arsenal at the end of the season.

The Young P'ayer of the Year award went to Cyrille Regis of West Bromwich Albion.

The Scottish Professional Footballers' Association chose Paul Hegarty (Dundee United) as their Player of the Year, a choice which was underlined when he later won his first cap for Scotland.

MANAGER OF THE YEAR: Bob Paisley (Liverpool).

Once again Bob Paisley took Liverpool to the League Championship. His team's continued success over so many seasons is in itself a tribute to Paisley in particular and the club in general.

EUROPEAN FOOTBALLER OF THE YEAR 1978: Kevin Keegan (SV Hamburg).

Previous winners: Stanley Matthews (1956), Alfredo Di Stefano (1957 & 1959), Raymond Kopa (1958), Luis Suarez (1960), Omar Sivori (1961), Josef Masopust (1962), Lev Yashin (1963), Denis Law (1964), Eusebio (1965), Bobby Charlton (1966), Florian Albert (1967), George Best (1968), Gianni Rivera (1969), Gerd Muller (1970), Johan Cruyff (1971, 1973, 1974), Franz Beckenbauer (1972, 1976), Oleg Blokhin (1975) and Alan Simonsen (1977).

FOOTBALL LEAGUE FIXTURES 1979–80

Copyright of the Football League Limited and not to be reproduced in whole or in part without their consent. *Fixtures are subject to alteration.*

DIVISION ONE

ARSENAL

Date 1979	Opponents	Ground
Aug. 18	Brighton & H.A.	A
Aug. 22	Ipswich T.	H
Aug. 25	Manchester U.	H
Sept. 1	Leeds U.	A
Sept. 8	Derby Co.	H
Sept. 15	Middlesbrough	A
Sept. 22	Aston Villa	H
Sept. 29	Wolverhampton W.	A
Oct. 6	Manchester C.	H
Oct. 9	Bristol C.	A
Oct. 13	Bolton W.	H
Oct. 20	Stoke C.	A
Oct. 27	Brighton & H.A.	H
Nov. 3	Bristol C.	A
Nov. 10	Crystal P.	H
Nov. 17	Everton	A
Nov. 24	Liverpool	H
Dec. 1	Nottingham F.	A
Dec. 8	Coventry C.	H
Dec. 15	W.B.A.	A
Dec. 21	Norwich C.	H
Dec. 26	Tottenham H.	A
Dec. 29	Manchester U.	A
1980		
Jan. 1	Southampton	A
Jan. 12	Leeds U.	H
Jan. 19	Derby Co.	A
Feb. 2	Middlesbrough	H
Feb. 9	Aston Villa	A
Feb. 16	Wolverhampton W.	H
Feb. 23	Bolton W.	A
Mar. 8	Bristol C.	H
Mar. 14	Manchester C.	A
Mar. 22	Crystal P.	A
Mar. 25	Ipswich T.	A
Mar. 29	Stoke C.	H
Apr. 5	Southampton	H
Apr. 7	Tottenham H.	H
Apr. 8	Norwich C.	A
Apr. 12	Nottingham F.	H
Apr. 19	Liverpool	A
Apr. 21	W.B.A.	H
Apr. 26	Coventry C.	A

ASTON VILLA

Date 1979	Opponents	Ground
Aug. 18	Bolton W.	A
Aug. 22	Brighton & H.A.	H
Aug. 25	Bristol C.	A
Sept. 1	Everton	H
Sept. 8	Manchester U.	A
Sept. 15	Crystal P.	H
Sept. 22	Arsenal	A
Sept. 29	Middlesbrough	H
Oct. 6	Southampton	A
Oct. 9	Brighton & H.A.	A
Oct. 13	Bristol C.	H
Oct. 20	Derby Co.	A
Oct. 27	Wolverhampton W.	H
Nov. 3	W.B.A.	A
Nov. 10	Ipswich T.	H
Nov. 17	Stoke C.	A
Nov. 24	Nottingham F.	H
Dec. 1	Liverpool	A
Dec. 8	Coventry C.	H
Dec. 15	Tottenham H.	A
Dec. 21	Norwich C.	H
Dec. 26	Leeds U.	A
Dec. 29	Bristol C.	A
1980		
Jan. 1	Manchester C.	H
Jan. 12	Everton	A
Jan. 19	Manchester U.	H
Feb. 2	Arsenal	A
Feb. 9	Middlesbrough	A
Feb. 16	Wolverhampton W.	A
Feb. 23	Derby Co.	H
Mar. 8	Crystal P.	A
Mar. 14	Southampton	H
Mar. 22	Ipswich T.	A
Mar. 25	Leeds U.	H
Mar. 29	Nottingham F.	A
Apr. 5	Coventry C.	H
Apr. 7	Tottenham H.	A
Apr. 8	Norwich C.	A
Apr. 12	Liverpool	H
Apr. 19	Leeds U.	A
Apr. 26	Tottenham H.	H
May 3	Liverpool	A

BOLTON WANDERERS

Date 1979	Opponents	Ground
Aug. 18	Aston Villa	H
Aug. 22	Liverpool	A
Aug. 25	Southampton	H
Sept. 1	Brighton & H.A.	A
Sept. 8	W.B.A.	H
Sept. 15	Coventry C.	A
Sept. 22	Leeds U.	H
Sept. 29	Norwich C.	A
Oct. 6	Derby Co.	H
Oct. 9	Arsenal	A
Oct. 13	Arsenal	A
Oct. 20	Crystal P.	A
Oct. 27	Nottingham F.	H
Nov. 3	Tottenham H.	A
Nov. 10	Manchester C.	A
Nov. 17	Manchester C.	H
Nov. 24	Stoke C.	A
Dec. 1	Wolverhampton W.	H
Dec. 8	Everton	A
Dec. 15	Ipswich T.	H
Dec. 21	Middlesbrough	A
Dec. 26	Manchester U.	H
Dec. 29	Southampton	A
1980		
Jan. 1	Manchester U.	A
Jan. 12	Brighton & H.A.	H
Jan. 19	W.B.A.	A
Feb. 2	Leeds U.	H
Feb. 9	Norwich C.	A
Feb. 16	Coventry C.	H
Feb. 23	Nottingham F.	H
Mar. 8	Derby Co.	A
Mar. 14	Crystal P.	H
Mar. 22	Tottenham H.	H
Mar. 25	Middlesbrough	A
Mar. 29	Everton	A
Apr. 5	Manchester C.	H
Apr. 7	Manchester U.	H
Apr. 8	Middlesbrough	A
Apr. 12	Stoke C.	H
Apr. 19	Stoke C.	A
Apr. 26	Ipswich T.	A
May 3	Wolverhampton W.	H

BRIGHTON & H.A.

Date 1979	Opponents	Ground
Aug. 18	Arsenal	H
Aug. 22	Aston Villa	A
Aug. 25	Manchester C.	H
Sept. 1	Bolton W.	H
Sept. 8	Tottenham H.	A
Sept. 15	Ipswich T.	H
Sept. 22	Southampton	A
Sept. 29	W.B.A.	H
Oct. 6	Aston Villa	H
Oct. 9	Aston Villa	H
Oct. 13	Leeds U.	A
Oct. 20	Coventry C.	H
Oct. 27	Norwich C.	A
Nov. 3	Arsenal	A
Nov. 10	Nottingham F.	H
Nov. 17	Middlesbrough	A
Nov. 24	Derby Co.	H
Dec. 1	Everton	A
Dec. 8	Stoke C.	H
Dec. 15	Stoke C.	A
Dec. 21	Wolverhampton W.	H
Dec. 26	Crystal P.	A
Dec. 29	Manchester C.	H
1980		
Jan. 1	Bristol C.	A
Jan. 12	Bolton W.	A
Feb. 2	Ipswich T.	H
Feb. 9	Southampton	A
Feb. 16	W.B.A.	A
Feb. 23	Tottenham H.	H
Mar. 1	Coventry C.	H
Mar. 8	Norwich C.	H
Mar. 14	Manchester U.	A
Mar. 22	Nottingham F.	A
Mar. 25	Leeds U.	H
Mar. 29	Derby Co.	A
Apr. 5	Bristol C.	H
Apr. 7	Crystal P.	H
Apr. 8	Derby Co.	H
Apr. 12	Liverpool	A
Apr. 19	Middlesbrough	H
Apr. 26	Stoke C.	A
May 3	Everton	H

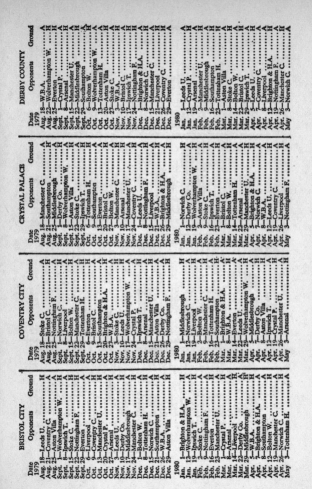

BRISTOL CITY

Date 1979	Opponents	Ground
Aug. 18	Leeds U.	H
Aug. 21	Wolverhampton W.	A
Aug. 25	Aston Villa	A
Sept. 1	Wolverhampton W.	H
Sept. 8	Ipswich T.	A
Sept. 15	Liverpool	H
Sept. 22	Nottingham F.	A
Sept. 29	Everton	H
Oct. 6	Liverpool	A
Oct. 9	Coventry C.	A
Oct. 13	Manchester U.	H
Oct. 20	Arsenal	A
Oct. 27	W.B.A.	H
Nov. 3	Leeds U.	A
Nov. 10	Derby Co.	H
Nov. 17	Middlesbrough	A
Nov. 24	Manchester C.	H
Dec. 1	Bolton W.	A
Dec. 8	Norwich C.	H
Dec. 15	Liverpool	H
Dec. 21	Southampton	A
Dec. 29	Aston Villa	A
1980		
Jan. 1	Brighton & H.A.	H
Jan. 12	Wolverhampton W.	A
Jan. 19	Ipswich T.	H
Jan. 26	Stoke C.	A
Feb. 2	Nottingham F.	H
Feb. 16	Everton	A
Feb. 23	Manchester U.	A
Mar. 1	Crystal P.	H
Mar. 8	Arsenal	H
Mar. 14	Liverpool	A
Mar. 22	Derby Co.	A
Mar. 29	Middlesbrough	H
Apr. 5	W.B.A.	A
Apr. 7	Brighton & H.A.	A
Apr. 8	Southampton	H
Apr. 12	Bolton W.	H
Apr. 19	Manchester C.	A
Apr. 26	Norwich C.	H
May 3	Tottenham H.	A

COVENTRY CITY

Date 1979	Opponents	Ground
Aug. 18	Stoke C.	H
Aug. 21	Bristol C.	H
Aug. 25	Nottingham F.	H
Sept. 1	Norwich C.	A
Sept. 8	Liverpool	H
Sept. 15	Everton	A
Sept. 22	Derby Co.	A
Sept. 29	Tottenham H.	A
Oct. 6	Everton	H
Oct. 9	Bristol C.	H
Oct. 13	Southampton	A
Oct. 20	Brighton & H.A.	H
Nov. 3	Stoke C.	A
Nov. 10	Leeds U.	H
Nov. 17	Wolverhampton W.	A
Nov. 24	Ipswich T.	H
Dec. 1	Arsenal	A
Dec. 8	Manchester U.	H
Dec. 15	Manchester C.	A
Dec. 21	Aston Villa	H
Dec. 29	Nottingham F.	A
1980		
Jan. 1	Middlesbrough	H
Jan. 12	Norwich C.	A
Jan. 19	Liverpool	H
Feb. 2	Bolton W.	A
Feb. 9	Manchester C.	H
Feb. 16	Everton	A
Feb. 23	Southampton	H
Mar. 1	Brighton & H.A.	A
Mar. 8	W.B.A.	H
Mar. 14	Everton	H
Mar. 22	Leeds U.	A
Mar. 29	Wolverhampton W.	W
Apr. 5	Middlesbrough	A
Apr. 7	Derby Co.	H
Apr. 8	Aston Villa	A
Apr. 12	Ipswich T.	H
Apr. 19	Crystal P.	A
Apr. 26	Manchester U.	A
May 3	Arsenal	H

CRYSTAL PALACE

Date 1979	Opponents	Ground
Aug. 18	Manchester C.	A
Aug. 21	Southampton	H
Aug. 25	Middlesbrough	A
Sept. 1	Wolverhampton W.	H
Sept. 8	Wolverhampton W.	A
Sept. 15	Stoke C.	H
Sept. 22	Stoke C.	A
Sept. 29	Ipswich T.	H
Oct. 6	Tottenham H.	A
Oct. 9	Southampton	H
Oct. 13	Everton	A
Oct. 20	Bolton W.	H
Oct. 27	Bolton W.	A
Nov. 10	Arsenal	H
Nov. 17	Manchester U.	A
Nov. 24	Leeds U. C.	H
Dec. 1	Leeds U. C.	A
Dec. 8	Liverpool	H
Dec. 15	Liverpool	A
Dec. 21	W.B.A.	H
Dec. 29	Brighton & H.A.	A
1980		
Jan. 1	Middlesbrough	H
Jan. 12	Norwich C.	H
Jan. 19	Derby Co.	A
Feb. 2	Wolverhampton W.	A
Feb. 9	Aston Villa	H
Feb. 16	Stoke C.	A
Feb. 23	Ipswich T.	H
Mar. 1	Bristol C.	A
Mar. 8	Bolton W.	H
Mar. 14	Tottenham H.	A
Mar. 22	Arsenal	A
Mar. 29	Manchester U. U.	A
Apr. 5	Brighton & H.A.	H
Apr. 7	Norwich C.	A
Apr. 8	W.B.A.	H
Apr. 12	Leeds U.	A
Apr. 19	Coventry C.	H
Apr. 26	Manchester C.	H
May 3	Nottingham F.	A

DERBY COUNTY

Date 1979	Opponents	Ground
Aug. 18	W.B.A.	A
Aug. 22	Wolverhampton W.	H
Aug. 25	Everton	A
Sept. 1	Crystal P.	H
Sept. 8	Arsenal	A
Sept. 15	Manchester U.	H
Sept. 22	Middlesbrough	A
Sept. 29	Southampton	H
Oct. 6	Bolton W.	A
Oct. 9	Wolverhampton W.	H
Oct. 13	Tottenham H.	A
Oct. 20	Aston Villa	H
Oct. 27	Stoke C.	A
Nov. 3	W.B.A.	H
Nov. 10	Bristol C.	A
Nov. 17	Ipswich T.	H
Nov. 24	Nottingham F.	A
Dec. 1	Brighton & H.A.	H
Dec. 8	Manchester C.	A
Dec. 15	Manchester C.	H
Dec. 21	Liverpool	A
Dec. 26	Coventry C.	A
Dec. 29	Everton	A
1980		
Jan. 1	Leeds U.	A
Jan. 12	Crystal P.	H
Jan. 19	Arsenal	A
Feb. 2	Middlesbrough	H
Feb. 9	Southampton	H
Feb. 16	Southampton	A
Feb. 23	Aston Villa	H
Mar. 1	Stoke C.	A
Mar. 8	Bolton W.	H
Mar. 14	Tottenham H.	A
Mar. 22	Bristol C.	H
Mar. 29	Ipswich T.	A
Apr. 5	Coventry C.	H
Apr. 7	Liverpool	A
Apr. 8	Brighton & H.A.	H
Apr. 12	Brighton & H.A.	H
Apr. 19	Nottingham F.	A
Apr. 26	Norwich C.	H
May 3	Everton	A

EVERTON

Date 1979	Opponents	Ground
Aug. 18	Norwich C.	H
Aug. 22	Leeds U.	A
Aug. 25	Derby Co.	H
Sept. 1	Aston Villa	A
Sept. 8	Stoke C.	H
Sept. 15	Wolverhampton W.	A
Sept. 22	Ipswich T.	H
Sept. 29	Bristol C.	A
Oct. 6	Coventry C.	H
Oct. 9	Leeds U.	H
Oct. 13	Crystal P.	A
Oct. 20	Liverpool	H
Oct. 27	Manchester U.	A
Nov. 3	Norwich C.	A
Nov. 10	Middlesbrough	H
Nov. 17	Arsenal	A
Nov. 24	Tottenham H.	H
Dec. 1	W.B.A.	A
Dec. 8	Brighton & H.A.	H
Dec. 15	Southampton	A
Dec. 22	Manchester C.	H
Dec. 26	Bolton W.	A
Dec. 29	Derby Co.	A

Date 1980	Opponents	Ground
Jan. 1	Nottingham F.	H
Jan. 12	Aston Villa	H
Jan. 19	Stoke C.	A
Feb. 2	Wolverhampton W.	H
Feb. 9	Ipswich T.	A
Feb. 16	Bristol C.	H
Feb. 23	Liverpool	A
Mar. 1	Manchester U.	H
Mar. 8	Manchester C.	A
Mar. 14	Coventry C.	A
Mar. 22	Middlesbrough	H
Mar. 29	Arsenal	H
Apr. 4	Bolton W.	A
Apr. 5	Norwich C.	H
Apr. 7	Nottingham F.	A
Apr. 12	W.B.A.	H
Apr. 19	Tottenham H.	A
Apr. 26	Southampton	H
May. 3	Brighton & H.A.	A

IPSWICH TOWN

Date 1979	Opponents	Ground
Aug. 18	Nottingham F.	A
Aug. 21	Arsenal	H
Aug. 25	Wolverhampton W.	H
Sept. 1	Stoke C.	A
Sept. 8	Bristol C.	H
Sept. 15	Brighton & H.A.	A
Sept. 22	Everton	A
Sept. 29	Crystal P.	H
Oct. 6	Leeds U.	A
Oct. 9	Arsenal	A
Oct. 13	Liverpool	H
Oct. 20	Manchester U.	A
Oct. 27	Middlesbrough	H
Nov. 3	Nottingham F.	H
Nov. 10	Aston Villa	A
Nov. 17	Derby Co.	H
Nov. 24	Coventry C.	A
Dec. 1	Manchester C.	H
Dec. 8	Bolton W.	A
Dec. 15	Bolton W.	H
Dec. 22	Norwich C.	A
Dec. 26	Tottenham H.	H
Dec. 29	Wolverhampton W.	A

Date 1980	Opponents	Ground
Jan. 1	W.B.A.	H
Jan. 12	Stoke C.	A
Jan. 19	Brighton & H.A.	H
Feb. 2	Everton	H
Feb. 9	Crystal P.	A
Feb. 16	Bristol C.	A
Mar. 1	Manchester U.	H
Mar. 8	Leeds U.	A
Mar. 14	Aston Villa	H
Mar. 22	Derby Co.	H
Mar. 29	Derby Co.	A
Apr. 4	Tottenham H.	H
Apr. 5	Norwich C.	H
Apr. 7	Coventry C.	A
Apr. 19	Southampton	A
Apr. 26	Bolton W.	A
May. 3	Manchester C.	A

LEEDS UNITED

Date 1979	Opponents	Ground
Aug. 18	Bristol C.	H
Aug. 22	Everton	H
Aug. 25	Norwich C.	A
Sept. 1	Coventry C.	A
Sept. 8	Nottingham F.	H
Sept. 15	Liverpool	A
Sept. 22	Bolton W.	H
Sept. 29	Manchester C.	A
Oct. 6	Ipswich T.	H
Oct. 9	Everton	A
Oct. 13	Brighton & H.A.	A
Oct. 20	Tottenham H.	H
Oct. 27	Southampton	A
Nov. 3	Bristol C.	A
Nov. 10	Coventry C.	H
Nov. 17	W.B.A.	A
Nov. 24	Crystal P.	H
Dec. 1	Aston Villa	A
Dec. 8	Manchester U.	H
Dec. 15	Arsenal	A
Dec. 22	Middlesbrough	H
Dec. 26	Derby Co.	A

Date 1980	Opponents	Ground
Jan. 1	Derby Co.	H
Jan. 12	Nottingham F.	A
Jan. 19	Liverpool	H
Feb. 2	Bolton W.	A
Feb. 9	Manchester C.	H
Feb. 23	Tottenham H.	H
Mar. 1	Ipswich T.	A
Mar. 8	Everton	A
Mar. 14	Ipswich T.	H
Mar. 22	Brighton & H.A.	H
Mar. 29	Tottenham H.	A
Apr. 4	Derby Co.	A
Apr. 5	Stoke C.	H
Apr. 7	Stoke C.	A
Apr. 12	Middlesbrough	A
Apr. 19	Aston Villa	H
Apr. 26	Wolverhampton W.	A
May. 3	Manchester U.	H

LIVERPOOL

Date 1979	Opponents	Ground
Aug. 18	Wolverhampton W.	A
Aug. 21	Bolton W.	H
Aug. 25	W.B.A.	H
Sept. 1	Southampton	A
Sept. 8	Derby Co.	H
Sept. 15	Leeds U.	H
Sept. 22	Nottingham F.	A
Sept. 29	Bristol C.	H
Oct. 6	Bolton W.	A
Oct. 9	Everton	W
Oct. 13	Ipswich T.	H
Oct. 20	Everton	A
Oct. 27	Crystal P.	A
Nov. 3	Wolverhampton W.	H
Nov. 10	Brighton & H.A.	A
Nov. 17	Tottenham H.	H
Nov. 24	Middlesbrough	A
Dec. 1	Crystal P.	H
Dec. 8	Manchester C.	A
Dec. 15	Manchester U.	H
Dec. 22	Manchester C.	A
Dec. 26	W.B.A.	A

Date 1980	Opponents	Ground
Jan. 1	Stoke C.	A
Jan. 12	Southampton	A
Jan. 19	Leeds U.	A
Feb. 2	Norwich C.	H
Feb. 9	Nottingham F.	H
Feb. 16	Derby C.	A
Feb. 23	Everton	H
Mar. 1	Manchester C.	A
Mar. 8	Brighton & H.A.	A
Mar. 22	Tottenham H.	A
Mar. 29	Stoke C.	H
Apr. 4	Manchester U.	H
Apr. 5	Bristol C.	A
Apr. 12	Middlesbrough	H
Apr. 19	Arsenal	H
Apr. 26	Crystal P.	A
May. 3	Aston Villa	H

MANCHESTER CITY

Date 1979	Opponents	Ground
Aug. 18	Crystal P.	H
Aug. 21	Middlesbrough	H
Aug. 25	Brighton & H.A.	A
Sept. 1	Tottenham H.	A
Sept. 8	Southampton	H
Sept. 15	W.B.A.	A
Sept. 22	Coventry C.	H
Sept. 29	Leeds U.	A
Oct. 6	Arsenal	H
Oct. 10	Middlesbrough	A
Oct. 13	Nottingham F.	H
Oct. 20	Norwich C.	A
Oct. 27	Liverpool	A
Nov. 3	Crystal P.	A
Nov. 10	Manchester U.	H
Nov. 17	Bolton W.	A
Nov. 24	Bristol C.	H
Dec. 1	Wolverhampton W.	A
Dec. 8	Leeds T.	H
Dec. 15	Derby Co.	A
Dec. 21	Everton	H
Dec. 26	Stoke C.	A
Dec. 29	Brighton & H.A.	H
1980		
Jan. 1	Aston Villa	A
Jan. 12	Tottenham H.	H
Jan. 19	Southampton	A
Feb. 2	W.B.A.	H
Feb. 9	Coventry C.	A
Feb. 16	Nottingham F.	A
Feb. 23	Norwich C.	H
Mar. 1	Liverpool	H
Mar. 8	Manchester U.	A
Mar. 15	Arsenal	A
Mar. 22	Leicester U.	H
Mar. 29	Bolton W.	H
Apr. 5	Stoke C.	A
Apr. 7	Aston Villa	H
Apr. 8	Everton	A
Apr. 12	Wolverhampton W.	H
Apr. 19	Bristol C.	A
Apr. 26	Derby Co.	H
May 3	Ipswich T.	A

MANCHESTER UNITED

Date 1979	Opponents	Ground
Aug. 18	Southampton	A
Aug. 22	W.B.A.	H
Aug. 25	Arsenal	H
Sept. 1	Middlesbrough	A
Sept. 8	Aston Villa	H
Sept. 15	Derby Co.	A
Sept. 22	Wolverhampton W.	H
Sept. 29	Stoke C.	H
Oct. 6	Brighton & H.A.	A
Oct. 10	Bristol C.	H
Oct. 13	Ipswich T.	A
Oct. 20	Everton	H
Oct. 27	Southampton	H
Nov. 3	Manchester C.	A
Nov. 10	Leeds U.	H
Nov. 17	Tottenham H.	A
Nov. 24	Norwich C.	H
Dec. 1	Coventry C.	A
Dec. 8	Nottingham F.	H
Dec. 15	Liverpool	A
Dec. 22	Arsenal	A
Dec. 26	Liverpool	H
Dec. 29	Arsenal	A
1980		
Jan. 1	Bolton W.	H
Jan. 12	Middlesbrough	A
Jan. 19	Aston Villa	A
Feb. 2	Derby Co.	H
Feb. 9	Wolverhampton W.	A
Feb. 16	Stoke C.	H
Feb. 23	Bristol C.	A
Mar. 1	Ipswich T.	H
Mar. 8	Everton	H
Mar. 15	Brighton & H.A.	H
Mar. 22	Coventry C.	H
Mar. 29	Crystal P.	A
Apr. 5	Tottenham H.	H
Apr. 7	Bolton W.	A
Apr. 8	Nottingham F.	A
Apr. 12	Southampton	A
Apr. 19	Norwich C.	A
Apr. 26	Coventry C.	H
May 3	Leeds U.	A

MIDDLESBROUGH

Date 1979	Opponents	Ground
Aug. 18	Tottenham H.	A
Aug. 22	Manchester C.	A
Aug. 25	Crystal P.	H
Sept. 1	Manchester U.	H
Sept. 8	Arsenal	A
Sept. 15	Aston Villa	H
Sept. 22	Bristol C.	A
Sept. 29	Aston Villa	H
Oct. 6	W.B.A.	A
Oct. 10	Manchester C.	H
Oct. 13	Wolverhampton W.	A
Oct. 20	Wolverhampton W.	H
Oct. 27	Ipswich T.	A
Nov. 3	Tottenham H.	H
Nov. 10	Everton	A
Nov. 17	Bristol C.	H
Nov. 24	Brighton & H.A.	A
Dec. 1	Liverpool	H
Dec. 8	Southampton	A
Dec. 15	Nottingham F.	H
Dec. 21	Arsenal	H
Dec. 26	Leeds U.	A
Dec. 29	Crystal P.	A
1980		
Jan. 1	Coventry C.	A
Jan. 12	Manchester U.	H
Jan. 19	Norwich C.	A
Feb. 2	Arsenal	H
Feb. 9	Aston Villa	A
Feb. 16	Aston Villa	H
Mar. 1	Wolverhampton W.	A
Mar. 8	W.B.A.	H
Mar. 15	Bristol C.	A
Mar. 22	Bristol C.	H
Apr. 5	Coventry C.	H
Apr. 7	Leeds U.	H
Apr. 8	Bolton W.	A
Apr. 12	Ipswich T.	H
Apr. 19	Brighton & H.A.	A
Apr. 26	Nottingham F.	A
May 3	Southampton	H

NORWICH CITY

Date 1979	Opponents	Ground
Aug. 18	Everton	A
Aug. 22	Tottenham H.	H
Aug. 25	Leeds U.	H
Sept. 1	Coventry C.	A
Sept. 8	Middlesbrough	H
Sept. 15	Arsenal	A
Sept. 22	Liverpool	H
Sept. 29	Bolton W.	A
Oct. 6	Stoke C.	A
Oct. 10	Tottenham H.	H
Oct. 13	Wolverhampton W.	A
Oct. 20	Manchester C.	H
Oct. 27	Brighton & H.A.	A
Nov. 3	Everton	H
Nov. 10	Southampton	A
Nov. 17	Nottingham F.	H
Nov. 24	Ipswich T.	A
Dec. 1	Aston Villa	H
Dec. 8	Bristol C.	A
Dec. 15	Derby Co.	H
Dec. 21	Arsenal	A
Dec. 26	Crystal P.	H
Dec. 29	Leeds U.	A
1980		
Jan. 1	Crystal P.	A
Jan. 12	Coventry C.	H
Jan. 19	Middlesbrough	H
Feb. 2	Liverpool	A
Feb. 9	Brighton & H.A.	H
Feb. 23	Manchester C.	A
Mar. 1	Manchester U.	H
Mar. 8	Manchester U.	H
Mar. 15	Stoke C.	A
Mar. 22	Arsenal	H
Mar. 24	Southampton	H
Apr. 5	Ipswich T.	H
Apr. 7	Crystal P.	H
Apr. 8	Arsenal	A
Apr. 12	Aston Villa	A
Apr. 19	Leicester U.	H
Apr. 26	Bristol C.	A
May 3	Derby Co.	A

NOTTINGHAM FOREST

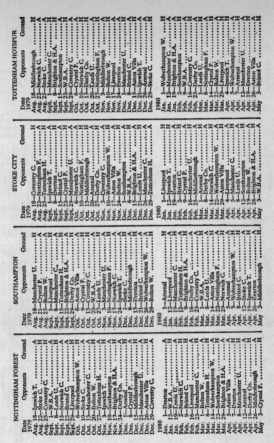

Date 1979	Opponents	Ground
Aug. 18	Ipswich T.	A
Aug. 21	Stoke C.	H
Aug. 25	Coventry C.	H
Sept. 1	W.B.A.	A
Sept. 8	Leeds U.	H
Sept. 15	Norwich C.	A
Sept. 22	Bristol C.	H
Sept. 29	Liverpool	A
Oct. 6	Wolverhampton W.	H
Oct. 13	Manchester C.	A
Oct. 20	Bolton W.	H
Oct. 27	Tottenham H.	A
Nov. 3	Derby Co.	H
Nov. 10	Arsenal	A
Nov. 17	Brighton & H.A.	H
Nov. 24	Crystal P.	A
Dec. 1	Middlesbrough	H
Dec. 8	Everton	A
Dec. 15	Manchester U.	H
Dec. 21	Aston Villa	A
Dec. 26	Coventry C.	H

Date 1980	Opponents	Ground
Jan.	Everton	A
Jan. 12	W.B.A.	H
Jan. 19	Leeds U.	A
Feb. 2	Bristol C.	H
Feb. 9	Liverpool	H
Feb. 16	Manchester C.	H
Feb. 23	Norwich C.	A
Mar. 1	Bolton W.	H
Mar. 8	Tottenham H.	H
Mar. 14	Wolverhampton W.	A
Mar. 22	Southampton	H
Mar. 29	Ipswich T.	A
Apr. 5	Aston Villa	H
Apr. 7	Everton	H
Apr. 8	Manchester U.	A
Apr.	Arsenal	H
Apr. 19	Ipswich T.	A
Apr. 26	Middlesbrough	H
May 3	Crystal P.	A

SOUTHAMPTON

Date 1979	Opponents	Ground
Aug. 18	Manchester U.	H
Aug. 21	Coventry C.	A
Aug. 25	Bolton W.	H
Sept. 1	W.B.A.	A
Sept. 8	Manchester C.	H
Sept. 15	Tottenham H.	A
Sept. 22	Brighton & H.A.	H
Sept. 29	Derby Co.	A
Oct. 6	Aston Villa	H
Oct. 10	Crystal P.	A
Oct. 13	Coventry C.	H
Oct. 20	W.B.A.	A
Oct. 27	Leeds U.	H
Nov. 3	Manchester U.	A
Nov. 10	Norwich C.	H
Nov. 17	Ipswich T.	A
Nov. 24	Stoke C.	H
Dec. 1	Middlesbrough	A
Dec. 8	Everton	H
Dec. 15	Bristol C.	A
Dec. 21	Nottingham F.?	H
Dec. 26	Wolverhampton W.	A
Dec. 29	Bolton W.	H

Date 1980	Opponents	Ground
Jan.	Arsenal	H
Jan. 12	Liverpool	A
Jan. 19	Manchester U.	H
Feb. 2	Everton	A
Feb. 9	Brighton & H.A.	H
Feb. 16	Derby Co.	A
Feb. 23	Coventry C.	H
Mar. 1	Bolton W.	A
Mar. 8	Leeds U.	H
Mar. 14	Aston Villa	A
Mar. 22	Nottingham F.	A
Mar. 29	Arsenal	H
Apr. 5	Wolverhampton W.	A
Apr. 7	Everton	H
Apr. 8	Bristol C.	A
Apr.	Manchester U.	H
Apr. 19	Ipswich T.	H
Apr. 26	Everton	A
May 3	Middlesbrough	H

STOKE CITY

Date 1979	Opponents	Ground
Aug. 18	Coventry C.	H
Aug. 22	Nottingham F.	A
Aug. 25	Tottenham H.	H
Sept. 1	Everton	A
Sept. 8	Bristol C.	H
Sept. 15	Crystal P.	A
Sept. 22	Manchester U.	H
Sept. 29	Manchester C.	A
Oct. 6	Norwich C.	H
Oct. 13	Middlesbrough	A
Oct. 20	Arsenal	H
Oct. 27	Derby Co.	A
Nov. 3	Coventry C.	H
Nov. 10	Wolverhampton W.	A
Nov. 17	Aston Villa	H
Nov. 24	Southampton	A
Dec. 1	W.B.A.	H
Dec. 8	W.B.A.	A
Dec. 15	Brighton & H.A.	H
Dec. 21	Leeds U.	A
Dec. 26	Manchester U.	H
Dec. 29	Tottenham H.	A

Date 1980	Opponents	Ground
Jan.	Liverpool	H
Jan. 12	Ipswich T.	A
Jan. 19	Everton	H
Feb. 2	Crystal P.	H
Feb. 9	Manchester U.	A
Feb. 16	Middlesbrough	H
Feb. 23	Arsenal	A
Mar. 1	Derby Co.	H
Mar. 8	Norwich C.	A
Mar. 14	Wolverhampton W.	H
Mar. 22	Aston Villa	A
Apr. 5	Liverpool	A
Apr. 7	Manchester C.	H
Apr. 8	Leeds U.	H
Apr.	Southampton	A
Apr. 19	Manchester C.	A
Apr. 26	Brighton & H.A.	H
May 3	Bristol C.	A

TOTTENHAM HOTSPUR

Date 1979	Opponents	Ground
Aug. 18	Middlesbrough	H
Aug. 22	Norwich C.	A
Aug. 25	Stoke C.	A
Sept. 1	Everton	H
Sept. 8	Brighton & H.A.	A
Sept. 15	Southampton	H
Sept. 22	W.B.A.	A
Sept. 29	Coventry C.	H
Oct. 6	Crystal P.	A
Oct. 13	Derby Co.	A
Oct. 20	Leeds U.	H
Oct. 27	Nottingham F.	H
Nov. 3	Middlesbrough	A
Nov. 10	Bolton W.	H
Nov. 17	Liverpool	A
Nov. 24	Everton	A
Dec. 1	Bristol C.	H
Dec. 8	Bristol C.	A
Dec. 15	Aston Villa	H
Dec. 21	Ipswich T.	A
Dec. 26	Manchester U.	H
Dec. 29	Stoke C.	H

Date 1980	Opponents	Ground
Jan.	Wolverhampton W.	A
Jan. 12	Manchester C.	A
Jan. 19	Brighton & H.A.	A
Feb. 2	Southampton	A
Feb. 9	W.B.A.	H
Feb. 16	Coventry C.	A
Feb. 23	Derby Co.	H
Mar. 1	Leeds U.	A
Mar. 8	Nottingham F.	A
Mar. 15	Crystal P.	H
Mar. 22	Norwich C.	H
Mar. 29	Liverpool	H
Apr. 5	Ipswich T.	A
Apr. 7	Everton	H
Apr. 8	Bolton W.	H
Apr. 12	Manchester U.	A
Apr. 19	Everton	A
Apr. 26	Aston Villa	H
May 3	Bristol C.	A

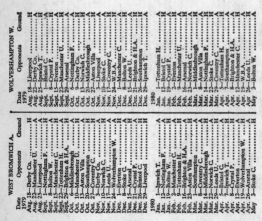

WEST BROMWICH A.

Date 1979	Opponents	Ground
Aug. 18	Derby Co.	A
Aug. 22	Manchester U.	A
Aug. 25	Liverpool	A
Sept. 1	Nottingham F.	H
Sept. 8	Bolton W.	H
Sept. 15	Manchester C.	A
Sept. 22	Tottenham H.	H
Sept. 29	Brighton & H.A.	A
Oct. 6	Middlesbrough	H
Oct. 10	Manchester U.	H
Oct. 13	Aston Villa	H
Oct. 20	Southampton	A
Oct. 27	Coventry C.	H
Nov. 3	Derby Co.	H
Nov. 10	Norwich C.	A
Nov. 17	Leeds U.	H
Nov. 24	Wolverhampton W.	A
Dec. 1	Everton	A
Dec. 8	Stoke C.	H
Dec. 21	Crystal P.	A
Dec. 26	Bristol C.	H
Dec. 29	Liverpool	H
1980		
Jan. 1	Ipswich T.	A
Jan. 12	Nottingham F.	A
Jan. 19	Bolton W.	H
Feb. 2	Manchester C.	H
Feb. 9	Tottenham H.	A
Feb. 16	Brighton & H.A.	H
Feb. 23	Aston Villa	A
Mar. 1	Southampton	H
Mar. 8	Middlesbrough	A
Mar. 14	Middlesbrough	A
Mar. 22	Norwich C.	H
Mar. 29	Leeds U.	A
Apr. 2	Bristol C.	A
Apr. 7	Ipswich T.	H
Apr. 8	Crystal P.	H
Apr. 12	Everton	H
Apr. 19	Wolverhampton W.	H
Apr. 26	Arsenal	A
May 3	Stoke C.	H

WOLVERHAMPTON W.

Date 1979	Opponents	Ground
Aug. 18	Liverpool	H
Aug. 22	Derby Co.	H
Aug. 25	Ipswich T.	A
Sept. 1	Bristol C.	H
Sept. 8	Crystal P.	A
Sept. 15	Everton	A
Sept. 22	Manchester U.	H
Sept. 29	Arsenal	A
Oct. 6	Nottingham F.	H
Oct. 9	Derby Co.	A
Oct. 13	Norwich C.	H
Oct. 20	Middlesbrough	A
Oct. 27	Aston Villa	H
Nov. 3	Liverpool	A
Nov. 10	Stoke C.	H
Nov. 17	Coventry C.	A
Nov. 24	W.B.A.	H
Dec. 1	Manchester C.	A
Dec. 8	Bolton W.	H
Dec. 15	Leeds U.	A
Dec. 21	Brighton & H.A.	H
Dec. 26	Southampton	A
Dec. 29	Ipswich T.	A
1980		
Jan. 1	Tottenham H.	A
Jan. 12	Bristol C.	A
Jan. 19	Crystal P.	H
Feb. 2	Everton	H
Feb. 9	Manchester U.	A
Feb. 16	Arsenal	H
Feb. 23	Norwich C.	A
Mar. 1	Middlesbrough	H
Mar. 8	Aston Villa	A
Mar. 14	Nottingham F.	A
Mar. 22	Stoke C.	H
Mar. 29	Coventry C.	H
Apr. 2	Tottenham H.	H
Apr. 7	Southampton	H
Apr. 8	Brighton & H.A.	A
Apr. 12	Manchester C.	H
Apr. 19	W.B.A.	A
Apr. 26	Leeds U.	H
May 3	Bolton W.	A

DIVISION TWO

BIRMINGHAM CITY

Date 1979	Opponents	Ground
Aug. 18	Fulham	H
Aug. 25	Sunderland	A
Sept. 1	Cardiff C.	A
Sept.	Bristol R.	H
Sept. 8	Chelsea	A
Sept. 15	Charlton Ath.	H
Sept. 22	Orient	A
Sept. 29	Newcastle U.	H
Oct. 6	P.N.E.	A
Oct. 13	Wrexham	H
Oct. 20	Swansea C.	A
Oct. 27	Shrewsbury T.	H
Nov. 3	Cambridge U.	A
Nov. 10	Watford	H
Nov. 17	Notts Co.	A
Nov. 24	Luton T.	H
Dec. 1	Leicester C.	A
Dec. 8	Notts Co.	H
Dec. 15	Burnley	A
Dec. 21	Oldham Ath.	H
Dec. 26	West Ham U.	A
Dec. 29	Cardiff C.	H
1980		
Jan. 1	Q.P.R.	H
Jan. 12	Bristol R.	A
Jan. 19	Chelsea	H
Feb. 2	Charlton Ath.	A
Feb. 9	Orient	H
Feb. 16	Newcastle U.	A
Feb. 23	Wrexham	H
Mar. 8	Swansea C.	A
Mar. 14	P.N.E.	H
Mar. 22	Cambridge U.	A
Mar. 29	Watford	H
Apr. 4	Q.P.R.	A
Apr. 7	West Ham U.	H
Apr. 8	Oldham Ath.	A
Apr. 12	Leicester C.	H
Apr. 19	Luton T.	A
Apr. 26	Burnley	H
May 3	Notts Co.	A

BRISTOL ROVERS

Date 1979	Opponents	Ground
Aug. 18	Q.P.R.	A
Aug. 21	Luton T.	H
Aug. 25	Shrewsbury T.	H
Sept. 1	Birmingham C.	A
Sept.	Watford	H
Sept. 8	Cambridge U.	A
Sept. 15	P.N.E.	H
Sept. 22	Cardiff C.	A
Sept. 29	Notts Co.	H
Oct. 6	Luton T.	A
Oct. 13	Chelsea	H
Oct. 20	Charlton Ath.	A
Oct. 27	Orient	H
Nov. 3	Q.P.R.	A
Nov. 10	Wrexham	H
Nov. 17	Newcastle U.	A
Nov. 24	Burnley	H
Dec. 1	West Ham U.	A
Dec. 8	West Ham U.	H
Dec. 15	Oldham Ath.	A
Dec. 21	Fulham	H
Dec. 26	Swansea C.	A
Dec. 29	Shrewsbury T.	A
1980		
Jan. 1	Leicester C.	A
Jan. 12	Birmingham C.	H
Jan. 19	Watford	A
Feb. 2	Cambridge U.	H
Feb. 9	P.N.E.	A
Feb. 16	Cardiff C.	H
Feb. 23	Chelsea	A
Mar. 8	Orient	H
Mar. 14	Notts Co.	A
Mar. 22	Wrexham	H
Mar. 29	Newcastle U.	A
Apr. 4	Fulham	H
Apr. 7	Swansea C.	A
Apr. 8	Leicester C.	H
Apr. 12	Sunderland	A
Apr. 19	Cambridge U.	H
Apr. 26	Oldham Ath.	A
May 3	West Ham U.	H

BURNLEY

Date 1979	Opponents	Ground
Aug. 18	Orient	A
Aug. 25	Notts Co.	H
Sept. 1	Birmingham C.	H
Sept.	Swansea C.	A
Sept. 15	Fulham	H
Sept. 22	P.N.E.	A
Sept. 29	West Ham U.	H
Oct. 6	Chelsea	A
Oct. 9	Charlton Ath.	A
Oct. 13	Cardiff C.	H
Oct. 20	P.N.E.	A
Nov. 3	Orient	H
Nov. 10	Leicester C.	A
Nov. 17	Luton T.	H
Nov. 24	Bristol R.	A
Dec. 1	Cambridge U.	H
Dec. 8	Watford	A
Dec. 15	Birmingham C.	H
Dec. 21	Wrexham	A
Dec. 26	Newcastle U.	H
Dec. 29	Notts Co.	A
1980		
Jan. 1	Shrewsbury T.	H
Jan. 12	Swansea C.	A
Jan. 19	Charlton Ath.	H
Feb. 2	Fulham	A
Feb. 9	Sunderland	H
Feb. 16	West Ham U.	A
Feb. 23	Cambridge U.	H
Mar. 8	P.N.E.	A
Mar. 14	Q.P.R.	H
Mar. 22	Chelsea	A
Mar. 29	Leicester C.	H
Apr. 4	Luton T.	A
Apr. 7	Wrexham	H
Apr. 8	Shrewsbury T.	A
Apr. 12	Bristol R.	H
Apr. 19	Cambridge U.	A
Apr. 26	Birmingham C.	A
May 3	Watford	H

CAMBRIDGE UNITED

Date 1979	Opponents	Ground
Aug. 18	Luton T.	A
Aug. 21	Leicester C.	H
Aug. 25	Watford	H
Sept. 1	Shrewsbury T.	A
Sept. 8	Bristol R.	H
Sept. 15	Bristol C.	A
Sept. 22	Chelsea	A
Sept. 29	Swansea C.	H
Oct. 6	Leicester C.	A
Oct. 9	Charlton Ath.	H
Oct. 13	Charlton Ath.	A
Oct. 20	Orient	H
Nov. 3	Luton T.	H
Nov. 10	Wrexham	A
Nov. 17	Birmingham C.	H
Dec. 1	Q.P.R.	A
Dec. 8	P.N.E.	H
Dec. 15	Fulham	A
Dec. 21	Burnley	A
Dec. 26	Oldham Ath.	H
Dec. 29	Watford	A
1980		
Jan. 1	Notts C.	H
Jan. 12	Shrewsbury T.	A
Jan. 19	Sunderland	H
Feb. 2	Bristol R.	A
Feb. 9	Chelsea	H
Feb. 16	Orient	A
Mar. 1	Newcastle U.	H
Mar. 8	Swansea C.	A
Mar. 14	Q.P.R.	H
Mar. 22	West Ham U.	H
Mar. 29	Wrexham	A
Apr. 4	Oldham Ath.	H
Apr. 7	Q.P.R.	A
Apr. 12	Burnley	A
Apr. 19	Fulham	H
Apr. 26	P.N.E.	A

CARDIFF CITY

Date 1979	Opponents	Ground
Aug. 18—	Notts Co.	H
Aug. 25—	Birmingham C.	A
Sept. 1—	Wrexham	H
Sept. 8—	Shrewsbury T.	A
Sept. 15—	Watford	H
Sept. 22—	Cambridge U.	A
Sept. 29—	Bristol R.	H
Oct. 6—	Luton T.	A
Oct. 9—	Q.P.R.	H
Oct. 13—	Burnley	A
Oct. 20—	Chelsea	H
Oct. 27—	Charlton Ath.	A
Nov. 3—	Notts Co.	A
Nov. 10—	Newcastle U.	H
Nov. 24—	Orient	A
Dec. 1—	West Ham U.	H
Dec. 8—	Sunderland	A
Dec. 15—	P.N.E.	H
Dec. 21—	Leicester C.	A
Dec. 29—	Birmingham C.	H
1980		
Jan. 1—	Swansea C.	A
Jan. 12—	Wrexham	A
Feb. 2—	Shrewsbury T.	H
Feb. 9—	Cambridge U.	H
Feb. 23—	Bristol R.	A
Mar. 1—	Burnley	H
Mar. 8—	Charlton Ath.	H
Mar. 14—	Luton T.	A
Mar. 22—	Newcastle U.	A
Mar. 29—	Orient	H
Apr. 4—	Swansea C.	H
Apr. 8—	Leicester C.	A
Apr. 12—	Oldham Ath.	A
Apr. 19—	West Ham U.	A
Apr. 26—	P.N.E.	A
May 3—	Sunderland	H

CHARLTON ATHLETIC

Date 1979	Opponents	Ground
Aug. 18—	P.N.E.	H
Aug. 25—	Burnley	A
Sept. 1—	Newcastle U.	H
Sept. 8—	Orient	A
Sept. 15—	Wrexham	H
Sept. 18—	Birmingham C.	H
Sept. 22—	Shrewsbury T.	A
Sept. 29—	Watford	H
Oct. 6—	Sunderland	A
Oct. 9—	Burnley	H
Oct. 13—	Cambridge U.	A
Oct. 20—	Bristol R.	H
Oct. 27—	Cardiff C.	H
Nov. 3—	P.N.E.	A
Nov. 10—	Oldham Ath.	H
Nov. 17—	Chelsea	A
Nov. 24—	Q.P.R.	A
Dec. 1—	Swansea C.	H
Dec. 8—	Leicester C.	A
Dec. 15—	Luton T.	H
Dec. 22—	Notts Co.	A
Dec. 29—	Newcastle U.	A
1980		
Jan. 1—	Fulham	H
Jan. 12—	Orient	H
Feb. 2—	Wrexham	A
Feb. 9—	Birmingham C.	H
Feb. 16—	Shrewsbury T.	H
Feb. 23—	Watford	A
Mar. 1—	Cambridge U.	H
Mar. 8—	Cardiff C.	A
Mar. 15—	Sunderland	H
Mar. 22—	Oldham Ath.	A
Mar. 29—	Chelsea	H
Apr. 4—	Notts Co.	A
Apr. 5—	Q.P.R.	H
Apr. 8—	Fulham	A
Apr. 12—	West Ham U.	A
Apr. 19—	Leicester C.	H
Apr. 26—	Swansea C.	A
May 3—	Swansea C.	H

CHELSEA

Date 1979	Opponents	Ground
Aug. 18—	Sunderland	A
Aug. 22—	West Ham U.	H
Aug. 25—	Wrexham	A
Sept. 1—	Newcastle U.	H
Sept. 8—	Shrewsbury T.	A
Sept. 15—	Watford	H
Sept. 22—	Cambridge U.	A
Sept. 29—	Watford	H
Oct. 6—	Burnley	A
Oct. 10—	West Ham U.	H
Oct. 13—	Bristol R.	A
Oct. 20—	Cardiff C.	A
Oct. 27—	Q.P.R.	H
Nov. 3—	Sunderland	H
Nov. 10—	Orient	A
Nov. 17—	Charlton Ath.	H
Nov. 24—	Notts Co.	A
Dec. 1—	P.N.E.	H
Dec. 8—	Oldham Ath.	A
Dec. 15—	Swansea C.	H
Dec. 21—	Q.P.R.	A
Dec. 26—	Leicester C.	H
Dec. 29—	Wrexham	H
1980		
Jan. 1—	Luton T.	A
Jan. 12—	Newcastle U.	A
Jan. 19—	Birmingham C.	H
Feb. 2—	Shrewsbury T.	H
Feb. 9—	Watford	A
Feb. 16—	Cambridge U.	H
Feb. 23—	Bristol R.	A
Mar. 1—	P.N.E.	A
Mar. 8—	Fulham	H
Mar. 14—	Orient	A
Mar. 22—	Orient	H
Mar. 29—	Charlton Ath.	A
Apr. 4—	Leicester C.	A
Apr. 5—	Q.P.R.	H
Apr. 12—	P.N.E.	H
Apr. 19—	Notts Co.	A
Apr. 26—	Swansea C.	H
May 3—	Oldham Ath.	H

FULHAM

Date 1979	Opponents	Ground
Aug. 18—	Birmingham C.	A
Aug. 22—	Orient	H
Aug. 25—	Sunderland	A
Sept. 1—	P.N.E.	H
Sept. 8—	Q.P.R.	A
Sept. 15—	Burnley	H
Sept. 22—	Leicester C.	A
Sept. 29—	Luton T.	H
Oct. 6—	Wrexham	A
Oct. 9—	Orient	H
Oct. 13—	Swansea C.	A
Oct. 20—	Notts Co.	H
Oct. 27—	Chelsea	A
Nov. 3—	Birmingham C.	H
Nov. 10—	West Ham U.	A
Nov. 17—	Oldham Ath.	H
Nov. 24—	Watford	A
Dec. 1—	Shrewsbury T.	H
Dec. 8—	Cambridge U.	A
Dec. 15—	Bristol R.	H
Dec. 21—	Cardiff C.	A
Dec. 29—	Sunderland	H
1980		
Jan. 1—	Charlton Ath.	A
Jan. 12—	Newcastle U.	H
Feb. 2—	Burnley	A
Feb. 9—	Luton T.	A
Feb. 16—	Swansea C.	H
Feb. 23—	Bristol R.	A
Mar. 1—	Chelsea	A
Mar. 8—	West Ham U.	H
Mar. 22—	West Ham U.	A
Mar. 29—	Orient	A
Apr. 4—	Cardiff C.	H
Apr. 5—	Leicester C.	A
Apr. 8—	Charlton Ath.	H
Apr. 12—	Newcastle U.	A
Apr. 19—	Watford	H
Apr. 26—	Cambridge U.	A
May 3—	Shrewsbury T.	H

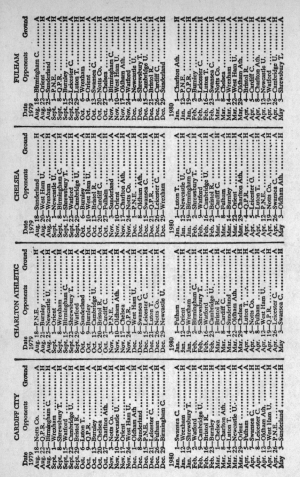

LEICESTER CITY

Date 1979	Opponents	Ground
Aug. 18	Watford	H
Aug. 21	Cambridge U.	A
Aug. 25	Q.P.R.	H
Sept. 1	Luton T.	A
Sept. 8	Notts Co.	H
Sept. 15	Newcastle U.	A
Sept. 22	Fulham	H
Sept. 29	Swansea	A
Oct. 6	Shrewsbury T.	A
Oct. 10	Cambridge U.	H
Oct. 13	West Ham U.	H
Oct. 20	Fulham	A
Oct. 27	Sunderland	H
Nov. 3	Watford	A
Nov. 10	Burnley	H
Nov. 17	P.N.E.	A
Nov. 24	Wrexham	H
Dec. 1	Birmingham C.	A
Dec. 8	Orient	H
Dec. 15	Cardiff C.	A
Dec. 22	Chelsea	H
Dec. 26	Q.P.R.	A
Dec. 29	Q.P.R.	A
1980		
Jan. 1	Bristol R.	H
Jan. 12	Notts Co.	A
Jan. 19	Cambridge U.	A
Feb. 2	Newcastle U.	H
Feb. 9	Fulham	A
Feb. 23	West Ham U.	H
Mar. 1	Oldham Ath.	A
Mar. 8	Sunderland	H
Mar. 15	Shrewsbury T.	A
Mar. 22	Burnley	H
Mar. 29	P.N.E.	A
Apr. 5	Chelsea	H
Apr. 8	Bristol R.	A
Apr. 12	Birmingham C.	H
Apr. 19	Wrexham	A
Apr. 26	Orient	H
May 3	Orient	A

LUTON TOWN

Date 1979	Opponents	Ground
Aug. 18	Cambridge U.	H
Aug. 21	Bristol R.	A
Aug. 25	Orient	H
Sept. 1	Leicester C.	H
Sept. 8	Swansea C.	A
Sept. 15	Notts Co.	H
Sept. 22	Oldham Ath.	A
Sept. 29	Fulham	H
Oct. 6	Cardiff C.	A
Oct. 9	Bristol R.	H
Oct. 13	Sunderland U.	H
Oct. 20	Watford	A
Oct. 27	P.N.E.	H
Nov. 3	Cambridge U.	A
Nov. 10	Burnley	H
Nov. 17	Wrexham	A
Dec. 1	Birmingham C.	H
Dec. 8	Newcastle U.	A
Dec. 15	Orient	A
Dec. 21	Charlton Ath.	H
Dec. 26	Watford	A
Dec. 29	Orient	H
1980		
Jan. 1	Chelsea	A
Jan. 12	Leicester C.	A
Jan. 18	Swansea C.	H
Feb. 2	Oldham Ath.	A
Feb. 9	Fulham	H
Feb. 23	Sunderland	A
Mar. 1	West Ham U.	H
Mar. 8	Cardiff C.	A
Mar. 15	Cardiff C.	H
Mar. 22	Q.P.R.	A
Mar. 29	Burnley Ath.	H
Apr. 4	Watford	A
Apr. 5	Chelsea	H
Apr. 12	Shrewsbury T.	A
Apr. 19	Birmingham C.	H
Apr. 26	Q.P.R.	A
May 3	Newcastle U.	H

NEWCASTLE UNITED

Date 1979	Opponents	Ground
Aug. 18	Oldham Ath.	H
Aug. 21	P.N.E.	A
Aug. 25	Charlton Ath.	A
Sept. 1	Chelsea	H
Sept. 8	Orient	A
Sept. 15	Leicester C.	H
Sept. 22	Wrexham	A
Sept. 29	Birmingham C.	H
Oct. 6	West Ham U.	A
Oct. 10	P.N.E.	H
Oct. 13	Shrewsbury T.	A
Oct. 20	Watford	H
Oct. 27	Cambridge U.	A
Nov. 3	Oldham Ath.	H
Nov. 10	Cardiff	A
Nov. 17	Fulham	H
Nov. 24	Swansea C.	A
Dec. 1	Fulham	A
Dec. 8	Q.P.R.	H
Dec. 15	Q.P.R.	A
Dec. 21	Charlton Ath.	H
Dec. 26	Burnley	A
Dec. 29	Charlton Ath.	H
1980		
Jan. 1	Sunderland	H
Jan. 12	Chelsea	A
Jan. 19	Orient	H
Feb. 2	Leicester C.	A
Feb. 9	Wrexham	H
Feb. 16	Birmingham C.	A
Feb. 23	Watford	H
Mar. 1	Cambridge U.	A
Mar. 8	West Ham U.	H
Mar. 14	Cardiff C.	A
Mar. 22	Cardiff C.	H
Mar. 29	P.N.E.	A
Apr. 5	Sunderland	A
Apr. 7	Fulham	H
Apr. 12	Swansea C.	A
Apr. 19	Q.P.R.	H
Apr. 26	Q.P.R.	A
May 3	Luton T.	A

NOTTS. COUNTY

Date 1979	Opponents	Ground
Aug. 18	Cardiff C.	H
Aug. 25	Shrewsbury T.	A
Sept. 1	Q.P.R.	H
Sept. 8	Leicester C.	A
Sept. 15	Luton T.	A
Sept. 22	Swansea C.	H
Sept. 29	Wrexham	A
Oct. 6	Bristol R.	H
Oct. 13	Birmingham C.	A
Oct. 20	Fulham	H
Oct. 27	West Ham U.	A
Nov. 3	Cardiff C.	H
Nov. 10	Watford	A
Nov. 17	Sunderland	H
Dec. 1	Chelsea	A
Dec. 8	Watford	H
Dec. 15	Orient	A
Dec. 15	Newcastle U.	H
Dec. 22	Charlton Ath.	A
Dec. 26	Burnley	H
1980		
Jan. 1	Cambridge U.	H
Jan. 12	Q.P.R.	A
Jan. 19	Leicester C.	H
Feb. 2	Luton T.	A
Feb. 9	Wrexham	H
Feb. 23	Birmingham C.	A
Mar. 1	Charlton Ath.	H
Mar. 8	Cambridge U.	A
Mar. 14	Fulham	H
Mar. 22	Bristol R.	A
Mar. 29	Sunderland U.	H
Apr. 5	Charlton Ath.	A
Apr. 8	Cambridge U.	H
Apr. 12	Watford	H
Apr. 19	Birmingham C.	A
Apr. 26	Orient	H
May 3	Birmingham C.	A

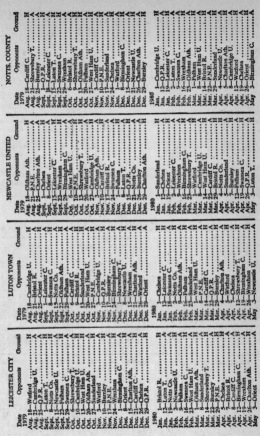

228

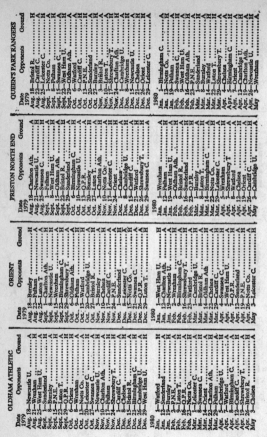

OLDHAM ATHLETIC

Date 1979	Opponents	Ground
Aug. 18	Newcastle U.	A
Aug. 21	Wrexham	H
Aug. 25	West Ham U.	H
Sept. 1	Sunderland	A
Sept. 8	Burnley	H
Sept. 15	P.N.E.	A
Sept. 22	Luton T.	H
Sept. 29	Q.P.R.	A
Oct. 6	Orient	H
Oct. 9	Wrexham	A
Oct. 13	Notts Co.	A
Oct. 20	Leicester C.	H
Oct. 27	Swansea C.	A
Nov. 3	Newcastle U.	H
Nov. 10	Charlton Ath.	A
Nov. 17	Fulham	H
Nov. 24	Shrewsbury T.	A
Dec. 1	Cardiff C.	H
Dec. 8	Chelsea	A
Dec. 15	Birmingham C.	H
Dec. 26	Cambridge U.	A
Dec. 29	West Ham U.	A
1980		
Jan. 1	Watford	H
Jan. 12	Sunderland	H
Jan. 19	Burnley	A
Feb. 2	P.N.E.	H
Feb. 9	Q.P.R.	H
Feb. 16	Notts Co.	A
Feb. 23	Leicester C.	H
Mar. 1	Swansea C.	A
Mar. 8	Orient	A
Mar. 22	Charlton Ath.	H
Mar. 29	Fulham	A
Apr. 5	Cambridge U.	H
Apr. 7	Birmingham C.	A
Apr. 12	Cardiff C.	A
Apr. 19	Shrewsbury T.	H
Apr. 26	Bristol R.	A
May 3	Chelsea	H

ORIENT

Date 1979	Opponents	Ground
Aug. 18	Burnley	A
Aug. 22	Fulham	H
Aug. 25	Luton T.	A
Sept. 1	Charlton Ath.	H
Sept. 8	Newcastle U.	H
Sept. 15	Wrexham	A
Sept. 22	Birmingham C.	H
Sept. 29	Shrewsbury T.	A
Oct. 6	Oldham Ath.	A
Oct. 9	Fulham	A
Oct. 13	Watford	H
Oct. 20	Cambridge U.	A
Oct. 27	Bristol R.	H
Nov. 3	Burnley	H
Nov. 10	Chelsea	A
Nov. 17	Cardiff C.	H
Nov. 24	Q.P.R.	A
Dec. 1	Sunderland	A
Dec. 8	Leicester C.	H
Dec. 15	Notts Co.	A
Dec. 22	Swansea C.	H
Dec. 26	Q.P.R.	H
Dec. 29	Luton T.	H
1980		
Jan. 1	West Ham U.	A
Jan. 19	Newcastle U.	A
Feb. 2	Wrexham	H
Feb. 9	Birmingham C.	A
Feb. 16	Shrewsbury T.	H
Feb. 23	Watford	A
Mar. 1	Bristol R.	A
Mar. 8	Oldham Ath.	H
Mar. 22	Chelsea	A
Mar. 29	Cardiff C.	H
Apr. 1	Swansea C.	A
Apr. 5	Cambridge U.	H
Apr. 8	Q.P.R.	H
Apr. 12	Sunderland	H
Apr. 19	P.N.E.	A
Apr. 26	Notts Co.	A
May 3	Leicester C.	H

PRESTON NORTH END

Date 1979	Opponents	Ground
Aug. 18	Charlton Ath.	H
Aug. 21	Newcastle U.	A
Aug. 25	Swansea C.	H
Sept. 1	Fulham	A
Sept. 8	West Ham U.	H
Sept. 15	Oldham Ath.	H
Sept. 22	Bristol R.	A
Sept. 29	Sunderland	A
Oct. 6	Wrexham	H
Oct. 10	Newcastle U.	H
Oct. 13	Q.P.R.	A
Oct. 20	Burnley	H
Oct. 27	Luton T.	A
Nov. 3	Charlton Ath.	A
Nov. 10	Notts Co.	H
Nov. 17	Leicester C.	A
Nov. 24	Cambridge U.	H
Dec. 1	Chelsea	A
Dec. 8	Cardiff C.	H
Dec. 15	Cardiff C.	A
Dec. 22	Birmingham C.	H
Dec. 26	Shrewsbury T.	H
Dec. 29	Swansea C.	A
1980		
Jan. 1	Wrexham	A
Jan. 12	West Ham U.	A
Jan. 19	Oldham Ath.	A
Feb. 2	Bristol R.	H
Feb. 9	Sunderland	H
Feb. 16	Q.P.R.	A
Mar. 1	Burnley	A
Mar. 8	Luton T.	H
Mar. 14	Birmingham C.	A
Mar. 22	Notts Co.	A
Mar. 29	Leicester C.	H
Apr. 5	Shrewsbury T.	A
Apr. 7	Watford	H
Apr. 12	Chelsea	H
Apr. 19	Orient	H
Apr. 26	Cardiff C.	A
May 3	Cambridge U.	A

QUEEN'S PARK RANGERS

Date 1979	Opponents	Ground
Aug. 18	Bristol R.	H
Aug. 22	Leicester C.	A
Aug. 25	Notts Co.	H
Sept. 1	Fulham	A
Sept. 8	Swansea C.	H
Sept. 15	Swansea C.	A
Sept. 22	West Ham U.	H
Sept. 29	Oldham Ath.	H
Oct. 6	Watford	A
Oct. 9	Cardiff C.	H
Oct. 13	P.N.E.	H
Oct. 20	Sunderland	A
Oct. 27	Burnley	H
Nov. 3	Bristol R.	A
Nov. 10	Luton T.	A
Nov. 17	Charlton Ath.	H
Nov. 24	Newcastle U.	A
Dec. 1	Swansea C.	H
Dec. 8	Wrexham	H
Dec. 15	Newcastle U.	A
Dec. 22	Chelsea	A
Dec. 26	Leicester C.	H
1980		
Jan. 1	Birmingham C.	A
Jan. 12	Notts Co.	A
Jan. 19	Swansea C.	H
Feb. 2	Birmingham C.	H
Feb. 9	West Ham U.	A
Feb. 16	Oldham Ath.	A
Mar. 1	Watford	H
Mar. 8	Burnley	A
Mar. 14	Watford	H
Mar. 22	Luton T.	H
Mar. 29	Shrewsbury T.	A
Apr. 4	Chelsea	H
Apr. 5	Birmingham C.	A
Apr. 7	Orient	A
Apr. 12	Orient	H
Apr. 19	Cardiff C.	A
Apr. 26	Charlton Ath.	H
May 3	Wrexham	A

SHREWSBURY TOWN

Date 1979	Opponents	Ground
Aug. 18—Swansea C.		H
Aug. 21—Notts Co.		A
Aug. 25—Bristol R.		H
Sept. 1—Cambridge U.		A
Sept. 8—Cardiff C.		H
Sept. 15—Chelsea		A
Sept. 22—Charlton Ath.		H
Sept. 29—Orient		A
Oct. 6—Watford		A
Oct. 13—Leicester C.		H
Oct. 20—Newcastle U.		A
Oct. 27—Birmingham C.		H
Nov. 3—Swansea C.		A
Nov. 10—Watford		H
Nov. 17—Q.P.R.		A
Nov. 24—Luton T.		H
Dec. 1—West Ham U.		A
Dec. 8—Fulham		H
Dec. 15—West Ham U.		A
Dec. 21—Sunderland		H
Dec. 26—P.N.E.		A
Dec. 29—Bristol R.		A
1980		
Jan. 1—Burnley		A
Jan. 12—Cardiff C.		H
Jan. 19—Chelsea		A
Feb. 2—Charlton Ath.		H
Feb. 9—Orient		A
Feb. 16—Newcastle U.		H
Feb. 23—Wrexham		A
Mar. 1—Leicester C.		H
Mar. 8—Birmingham C.		A
Mar. 15—Q.P.R.		H
Mar. 22—Watford		A
Mar. 29—Q.P.R.		A
Apr. 1—Burnley		H
Apr. 5—P.N.E.		H
Apr. 8—Sunderland		A
Apr. 12—Luton T.		A
Apr. 19—West Ham U.		H
May 3—Fulham		A

SUNDERLAND

Date 1979	Opponents	Ground
Aug. 18—Chelsea		A
Aug. 22—Birmingham C.		H
Aug. 25—Fulham		H
Sept. 1—Oldham Ath.		A
Sept. 8—Cambridge U.		H
Sept. 15—West Ham U.		A
Sept. 22—Burnley		H
Sept. 29—Charlton Ath.		A
Oct. 6—Charlton Ath.		H
Oct. 9—Birmingham C.		A
Oct. 13—Q.P.R.		H
Oct. 20—Leicester C.		A
Oct. 27—Chelsea		H
Nov. 3—Chelsea		A
Nov. 10—Notts Co.		H
Nov. 17—Bristol R.		A
Nov. 24—Orient		H
Dec. 1—Orient		A
Dec. 8—Watford		H
Dec. 15—West Ham U.		H
Dec. 21—Shrewsbury T.		A
Dec. 26—Wrexham		H
Dec. 29—Fulham		A
1980		
Jan. 1—Newcastle U.		A
Jan. 12—Oldham Ath.		H
Jan. 19—Cambridge U.		A
Feb. 2—West Ham U.		H
Feb. 9—Burnley		A
Feb. 16—P.N.E.		H
Feb. 23—Luton T.		A
Mar. 1—Q.P.R.		H
Mar. 8—Cambridge U.		H
Mar. 14—Charlton Ath.		A
Mar. 22—Swansea C.		H
Mar. 28—Notts Co.		A
Apr. 4—Orient		H
Apr. 5—Shrewsbury T.		H
Apr. 7—Wrexham		A
Apr. 8—Shrewsbury T.		H
Apr. 12—Orient		A
Apr. 19—Bristol R.		H
Apr. 26—Sunderland		A
May 3—Cardiff C.		A

SWANSEA CITY

Date 1979	Opponents	Ground
Aug. 18—Shrewsbury T.		A
Aug. 21—Watford		H
Aug. 25—P.N.E.		A
Sept. 1—Burnley		H
Sept. 4—Luton T.		A
Sept. 8—Q.P.R.		H
Sept. 15—Notts Co.		A
Sept. 22—Leicester C.		H
Sept. 29—Cambridge U.		A
Oct. 6—Cambridge U.		H
Oct. 13—Watford		A
Oct. 20—Birmingham C.		H
Oct. 27—Oldham Ath.		A
Nov. 3—Shrewsbury T.		H
Nov. 10—Sunderland		A
Nov. 17—West Ham U.		H
Nov. 24—Newcastle U.		A
Dec. 1—Charlton Ath.		H
Dec. 8—Chelsea		A
Dec. 15—Chelsea		H
Dec. 21—Bristol R.		A
Dec. 29—P.N.E.		H
1980		
Jan. 1—Cardiff C.		H
Jan. 12—Luton T.		H
Feb. 2—Q.P.R.		A
Feb. 9—Notts Co.		H
Feb. 16—Leicester C.		A
Feb. 23—Birmingham C.		H
Mar. 1—Oldham Ath.		A
Mar. 8—Cambridge U.		H
Mar. 14—Sunderland		H
Mar. 22—Sunderland		A
Mar. 28—Newcastle U.		H
Apr. 4—Orient		A
Apr. 5—Bristol R.		H
Apr. 7—Cardiff C.		A
Apr. 12—Newcastle U.		A
Apr. 19—Fulham		H
Apr. 26—Chelsea		A
May 3—Charlton Ath.		A

WATFORD

Date 1979	Opponents	Ground
Aug. 18—Leicester C.		A
Aug. 25—Swansea C.		H
Sept. 1—West Ham U.		A
Sept. 8—Bristol R.		H
Sept. 15—Cardiff C.		A
Sept. 22—Chelsea		H
Sept. 29—Charlton Ath.		A
Oct. 6—Q.P.R.		H
Oct. 13—Orient		A
Oct. 20—Newcastle U.		H
Nov. 10—Shrewsbury T.		A
Nov. 17—Birmingham C.		H
Nov. 24—Fulham		A
Dec. 8—Sunderland		H
Dec. 15—Sunderland		A
Dec. 21—P.N.E.		H
Dec. 26—P.N.E.		A
Dec. 29—Cambridge U.		H
1980		
Jan. 1—Oldham Ath.		H
Jan. 12—West Ham U.		H
Feb. 2—Cardiff C.		A
Feb. 9—Notts Co.		H
Feb. 16—Charlton Ath.		A
Feb. 23—Birmingham C.		H
Mar. 8—Wrexham		A
Mar. 15—Q.P.R.		H
Mar. 22—Birmingham C.		A
Mar. 29—Luton T.		A
Apr. 5—Oldham Ath.		A
Apr. 7—Cardiff C.		H
Apr. 8—Charlton Ath.		H
Apr. 19—Notts Co.		A
Apr. 22—Fulham		H
Apr. 26—Sunderland		H
May 3—Burnley		H

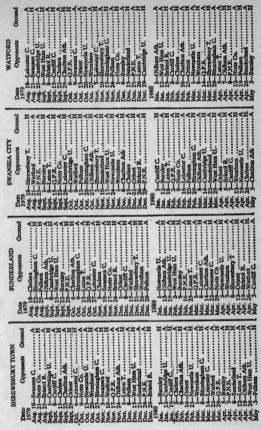

230

WEST HAM UNITED		
Date 1979	Opponents	Ground
Aug. 18	Wrexham	A
Aug. 20	Chelsea	H
Aug. 25	Oldham Ath.	H
Sept. 1	Watford	A
Sept. 8	P.N.E.	H
Sept. 15	Sunderland	A
Sept. 22	Q.P.R.	H
Sept. 29	Burnley	A
Oct. 6	Newcastle U.	H
Oct. 10	Chelsea	A
Oct. 13	Leicester C.	A
Oct. 20	Luton T.	H
Oct. 27	Notts Co.	A
Nov. 3	Wrexham	H
Nov. 10	Fulham	H
Nov. 17	Swansea C.	A
Nov. 24	Cardiff C.	H
Dec. 1	Charlton Ath.	A
Dec. 8	Bristol R.	H
Dec. 21	Shrewsbury T.	A
Dec. 26	Cambridge U.	H
Dec. 28	Birmingham C.	H
Dec. 29	Oldham Ath.	A
1980		
Jan. 1	Orient	H
Jan. 12	Watford	H
Jan. 19	P.N.E.	A
Feb. 2	Sunderland	H
Feb. 9	Q.P.R.	A
Feb. 23	Leicester C.	H
Mar. 1	Luton T.	A
Mar. 8	Notts Co.	H
Mar. 22	Newcastle U.	A
Mar. 29	Swansea	H
Apr. 2	Cambridge U.	A
Apr. 5	Fulham	A
Apr. 7	Birmingham C.	H
Apr. 12	Charlton Ath.	H
Apr. 19	Cardiff C.	A
Apr. 26	Shrewsbury T.	H
May 3	Bristol R.	A

WREXHAM		
Date 1979	Opponents	Ground
Aug. 18	West Ham U.	H
Aug. 21	Oldham Ath.	A
Aug. 25	Chelsea	A
Sept. 1	Cardiff C.	H
Sept. 8	Charlton Ath.	A
Sept. 15	Orient	H
Sept. 22	Newcastle U.	A
Sept. 29	Notts Co.	H
Oct. 6	Fulham	A
Oct. 8	Oldham Ath.	H
Oct. 13	Birmingham C.	A
Oct. 20	Shrewsbury T.	H
Oct.	Watford	A
Nov. 3	West Ham U.	A
Nov. 10	Bristol R.	H
Nov. 17	Cambridge U.	A
Nov. 24	Leicester C.	A
Dec. 1	Swansea C.	H
Dec. 8	Luton T.	A
Dec. 15	Burnley	H
Dec. 21	Q.P.R.	A
Dec. 26	Sunderland	A
Dec. 29	Chelsea	H
1980		
Jan. 1	P.N.E.	H
Jan. 12	Cardiff C.	A
Jan. 19	Charlton Ath.	H
Feb. 2	Orient	A
Feb. 9	Newcastle U.	H
Feb. 16	Notts Co.	A
Feb. 23	Birmingham C.	H
Mar. 1	Shrewsbury T.	A
Mar. 8	Watford	H
Mar. 14	Fulham	H
Mar. 22	Bristol R.	A
Mar. 29	Cambridge U.	H
Apr. 4	Burnley	A
Apr. 5	P.N.E.	A
Apr. 7	Sunderland	H
Apr. 12	Swansea C.	A
Apr. 19	Leicester C.	H
May 3	Q.P.R.	A

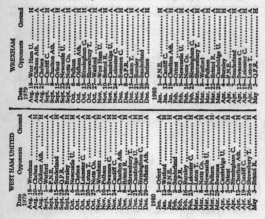

BARNSLEY

Date 1979	Opponents	Ground
Aug. 18	Sheffield Wed.	H
Aug. 21	Chesterfield	A
Aug. 25	Blackpool	H
Sept. 1	Oxford U.	A
Sept. 8	Mansfield T.	H
Sept. 15	Sheffield U.	A
Sept. 18	Colchester U.	A
Sept. 22	Millwall	H
Sept. 29	Colchester U.	H
Oct. 2	Blackburn R.	A
Oct. 6	Carlisle U.	H
Oct. 9	Chesterfield	A
Oct. 20	Carlisle U.	H
Oct. 23	Bury	A
Oct. 27	Sheffield Wed.	A
Nov. 3	Sheffield Wed.	H
Nov. 6	Hull C.	H
Nov. 10	Hull C.	A
Dec. 1	Southend U.	H
Dec. 8	Plymouth Argyle	A
Dec. 21	Brentford	H
Dec. 26	Brentford	A
Dec. 29	Reading	A
1980		
Jan. 1	Rotherham U.	H
Jan. 5	Wimbledon	A
Jan. 19	Mansfield T.	H
Jan. 26	Oxford U.	H
Feb. 2	Sheffield U.	A
Feb. 9	Colchester U.	A
Feb. 23	Gillingham	H
Mar. 1	Carlisle U.	A
Mar. 14	Brentford	A
Mar. 22	Exeter C.	H
Mar. 29	Hull C.	H
Apr. 1	Grimsby T.	A
Apr. 5	Rotherham U.	A
Apr. 7	Mansfield T.	A
Apr. 12	Wimbledon	H
Apr. 15	Exeter C.	A
Apr. 19	Oxford U.	H
Apr. 26	Plymouth Argyle	H
May	Swindon T.	A

BLACKBURN ROVERS

Date 1979	Opponents	Ground
Aug. 18	Millwall	A
Aug. 21	Carlisle U.	H
Aug. 25	Sheffield Wed.	H
Sept. 1	Grimsby T.	A
Sept. 8	Wimbledon	H
Sept. 15	Southend U.	A
Sept. 18	Blackpool	H
Sept. 22	Blackpool	A
Sept. 29	Rotherham U.	H
Oct. 2	Barnsley	H
Oct. 6	Gillingham	A
Oct. 10	Carlisle U.	A
Oct. 20	Brentford	A
Oct. 23	Colchester U.	H
Oct. 27	Millwall	H
Nov. 3	Millwall	A
Nov. 6	Chester	H
Nov. 10	Swindon T.	H
Dec. 1	Southend U.	H
Dec. 8	Oxford U.	A
Dec. 21	Plymouth Argyle	H
Dec. 26	Brentford	H
Dec. 29	Bury	A
1980		
Jan. 1	Sheffield U.	A
Jan. 12	Exeter C.	H
Jan. 19	Wimbledon	A
Jan. 26	Sheffield Wed.	A
Feb. 2	Oxford U.	A
Feb. 9	Southend U.	H
Feb. 16	Rotherham U.	A
Feb. 23	Plymouth Argyle	H
Mar. 1	Brentford	H
Mar. 8	Gillingham	A
Mar. 14	Gillingham	H
Mar. 22	Chesterfield	A
Mar. 29	Swindon T.	A
Apr. 1	Mansfield T.	H
Apr. 5	Sheffield U.	H
Apr. 12	Exeter C.	A
Apr. 15	Exeter C.	H
Apr. 22	Oxford U.	A
May	Bury	H

BLACKPOOL

Date 1979	Opponents	Ground
Aug. 18	Gillingham	H
Aug. 21	Carlisle U.	A
Aug. 25	Barnsley	A
Sept. 1	Wimbledon	H
Sept. 8	Brentford	A
Sept. 15	Rotherham U.	H
Sept. 18	Blackburn R.	A
Sept. 22	Blackburn R.	H
Sept. 29	Plymouth Argyle	A
Oct. 2	Sheffield U.	H
Oct. 10	Bury	A
Oct. 20	Colchester U.	H
Oct. 23	Swindon T.	A
Oct. 27	Brentford	H
Nov. 3	Gillingham	A
Nov. 6	Chesterfield Wed.	H
Nov. 17	Millwall	A
Dec. 1	Mansfield T.	H
Dec. 8	Reading	A
Dec. 21	Southend U.	H
Dec. 26	Hull C.	A
Dec. 29	Chester	H
1980		
Jan. 1	Carlisle U.	H
Jan. 12	Oxford U.	A
Jan. 19	Wimbledon	A
Jan. 26	Southend U.	H
Feb. 2	Rotherham U.	A
Feb. 9	Blackburn R.	H
Feb. 16	Brentford	A
Feb. 23	Colchester U.	H
Mar. 1	Exeter C.	A
Mar. 14	Gillingham	H
Mar. 22	Millwall	A
Mar. 29	Mansfield T.	H
Apr. 5	Hull C.	A
Apr. 7	Carlisle U.	H
Apr. 12	Oxford U.	H
Apr. 15	Bury	A
Apr. 22	Reading	H
May 3	Chester	A

BRENTFORD

Date 1979	Opponents	Ground
Aug. 18	Reading	A
Aug. 21	Carlisle U.	H
Aug. 25	Swindon T.	A
Sept. 1	Chesterfield	H
Sept. 8	Sheffield Wed.	A
Sept. 15	Grimsby T.	H
Sept. 18	Bury	H
Sept. 22	Wimbledon	A
Sept. 25	Blackburn R.	H
Sept. 29	Southend U.	H
Oct. 2	Exeter C.	A
Oct. 6	Oxford U.	H
Oct. 10	Oxford U.	A
Oct. 13	Blackpool	A
Oct. 20	Blackburn R.	H
Oct. 23	Sheffield U.	A
Oct. 27	Plymouth Argyle	H
Nov. 3	Reading	A
Nov. 6	Rotherham U.	A
Nov. 17	Rotherham U.	H
Dec. 1	Carlisle U.	H
Dec. 8	Hull C.	A
Dec. 21	Barnsley	A
Dec. 26	Chester	H
Dec. 29	Swindon T.	H
1980		
Jan. 1	Mansfield T.	A
Jan. 5	Gillingham	H
Jan. 12	Sheffield U.	A
Jan. 19	Sheffield Wed.	H
Jan. 26	Millwall	A
Feb. 2	Grimsby T.	A
Feb. 9	Southend U.	A
Feb. 23	Blackpool	H
Mar. 1	Blackburn R.	A
Mar. 8	Colchester U.	H
Mar. 14	Barnsley	H
Mar. 22	Colchester U.	A
Mar. 29	Rotherham U.	H
Apr. 5	Bury	A
Apr. 7	Gillingham	A
Apr. 12	Oxford U.	H
Apr. 19	Gillingham	A
Apr. 22	Hull C.	H
Apr. 26	Hull C.	A
May 3	Millwall	H

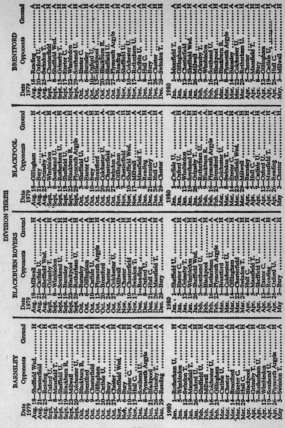

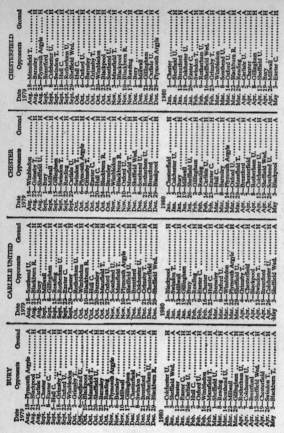

BURY

Date 1979	Opponents	Ground
Aug. 18	Plymouth Argyle	A
Aug. 25	Oxford U.	H
Sept. 1	Carlisle U.	H
Sept. 4	Chester	A
Sept. 8	Exeter C.	A
Sept. 15	Reading	H
Sept. 18	Grimsby T.	A
Sept. 22	Oxford U.	A
Sept. 29	Wimbledon U.	H
Oct. 6	Southend U.	A
Oct. 10	Blackpool	H
Oct. 13	Mansfield T.	A
Oct. 20	Sheffield U.	H
Oct. 23	Barnsley	A
Oct. 27	Reading	A
Nov. 3	Plymouth Argyle	H
Nov. 10	Millwall	A
Nov. 17	Gillingham	H
Dec. 1	Chesterfield	A
Dec. 8	Southend U.	H
Dec. 22	Rotherham U.	H
Dec. 26	Blackburn R.	A
1980		
Jan. 5	Colchester U.	H
Jan. 12	Sheffield Wed.	A
Jan. 19	Chester	H
Jan. 26	Exeter C.	H
Feb. 5	Halifax U.	A
Feb. 9	Oxford U.	H
Feb. 16	Wimbledon	A
Feb. 23	Mansfield T.	H
Mar. 1	Reading	A
Mar. 8	Southend U.	H
Mar. 15	Millwall	A
Mar. 22	Rotherham U.	H
Apr. 5	Colchester U.	A
Apr. 7	Brentford	H
Apr. 8	Rotherham Wed.	A
Apr. 19	Chesterfield	H
Apr. 26	Swindon T.	A
May 3	Blackburn T.	A

CARLISLE UNITED

Date 1979	Opponents	Ground
Aug. 18	Southend U.	H
Aug. 25	Blackburn R.	A
Sept. 1	Bury	A
Sept. 4	Millwall	H
Sept. 8	Gillingham	A
Sept. 15	Reading	H
Sept. 18	Rotherham U.	A
Sept. 22	Exeter C.	H
Sept. 29	Chester	A
Oct. 6	Rotherham U.	H
Oct. 10	Blackburn R.	A
Oct. 13	Hull C.	A
Oct. 20	Barnsley	H
Oct. 27	Oxford U.	A
Nov. 3	Southend U.	H
Nov. 10	Mansfield T.	A
Nov. 17	Sheffield U.	H
Dec. 1	Brentford	A
Dec. 8	Colchester U.	H
Dec. 22	Chesterfield	A
Dec. 29	Sheffield Wed.	H
1980		
Jan. 5	Blackpool	H
Jan. 12	Millwall	A
Jan. 19	Gillingham	H
Jan. 26	Bury	A
Feb. 5	Exeter C.	A
Feb. 9	Chester	H
Feb. 16	Hull C.	A
Mar. 1	Barnsley	H
Mar. 8	Wimbledon	A
Mar. 15	Plymouth Argyle	H
Mar. 22	Sheffield U.	A
Mar. 29	Chesterfield	H
Apr. 5	Reading	A
Apr. 8	Swindon T.	H
Apr. 12	Chester	H
Apr. 19	Colchester U.	A
Apr. 26	Southend U.	H
May 3	Sheffield Wed.	A

CHESTER

Date 1979	Opponents	Ground
Aug. 18	Wimbledon	H
Aug. 22	Grimsby T.	A
Aug. 25	Oxford U.	H
Sept. 1	Bury	A
Sept. 4	Millwall	H
Sept. 15	Gillingham	H
Sept. 18	Exeter C.	A
Sept. 22	Reading	A
Sept. 29	Carlisle U.	H
Oct. 3	Swindon T.	A
Oct. 6	Grimsby T.	H
Oct. 13	Exeter C.	A
Oct. 20	Hull C.	H
Oct. 23	Barnsley	A
Nov. 3	Wimbledon	H
Nov. 10	Blackburn R.	A
Nov. 17	Mansfield U.	H
Dec. 1	Sheffield Wed.	A
Dec. 8	Southend U.	H
Dec. 22	Brentford	A
Dec. 29	Bishopcol	H
1980		
Jan. 5	Chesterfield	H
Jan. 12	Colchester U.	A
Jan. 19	Colchester U.	H
Jan. 26	Sheffield U.	A
Feb. 2	Swindon T.	A
Feb. 9	Carlisle U.	A
Feb. 23	Exeter C.	H
Mar. 1	Hull C.	A
Mar. 8	Plymouth Argyle	H
Mar. 14	Mansfield U.	A
Mar. 29	Mansfield U.	H
Apr. 5	Chesterfield	A
Apr. 8	Rotherham U.	H
Apr. 12	Colchester U.	A
Apr. 19	Southend U.	H
May 3	Blackpool	A

CHESTERFIELD

Date 1979	Opponents	Ground
Aug. 18	Mansfield T.	A
Aug. 21	Barnsley	H
Aug. 25	Plymouth Argyle	A
Sept. 1	Bury	H
Sept. 8	Colchester U.	A
Sept. 15	Swindon U.	H
Sept. 18	Swindon U.	A
Sept. 22	Rotherham U.	A
Sept. 29	Sheffield Wed.	A
Oct. 2	Hull C.	H
Oct. 6	Oxford U.	A
Oct. 13	Grimsby T.	H
Oct. 20	Wimbledon	A
Oct. 23	Southend U.	H
Nov. 3	Mansfield T.	A
Nov. 7	Blackpool	H
Nov. 10	Bury	A
Nov. 24	Gillingham	H
Dec. 1	Millwall	A
Dec. 8	Gillingham	H
Dec. 22	Carlisle U.	H
Dec. 29	Plymouth Argyle	A
1980		
Jan. 5	Chester	A
Jan. 12	Sheffield U.	H
Jan. 19	Colchester U.	H
Jan. 26	Exeter C.	A
Feb. 2	Swindon T.	A
Feb. 9	Carlisle U.	H
Feb. 23	Sheffield Wed.	H
Mar. 1	Grimsby T.	A
Mar. 8	Wimbledon	H
Mar. 14	Southend U.	A
Mar. 22	Blackburn R.	H
Mar. 29	Reading	A
Apr. 5	Chester	H
Apr. 8	Gillingham	A
Apr. 12	Sheffield U.	A
Apr. 19	Bury	A
May 3	Exeter C.	H

233

COLCHESTER UNITED

Date 1979	Opponents	Ground
Aug. 18	Hull U.	A
Aug. 25	Sheffield U.	H
Aug. 28	Rotherham U.	A
Aug. 31	Swindon T.	H
Sept. 1	Chesterfield	A
Sept. 8	Sheffield Wed.	H
Sept. 15	Millwall	A
Sept. 18	Mansfield T.	A
Sept. 22	Grimsby T.	H
Sept. 29	Barnsley	A
Oct. 2	Mansfield T.	H
Oct. 6	Reading	H
Oct. 9	Sheffield U.	A
Oct. 13	Southend U.	H
Oct. 20	Blackpool	A
Oct. 23	Wimbledon	A
Oct. 27	Blackburn R.	H
Nov. 3	Hull C.	A
Nov. 6	Wimbledon	H
Nov. 10	Brentford	A
Nov. 17	Plymouth Argyle	H
Nov. 24	Millwall	H
Dec. 1	Rotherham U.	A
Dec. 8	Sheffield Wed.	A
Dec. 21	Exeter C.	H
Dec. 26	Gillingham	A
Dec. 29	Rotherham U.	A
1980		
Jan. 1	Bury	H
Jan. 12	Oxford U.	A
Jan. 19	Chesterfield	H
Jan. 26	Swindon T.	A
Feb. 9	Millwall	A
Feb. 16	Barnsley	H
Feb. 23	Southend U.	A
Mar. 1	Blackburn R.	H
Mar. 14	Reading	A
Mar. 18	Brentford	H
Mar. 22	Oxford U.	H
Mar. 29	Gillingham	A
Apr. 5	Swindon T.	H
Apr. 7	Exeter C.	A
Apr. 12	Plymouth Argyle	H
Apr. 19	Millwall	A
May. 3	Oxford U.	H

EXETER CITY

Date 1979	Opponents	Ground
Aug. 18	Grimsby T.	A
Aug. 22	Wimbledon	H
Aug. 25	Mansfield T.	H
Sept. 1	Sheffield U.	H
Sept. 8	Gillingham	H
Sept. 15	Millwall	A
Sept. 18	Brentford	A
Sept. 22	Carlisle U.	H
Sept. 25	Gillingham	H
Sept. 29	Barnsley	A
Oct. 2	Brentford	H
Oct. 6	Blackpool	A
Oct. 9	Wimbledon	A
Oct. 13	Southend U.	H
Oct. 20	Reading	A
Oct. 24	Southend U.	A
Oct. 27	Hull C.	H
Nov. 3	Grimsby T.	H
Nov. 10	Barnsley	A
Nov. 17	Oxford U.	H
Dec. 1	Wimbledon	A
Dec. 8	Sheffield Wed.	H
Dec. 21	Colchester U.	A
Dec. 26	Swindon T.	H
Dec. 29	Mansfield T.	A
1980		
Jan. 1	Plymouth Argyle	H
Jan. 5	Blackburn R.	A
Jan. 12	Sheffield U.	A
Jan. 19	Bury	H
Jan. 26	Chesterfield	A
Feb. 2	Carlisle U.	A
Feb. 9	Gillingham	H
Feb. 16	Gillingham	A
Feb. 23	Reading	A
Mar. 1	Hull C.	H
Mar. 8	Blackpool	H
Mar. 14	Reading	A
Mar. 22	Oxford U.	A
Apr. 5	Swindon T.	A
Apr. 7	Plymouth Argyle	A
Apr. 12	Blackburn R.	H
Apr. 15	Exeter C.	A
Apr. 19	Rotherham U.	A
Apr. 26	Sheffield Wed.	H
May. 3	Chesterfield	A

GILLINGHAM

Date 1979	Opponents	Ground
Aug. 18	Blackpool	A
Aug. 21	Southend U.	H
Aug. 25	Sheffield U.	A
Sept. 1	Carlisle U.	H
Sept. 8	Exeter C.	A
Sept. 15	Chester	H
Sept. 18	Hull C.	A
Sept. 22	Hull C.	H
Sept. 29	Exeter C.	A
Oct. 2	Wimbledon	H
Oct. 6	Blackburn R.	A
Oct. 9	Southend U.	H
Oct. 13	Bury	A
Oct. 20	Grimsby T.	H
Oct. 23	Oxford U.	A
Oct. 27	Mansfield T.	A
Nov. 3	Oxford U.	H
Nov. 10	Sheffield U.	H
Nov. 17	Bury	A
Nov. 21	Brentford	H
Dec. 1	Chesterfield	A
Dec. 8	Mansfield T.	H
Dec. 21	Colchester U.	H
Dec. 26	Swindon T.	A
Dec. 29	Millwall	A
1980		
Jan. 1	Sheffield Wed.	H
Jan. 5	Brentford	A
Jan. 12	Reading	H
Jan. 19	Carlisle U.	A
Jan. 26	Plymouth Argyle	H
Feb. 2	Chester	A
Feb. 9	Hull C.	H
Feb. 16	Exeter C.	A
Feb. 23	Grimsby T.	H
Mar. 1	Mansfield T.	A
Mar. 8	Blackburn R.	H
Mar. 15	Southend U.	A
Mar. 22	Bury	H
Mar. 29	Colchester U.	A
Apr. 5	Sheffield Wed.	H
Apr. 7	Oxford U.	A
Apr. 12	Brentford	H
Apr. 15	Swindon T.	A
Apr. 19	Rotherham U.	H
Apr. 26	Plymouth Argyle	A
May. 3	Millwall	H

GRIMSBY TOWN

Date 1979	Opponents	Ground
Aug. 18	Exeter C.	H
Aug. 22	Chester	A
Aug. 25	Blackpool	A
Sept. 1	Millwall	H
Sept. 8	Plymouth Argyle	A
Sept. 15	Brentford	H
Sept. 18	Bury	A
Sept. 22	Swindon T.	A
Sept. 29	Swindon T.	H
Oct. 2	Bury	H
Oct. 6	Millwall	A
Oct. 13	Chesterfield	H
Oct. 20	Gillingham	A
Oct. 23	Sheffield Wed.	H
Nov. 3	Rotherham U.	A
Nov. 6	Sheffield Wed.	A
Nov. 10	Southend U.	H
Nov. 17	Oxford U.	A
Dec. 1	Oxford U.	H
Dec. 8	Mansfield T.	A
Dec. 21	Carlisle U.	H
Dec. 26	Barnsley	A
1980		
Jan. 1	Hull C.	A
Jan. 5	Reading	A
Jan. 12	Blackburn R.	H
Jan. 19	Plymouth Argyle	A
Jan. 26	Blackpool	H
Feb. 2	Brentford	A
Feb. 9	Colchester U.	H
Feb. 23	Chesterfield	A
Mar. 1	Gillingham	H
Mar. 8	Mansfield T.	A
Mar. 15	Blackburn R.	H
Mar. 22	Southend U.	A
Mar. 29	Wimbledon	H
Apr. 5	Carlisle U.	A
Apr. 7	Hull C.	H
Apr. 12	Reading	A
Apr. 15	Oxford U.	H
Apr. 19	Mansfield U.	A
May. 3	Sheffield U.	H

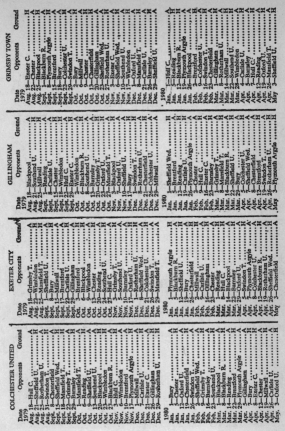

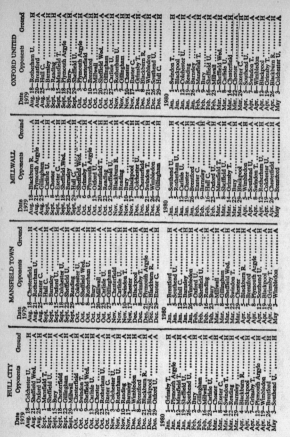

HULL CITY

Date 1979	Opponents	Ground
Aug. 18	Colchester U.	H
Aug. 21	Sheffield Wed.	A
Aug. 25	Oxford U.	A
Sept. 1	Barnsley	H
Sept. 8	Mansfield T.	A
Sept. 15	Bury	H
Sept. 18	Chesterfield	A
Sept. 22	Millwall	A
Sept. 29	Gillingham	H
Oct. 2	Chesterfield	H
Oct. 6	Swindon T.	A
Oct. 9	Sheffield Wed.	H
Oct. 13	Carlisle U.	A
Oct. 20	Chester	H
Oct. 23	Rotherham U.	A
Nov. 6	Rotherham U.	H
Nov. 10	Reading	A
Nov. 17	Wimbledon	H
Dec. 1	Brentford	A
Dec. 8	Blackburn R.	H
Dec. 21	Blackpool	A
Dec. 29	Oxford U.	H
1980		
Jan. 1	Grimsby T.	H
Jan. 5	Plymouth Argyle	A
Jan. 12	Mansfield T.	H
Jan. 19	Swindon T.	A
Jan. 26	Barnsley	A
Feb. 2	Bury	H
Feb. 9	Gillingham	A
Feb. 23	Carlisle U.	H
Mar. 1	Chester	A
Mar. 8	Exeter C.	H
Mar. 15	Swindon T.	A
Mar. 22	Barnsley	H
Mar. 29	Barnsley	A
Apr. 5	Blackburn R.	H
Apr. 7	Grimsby T.	A
Apr. 12	Plymouth Argyle	H
Apr. 19	Wimbledon	A
Apr. 26	Brentford	H
May 3	Southend U.	H

MANSFIELD TOWN

Date 1979	Opponents	Ground
Aug. 18	Chesterfield	H
Aug. 21	Rotherham U.	A
Aug. 25	Exeter C.	H
Sept. 1	Hull C.	A
Sept. 8	Sheffield U.	A
Sept. 15	Oxford U.	H
Sept. 18	Colchester U.	A
Sept. 22	Sheffield U.	H
Sept. 29	Reading	H
Oct. 2	Colchester U.	A
Oct. 6	Sheffield U.	A
Oct. 9	Rotherham U.	H
Oct. 13	Bury	A
Oct. 20	Millwall	A
Oct. 23	Carlisle U.	H
Oct. 27	Gillingham	H
Nov. 3	Chesterfield	A
Nov. 6	Carlisle U.	A
Nov. 10	Swindon T.	H
Nov. 17	Chester	A
Dec. 1	Grimsby T.	H
Dec. 8	Plymouth Argyle	A
Dec. 25	Blackburn R.	H
Dec. 29	Exeter C.	A
1980		
Jan. 1	Brentford	H
Jan. 5	Southend U.	A
Jan. 12	Hull C.	H
Jan. 19	Barnsley	A
Jan. 26	Oxford U.	A
Feb. 2	Bury	H
Feb. 9	Sheffield U.	A
Feb. 16	Reading	H
Feb. 23	Millwall	A
Mar. 1	Gillingham	H
Mar. 8	Sheffield Wed.	A
Mar. 14	Chester	H
Mar. 22	Blackburn R.	A
Mar. 29	Brentford	A
Apr. 5	Southend U.	H
Apr. 7	Grimsby T.	A
Apr. 12	Grimsby T.	H
Apr. 19	Blackpool	A
May 3	Wimbledon	H

MILLWALL

Date 1979	Opponents	Ground
Aug. 18	Blackburn R.	A
Aug. 21	Plymouth Argyle	H
Aug. 25	Gillingham	A
Sept. 1	Chester	H
Sept. 8	Chesterfield	A
Sept. 18	Sheffield Wed.	H
Sept. 22	Barnsley	A
Sept. 29	Hull C.	H
Oct. 2	Sheffield Wed.	A
Oct. 6	Grimsby T.	H
Oct. 9	Plymouth Argyle	A
Oct. 20	Oxford U.	H
Oct. 23	Reading	A
Oct. 27	Sheffield U.	H
Nov. 3	Blackburn R.	H
Nov. 17	Bury	A
Dec. 1	Colchester U.	H
Dec. 8	Swindon T.	A
Dec. 21	Wimbledon	H
Dec. 26	Gillingham	A
1980		
Jan. 1	Southend U.	H
Jan. 5	Rotherham U.	A
Jan. 12	Carlisle U.	H
Jan. 19	Chester	A
Feb. 9	Brentford	H
Feb. 2	Exeter C.	A
Feb. 16	Hull C.	H
Feb. 23	Oxford U.	A
Mar. 1	Mansfield T.	H
Mar. 8	Sheffield U.	A
Mar. 14	Grimsby T.	H
Mar. 22	Bury	A
Apr. 5	Wimbledon	H
Apr. 8	Southend U.	A
Apr. 19	Swindon T.	H
Apr. 19	Colchester U.	A
Apr. 26	Chesterfield	H
May 3	Brentford	A

OXFORD UNITED

Date 1979	Opponents	Ground
Aug. 18	Rotherham U.	A
Aug. 25	Bradford	A
Aug. 25	Hull C.	H
Sept. 1	Barnsley	A
Sept. 8	Reading	H
Sept. 15	Mansfield T.	A
Sept. 18	Plymouth Argyle	H
Sept. 22	Bury	A
Sept. 29	Sheffield U.	H
Oct. 2	Plymouth Argyle	A
Oct. 6	Brentford	H
Oct. 10	Brentford	A
Oct. 13	Millwall	A
Oct. 20	Sheffield Wed.	H
Oct. 23	Gillingham	A
Oct. 27	Carlisle U.	H
Nov. 3	Gillingham	H
Nov. 10	Grimsby T.	A
Dec. 1	Exeter C.	H
Dec. 8	Blackburn R.	A
Dec. 21	Swindon T.	H
Dec. 25	Southend R.	A
Dec. 29	Hull C.	A
1980		
Jan. 1	Swindon T.	H
Jan. 12	Colchester U.	H
Jan. 19	Reading	A
Jan. 26	Barnsley	A
Feb. 2	Mansfield T.	H
Feb. 9	Sheffield U.	A
Feb. 16	Sheffield U.	H
Feb. 23	Carlisle U.	A
Mar. 1	Chesterfield	H
Mar. 14	Carlisle U.	A
Mar. 22	Chester	H
Mar. 28	Exeter C.	A
Apr. 5	Swindon T.	H
Apr. 7	Wimbledon	A
Apr. 12	Blackpool	H
Apr. 26	Brentford	H
May 3	Colchester U.	A

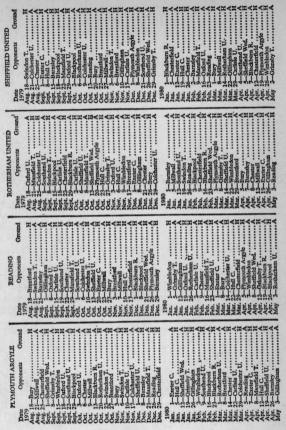

PLYMOUTH ARGYLE

Date 1979	Opponents	Ground
Aug. 18	Bury	H
Aug. 21	Millwall	A
Aug. 25	Chesterfield	A
Sept. 1	Sheffield Wed.	H
Sept. 8	Grimsby T.	A
Sept. 15	Wimbledon	H
Sept. 18	Oxford U.	A
Sept. 22	Southend U.	H
Sept. 29	Blackpool	A
Oct. 6	Chester	H
Oct. 13	Blackburn R.	A
Oct. 20	Rotherham U.	H
Oct. 23	Swindon T.	A
Oct. 27	Brentford	H
Nov. 3	Bury	A
Nov. 6	Swindon T.	H
Nov. 10	Carlisle U.	H
Nov. 17	Sheffield Utd.	A
Dec. 1	Barnsley	H
Dec. 8	Mansfield T.	A
Dec. 21	Reading	H
Dec. 26	Chesterfield	H
1980		
Jan. 1	Exeter C.	A
Jan. 5	Hull C.	H
Jan. 12	Sheffield Wed.	A
Jan. 19	Grimsby	H
Jan. 26	Wimbledon	A
Feb. 2	Southend U.	A
Feb. 9	Blackpool	H
Feb. 23	Blackburn R.	H
Mar. 1	Rotherham U.	A
Mar. 8	Brentford	A
Mar. 15	Colchester U.	H
Mar. 22	Gillingham	A
Mar. 29	Colchester U.	H
Apr. 5	Reading	A
Apr. 8	Mansfield T.	H
Apr. 12	Hull C.	A
Apr. 19	Sheffield U.	H
Apr. 26	Barnsley	A
May 3	Gillingham	A

READING

Date 1979	Opponents	Ground
Aug. 18	Brentford	H
Aug. 25	Swindon T.	A
Sept. 1	Gillingham	A
Sept. 8	Oxford U.	H
Sept. 15	Carlisle U.	A
Sept. 18	Chester	H
Sept. 22	Chester	A
Sept. 29	Mansfield T.	H
Oct. 6	Southend U.	A
Oct. 10	Swindon T.	H
Oct. 13	Sheffield U.	A
Oct. 20	Exeter C.	H
Oct. 27	Millwall	A
Nov. 3	Brentford	H
Nov. 6	Millwall	H
Nov. 10	Chesterfield	A
Dec. 1	Blackburn R.	H
Dec. 8	Blackpool	A
Dec. 21	Plymouth Wed.	A
Dec. 26	Plymouth Argyle	A
Dec. 29	Barnsley	H
1980		
Jan. 1	Wimbledon	H
Jan. 5	Grimsby T.	A
Jan. 12	Oxford U.	H
Jan. 19	Rotherham U.	A
Jan. 26	Carlisle U.	A
Feb. 2	Mansfield T.	H
Feb. 16	Sheffield U.	A
Feb. 23	Exeter C.	H
Mar. 1	Colchester U.	A
Mar. 14	Hull C.	H
Mar. 22	Chesterfield	A
Mar. 29	Wimbledon	A
Apr. 5	Plymouth Argyle	H
Apr. 8	Sheffield Wed.	H
Apr. 12	Grimsby T.	H
Apr. 19	Southend U.	A
Apr. 26	Blackpool	H
May 3	Rotherham U.	A

ROTHERHAM UNITED

Date 1979	Opponents	Ground
Aug. 18	Oxford U.	A
Aug. 25	Mansfield T.	H
Sept. 1	Colchester U.	A
Sept. 8	Southend U.	H
Sept. 15	Carlisle U.	A
Sept. 18	Carlisle U.	H
Sept. 22	Chesterfield	A
Sept. 29	Blackburn R.	H
Oct. 6	Carlisle U.	A
Oct. 13	Sheffield Wed.	H
Oct. 20	Plymouth Argyle	A
Oct. 23	Hull C.	H
Oct. 27	Grimsby T.	A
Nov. 3	Oxford U.	H
Nov. 10	Millwall	A
Nov. 17	Brentford	H
Dec. 1	Bingham	A
Dec. 8	Wimbledon	H
Dec. 22	Bury	A
Dec. 26	Bury	H
Dec. 29	Colchester U.	A
1980		
Jan. 1	Barnsley	H
Jan. 5	Millwall	A
Jan. 12	Swindon T.	H
Jan. 19	Swindon T.	A
Jan. 26	Reading	H
Feb. 9	Blackpool	A
Feb. 16	Chesterfield	H
Feb. 23	Sheffield Wed.	A
Mar. 1	Plymouth Argyle	H
Mar. 8	Sheffield U.	A
Mar. 14	Sheffield U.	H
Mar. 22	Grimsby T.	H
Mar. 29	Bury	A
Apr. 5	Barnsley	A
Apr. 7	Chester	H
Apr. 8	Chester	A
Apr. 19	Gillingham	H
Apr. 26	Exeter C.	A
May 3	Reading	H

SHEFFIELD UNITED

Date 1979	Opponents	Ground
Aug. 18	Swindon T.	H
Aug. 21	Colchester U.	A
Aug. 25	Chester	A
Sept. 1	Exeter C.	H
Sept. 8	Barnsley	A
Sept. 15	Barnsley	H
Sept. 18	Blackpool	A
Sept. 22	Mansfield T.	H
Sept. 29	Southend U.	A
Oct. 3	Blackpool	H
Oct. 6	Rotherham U.	H
Oct. 9	Colchester U.	A
Oct. 13	Reading	H
Oct. 20	Brentford	A
Oct. 27	Millwall	H
Nov. 3	Exeter C.	A
Nov. 10	Gillingham	H
Nov. 17	Carlisle U.	A
Dec. 1	Wimbledon	H
Dec. 8	Wimbledon	A
Dec. 21	Southend U.	H
Dec. 29	Grimsby T.	A
1980		
Jan. 1	Blackburn R.	H
Jan. 5	Chesterfield	A
Jan. 12	Hull C.	A
Jan. 19	Hull C.	H
Feb. 2	Barnsley	A
Feb. 9	Mansfield T.	H
Feb. 16	Oxford U.	H
Feb. 23	Reading	A
Mar. 1	Bury	H
Mar. 8	Millwall	A
Mar. 14	Rotherham U.	A
Mar. 22	Carlisle U.	H
Mar. 29	Southend U.	A
Apr. 5	Sheffield Wed.	H
Apr. 8	Chesterfield	H
Apr. 12	Plymouth Argyle	A
Apr. 19	Wimbledon	A
May 3	Grimsby T.	H

236

SHEFFIELD WEDNESDAY

Date 1979	Opponents	Ground
Aug. 18—Barnsley		H
Aug. 21—Blackburn R.		H
Aug. 25—Plymouth Argyle		A
Sept. 1—Reading		H
Sept. 8—Colchester U.		A
Sept. 15—Millwall		H
Sept. 18—Swindon T.		A
Sept. 22—Chesterfield		A
Sept. 29—Mansfield T.		H
Oct. 6—Mansfield T.		A
Oct. 13—Hull C.		H
Oct. 20—Oxford U.		A
Oct. 24—Grimsby T.		H
Oct. 27—Wimbledon		H
Nov. 3—Chester		A
Nov. 10—Blackpool		H
Nov. 17—Southend U.		A
Dec. 1—Bury		H
Dec. 8—Exeter C.		A
Dec. 21—Reading		A
Dec. 26—Sheffield U.		H
Dec. 29—Carlisle U.		A

Date 1980	Opponents	Ground
Jan. 1—Gillingham		H
Jan. 5—Bury		H
Jan. 12—Plymouth Argyle		A
Jan. 19—Brentford		A
Jan. 26—Blackpool		H
Feb. 2—Swindon T.		H
Feb. 9—Colchester U.		A
Feb. 16—Chesterfield		H
Mar. 1—Rotherham U.		A
Mar. 8—Wimbledon		A
Mar. 15—Mansfield T.		H
Mar. 22—Southend U.		A
Mar. 29—Sheffield U.		A
Apr. 5—Gillingham		A
Apr. 8—Reading		H
Apr. 12—Bury		A
Apr. 19—Exeter C.		H
May 3—Carlisle U.		H

SOUTHEND UNITED

Date 1979	Opponents	Ground
Aug. 18—Carlisle U.		H
Aug. 21—Wimbledon		A
Aug. 25—Wimbledon		A
Sept. 1—Rotherham U.		H
Sept. 8—Blackpool		H
Sept. 15—Blackburn R.		A
Sept. 18—Reading		H
Sept. 22—Plymouth Argyle		H
Sept. 29—Brentford		A
Oct. 6—Bury		A
Oct. 8—Gillingham		H
Oct. 13—Colchester U.		A
Oct. 20—Swindon T.		A
Oct. 24—Exeter C.		H
Oct. 27—Chesterfield		H
Nov. 3—Carlisle U.		A
Nov. 10—Grimsby T.		H
Nov. 17—Sheffield Wed.		H
Dec. 1—Barnsley		A
Dec. 8—Reading		A
Dec. 21—Oxford U.		H
Dec. 26—Oxford U.		A
Dec. 29—Wimbledon		A

Date 1980	Opponents	Ground
Jan. 1—Millwall		H
Jan. 5—Mansfield T.		A
Jan. 12—Rotherham U.		A
Jan. 19—Blackpool		H
Jan. 26—Hull C.		A
Feb. 2—Blackburn R.		H
Feb. 9—Plymouth Argyle		A
Feb. 16—Brentford		H
Feb. 23—Colchester U.		H
Mar. 1—Chesterfield		A
Mar. 8—Bury		H
Mar. 15—Bury		A
Mar. 22—Grimsby T.		A
Mar. 29—Sheffield Wed.		H
Apr. 5—Sheffield U.		A
Apr. 7—Oxford U.		H
Apr. 12—Millwall		A
Apr. 19—Sheffield U.		H
Apr. 26—Barnsley		H
May 3—Hull C.		H

SWINDON TOWN

Date 1979	Opponents	Ground
Aug. 18—Sheffield U.		A
Aug. 22—Reading		H
Aug. 31—Colchester U.		A
Sept. 1—Rotherham U.		A
Sept. 8—Rotherham U.		H
Sept. 15—Reading		A
Sept. 22—Sheffield Wed.		H
Sept. 29—Grimsby T.		A
Oct. 2—Chester		H
Oct. 6—Hull C.		H
Oct. 10—Reading		A
Oct. 13—Wimbledon		A
Oct. 20—Southend U.		H
Oct. 24—Plymouth Argyle		A
Oct. 27—Blackpool		H
Nov. 3—Chesterfield		A
Nov. 10—Plymouth Argyle		H
Nov. 17—Blackburn R.		A
Dec. 1—Gillingham		H
Dec. 8—Bury		A
Dec. 21—Exeter C.		H
Dec. 26—Brentford		A
Dec. 29—Brentford		H

Date 1980	Opponents	Ground
Jan. 1—Oxford U.		H
Jan. 5—Bury		A
Jan. 12—Rotherham U.		A
Jan. 19—Barnsley		H
Feb. 2—Colchester U.		H
Feb. 9—Sheffield Wed.		A
Feb. 16—Grimsby T.		H
Feb. 23—Wimbledon		H
Mar. 1—Blackpool		A
Mar. 8—Blackpool		H
Mar. 14—Hull C.		A
Mar. 22—Mansfield T.		H
Mar. 29—Exeter C.		A
Apr. 5—Exeter C.		H
Apr. 7—Oxford U.		A
Apr. 12—Reading		A
Apr. 19—Gillingham		H
Apr. 26—Gillingham		A
May 3—Barnsley		A

WIMBLEDON

Date 1979	Opponents	Ground
Aug. 18—Chester		H
Aug. 22—Exeter C.		A
Aug. 25—Hull C.		H
Sept. 1—Blackpool		A
Sept. 8—Blackburn R.		H
Sept. 15—Plymouth Argyle		A
Sept. 22—Brentford		H
Sept. 29—Bury		A
Oct. 2—Gillingham		A
Oct. 6—Gillingham		H
Oct. 13—Swindon T.		H
Oct. 20—Southend U.		A
Oct. 23—Chesterfield		H
Oct. 27—Sheffield Wed.		A
Nov. 3—Chester		A
Nov. 10—Colchester U.		H
Nov. 17—Grimsby T.		A
Dec. 1—Hull C.		H
Dec. 8—Reading		A
Dec. 21—Colchester U.		H
Dec. 26—Millwall		A
Dec. 29—Southend U.		H

Date 1980	Opponents	Ground
Jan. 1—Reading		H
Jan. 12—Blackpool		H
Jan. 19—Blackburn R.		A
Jan. 26—Mansfield T.		H
Feb. 2—Plymouth Argyle		A
Feb. 9—Brentford		A
Feb. 16—Bury		H
Feb. 23—Swindon T.		A
Mar. 1—Chesterfield		H
Mar. 8—Sheffield Wed.		H
Mar. 14—Carlisle U.		A
Mar. 22—Rotherham U.		A
Apr. 5—Grimsby T.		A
Apr. 7—Reading		A
Apr. 8—Oxford U.		H
Apr. 12—Barnsley		A
Apr. 19—Sheffield U.		H
May 3—Mansfield T.		H

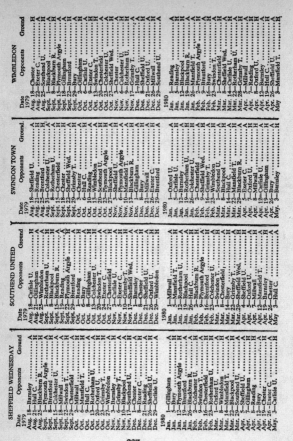

DIVISION FOUR

A.F.C. BOURNEMOUTH		
Date 1979	Opponents	Ground
Aug. 18	Rochdale	A
Aug. 21	Wigan Ath.	H
Aug. 25	Port Vale	H
Sept. 1	Scunthorpe U.	H
Sept. 8	Wigan Ath.	A
Sept. 15	Rochdale	H
Sept. 18	Portsmouth	A
Sept. 22	Halifax T.	A
Sept. 29	Tranmere R.	H
Oct. 2	Portsmouth	A
Oct. 6	Walsall	A
Oct. 9	York C.	H
Oct. 12	Hereford U.	A
Oct. 20	Huddersfield T.	H
Oct. 27	Bradford C.	H
Nov. 3	Rochdale	A
Nov. 6	Hereford	A
Nov. 10	Lincoln C.	H
Nov. 17	Doncaster R.	A
Dec. 1	Peterborough U.	H
Dec. 8	Crewe Alex.	A
Dec. 26	Northampton T.	H
Dec. 29	Darlington	A
1980		
Jan. 1	Torquay U.	H
Jan. 5	Port Vale	A
Jan. 12	Wigan Ath.	H
Jan. 19	Newport Co.	A
Jan. 26	Stockport Co.	H
Feb. 9	Tranmere R.	A
Feb. 16	York C.	A
Feb. 23	Huddersfield T.	A
Mar. 1	Hartlepool U.	H
Mar. 8	Hereford U.	H
Mar. 14	Lincoln C.	A
Mar. 22	Doncaster R.	H
Mar. 29	Northampton T.	A
Apr. 1	Aldershot	H
Apr. 5	Torquay U.	A
Apr. 8	Scunthorpe U.	A
Apr. 12	Northampton T.	H
Apr. 19	Portsmouth	A
Apr. 26	Crewe Alex.	A
May 3	Darlington	H

ALDERSHOT		
Date 1979	Opponents	Ground
Aug. 18	Huddersfield T.	A
Aug. 21	Newport Co.	H
Aug. 25	Port Vale	H
Sept. 1	Hartlepool U.	A
Sept. 8	Scunthorpe U.	H
Sept. 15	Bradford C.	A
Sept. 19	Peterborough U.	H
Sept. 22	Crewe Alex.	A
Sept. 29	Walsall	H
Oct. 2	Peterborough U.	A
Oct. 6	Bradford C.	H
Oct. 9	Newport Co.	A
Oct. 13	Northampton T.	H
Oct. 20	Torquay U.	A
Oct. 23	Lincoln C.	H
Oct. 27	Hereford U.	A
Nov. 3	Huddersfield T.	H
Nov. 10	Rochdale	A
Nov. 17	Halifax T.	H
Dec. 1	Doncaster R.	H
Dec. 8	Tranmere R.	A
Dec. 22	A.F.C. Bournemouth	A
Dec. 29	Port Vale	A
1980		
Jan. 1	Portsmouth	H
Jan. 5	Stockport Co.	H
Jan. 12	Hartlepool U.	H
Jan. 19	Scunthorpe U.	A
Jan. 26	Wigan Ath.	A
Feb. 2	Darlington	H
Feb. 9	Crewe Alex.	H
Feb. 16	Northampton T.	A
Feb. 23	Hereford U.	H
Mar. 1	Bradford U.	A
Mar. 8	Rochdale	H
Mar. 15	Torquay U.	A
Mar. 22	A.F.C. Bournemouth	H
Mar. 29	Tranmere R.	H
Apr. 1	Portsmouth	A
Apr. 5	York C.	A
Apr. 8	Doncaster R.	A
Apr. 26	York C.	H
May 3	Wigan Ath.	H

BRADFORD CITY		
Date 1979	Opponents	Ground
Aug. 18	Crewe Alex.	H
Aug. 21	Northampton T.	A
Aug. 25	Tranmere R.	A
Sept. 1	Lincoln C.	H
Sept. 8	Peterborough U.	A
Sept. 15	Port Vale	H
Sept. 19	Crewe Alex.	A
Sept. 22	Halifax T.	H
Sept. 29	Port Vale	A
Oct. 3	Aldershot	A
Oct. 6	Northampton Co.	A
Oct. 10	Stockport Co.	H
Oct. 20	Portsmouth	A
Oct. 23	Halifax T.	A
Oct. 27	A.F.C. Bournemouth	A
Nov. 3	Bradford U.	A
Nov. 10	Huddersfield T.	H
Nov. 17	York C.	A
Dec. 1	Hereford U.	H
Dec. 8	Stockport Co.	A
Dec. 21	Hartlepool U.	H
Dec. 26	Crewe Alex.	H
Dec. 29	Tranmere R.	A
1980		
Jan. 1	Rochdale	H
Jan. 12	Torquay U.	H
Jan. 19	Peterborough U.	A
Jan. 26	Lincoln C.	A
Feb. 2	Newport Co.	H
Feb. 9	Scunthorpe U.	A
Feb. 16	Wigan Ath.	H
Feb. 23	Crewe Alex.	A
Mar. 1	Portsmouth	H
Mar. 8	A.F.C. Bournemouth	H
Mar. 14	Huddersfield T.	A
Mar. 15	Aldershot	H
Mar. 22	Newport Co.	A
Mar. 29	York C.	H
Apr. 1	Hartlepool U.	A
Apr. 5	Rochdale	H
Apr. 7	Torquay U.	A
Apr. 12	Walsall	H
Apr. 19	Hereford U.	A
May 3	Peterborough U.	H

CREWE ALEXANDRA		
Date 1979	Opponents	Ground
Aug. 18	Bradford C.	A
Aug. 22	Lincoln C.	H
Aug. 25	Halifax T.	H
Sept. 1	Port Vale	H
Sept. 8	Peterborough U.	A
Sept. 15	Scunthorpe T.	H
Sept. 22	Aldershot	H
Sept. 29	Northampton T.	A
Oct. 2	Huddersfield T.	H
Oct. 6	Doncaster R.	A
Oct. 13	Hereford U.	H
Oct. 20	Rochdale	A
Oct. 24	Walsall	H
Oct. 27	Hartlepool U.	H
Nov. 3	Bradford U.	A
Nov. 10	Newport Co.	A
Nov. 17	Walsall	H
Dec. 1	Stockport Co.	H
Dec. 8	A.F.C. Bournemouth	H
Dec. 21	Wigan Ath.	A
Dec. 26	Bradford C.	A
Dec. 29	Torquay U.	H
1980		
Jan. 1	Scunthorpe U.	A
Jan. 5	Portsmouth	H
Jan. 12	Halifax T.	A
Jan. 19	Port Vale	A
Jan. 26	York C.	H
Feb. 2	Hartlepool U.	A
Feb. 16	Huddersfield T.	H
Feb. 23	Aldershot	A
Mar. 1	Rochdale	A
Mar. 8	Peterborough U.	H
Mar. 15	Newport Co.	H
Mar. 29	Darlington	A
Apr. 5	Wigan Ath.	A
Apr. 7	Tranmere R.	H
Apr. 12	Scunthorpe U.	H
Apr. 15	Portsmouth	A
Apr. 19	Stockport Co.	A
Apr. 26	A.F.C. Bournemouth	H
May 3	York C.	A

238

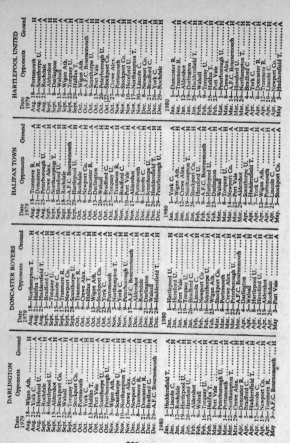

DARLINGTON

Date 1979	Opponents	Ground
Aug. 18	Wigan Ath.	A
Aug. 21	York C.	A
Aug. 25	Hereford U.	H
Sept. 1	Hartlepool U.	A
Sept. 8	Hartlepool U.	H
Sept. 15	Aldershot	A
Sept. 18	Port Vale	H
Sept. 22	Walsall	A
Sept. 29	Torquay U.	H
Oct. 2	Stockport Co.	H
Oct. 6	Portsmouth	A
Oct. 13	Halifax T.	H
Oct. 20	Port Vale	A
Oct. 23	Scunthorpe U.	A
Oct. 27	Peterborough U.	H
Nov. 3	Wigan Ath.	H
Nov. 6	Scunthorpe U.	H
Nov. 10	Northampton T.	A
Nov. 17	Newport Co.	H
Dec. 1	Tranmere R.	A
Dec. 8	Doncaster R.	H
Dec. 26	Tranmere R.	H
Dec. 29	A.F.C. Bournemouth	A
1980		
Jan. 1	Huddersfield T.	A
Jan. 12	Lincoln C.	H
Jan. 19	Rochdale	H
Jan. 26	Hereford U.	A
Feb. 2	Aldershot	H
Feb. 9	Torquay U.	A
Feb. 23	Halifax T.	A
Mar. 1	Port Vale	H
Mar. 8	Peterborough U.	A
Mar. 22	Northampton T.	H
Mar. 29	Crewe Alex.	A
Apr. 4	Bradford C.	H
Apr. 8	Huddersfield T.	H
Apr. 12	Lincoln C.	A
Apr. 19	Newport Co.	A
Apr. 26	Tranmere R. B.	H
May 3	A.F.C. Bournemouth	H

DONCASTER ROVERS

Date 1979	Opponents	Ground
Aug. 18	Northampton T.	H
Aug. 21	Halifax T.	H
Aug. 25	Huddersfield T.	A
Sept. 1	Bradford C.	H
Sept. 8	Crewe Alex.	A
Sept. 15	Lincoln C.	A
Sept. 17	Tranmere R.	H
Sept. 22	Newport Co.	A
Sept. 29	Tranmere R.	A
Oct. 2	Crewe Alex.	H
Oct. 6	Halifax T.	H
Oct. 13	Wigan Ath.	A
Oct. 20	Stockport Co.	H
Oct. 23	York C.	A
Oct. 27	Portsmouth	H
Nov. 3	Northampton T.	A
Nov. 6	York C.	H
Nov. 10	Peterborough U.	A
Nov. 17	A.F.C. Bournemouth	H
Dec. 1	Aldershot	A
Dec. 8	Darlington	A
Dec. 21	Darlington	H
Dec. 26	Walsall	A
Dec. 29	Huddersfield T.	H
1980		
Jan. 1	Hartlepool U.	H
Jan. 5	Hereford U.	A
Jan. 12	Port Vale	H
Jan. 19	Bradford C.	A
Jan. 26	Newport Co.	H
Feb. 2	Lincoln C.	A
Feb. 9	Scunthorpe U.	H
Feb. 16	Stockport Co.	A
Mar. 1	Portsmouth	H
Mar. 8	Peterborough U.	A
Mar. 22	A.F.C. Bournemouth	A
Apr. 4	Darlington	H
Apr. 8	Huddersfield T.	A
Apr. 12	Hereford U.	H
Apr. 19	Aldershot	A
Apr. 26	Rochdale	H
May 3	Port Vale	A

HALIFAX TOWN

Date 1979	Opponents	Ground
Aug. 18	Tranmere R.	A
Aug. 25	Peterborough U.	H
Sept. 1	Crewe Alex.	A
Sept. 8	Northampton T.	H
Sept. 15	Rochdale	A
Sept. 18	Rochdale	H
Sept. 22	A.F.C. Bournemouth	A
Sept. 29	Hartlepool U.	H
Oct. 2	Rochdale	H
Oct. 6	Doncaster R.	A
Oct. 9	Newport Co.	H
Oct. 13	Darlington	A
Oct. 20	Walsall	H
Oct. 23	Bradford C.	A
Nov. 3	Tranmere R.	H
Nov. 6	Brentford	A
Nov. 10	Port Vale	A
Nov. 17	Aldershot	H
Dec. 1	Lincoln C.	A
Dec. 8	Scunthorpe U.	H
Dec. 26	Huddersfield T.	A
Dec. 29	Peterborough U.	A
1980		
Jan. 1	York C.	H
Jan. 5	Wigan Ath.	A
Jan. 12	Crewe Alex.	H
Jan. 19	Northampton T.	A
Jan. 26	Hereford U.	H
Feb. 2	A.F.C. Bournemouth	H
Feb. 16	Hartlepool U.	H
Feb. 23	Darlington	A
Mar. 1	Torquay U.	H
Mar. 8	Newport Co.	A
Mar. 14	Port Vale	H
Mar. 22	Scunthorpe U.	A
Apr. 5	Huddersfield T.	H
Apr. 8	York C.	A
Apr. 12	Wigan Ath.	H
Apr. 19	Portsmouth	A
Apr. 25	Lincoln C.	H
May 3	Stockport Co.	A

HARTLEPOOL UNITED

Date 1979	Opponents	Ground
Aug. 18	Portsmouth	H
Aug. 25	Peterborough U.	A
Sept. 1	Aldershot	H
Sept. 8	Darlington	H
Sept. 15	Wigan Ath.	A
Sept. 22	Torquay U.	H
Sept. 29	Halifax T.	A
Oct. 2	Wigan Ath.	H
Oct. 6	A.F.C. Bournemouth	A
Oct. 13	Scunthorpe U.	A
Oct. 20	Port Vale	H
Oct. 22	Stockport Co.	H
Oct. 27	Crewe Alex.	A
Nov. 3	Portsmouth	A
Nov. 6	Stockport Co.	A
Nov. 10	Hereford U.	H
Nov. 17	Northampton T.	H
Nov. 30	Lincoln C.	A
Dec. 8	Newport Co.	H
Dec. 26	York C.	H
Dec. 29	Rochdale	A
1980		
Jan. 1	Doncaster R.	A
Jan. 12	Tranmere R.	A
Jan. 19	Darlington	A
Jan. 26	Huddersfield T.	H
Feb. 2	Walsall	H
Feb. 9	Torquay U.	H
Feb. 16	Halifax T.	A
Mar. 1	Peterborough U.	H
Mar. 8	A.F.C. Bournemouth	A
Mar. 14	Hereford U.	A
Mar. 22	Northampton T.	A
Mar. 26	Scunthorpe U.	H
Apr. 5	York C.	A
Apr. 8	Doncaster R.	H
Apr. 12	Tranmere R.	H
Apr. 19	Newport Co.	A
Apr. 26	Port Vale	A
May 3	Huddersfield T.	A

HEREFORD UNITED

Date 1979	Opponents	Ground
Aug. 18	York C.	H
Aug. 21	Port Vale	A
Aug. 25	Darlington	A
Sept. 1	Walsall	H
Sept. 8	Tranmere R.	A
Sept. 15	Halifax T.	H
Sept. 18	Wigan Ath.	A
Sept. 22	Torquay U.	H
Sept. 29	Peterborough U.	A
Oct. 2	Torquay U.	A
Oct. 6	Port Vale	H
Oct. 10	Port Co.	H
Oct. 20	Northampton	A
Oct. 27	Aldershot	H
Nov. 3	York C.	A
Nov. 6	A.F.C. Bournemouth	H
Nov. 17	Rochdale	A
Dec. 1	Huddersfield T.	H
Dec. 8	Bradford C.	A
Dec. 15	Lincoln C.	H
Dec. 26	Portsmouth	A
Dec. 29	Scunthorpe U.	H

Date 1980	Opponents	Ground
Jan. 1	Newport Co.	A
Jan. 5	Doncaster R.	H
Jan. 19	Tranmere R.	H
Jan. 26	Darlington	A
Feb. 2	Peterborough U.	H
Feb. 9	Halifax T.	A
Feb. 16	Peterborough Co.	H
Feb. 23	Crewe Alex.	A
Mar. 1	Northampton T.	H
Mar. 8	Aldershot	A
Mar. 14	Stockport Co.	H
Mar. 22	Hartlepool U.	A
Mar. 26	Rochdale	H
Apr. 5	Portsmouth	H
Apr. 7	Newport Co.	H
Apr. 12	Lincoln C.	A
Apr. 19	Doncaster R.	A
Apr. 26	Bradford C.	H
May 3	Scunthorpe U.	A

HUDDERSFIELD TOWN

Date 1979	Opponents	Ground
Aug. 18	Aldershot	H
Aug. 21	Wigan Ath.	A
Aug. 25	Darlington	A
Sept. 1	Lincoln C.	H
Sept. 8	Newport Co.	A
Sept. 15	Crewe Alex.	H
Sept. 19	Port Vale	A
Sept. 22	Stockport Co.	H
Sept. 29	Port Vale	H
Oct. 2	Crewe Alex.	A
Oct. 6	Peterborough U.	H
Oct. 13	Portsmouth	A
Oct. 20	A.F.C. Bournemouth	H
Oct. 23	Northampton T.	A
Oct. 27	York C.	H
Nov. 3	Aldershot	A
Nov. 10	Bradford C.	H
Nov. 17	Hereford U.	A
Dec. 1	Tranmere R.	H
Dec. 8	Rochdale	A
Dec. 21	Halifax T.	H
Dec. 29	Doncaster R.	A

Date 1980	Opponents	Ground
Jan. 1	Darlington	H
Jan. 12	Lincoln C.	A
Jan. 19	Newport Co.	A
Jan. 26	A.F.C. Bournemouth	H
Feb. 2	Scunthorpe U.	A
Feb. 9	Stockport Co.	H
Feb. 16	Peterborough U.	A
Feb. 23	Portsmouth	H
Mar. 1	York C.	A
Mar. 14	Peterborough U.	H
Mar. 22	Bradford C.	A
Mar. 26	Rochdale	H
Apr. 5	Halifax T.	A
Apr. 7	Darlington	H
Apr. 12	Hereford U.	H
Apr. 19	Torquay U.	A
Apr. 26	Hartlepool U.	H
May 3	Hartlepool U.	A

LINCOLN CITY

Date 1979	Opponents	Ground
Aug. 18	Peterborough U.	A
Aug. 22	Crew Alex.	A
Aug. 25	York C.	A
Sept. 1	Huddersfield T.	A
Sept. 8	Doncaster R.	A
Sept. 15	Walsall	A
Sept. 18	Tranmere R.	A
Sept. 22	Scunthorpe Co.	A
Oct. 2	Walsall	A
Oct. 6	Port Vale	A
Oct. 10	Crewe Alex.	A
Oct. 13	Hartlepool U.	A
Oct. 20	Aldershot	A
Oct. 23	Stockport Co.	A
Nov. 3	Peterborough U.	A
Nov. 10	A.F.C. Bournemouth	A
Nov. 17	Portsmouth	A
Nov. 30	Halifax T.	A
Dec. 15	Hereford U.	A
Dec. 21	Hereford U.	A
Dec. 26	York C.	A

Date 1980	Opponents	Ground
Jan. 1	Northampton T.	H
Jan. 5	Darlington	A
Jan. 12	Huddersfield T.	H
Jan. 19	Bradford C.	A
Jan. 26	Crewe Alex.	H
Feb. 2	Doncaster R.	A
Feb. 9	Tranmere R.	H
Feb. 16	Scunthorpe U.	A
Feb. 23	Wigan Ath.	H
Mar. 8	Port Vale	A
Mar. 14	Port Vale	H
Mar. 22	A.F.C. Bournemouth	A
Apr. 5	Rochdale	H
Apr. 7	Northampton T.	A
Apr. 12	Bradford C.	H
Apr. 19	Halifax T.	A
Apr. 26	Halifax T.	H
May 3	Torquay U.	A

NEWPORT COUNTY

Date 1979	Opponents	Ground
Aug. 18	Port Vale	A
Aug. 21	Aldershot	H
Aug. 25	A.F.C. Bournemouth	A
Sept. 1	York C.	H
Sept. 8	Huddersfield T.	H
Sept. 15	Bradford C.	A
Sept. 18	Northampton T.	H
Sept. 22	Lincoln C.	A
Oct. 2	Northampton T.	A
Oct. 6	Halifax T.	H
Oct. 9	Aldershot	A
Oct. 13	Crewe Alex.	H
Oct. 20	Scunthorpe U.	A
Oct. 23	Portsmouth	H
Nov. 6	Portsmouth	A
Nov. 17	Stockport Co.	A
Nov. 21	Peterborough U.	H
Dec. 8	Peterborough U.	A
Dec. 26	Torquay U.	A
Dec.	Walsall	A

Date 1980	Opponents	Ground
Jan. 1	Hereford U.	H
Jan. 12	York C.	A
Jan. 19	Huddersfield T.	H
Jan. 26	A.F.C. Bournemouth	H
Feb. 2	Bradford C.	A
Feb. 9	Doncaster R.	H
Feb. 16	Tranmere R.	A
Feb. 29	Scunthorpe U.	H
Mar. 8	Lincoln C.	H
Mar. 22	Crewe Alex.	A
Mar. 29	Stockport Co.	H
Apr. 5	Torquay U.	A
Apr. 12	Rochdale	H
Apr. 19	Darlington	A
Apr. 19	Hartlepool U.	H
May 3	Walsall	A

240

NORTHAMPTON TOWN

Date 1979	Opponents	Ground
Aug. 18	Doncaster R.	A
Aug. 22	York C.	H
Aug. 25	Walsall	H
Sept. 1	Torquay U.	A
Sept. 5	Port Vale	H
Sept. 8	Newport Co.	A
Sept. 15	Aldershot	A
Sept. 18	Peterborough U.	A
Sept. 22	Crewe Alex.	H
Sept. 29	Hereford U.	H
Oct. 2	Hartlepool U.	H
Oct. 6	Tranmere R.	A
Oct. 10	Bradford C.	H
Oct. 13	Aldershot	A
Oct. 20	Hartlepool U.	H
Oct. 23	Huddersfield T.	A
Oct. 27	Rochdale	A
Nov. 3	Darlington	H
Nov. 6	Lincoln C.	A
Nov. 10	Doncaster R.	H
Nov. 17	Torquay U.	A
Dec. 1	Wigan Ath.	H
Dec. 8	Hartlepool U.	A
Dec. 15	Stockport Co.	H
Dec. 21	A.F.C. Bournemouth	H
Dec. 26	Scunthorpe U.	A
Dec. 29	Portsmouth	H
1980		
Jan. 1	Lincoln C.	H
Jan. 5	York C.	A
Jan. 12	Torquay U.	H
Jan. 19	Halifax T.	A
Feb. 2	Port Vale	A
Feb. 9	Peterborough U.	H
Feb. 16	Crewe Alex.	A
Feb. 23	Hereford U.	A
Mar. 1	Rochdale	H
Mar. 8	Darlington	A
Mar. 14	Tranmere R.	H
Mar. 22	Hartlepool U.	A
Mar. 25	Huddersfield T.	H
Mar. 29	Halifax T.	H
Apr. 5	Stockport Co.	A
Apr. 8	A.F.C. Bournemouth	A
Apr. 12	Lincoln C.	H
Apr. 19	Wigan Ath.	A
Apr. 25	Scunthorpe U.	H
May 3	Portsmouth	A

PETERBOROUGH UNITED

Date 1979	Opponents	Ground
Aug. 18	Lincoln C.	A
Aug. 22	Tranmere R.	H
Aug. 25	Halifax T.	H
Sept. 1	Port Vale	A
Sept. 5	York C.	H
Sept. 8	Aldershot	A
Sept. 15	Aldershot	H
Sept. 18	Northampton T.	A
Sept. 22	Hereford U.	H
Sept. 29	Crewe Alex.	A
Oct. 2	Darlington	H
Oct. 6	Huddersfield T.	A
Oct. 13	Rochdale	H
Oct. 20	Torquay U.	A
Oct. 24	Hartlepool U.	A
Oct. 27	Darlington	H
Nov. 3	Lincoln C.	A
Nov. 10	Doncaster R.	H
Nov. 17	Walsall	A
Dec. 1	A.F.C. Bournemouth	H
Dec. 8	Scunthorpe U.	A
Dec. 15	Wigan Ath.	H
Dec. 29	Halifax T.	A
1980		
Jan. 1	Stockport Co.	H
Jan. 5	Scunthorpe U.	H
Jan. 12	Bradford C.	A
Jan. 19	York C.	A
Jan. 26	Port Vale	H
Feb. 2	Aldershot	A
Feb. 9	Northampton T.	A
Feb. 16	Hereford U.	H
Feb. 23	Huddersfield T.	A
Mar. 1	Darlington	H
Mar. 8	Darlington	A
Mar. 14	Huddersfield T.	H
Mar. 22	Doncaster R.	A
Mar. 28	Wigan Ath.	A
Apr. 5	Newport Co.	H
Apr. 8	Aldershot	H
Apr. 12	Tranmere R.	A
Apr. 19	A.F.C. Bournemouth	A
Apr. 25	Stockport Co.	A
May 3	Bradford C.	H

PORTSMOUTH

Date 1979	Opponents	Ground
Aug. 18	Hartlepool U.	H
Aug. 22	Tranmere R.	A
Aug. 25	Scunthorpe U.	A
Sept. 1	Wigan Ath.	H
Sept. 5	Stockport Co.	A
Sept. 8	Aldershot	H
Sept. 15	A.F.C. Bournemouth	A
Sept. 22	Rochdale	H
Sept. 29	York C.	H
Oct. 2	A.F.C. Bournemouth	A
Oct. 6	Darlington	A
Oct. 10	Torquay U.	H
Oct. 13	Huddersfield T.	A
Oct. 20	Bradford C.	H
Oct. 23	Newport Co.	H
Oct. 27	Doncaster R.	A
Nov. 3	Hartlepool U.	A
Nov. 10	Newport Co.	H
Nov. 17	Lincoln C.	A
Dec. 1	Halifax T.	H
Dec. 8	Peterborough U.	H
Dec. 15	Torquay U.	A
Dec. 22	Doncaster R.	H
Dec. 26	Hereford U.	A
Dec. 29	Northampton T.	A
1980		
Jan. 1	Aldershot	H
Jan. 5	Crewe Alex.	A
Jan. 12	Wigan Ath.	A
Jan. 19	Scunthorpe U.	H
Feb. 2	Tranmere R.	H
Feb. 9	Rochdale	A
Feb. 16	York C.	A
Feb. 23	Huddersfield T.	H
Mar. 1	Doncaster R.	A
Mar. 8	Darlington	H
Mar. 15	Walsall	A
Mar. 22	Walsall	H
Mar. 25	Lincoln C.	H
Mar. 29	Aldershot	A
Apr. 5	Stockport Co.	H
Apr. 8	Crewe Alex.	H
Apr. 12	Port Vale	A
Apr. 19	Bradford C.	A
Apr. 26	Peterborough U.	A
May 3	Northampton T.	H

PORT VALE

Date 1979	Opponents	Ground
Aug. 18	Newport Co.	A
Aug. 22	Aldershot	H
Aug. 25	Aldershot	A
Sept. 1	Peterborough U.	H
Sept. 5	Northampton T.	A
Sept. 8	Crewe Alex.	H
Sept. 15	Hartlepool U.	A
Sept. 22	Huddersfield T.	H
Sept. 29	Rochdale	A
Oct. 2	Bradford C.	A
Oct. 6	Lincoln C.	H
Oct. 10	Hartlepool U.	A
Oct. 13	Hartlepool U.	H
Oct. 20	Darlington	A
Oct. 27	Walsall	H
Nov. 3	Newport Co.	A
Nov. 10	Tranmere R.	H
Nov. 17	Torquay U.	A
Dec. 1	York C.	H
Dec. 8	Stockport Co.	A
Dec. 15	Scunthorpe U.	H
Dec. 26	Doncaster R.	A
Dec. 29	Aldershot	H
1980		
Jan. 1	Wigan Ath.	A
Jan. 5	A.F.C. Bournemouth	A
Jan. 12	Doncaster R.	H
Jan. 19	Crewe Alex.	A
Jan. 26	Peterborough U.	A
Feb. 2	Northampton T.	H
Feb. 9	Hartlepool U.	H
Feb. 16	Rochdale	H
Feb. 23	Hartlepool U.	A
Mar. 1	Darlington	H
Mar. 8	Halifax T.	A
Mar. 14	Lincoln C.	A
Mar. 22	Torquay U.	H
Mar. 25	Wigan Ath.	H
Mar. 29	Portsmouth	H
Apr. 5	Walsall	A
Apr. 8	Portsmouth	H
Apr. 12	A.F.C. Bournemouth	H
Apr. 25	A.F.C. Bournemouth	A
May 3	Doncaster R.	H

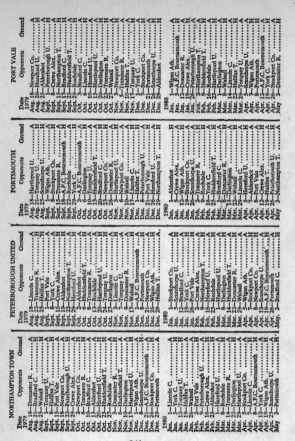

ROCHDALE

Date 1979	Opponents	Ground
Aug. 18	A.F.C. Bournemouth	H
Aug. 20	Stockport Co.	A
Aug. 25	Hartlepool U.	H
Sept. 1	Aldershot	A
Sept. 8	Tranmere R.	A
Sept. 15	Torquay U.	H
Sept. 18	Portsmouth	A
Sept. 22	Port Vale	A
Sept. 29	Halifax T.	H
Oct. 2	York C.	H
Oct. 6	Northampton T.	A
Oct. 8	Crewe Alex.	A
Oct. 13	Hereford U.	H
Oct. 20	Newport Co.	A
Oct. 23	Huddersfield T.	A
Oct. 27	Lincoln C.	H
Nov. 3	Newport Co.	A
Nov. 6	Peterborough U.	H
Nov. 10	Port Vale	H
Nov. 17	Peterborough U.	A
Nov. 24	Scunthorpe U.	H
Dec. 1	Darlington	A
Dec. 8	Doncaster R.	H
Dec. 26	Scunthorpe U.	A
Dec. 29	Tranmere R.	A
1980		
Jan. 1	Bradford C.	A
Jan. 5	Newport Co.	A
Jan. 12	Darlington	H
Jan. 19	Walsall	A
Jan. 26	Tranmere R.	H
Feb. 2	Torquay U.	H
Feb. 9	Portsmouth	H
Feb. 16	Port Vale	A
Feb. 23	Peterborough U.	H
Mar. 1	Crewe Alex.	A
Mar. 8	Northampton T.	H
Mar. 11	York C.	A
Mar. 15	Hereford U.	A
Mar. 22	Huddersfield T.	H
Apr. 1	Lincoln C.	A
Apr. 5	Newport Co.	H
Apr. 8	Crewe Alex.	H
Apr. 12	Scunthorpe U.	A
Apr. 19	Scunthorpe U.	H
Apr. 26	Doncaster R.	A
May 3	Tranmere R.	A

SCUNTHORPE UNITED

Date 1979	Opponents	Ground
Aug. 18	Torquay U.	A
Aug. 21	Hartlepool U.	A
Aug. 25	Portsmouth	A
Sept. 1	A.F.C. Bournemouth	H
Sept. 8	Aldershot	A
Sept. 15	Huddersfield T.	H
Sept. 18	York C.	A
Sept. 22	Bradford C.	H
Sept. 28	Doncaster R.	A
Oct. 2	York C.	H
Oct. 6	Walsall	A
Oct. 9	Hartlepool U.	H
Oct. 13	Lincoln C.	A
Oct. 20	Newport Co.	H
Oct. 23	Darlington	A
Oct. 27	Tranmere R.	A
Nov. 3	Peterborough U.	H
Nov. 6	Darlington	H
Nov. 10	Stockport Co.	A
Nov. 17	Wigan Ath.	H
Nov. 30	Wigan Ath.	A
Dec. 1	Northampton T.	H
Dec. 8	Halifax T.	A
Dec. 21	Port Vale	H
Dec. 26	Hereford U.	A
1980		
Jan. 1	Crewe Alex.	H
Jan. 5	Peterborough U.	A
Jan. 12	A.F.C. Bournemouth	A
Jan. 19	Aldershot	H
Jan. 26	Huddersfield T.	A
Feb. 2	Bradford C.	A
Feb. 16	Doncaster R.	H
Feb. 23	Lincoln C.	H
Feb. 29	Newport Co.	A
Mar. 8	Tranmere R.	H
Mar. 15	Peterborough U.	A
Mar. 22	Wigan Ath.	A
Mar. 29	Halifax T.	H
Apr. 1	Crewe Alex.	A
Apr. 5	Rochdale	H
Apr. 12	Peterborough U.	A
Apr. 19	Rochdale	A
Apr. 26	Hereford U.	H
May 3	Hereford U.	A

STOCKPORT COUNTY

Date 1979	Opponents	Ground
Aug. 18	Walsall	H
Aug. 21	Rochdale	H
Aug. 25	Tranmere R.	A
Sept. 1	Tranmere R.	A
Sept. 8	A.F.C. Bournemouth	A
Sept. 15	A.F.C. Bournemouth	H
Sept. 18	York C.	A
Sept. 22	Huddersfield T.	H
Sept. 29	Darlington	A
Oct. 2	Hereford U.	H
Oct. 6	Rochdale	A
Oct. 13	Bradford C.	H
Oct. 20	Doncaster R.	A
Oct. 23	Hartlepool U.	A
Oct. 27	Lincoln C.	H
Nov. 3	Walsall	A
Nov. 6	Hartlepool U.	H
Nov. 10	Scunthorpe U.	H
Nov. 17	Port Vale	A
Dec. 1	Crewe Alex.	H
Dec. 8	Torquay U.	A
Dec. 21	Northampton T.	H
Dec. 26	Port Vale	A
Dec. 29	Wigan Ath.	A
1980		
Jan. 1	Peterborough U.	H
Jan. 5	Portsmouth	A
Jan. 12	Tranmere R.	H
Jan. 19	Portsmouth	H
Jan. 26	Halifax T.	A
Feb. 2	A.F.C. Bournemouth	A
Feb. 9	Huddersfield T.	A
Feb. 23	Bradford C.	A
Feb. 29	Hereford U.	H
Mar. 1	Darlington	H
Mar. 8	Hereford U.	H
Mar. 22	Scunthorpe U.	A
Mar. 29	Newport Co.	H
Apr. 1	Newport Co.	H
Apr. 5	Peterborough U.	A
Apr. 12	Aldershot	A
Apr. 19	Crewe Alex.	A
Apr. 26	Port Vale	H
May 3	Halifax T.	H

TORQUAY UNITED

Date 1979	Opponents	Ground
Aug. 18	Scunthorpe U.	H
Aug. 21	Portsmouth	A
Aug. 25	Crewe Alex.	A
Sept. 1	Northampton T.	H
Sept. 8	Portsmouth	H
Sept. 15	Hereford U.	A
Sept. 19	Hereford U.	H
Sept. 22	Darlington	A
Sept. 29	Hartlepool U.	H
Oct. 2	Wigan Ath.	A
Oct. 6	Portsmouth	H
Oct. 10	Walsall	A
Oct. 13	Bradford C.	A
Oct. 24	Peterborough U.	H
Oct. 27	Halifax T.	A
Nov. 3	Scunthorpe U.	A
Nov. 10	York C.	H
Nov. 17	Port Vale	H
Dec. 1	Tranmere R.	A
Dec. 8	Hartlepool U.	H
Dec. 21	Stockport Co.	H
Dec. 26	Newport Co.	A
Dec. 29	Crewe Alex.	H
1980		
Jan. 1	A.F.C. Bournemouth	A
Jan. 12	Bradford C.	H
Jan. 19	Northampton T.	A
Jan. 26	Doncaster R.	H
Feb. 2	Lincoln C.	A
Feb. 9	Rochdale	A
Feb. 16	Hartlepool U.	H
Feb. 23	Aldershot	A
Mar. 1	Walsall	H
Mar. 8	Halifax T.	A
Mar. 14	Wigan Ath.	H
Mar. 22	Newport Co.	A
Apr. 1	Stockport Co.	A
Apr. 5	Newport Co.	H
Apr. 12	A.F.C. Bournemouth	H
Apr. 19	Lincoln C.	A
Apr. 22	Tranmere R.	H
Apr. 26	Huddersfield T.	A
May 3	Lincoln C.	H

TRANMERE ROVERS

Date 1979	Opponents	Ground
Aug. 18	Halifax T.	H
Aug. 22	Hartlepool U.	A
Aug. 25	Bradford C.	A
Sept. 1	Stockport Co.	H
Sept. 8	Hereford U.	A
Sept. 15	Rochdale	H
Sept. 18	Port Vale	H
Sept. 22	Lincoln C.	A
Sept. 29	Darlington	H
Oct. 2	Doncaster R.	A
Oct. 6	Northampton U.	H
Oct. 13	Newport Co.	A
Oct. 20	York C.	H
Oct. 23	Crewe Alex.	H
Oct. 27	Scunthorpe U.	A
Nov. 3	Halifax T.	A
Nov. 10	Wigan Ath.	H
Nov. 17	Huddersfield T.	A
Dec. 1	Torquay U.	H
Dec. 8	Wigan Ath.	A
Dec. 21	Aldershot	H
Dec. 26	Crewe Alex.	A
Dec. 29	Bradford C.	H
1980		
Jan. 1	Walsall	H
Jan. 5	Hartlepool U.	A
Jan. 12	Stockport Co.	A
Jan. 19	Hereford U.	H
Jan. 26	Rochdale	A
Feb. 1	Lincoln C.	H
Feb. 16	A.F.C. Bournemouth	A
Feb. 23	Newport Co.	H
Mar. 1	York C.	A
Mar. 8	Scunthorpe U.	H
Mar. 14	Northampton T.	A
Mar. 22	Wigan Ath.	H
Mar. 28	Huddersfield T.	H
Apr. 5	Crewe Alex.	A
Apr. 7	Walsall	A
Apr. 8	Aldershot	A
Apr. 12	Hartlepool U.	H
Apr. 19	Darlington	A
Apr. 26	Darlington	H
May 3	Rochdale	A

WALSALL

Date 1979	Opponents	Ground
Aug. 18	Stockport Co.	H
Aug. 25	A.F.C. Bournemouth	A
Sept. 1	Northampton T.	H
Sept. 8	Hereford U.	A
Sept. 15	Hartlepool U.	H
Sept. 18	Rochdale	A
Sept. 22	Darlington	H
Sept. 29	Aldershot	A
Oct. 2	Lincoln C.	A
Oct. 6	Scunthorpe U.	H
Oct. 9	A.F.C. Bournemouth	H
Oct. 13	Halifax T.	A
Oct. 20	Torquay U.	H
Oct. 23	Crewe Alex.	A
Oct. 27	Port Vale	H
Nov. 3	Bradford C.	A
Nov. 10	Portsmouth	H
Nov. 17	Peterborough U.	A
Dec. 1	Bradford C.	H
Dec. 8	Wigan Ath.	A
Dec. 21	Doncaster R.	H
Dec. 29	Newport Co.	A
1980		
Jan. 1	Tranmere R.	A
Jan. 12	Huddersfield T.	H
Jan. 19	Hereford U.	H
Jan. 26	Rochdale	H
Feb. 2	Northampton T.	A
Feb. 9	Hartlepool U.	A
Feb. 16	Aldershot	H
Feb. 23	Torquay U.	A
Mar. 1	Halifax T.	H
Mar. 8	Scunthorpe U.	H
Mar. 14	Portsmouth	A
Mar. 22	Peterborough U.	H
Mar. 29	Peterborough U.	H
Apr. 5	Wigan Ath.	A
Apr. 7	Tranmere R.	H
Apr. 8	York C.	A
Apr. 12	Huddersfield T.	A
Apr. 19	Bradford C.	H
Apr. 26	Newport Co.	A
May 3	Newport Co.	H

WIGAN ATHLETIC

Date 1979	Opponents	Ground
Aug. 18	Darlington	A
Aug. 22	Huddersfield T.	A
Aug. 25	Portsmouth	H
Sept. 8	A.F.C. Bournemouth	A
Sept. 15	Hereford U.	H
Sept. 19	Hereford U.	H
Sept. 22	Hartlepool U.	A
Sept. 29	Bradford C.	H
Oct. 2	Hartlepool U.	A
Oct. 6	Torquay U.	H
Oct. 9	Huddersfield T.	H
Oct. 13	Lincoln C.	A
Oct. 20	Rochdale	A
Oct. 23	Darlington	A
Nov. 3	Rochdale	H
Nov. 10	Rochdale	A
Nov. 17	Northampton T.	H
Dec. 1	Walsall	H
Dec. 8	Crewe Alex.	H
Dec. 22	Hereford U.	A
Dec. 29	Stockport Co.	A
1980		
Jan. 1	Port Vale	H
Jan. 5	Halifax T.	A
Jan. 12	Newport Co.	H
Jan. 19	A.F.C. Bournemouth	A
Jan. 26	Aldershot	H
Feb. 2	York C.	H
Feb. 9	Bradford C.	A
Feb. 16	Doncaster R.	H
Feb. 23	Lincoln C.	A
Feb. 29	Tranmere R.	A
Mar. 1	Torquay U.	H
Mar. 14	Scunthorpe U.	A
Mar. 22	Scunthorpe U.	A
Mar. 29	Peterborough U.	A
Apr. 5	Walsall	H
Apr. 7	Port Vale	A
Apr. 12	Halifax T.	H
Apr. 19	Northampton T.	A
May 3	Aldershot	A

YORK CITY

Date 1979	Opponents	Ground
Aug. 18	Hereford U.	A
Aug. 21	Darlington	H
Aug. 25	Lincoln C.	H
Sept. 1	Hartlepool U.	A
Sept. 8	Peterborough U.	H
Sept. 15	Wigan Ath.	H
Sept. 18	Scunthorpe U.	A
Sept. 22	Stockport Co.	H
Sept. 29	Portsmouth	A
Oct. 2	Scunthorpe U.	H
Oct. 6	Darlington	A
Oct. 13	A.F.C. Bournemouth	H
Oct. 19	Tranmere R.	A
Oct. 23	Doncaster R.	H
Oct. 27	Hereford U.	A
Nov. 3	Doncaster R.	A
Nov. 10	Torquay U.	H
Nov. 17	Port Vale	A
Dec. 1	Aldershot	H
Dec. 21	Walsall	H
Dec. 29	Lincoln C.	A
1980		
Jan. 1	Northampton T.	H
Jan. 5	Northampton T.	A
Jan. 12	Newport Co.	A
Jan. 19	A.F.C. Bournemouth	A
Feb. 2	Crewe Alex.	H
Feb. 9	Wigan Ath.	A
Feb. 16	Stockport Co.	H
Feb. 23	A.F.C. Bournemouth	A
Mar. 1	Tranmere R.	H
Mar. 8	Huddersfield T.	A
Mar. 22	Torquay U.	H
Mar. 29	Bradford C.	A
Apr. 4	Hartlepool U.	H
Apr. 7	Walsall	H
Apr. 12	Northampton T.	A
Apr. 19	Port Vale	H
May 3	Aldershot	A

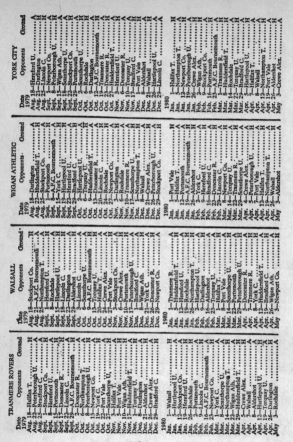

THE ALLIANCE PREMIER FOOTBALL LEAGUE FIXTURES 1979-80

Saturday August 18
Bangor C v A P Leamington
Barrow v Yeovil T
Boston U v Bath C
Maidstone U v Scarborough
Northwich Vic v Redditch U
Nuneaton Bor v Barnet
Stafford R v Kettering T
Telford U v Gravesend & Northfleet

Weymouth v Altrincham
Worcester C v Wealdstone

Monday August 20
Altrincham v Telford U
Northwich Vic v Bangor C
Worcester C v Weymouth

Tuesday August 21
A P Leamington v Nuneaton Bor
Barnet v Boston U
Gravesend & Northfleet v Bath C
Redditch U v Stafford R

Wednesday August 22
Kettering T v Wealdstone
Scarborough v Barrow

Yeovil T v Maidstone U
Saturday August 25
Altrincham v Maidstone U
A P Leamington v Northwich Vic
Barnet v Stafford R
Bath C v Barrow
Gravesend & Northfleet v Bangor C

Kettering T v Worcester C
Redditch U v Telford U
Scarborough v Weymouth
Wealdstone v Nuneaton Bor
Yeovil T v Boston U

Monday August 27
ALLIANCE PREMIER
FOOTBALL LEAGUE CUP
First Round
Scarborough v Northwich Vic
Stafford R v Nuneaton Bor
Wealdstone v Maidstone U
Worcester C v Weymouth

Tuesday August 28
A P Leamington v Boston U
Bangor C v Altrincham

Saturday September 1
Bangor C v Redditch U

Barrow v A P Leamington
Boston U v Gravesend & Northfleet

Maidstone U v Wealdstone
Northwich Vic v Bath C
Nuneaton Bor v Kettering T
Stafford R v Scarborough
Telford U v Yeovil T
Weymouth v Barnet
Worcester C v Altrincham

Monday September 3
Bath C v Gravesend & Northfleet
Nuneaton Bor v A P Leamington
Telford U v Altrincham
Wealdstone v Kettering

Tuesday September 4
Bangor C v Northwich Vic
Barrow v Scarborough
Maidstone U v Yeovil T
Stafford R v Redditch U

Wednesday September 5
Boston U v Barnet
Weymouth v Worcester C

Saturday September 8
Altrincham v Nuneaton Bor
A P Leamington v Telford U
Barnet v Maidstone U
Bath C v Bangor C
Gravesend & Northfleet v Barrow
Kettering T v Weymouth
Redditch U v Boston U
Scarborough v Worcester C
Wealdstone v Stafford R
Yeovil T v Northwich Vic

Monday September 10
Bath C v Nuneaton Bor
Telford U v Northwich Vic

Tuesday September 11
Barrow v Stafford R

Wednesday September 12
Kettering T v A P Leamington

Saturday September 15
Maidstone U v Kettering T
Nuneaton Bor v Scarborough
Stafford R v Altrincham
Weymouth v Wealdstone
Worcester C v Barnet

Saturday September 22
Barnet v Redditch U

Barrow v Weymouth
Boston U v Nuneaton Bor
Gravesend & N'fleet v Scarborough
Kettering T v Bath C
Maidstone U v Bangor C
Northwich Vic v Worcester C
Telford U v Stafford R
Wealdstone v A P Leamington
Yeovil T v Altrincham

Saturday September 29
ALLIANCE PREMIER
FOOTBALL LEAGUE CUP
Second Round
A P Leamington v Kettering T
Scarborough or
Northwich v Redditch U
Gravesend & N'fleet v
 Worcester C or Weymouth
Altrincham v Bangor C
Barnet v Bath C
Boston U v Wealdstone or
 Maidstone U

Stafford R or
Nuneaton Bor v Yeovil
Telford U v Barrow

Saturday October 6
A P Leamington v Scarborough
Bath C v Barnet.
Gravesend & N'fleet v Wealdstone
Maidstone U v Boston U
Nuneaton Bor v Northwich Vic

Redditch U v Altrincham
Stafford R v Bangor C
Weymouth v Telford U
Worcester C v Barrow
Yeovil T v Kettering T

Saturday October 13
Altrincham v Bath C
Bangor C v Weymouth
Boston U v Worcester C
Northwich Vic v Maidstone U
Scarborough v Yeovil T
Telford U v Nuneaton Bor

Saturday October 20
A P Leamington v Altrincham
Bath C v Wealdstone
Gravesend & N'fleet v Kettering T

Maidstone U v Telford U
Nuneaton Bor v Barrow
Redditch U v Scarborough
Stafford R v Northwich Vic
Weymouth v Boston U
Worcester C v Bangor C
Yeovil T v Barnet

Saturday October 27
Altrincham v Gravesend

Bangor C v Nuneaton Bor
Barnet v A P Leamington

Barrow v Maidstone U
Boston U v Stafford R
Kettering T v Redditch U
Northwich Vic v Weymouth
Scarborough v Bath C
Telford U v Worcester C
Wealdstone v Yeovil T

Saturday November 3
Bath C v Telford U
Gravesend & Northfleet v
    Northwich V
Redditch U v Barrow
Scarborough v Kettering
Yeovil T v Bangor C

Saturday November 10
A P Leamington v Yeovil T
Bangor C v Scarborough
Barnet v Telford U
Barrow v Altrincham
Bath C v Maidstone U
Boston U v Wealdstone
Northwich Vic v Kettering T
Nuneaton Bor v Redditch
Weymouth v Gravesend & Northfleet
Worcester C v Stafford R

Saturday November 17
Altrincham v Boston U
Gravesend & N'fleet v Worcester C
Kettering T v Barnet
Maidstone U v Nuneaton Bor
Redditch U v Weymouth

Scarborough v Northwich Vic
Stafford R v A P Leamington
Telford U v Barrow
Wealdstone v Bangor C
Yeovil T v Bath C

Saturday November 24
A P Leamington v Bath C
Barnet v Barrow
Boston U v Telford U
Northwich Vic v Wealdstone
Nuneaton Bor v Yeovil T
Weymouth v Maidstone U
Worcester C v Redditch U

Saturday December 1
Altrincham v Barnet
Barrow v Boston U
Kettering T v Bangor C
Maidstone U v A P Leamington
Redditch U v Gravesend
    & Northfleet
Stafford R v Weymouth
Wealdstone v Scarborough
Yeovil T v Worcester C

Saturday December 8
A P Leamington v Worcester C
Bangor C v Barnet
Bath C v Redditch U
Kettering T v Barrow
Maidstone U v Stafford R

Northwich Vic v Boston U
Nuneaton Bor v Weymouth
Scarborough v Telford U
Wealdstone v Altrincham
Yeovil T v Gravesend and
    Northfleet

Saturday December 15
Altrincham v Kettering T
Barnet v Northwich Vic
Barrow v Bangor C
Boston U v Scarborough
Gravesend & N'fleet v Nuneaton B
Redditch U v Yeovil T
Stafford R v Bath C
Telford U v Wealdstone
Weymouth v A P Leamington
Worcester C v Maidstone U

Saturday December 22
Altrincham v Scarborough
A P Leamington v Redditch U
Bangor C v Telford U
Barnet v Wealdstone
Bath C v Worcester C
Gravesend & Northfleet v
    Maidstone U
Kettering T v Boston U
Northwich Vic v Barrow
Nuneaton Bor v Stafford R
Yeovil T v Weymouth

Saturday December 29
Altrincham v Northwich Vic
Barnet v Scarborough
Barrow v Wealdstone
Boston U v Bangor C
Gravesend & Northfleet v A P Leamington
Redditch U v Maidstone U
Stafford R v Yeovil T
Telford U v Kettering T
Weymouth v Bath C
Worcester C v Nuneaton Bor

Tuesday January 1 1980
Barrow v Northwich Vic
Boston U v Kettering T
Maidstone U v Gravesend
Redditch U v A P Leamington
Scarborough v Altrincham
Stafford R v Nuneaton Bor
Telford U v Bangor C
Wealdstone v Barnet
Weymouth v Yeovil T
Worcester C v Bath C

Saturday January 5
A P Leamington v Weymouth
Bangor C v Barrow
Bath C v Stafford R
Kettering T v Altrincham
Maidstone U v Worcester C
Northwich Vic v Barnet
Nuneaton Bor v Gravesend & Northfleet
Scarborough v Boston U
Wealdstone v Telford U
Yeovil T v Redditch U

Saturday January 12
Barnet v Gravesend & Northfleet
Wealdstone v Redditch U

Saturday January 19
Altrincham v Wealdstone
Barnet v Bangor C
Barrow v Kettering T
Boston U v Northwich Vic
Gravesend & Northfleet v Yeovil T
Redditch U v Bath C
Stafford R v Maidstone U
Telford U v Scarborough
Weymouth v Nuneaton Bor
Worcester C v A P Leamington

Saturday January 26
A P Leamington v Gravesend & Northfleet
Bangor C v Boston U
Bath C v Weymouth
Kettering T v Telford U
Maidstone U v Redditch U
Northwich Vic v Altrincham
Nuneaton Bor v Worcester C
Scarborough v Barnet
Wealdstone v Barrow
Yeovil T v Stafford R

Saturday February 2
A P Leamington v Maidstone U
Bangor C v Kettering T
Barnet v Altrincham
Boston U v Barrow
Gravesend & N'fleet v Redditch U
Northwich Vic v Telford U
Nuneaton Bor v Bath C
Scarborough v Wealdstone
Weymouth v Stafford R
Worcester C v Yeovil T

Saturday February 9
Altrincham v Bangor C
Barrow v Barnet
Bath C v A P Leamington
Kettering T v Scarborough
Maidstone U v Telford U
Redditch U v Worcester C
Stafford R v Gravesend & Northfleet
Telford U v Boston U
Wealdstone v Northwich Vic
Yeovil T v Nuneaton Bor

Saturday February 16
A P Leamington v Stafford R
Bangor C v Wealdstone
Barnet v Kettering T
Barrow v Telford U
Bath C v Yeovil T
Boston U v Altrincham
Northwich Vic v Scarborough
Nuneaton Bor v Maidstone U

Weymouth v Redditch U
Worcester C v Gravesend
                & Northfleet

Saturday February 23
Altrincham v Barrow
Gravesend & Northfleet v
                Weymouth
Kettering T v Northwich Vic
Maidstone U v Bath C
Redditch U v Nuneaton Bor
Scarborough v Bangor C
Stafford R v Worcester C
Telford U v Barnet
Wealdstone v Boston U
Yeovil T v A P Leamington

Saturday March 1
Altrincham v Weymouth
Bangor C v Gravesend & Northfleet
Barnet v Nuneaton Bor
Barrow v Bath C
Boston U v Yeovil T
Kettering T v Stafford R
Northwich Vic v A P Leamington
Scarborough v Maidstone U
Telford U v Redditch U
Wealdstone v Worcester C

Saturday March 8
A P Leamington v Bangor C
Bath C v Boston U

Gravesend & Northfleet v
                Telford U
Maidstone U v Altrincham
Nuneaton Bor v Wealdstone
Redditch U v Northwich Vic
Stafford R v Barnet
Worcester C v Kettering T
Yeovil T v Barrow

Saturday March 15
Altrincham v Redditch U
Bangor C v Stafford R
Barnet v Bath C
Barrow v Worcester C
Boston U v Maidstone U
Kettering T v Yeovil T
Northwich Vic v Nuneaton Bor
Scarborough v A P Leamington
Telford U v Weymouth
Wealdstone v Gravesend
                & Northfleet

Saturday March 22
A P Leamington v Barrow
Bath C v Northwich Vic
Gravesend & Northfleet v
                Boston U
Maidstone U v Barnet
Nuneaton Bor v Altrincham
Redditch U v Bangor C
Stafford R v Wealdstone
Weymouth v Kettering T
Worcester C v Scarborough
Yeovil T v Telford U

Saturday March 29
Altrincham v Stafford R
Bangor v Yeovil T
Barnet v Worcester C
Barrow v Redditch U
Boston U v A P Leamington
Kettering T v Maidstone U
Northwich Vic v Gravesend
                & Northfleet
Scarborough v Nuneaton Bor
Telford U v Bath C
Wealdstone v Weymouth

Saturday April 5
A P Leamington v Kettering T
Bath C v Altrincham
Gravesend & N'fleet v Barnet
Maidstone U v Northwich Vic
Nuneaton Bor v Telford U
Redditch U v Wealdstone
Stafford R v Barrow
Weymouth v Bangor C
Worcester C v Boston U
Yeovil T v Scarborough

Monday April 7
A P Leamington v Wealdstone
Bangor C v Maidstone U
Bath C v Kettering T
Scarborough v Gravesend
                & Northfleet
Nuneaton Bor v Boston U
Redditch U v Barnet
Stafford R v Telford U

Weymouth v Barrow
Worcester C v Northwich Vic
Altrincham v Yeovil

Saturday April 12
Altrincham v Worcester C
Bangor C v Bath C
Barnet v Weymouth
Barrow v Gravesend & Northfleet
Boston U v Redditch U
Kettering T v Nuneaton B
Northwich Vic v Yeovil T
Scarborough v Stafford R
Telford U v A P Leamington
Wealdstone v Maidstone U

Saturday April 19
Altrincham v A P Leamington
Bangor C v Worcester C
Barnet v Yeovil T
Barrow v Nuneaton Bor
Boston U v Weymouth
Kettering T v Gravesend
    & Northfleet
Northwich Vic v Stafford R
Scarborough v Redditch U
Telford U v Maidstone U
Wealdstone v Bath C

Saturday April 26
Gravesend & Northfleet v
    Stafford R

Saturday May 3
A P Leamington v Barnet
Bath C v Scarborough
Gravesend & Northfleet v
    Altrincham
Maidstone U v Barrow
Nuneaton v Bangor C
Redditch U v Kettering T
Stafford R v Boston U
Weymouth v Northwich Vic
Worcester C v Telford U
Yeovil T v Wealdstone

ROTHMANS FOOTBALL YEARBOOK 1979-80
Edited by Jack Rollin

The tenth edition of the most successful
yearbook ever published.
1000pp £5.50 hardback £3.75 limp bound

ROTHMANS BOOK OF FOOTBALL LEAGUE RECORDS 1888-89 TO 1978-79
Ian Laschke

How to settle who won which game and when.
The book contains the result of every Football
League match since 1888-89.
352pp £10.00 hardback (available from
November)

F.A. NON-LEAGUE FOOTBALL ANNUAL 1979-80
A Playfair Annual
Edited by Tony Williams

The only annual of its kind, containing
information on more than 300 leading non-
league clubs.
304pp 85p paperback 4pp black and white
photos

M&J Queen Anne Press

INTERNATIONAL, REPRESENTATIVE AND CUP DATES, 1979-80

All fixtures subject to alteration.

September
Sat. 15	F.A. Challenge Cup First Round Qualifying
Wed. 19	European Cups Preliminary Round (*First Leg*)
Wed. 26	Football League Cup Third Round
Sat. 29	F.A. Challenge Vase Preliminary Round

October
Wed. 3	European Cups Preliminary Round (*Second Leg*)
Sat. 6	F.A. Challenge Cup Second Round Qualifying
Sun. 7	F.A. Sunday Cup First Round
Sat. 13	F.A. Challenge Trophy First Round Qualifying
Sat. 20	F.A. Challenge Cup Third Round Qualifying
Wed. 24	European Cups Second Round (*First Leg*)
Sat. 27	F.A. Challenge Vase First Round
Wed. 31	Football League Cup Fourth Round

November
Sat. 3	F.A. Challenge Cup Fourth Round Qualifying
Sun. 4	F.A. Sunday Cup Second Round
Wed. 7	European Cups Second Round (*Second Leg*)
Sat. 10	F.A. Challenge Trophy Second Round Qualifying
Sat. 24	F.A. Challenge Cup First Round Proper
Sat. 24	F.A. Challenge Vase Second Round
Wed. 28	UEFA Cup Third Round (*First Leg*)

December
Sat. 1	F.A. Challenge Trophy Third Round Qualifying
Sun. 2	F.A. Sunday Cup Third Round
Wed. 5	Football League Cup Fifth Round
Wed. 12	UEFA Cup Third Round (*Second Leg*)
Sat. 15	F.A. Challenge Cup Second Round Proper
Sat. 15	F.A. Challenge Vase Third Round

January 1980
Sat. 5	F.A. Challenge Cup Third Round Proper
Sat. 12	F.A. Challenge Trophy First Round Proper
Sun. 13	F.A. Sunday Cup Fourth Round
Wed. 16	Football League Cup Semi-Finals (*First Leg*)
Sat. 19	F.A. Challenge Vase Fourth Round
Sat. 26	F.A. Challenge Cup Fourth Round Proper

February

Sat. 2	F.A. Challenge Trophy Second Round Proper
Sat. 9	F.A. Challenge Vase Fifth Round
Sun. 10	F.A. Sunday Cup Fifth Round
Wed. 13	Football League Cup Semi-Finals (*Second Leg*)
Sat. 16	F.A. Challenge Cup Fifth Round Proper
Sat. 23	F.A. Challenge Trophy Third Round Proper

March

Sat. 1	F.A. Challenge Vase Sixth Round
Wed. 5	European Champion Clubs' Cup Third Round (*First Leg*)
Wed. 5	European Cup Winners' Cup Third Round (*First Leg*)
Wed. 5	UEFA Cup Fourth Round (*First Leg*)
Sat. 8	F.A. Challenge Cup Sixth Round Proper
Sat. 15	F.A. Challenge Trophy Fourth Round Proper
Sat. 15	Football League Cup Final
Sun. 16	F.A. Sunday Cup Semi-Finals
Wed. 19	European Champion Clubs' Cup Third Round (*Second Leg*)
Wed. 19	European Cup Winners' Cup Third Round (*Second Leg*)
Wed. 19	UEFA Cup Fourth Round (*Second Leg*)
Sat. 22	F.A. Challenge Vase Semi-Finals (*First Leg*)
Sat. 29	F.A. Challenge Vase Semi-Finals (*Second Leg*)

April

Wed. 9	European Cups Semi-Finals (*First Leg*)
Sat. 12	F.A. Challenge Cup Semi-Finals
Sat. 12	F.A. Challenge Trophy Semi-Finals (*First Leg*)
Sat. 19	F.A. Challenge Trophy Semi-Finals (*Second Leg*)
Wed. 23	European Cups Semi-Finals (*Second Leg*)
Sat. 26	F.A. Challenge Vase Final

May

Sun. 4	F.A. Sunday Cup Final
Wed. 7	UEFA Cup Final (*First Leg*)
Sat. 10	F.A. Challenge Cup Final
Wed. 14	European Cup Winners' Cup Final
Sat. 17	F.A. Challenge Trophy Final
Wed. 21	UEFA Cup Final (*Second Leg*)
Wed. 28	European Champion Clubs' Cup Final

INTERNATIONALS

October
Wed. 17	N. Ireland v England (*European Championship*)
Wed. 17	Rep. of Ireland v Bulgaria (*European Championship*)
Wed. 17	Scotland v Austria (*European Championship*)
Wed. 17	West Germany v Wales (*European Championship*)

November
Wed. 21	England v Bulgaria (*European Championship*)
Wed. 21	Turkey v Wales (*European Championship*)
Wed. 21	N. Ireland v Rep. of Ireland (*European Championship*)
Wed. 21	Belgium v Scotland (*European Championship*)

December
Wed. 19	Scotland v Belgium (*European Championship*)

February 1980
Wed 6	England v Rep. of Ireland (*European Championship*)
Wed. 6	Scotland v Portugal (*European Championship*)

March
Wed. 26	Spain v England
Wed. 26	England v Spain ('*B*')

May
Tue. 13	England v Argentina
Sat. 17	Wales v England
Sat. 17	N. Ireland v Scotland
Tue. 20	England v N. Ireland
Wed. 21	Scotland v Wales
Fri. 23	Wales v N. Ireland
Sat. 24	Scotland v England

June
Sun. 1	Australia v England (*Australian Soccer Federation Centenary Match*)
11–22	European Championship Final Tournament

U.E.F.A. UNDER-21 COMPETITION 1979-80

September 1979
Tue. 11	England v Denmark

November
Tue. 20	England v Bulgaria

IMPORTANT ADDRESSES

FOOTBALL ASSOCIATION: E. A. Croker, 16 Lancaster Gate, London W2 3LW.

SCOTTISH F.A.: E. Walker, 6 Park Gardens, Glasgow G3 7YE.

IRISH F.A.: W. J. Drennan, JP, 20 Windsor Avenue, Belfast BT9 6EG.

WELSH F.A.: Trevor Morris, OBE, 3 Fairy Road, Wrexham, LL13 7PS.

F.A. of IRELAND (Eire): P. J. O'Driscoll, 80 Merrion Square, Dublin 2.

LEAGUE OF IRELAND: E. J. Dowling, 80 Merrion Square, Dublin 2.

FEDERATION INTERNATIONALE DE FOOTBALL ASSOCIATION (FIFA): Dr Helmut Kaser, FIFA House, 11 Hitzigweg, 8032 Zurich, Switzerland.

UNION DES ASSOCIATIONS EUROPEENES DE FOOTBALL (UEFA· H. Bangerter, PO Box 16, CH-3000 Berne 15, Switzerland.

FOOTBALL LEAGUE: A. Hardaker, OBE, Lytham St Annes, Lancs. FY8 1JG.

SCOTTISH LEAGUE: J. Farry, 188 West Regent Street, Glasgow, G2 4RY.

IRISH LEAGUE: W. J. Drennan, 20 Windsor Avenue, Belfast BT9 6EG.

WELSH LEAGUE: J. T. Burrows, 16 Meyer Street, Thomastown, Tonyrefail, Glamorganshire.

ALLIANCE PREMIER LEAGUE: G. B. Graham, 36 Foregate, Highgate Park, Fulwood, Preston, Lancashire PR2 4LA.

SOUTHERN LEAGUE: W. E. Dellow, FCCS, 1 Cartmel Close, Reigate, Surrey, RH2 0LS.

NORTHERN PREMIER LEAGUE: R. D. Bayley, 228 Grove Lane, Hale, Altrincham, Cheshire, WA15 8PR.

THE ASSOCIATION OF FOOTBALL LEAGUE REFEREES AND LINESMEN: R. G. Warnke, 7 Ferndale Road, Binley Woods, Nr. Coventry, CV3 2BG.

FOOTBALL LEAGUE MANAGERS AND SECRETARIES ASSOCIATION: K. Friar, c/o Arsenal FC, Arsenal Stadium, Highbury, London, N5.

WOMEN'S FOOTBALL ASSOCIATION: Miss P. Gregory, 7 Mayfield Road, London, N8.

UNIVERSITIES ATHLETIC UNION: B. Byrne, 28 Woburn Square, London, WC1.

ENGLISH SCHOOLS F.A.: G. Evans, 4a Eastgate Street, Stafford, ST16 2NN.

PROFESSIONAL FOOTBALLERS' ASSOCIATION: C. Lloyd, 124 Corn Exchange Buildings, Hanging Ditch, Manchester, M4 3BN.

ENGLAND SUPPORTERS' ASSOCIATION: R. Coates, Hill End House, Butlers Cross, Aylesbury, Buckinghamshire.